PSYCHOTHERAPY
AS A
DEVELOPMENTAL
PROCESS

PSYCHOTHERAPY
AS A
DEVELOPMENTAL
PROCESS

MICHAEL BASSECHES AND MICHAEL F. MASCOLO

Routledge
Taylor & Francis Group
New York London

Routledge
Taylor & Francis Group
270 Madison Avenue
New York, NY 10016

Routledge
Taylor & Francis Group
2 Park Square
Milton Park, Abingdon
Oxon OX14 4RN

© 2010 by Taylor & Francis Group, LLC
Routledge is an imprint of Taylor & Francis Group, an Informa business

Printed in the United States of America on acid-free paper
10 9 8 7 6 5 4 3 2 1

International Standard Book Number-13: 978-0-8058-5730-6 (Hardcover)

Library of Congress Cataloging-in-Publication Data

Basseches, Michael.
    Psychotherapy as a developmental process / Michael Basseches and Michael F. Mascolo.
        p. cm.
    Includes bibliographical references.
    ISBN 978-0-8058-5730-6 (hbk. : alk. paper)
    1. Psychotherapy. I. Mascolo, Michael F. II. Title.

RC480.B3176 2009
616.89'14--dc22   2009002598

Visit the Taylor & Francis Web site at
http://www.taylorandfrancis.com

and the Routledge Web site at
http://www.routledge.com

To Our Children:

Josh and Ben

Seth, Mica, and Jake

Contents

Part III   Method

Part IV   Case Analyses

Part V Implications

List of Tables

List of Figures

Acknowledgments

From beginning to end of the process of work on this book, my two strongest and most consistent supporters have been Joshua Basseches and Benjamin Basseches, my two sons. I want to begin by acknowledging how much their interest, support, encouragement, and even gentle "limit setting" regarding my trying to put paying attention to them ahead of writing, have helped me. Also, in particular, near the outset Josh provided much valued help with the naming of the book, and at the end Ben provided much valued help with the cover design.

Others have provided crucial contributions, encouragement, and support at different points in what has been a very long process leading up to the publication of this book. My psychotherapy clients, mentors, supervisees, and therapists over the years have definitely played central roles in teaching me what psychotherapy is and can be. Meanwhile my colleagues and students, past and present, at the Bureau of Study Counsel at Harvard University and the Psychology Department at Suffolk University, have created two rich professional environments that both separately and in the dialectic between them have nurtured the ideas and experiences that constitute my contributions to this book. For reasons of privacy and space economy I won't list the names of all members of these groups — some are cited in the text itself — but you all know who you are and I thank you. Special thanks to "Eva," a pseudonym, but you also know who you are, for many years ago generously giving me your permission to write about our work together so others might learn from it. And along these lines, special thanks also go to Dr. Abigail Lipson, for editing a project that gave me a chance to write about the work Eva and I did, long before things fell into place to write this book.

Nineteen eighty-four was the year that I began my journey to becoming a psychotherapist. It was also the year that I completed my previous book on Dialectical Thinking and Adult Development and I thanked all those who contributed to my education and professional development as a developmental psychologist exploring adult intellectual development in the contexts of higher education and work. That brings me to a special group of people who that same year invited me into what has been an enduring intellectual and social context for my efforts to build a bridge from developmental psychology first to psychotherapy practice and ultimately to psychotherapy research. It is a great experience to be able to articulate the nature of the bridge in this book, now that it feels firmly anchored on both sides. But in the beginning, when I was a novice therapist, the bridge was not so well anchored, and required a community to provide scaffolding for the work ahead. The community called itself The Clinical-Developmental Institute and included over the years good friends and colleagues Bob Goodman, Ann Fleck-Henderson, Bob Kegan, Gil Noam, Gina O'Connell Higgins, Sharon Parks-Daloz, Laura Rogers, and Betsy Speicher, as well as many students who participated in Clinical-Developmental Institute Programs.

In thinking about the importance of building this bridge, I want also to acknowledge my gratitude to a mentor who in a wonderful way has both supported me and argued with me throughout my career as a student and a psychologist. Ken Gergen actually helped shape my experience of a chasm that needed to be bridged and then fully supported my efforts to bridge it. When I was at the tender age of 21, Ken encouraged me to study personality and developmental psychology in graduate school in order to develop a broad conceptual framework in which to think about psychological theory and practice. Then, when I told him 12 years later that for both intellectual and personal reasons, I wanted to learn to practice psychotherapy, he "met me where I was" in several senses. First, he essentially said, "Of course, go for it, what can I do to help?" Second, he met me in the sense that he had also become interested in psychotherapy himself and was very eager to discuss its vicissitudes. Finally, he agreed to meet me in person at a conference near Boston on Social Construction and Relational Practices. Had I not gone to that conference to catch up with Ken, I might not have ever met my esteemed coauthor and dear friend, Mike Mascolo, and this book might have never come to be.

At the conference, after a wonderful time hanging out with Ken and Mary Gergen, I attended a presentation Mike Mascolo was giving. I was awed by the depth and breadth of his thinking in integrating a range of developmental models. Furthermore, Mike's experience as a developmental psychologist studying development in the context of relationships, and his eagerness to look at psychotherapy as one such relational context, made him a wonderful partner for the endeavor of this book. I believe that this book is much stronger than anything that either of us could have written himself. Though of course collaboration has entailed facing and overcoming conflicts along the way, Mike's reliable dedication to this project across all the moments of excitement as well as frustration has been a bulwark upon which the work of the book has been accomplished.

Collaborating with a coauthor for whom I had great respect was a wonderful and motivating aspect of the experience of working on this book. However, for me at least, the will to write a book depends for its maintenance over time on the awareness of an audience that will be interested in reading it. Every practitioner, researcher, and student of psychotherapy I've met who has longed for improved communication within the field of psychotherapy has thus contributed to the motivation and energy it took to complete this project. However, the Society for the Exploration of Psychotherapy Integration made a special contribution to this book by establishing a location where I could reliably find representatives of the full diversity of this audience gathered under one roof, engaged in constructive, integrative dialogue. Within SEPI, Tullio Carere-Comes, Leigh McCullough (who also contributed case material to this book), Hilde Rapp, and Antonio Branco Vasco have been especially encouraging of the work that led to this book.

Many PhD students at Suffolk University have contributed at different stages to the research foundations on which this book has been built. Thomas Q. Peters' contribution stands out as he participated in every stage from developing the first coding manual for developmental analysis of psychotherapy process (DAPP), to conducting research on both the reliability of the coding process and its usefulness for understanding psychotherapy case material, to the actual writing of this book. Others who contributed to the development of the first coding manual included Charles Dooley, Melissa Rideout, Ritu Sharma, and Stacy Thayer. Those who have contributed to different aspects of the ongoing research have included Daniel J. Richard, Anthony Annunziata, Ilana Licht, Shana Dangelo, Carla Gabris, Adriana DeAmicis, Stephanie Berube, and Kristen Batejan. Rebecca L. Billings has contributed to the actual writing of this book.

In addition to all of the people mentioned above, several friends stand out in my mind for having "gotten it" about the importance of the book and in that context encouraging my work on it. These include David Blustein, Ann Densmore, Barbara Krieger, Julie Oxenberg, D. J. Prowell, and Paul Saint-Amand.

Both of my parents, Maurice Basseches and Beatrice Goodman Basseches, as well as "my cousin, the psychoanalyst," Carol Kaye, died during the process of my work on this book. Though they can't join in the celebration with me, their interest in and support of my work, and all the ways in which it was expressed, are very much present parts of this moment for me.

Allen Ivey, a scholar who did pioneering work bringing developmental psychology and psychotherapy together, also deserves much of the credit for this book appearing in its current form. His request and encouragement for our writing a proposal for what such a book might look like truly marked the date of conception of the book in its current form. Allen continued to support our carrying out the proposal that we wrote, even as we confronted obstacles along the way. With the help of editors Susan Milmoe and Steve Rutter, Allen was the main person responsible for prenatal care for the book. Now, as we write these words, the delivery is in the able hands of Midwife Dana Bliss, our current editor at Taylor & Francis/Routledge. While Dana's contribution has included bringing clarity to the topic of timetables, it is one thing to set timetables for work, and it is quite another thing to organize one's time to keep up with the timetables, while also maintaining order and "living peace" in the rest of one's life. Here, I want to acknowledge the essential role played by therapeutic organizer extraordinaire Erin Elizabeth Wells, who contributed both a skill set that I sorely lacked and a vision of how to offer resources in the service of clients' evolving constructions of meaning that is entirely consistent with the framework presented in this book.

Finally, I want to express my utmost gratitude to one member of the Society for the Exploration of Psychotherapy Integration, Angela Brandão, who took a particular interest in both me and my work and played essential roles in bringing the writing process to completion. There is something about the last few months of a project that has lasted years that is especially difficult. It was in that critical time that Angela insisted that it could be done and must be done, even if it meant putting everything else aside. Angela infused my efforts with energy, helping me not only to keep in mind the contribution that getting the book in the public domain could make but also to look forward with tremendous enthusiasm to life after the book was done. Angela reviewed my writing with a keen eye and sharp mind, offered insightful and constructive comments, and put in the hard and pressured work needed to help polish the final manuscript in the final hours. And she did all this over what she had intended to be her winter vacation, before the realities of the book timetable became clear. Finishing the book together, with a deep sense of partnership, is a process that I will always remember; and Angela's role in helping push the book across the finish line is one for which I will always be grateful.

Michael Basseches

To the intellectual giants who have contributed directly to the thinking that has informed this book: Kurt Fischer, Alan Fogel, Marc Lewis, Isabela Granic, Joe DeRivera, Bob Neimeyer, Jim Mancuso, Ted Sarbin, Jaan Valsiner and Jim Wertsch. I also want to acknowledge the friendship, support and valued contributions of Carol Ann Dalto, Nira Granott, Debra Harkins, Catherine Raeff, Ruth Propper and Carol Reichenthal. And, as well, to those with whom I have only passing acquaintance, but who have nonetheless deeply shaped my thinking: Shaun Gallagher, Gilbert Gottlieb, Kenneth Gergen, Rom Harre, Mark Johnson, Barbara Rogoff, John Shotter, and Evan Thompson. Thank you, Leigh McCollough, for the courage and compassion to make your clinical work and expertise available for analysis, and to "Eva" and "the Lady." To my coauthor, Mike Basseches, I thank you for your brilliance, your deep friendship, and for the personal development that you fostered in me through our many interactions. I want to acknowledge the able collaboration and hard work provided by the students who have worked with me on this project: Paul Ebbinghausen, Frances Devine, Christina George, Michael Tartaglia, Greta Thomsen, and Julie Norman. Thank you Seth, Mica and Jake for your patience and inspiration. And finally, I am forever indebted to my wife, Alicia Diozzi, who has supported me throughout this process with her patience and understanding and who has given me the gift of happiness.

Michael F. Mascolo

PART 1

Introduction

CHAPTER 1

Psychotherapy and Development
Goals of This Book

Psychotherapy and *development* represent two central concerns of practitioners, theorists, and researchers—both within the field of psychology and far beyond disciplinary bounds; both within the contemporary zeitgeist and over the histories of various related disciplines. How are we bringing these concerns together in this book, and why?

Our primary audience is the broad community of practitioners, researchers, and students of psychotherapy.[1] The term *psychotherapy practice* refers to an extremely broad and variegated set of phenomena. The tremendous variation in manifestations of psychotherapy practice is attributable to at least the following five factors, among others: (a) variation among the personal styles, repertoires, and relationship histories of individual practitioners, all of which influence the way the psychotherapy process unfolds; (b) variation in the schools, theories, and techniques in which therapists have been trained, in which the differences appear so great that practitioners trained in these traditions seem to speak in technical languages that are often so different from one another that communication across the boundaries of these traditions is an almost overwhelming challenge;[2]

---

[1] Writings closely related to the themes of this book, but addressed equally if not more so to the community of life span developmental psychologists, can be found in Basseches (1997a, 1997b, 2003).

[2] Consider the experience of moving between meetings of professional associations of therapists, such as the American Association of Behavior Therapy (AABT) and Division 39 (division of psychoanalysis) of the American Psychological Association—the discourses are so different that simultaneous translation, as from Japanese to English, would be hard to imagine.

(c) variation in the forms of therapy (group therapy, couple therapy, family therapy, individual therapy, milieu therapy, psychodrama, community intervention, etc.), which leads to very different patterns of interaction; (d) variation in the setting of therapy (private practice, college or school counseling center, community health center, hospital, etc.), which also leads to major differences in how the process is manifest; and (e) variation among the clients—in terms of age, gender, culture, socioeconomic class, and the problems and processes that led to their presenting themselves for psychotherapy. For *all* those engaged in psychotherapy practice, our goal in this book is to provide a framework and method for thinking about their work that allows for critical reflection on their own successes and disappointments, and on the similarities and differences among their own and other practitioners' work with different clients.

Our approach to providing such a framework and method is a "common factors" (Carere-Comes, 1999, 2001) approach, based on the idea that some form of development is the common outcome of *all* effective psychotherapy, all differences notwithstanding. Our effort is to describe and track the fundamental common processes that facilitate development within all forms of therapy, and to understand how these processes are obstructed in cases where the therapy is not effective.

Psychotherapy research also comprises a wide range of activities. Nevertheless, one basic research paradigm has dominated such research (Peters, 2008). This paradigm entails treating outcomes, primarily measured in terms of symptom reduction (both immediately after therapy and over time), as dependent variables, and treating client diagnosis, therapist technique and training, and length of therapy as primary independent or mediating variables. There is also a concomitant attempt to develop quantitative measures of other mediating variables, such as strength of therapeutic alliance, degree of therapist–client demographic match, and aspects of therapists' and clients' personalities. Although many therapists are indeed concerned with reducing some of their clients' "symptoms," and that this is done in a cost-efficient manner is certainly a major concern of third-party payers who fund a great deal of psychotherapy, in our view this research paradigm generates understandings that are only tangentially related to what inspires, guides, and motivates most therapists in their work. Furthermore, most meta-analyses of psychotherapy research studies have suggested that no one therapeutic approach is clearly superior to others in terms of outcomes (Cuijpers, van Straten, & Warmerdam, 2008; Luborsky et al., 2003), and some research has cast doubt on whether a therapist's training makes any significant difference in therapeutic outcome (Dawes, 1994). Although research that leads to the documentation of a particular standardized therapy technique as an "empirically supported treatment" does provide some encouragement to practitioners, teachers, funders, and consumers of psychotherapy, it is debatable whether this entire outcome-oriented research enterprise has led to a greater overall success rate in psychotherapy practice.

For all those interested in psychotherapy research, our goal in this book is to offer an alternative research approach that systematically tracks the psychotherapy process itself and describes each case's unique developmental outcome (rather than relying on more general outcome measures that do not relate to the client's unique individual concerns). In tracking the psychotherapy process, we focus on the questions of what kinds of therapeutic resources therapists are offering to their clients (and clients to each other when the therapy involves more than one client), and whether and how clients are able to make use of these resources in the service of their own development. We also look at processes of mutual adjustment of what therapists learn to offer and what clients learn to use. We believe that this research approach is more compatible with the way most therapists approach their practice than the search for technique–outcome correlations. We furthermore hope that this type of process-focused research will complement existing outcome research, and be more likely than further symptom reduction studies to result in the improvement of overall psychotherapy success rates.

So our starting point is the idea that psychological development represents a common outcome of all effective psychotherapy. Is this a radical idea, or is this an assumption that most therapists, across the widely divergent psychotherapeutic traditions, already make? Perhaps this depends on how *psychological development* is defined and conceptualized. Is it methodologically possible to rigorously assess and track psychological development as it occurs within the psychotherapy process? Again, this depends on our ability to conceptualize psychological development and to operationalize the measurement of psychological development as it occurs in the context of human relationships.

For these reasons, we will turn our attention at the outset of this book to what we mean by *development*, and how we study it. We will clarify the intellectual traditions on which we draw in understanding the concept of human development. Also, we will try to locate where we stand on some of the controversial issues that have arisen in life span developmental psychology, particularly as it is applied to professional practice.

This will provide a foundation for the work that will make up the core of this book—the presentation of our proposed method of analysis; a discussion of its relationship to the goals, models, and methods of extant approaches to psychotherapy; an analysis of the role of emotion in psychotherapy; and illustrative applications of this method to psychotherapeutic case material. In the final section of the book, we will consider the implications of our approach for psychotherapy practice, research, and training, as well as for developmental psychology.

Before initiating our systematic discussion of how we conceptualize development, and the intellectual traditions on which we draw, we would like to share an anecdotal account of what happened when the first author presented this work for discussion to a group of his practitioner colleagues. The discussion that ensued quickly raised issues of the ways that a book like this might be appropriated and/or misappropriated.

The presentation began with the statements that the authors are interested in "common factors" in all forms of psychotherapy practice; that our focus is on the common processes that foster development within all forms of psychotherapy, in cases in which the therapy is successful; that we are particularly interested in the range of additional resources that therapists offer that can be utilized by clients in the service of their development; and that we believe that cases in which psychotherapy is unsuccessful can be understood as instances of the client being unable to make developmental use of the resources that the therapist is offering and, conversely, of the therapist being unable to offer resources that the client can use. Then, our research method for tracking the developmental movements that occur within psychotherapy, the resources that the therapist offers, and the client's use of these resources was described in a bit more detail.

In the ensuing discussion, following an exercise in which participants were invited to look at their own experience of practice through the lens of developmental analysis, two participants[3] soon articulated the key question: Is this framework intended to be descriptive or prescriptive? This question strikes to the heart of the current relationship between psychotherapy practice and psychotherapy research, and to the contribution to that relationship that this book is intended to offer.

If one looks at what currently guides psychotherapy practitioners in their practice, one finds an abundance of theoretical frameworks and therapeutic techniques. Each practitioner describes his or her work in the languages of the theoretical model(s) in which he or she has been trained, and cites any specific techniques that he or she has learned to employ. Most therapists further acknowledge the role of their own personal styles in the way in which they build relationships with clients and make choices about which conceptual and technical tools to employ in their work with any given client. Most therapists also acknowledge that various kinds of "value judgments" influence their choices throughout the entire process of therapy, from the establishment of goals, through choices of where to

---

[3] Ariel Phillips and Craig Rodgers of the Harvard University Bureau of Study Counsel, December 16, 2005.

focus and what positions to adopt in any given session, to decisions related to termination.

It is not unusual for therapists to encounter reports or presentations on new research and/or on innovations in therapeutic technique. (The techniques and research findings may be conjoined when a technique is presented as an "empirically supported treatment.") Sometimes these encounters occur in the context of continuing education, which the therapist seeks to foster his or her own professional development. Sometimes the encounters occur in the context of the pressure that therapists may feel from third-party payers or regulators, to make sure that their practice is both efficient and consistent with evolving standards of care. But in either case, the therapists are often asking the questions "What is this presentation suggesting that I do that is new and different from what I am already doing?" and "Is this adaptation one that I am willing and able to make?"

In this context, it seems important for us to clarify that the *primary* effort of this book is *descriptive*. The goal is to describe systematically how therapists, *in doing the range of things that they already do*, help to support their clients' development. A further goal is to provide a common language in which therapists trained in differing approaches and techniques can discuss and appreciate the similarities, differences, and complementarities within what they already do. But the goal is *not* to present a new and different approach for therapists to adopt in working with their clients, nor to suggest that therapists abandon their particular ways of working in favor of a more standardized approach.

On the other hand, there is another sense in which the intent of this book is *prescriptive*. First, we are prescribing *that* therapists reflect on whether progress is being made in their work with each individual client. Although this is something that conscientious therapists already do, and that psychotherapy research is intended to support, we offer a set of concepts and methods that we hope will be more helpful in this effort. And although these methods may entail the therapist taking a step outside the conceptual framework through which he or she usually, on a day-to-day basis, views his or her practice, they involve close inspection of the presence or absence of movement in the client's own unique meaning making. They are not likely to be experienced by the therapist as the imposition of assessment of the relationship from an external, nomothetic frame of reference, as is often the case when therapy is subjected to evaluation by managed care reviews or efficacy research. Finally, we are indeed prescribing that when therapists discover that their work with a client is stuck with respect to developmental progress, they attempt to diagnose and treat these obstacles to development by considering the alternative forms in which they may offer developmental resources to this client.

In sum, the current relationship between psychotherapy practice and psychotherapy research is often experienced as a struggle, in which psychotherapy research is experienced as prescriptive, using large numbers of research subjects and general measures to establish "standards of care" to which practitioners are expected to adapt. Therapists often respond by rejecting research that seems to come from a foreign frame of reference, uncritically reasserting their personal "intuition," "clinical experience," and "knowledge of the particular client" as adequate foundations for their work. In contrast, this book is an effort to provide a *descriptive* framework that can be used to appreciate the highly varied ways in which particular therapists tailor their work to unique clients' developmental needs, while at the same time offering a *prescription* of a more rigorous method for recognizing and correcting the problem when a particular therapist's way of working is not serving the client well.

It would be a misappropriation of this book to interpret it as offering a novel way of doing therapy, or as suggesting the substitution of "developmental theory" or "developmental techniques" for the approaches to their work on which variously trained therapists have learned to rely. On the other hand, this work was appropriated by another one of the first author's practitioner colleagues in exactly the way we as authors intend when she said at the end of the presentation,

> It's so important that we find ways to be reflective and self-critical about our work. I share with others here the sense that the work is really about "being with" the client. But I don't want to assume I'm doing that just fine, that it doesn't need any self-reflection. You're offering a way to examine our work.[4]

With respect to the "value judgments" that the vast majority of therapists acknowledge repeatedly making, another advantage of viewing psychotherapy as a developmental process is that doing so provides a comprehensive framework in which these value judgments can be located and subjected to constructive, critical reflection. In the absence of such a comprehensive framework, we believe therapists rely on some combination of values drawn from a "medical model of psychotherapy," the problems of which are considered in the implications section of the book;[5] the therapists' own personal likes and dislikes, whether (a) implicit or even outside of consciousness but reflected in their action choices, (b) explicitly but uncritically asserted, and/or (c) located and supported within a broader set of assumptions adopted by the particular therapist but not necessarily consensually validated by other therapists; and (d) values implicit or explicit in the theories of personality and psychotherapy on which they rely in their practice. Developmental frameworks, understood in the way

---

[4] Diane Weinstein, Harvard University Bureau of Study Counsel, December 16, 2005.
[5] A more extended discussion of these problems can be found in Basseches (2003).

we articulate in the next two chapters, do incorporate evaluative perspectives and assumptions. We hold that it is precisely because these frameworks have this *prescriptive* aspect that developmental approaches are appropriate frameworks for *describing* psychotherapeutic practice (and we hope and expect that they will be so experienced by psychotherapists).

Psychotherapeutic practice, like all educational practice, is not a value-neutral enterprise. It will inevitably be guided either by values that can be articulated and subjected to consensual affirmation, or by values that remain unarticulated and are more likely to be idiosyncratic, ethnocentric, or shared only by self-defined communities of "experts."[6] In the course of the chapters that follow, we will introduce discussion of the values or prescriptive assumptions that are entailed by our "coactive systems" view of psychotherapy as a developmental process, and how they might guide psychotherapeutic practice. This approach represents an alternative to the implicit prescriptivity of the medical model, which has a significant impact on how psychotherapy is currently and has historically been conducted. Because the coactive systems view itself represents an integration of genetic epistemological structuralist (Piaget, 1970, 1985) and sociocultural traditions (Cole, 1996; Vygotsky, 1978; Wertsch, 1998), and systems approaches (Fischer & Bidell, 2006; Gottlieb, Wahlsten, & Lickliter, 2006) to thinking about development, we will attempt to clarify where we stand on foundational issues related to the nature of psychological functioning, social relations, and development, especially as they relate to psychotherapy.

---

[6] Kohlberg and Mayer's (1972) article, "Development as the Aim of Education," presents the argument that developmental models provide sounder philosophical bases for educational practice than cultural socialization models or romantic models—which tend, by intention or default, to be offered as alternative bases.

PART **II**

Conceptual Foundations

CHAPTER 2

The Concept of Development and Its Implications for Psychotherapy

In order to understand what it means to think of psychotherapy as a developmental process, it is important to thoroughly consider the concept of *development*. The concept of development is often taken to be a synonym for terms such as *change, growth, age-related change, history,* or even *evolution.* Although development may involve some or all of these various processes, in our view, it cannot be reduced to any of them. Our conception of development is an explicitly dialectical one (see Basseches, 1984).[1] For our purposes here, a dialectical model can be understood as one that conceptualizes structural transformations in the organization of wholes as evolving from the dynamic relationships of multiple interacting systems and their components with each other. From this view, at its most general level, we understand *development* to refer to *transformations in the forms of organization of systems that occur in the context of adaptation* in response

---

[1] Basseches (1984) has provided a comprehensive analysis of the nature of dialectical thinking, both as an intellectual tradition and as an adult form of cognitive organization. As described by Basseches, the manifestations of both dialectical cognitive organization and dialectical philosophical traditions are many and varied. Dialectical thinking has played central roles in the natural sciences, social sciences, and humanities, and all the phenomena studied across these intellectual disciplines are susceptible to being understood in the context of dialectical processes. Furthermore, dialectical thinking is manifest in the ways in which some adults learn to approach challenges of adult life (see Kegan, 1982, 1994). What ties together the varied manifestations of dialectical thinking is a combination of cognitive organizational principles, epistemological assumptions, and ontological assumptions. The reader is referred to Basseches (1984) for a fuller understanding of the broad intellectual traditions that shape our approach in this book.

to interactions with other systems in the physical and social environment.[2] In the presentation of a dialectical model of development that follows, we will introduce a distinction between a focus on development as structural transformation and a focus on the processes by which structural change occurs over time as a product of dialectical interaction among elements of interacting systems. Our dialectical model of development relates these two aspects of development to each other, in that the structural transformations are understood as resulting from the interaction of elements. However, the method of analysis of psychotherapy process that we offer throughout this book will at moments focus more on the structural difference between more developed and less developed forms of organization of a client's activity, whereas at other moments it focuses on the intrapsychic and interpersonal processes by which these developments occur. In presenting a method of analysis that combines these two foci, we will examine how a developmental perspective can illuminate both the types of changes and the change processes that occur in successful psychotherapy.

Development as Structural Transformation

A fundamental premise of this book is that when psychotherapy is effective, it fosters psychological development in clients.[3] The prescriptive assertion articulated above—that practitioners should assess their work by observing whether development is occurring—raises fundamental questions: What counts as development? What sorts of changes can be considered developmental change? These are not simply empirical questions to be answered by simple observation. Instead, the issue of the nature of developmental change is a conceptual question that must be addressed before one begins the process of assessing any given course of psychotherapy.

Our conception of structural transformation draws upon Werner and Kaplan's (1962/1984) articulation of the *"orthogenetic principle" of development within the context of an overall dialectical approach.* The orthogenetic principle stipulates that when an entity undergoes development, it moves from a relatively global and undifferentiated state to states of increasing differentiation, integration, and hierarchic integration. This conception of development may be illustrated using the metaphor of the *developing embryo.* From conception to the development of the infant, the ovum moves through a series of stages that reflect increasing levels of

---

[2] In Chapter 3, we explain the coactive systems model, which for us serves as context for understanding these adaptive challenges.

[3] We also view effective psychotherapy as resulting in practitioners constructing new knowledge and developing psychologically, but we will defer until later discussion of practitioner development and its relationship to client development.

differentiation, integration, and hierarchic integration. At conception, the embryo begins as a single-celled ovum. Relative to the structures that will develop later, the ovum is global and undifferentiated. None of the structures that will form the infant are present in the single-celled ovum. Soon after fertilization, the ovum begins to undergo continuous cell division (cleavage). In so doing, this is a first step in the differentiation of the cells that will eventually form the fetus. After cleavage, cells begin to specialize and take on different forms and functions. Such specialization involves both increased differentiation (cell assemblies become increasingly distinct from each other) and integration (cells come together to begin to form interconnected organ systems). Over time, the various organ systems become *hierarchically integrated* to form a single, integral organism—the infant.

Development as a Dialectical Process

Within a dialectical model of development, development occurs when in the context of mutual adaptation, systems move from more global and undifferentiated states to increasingly more differentiated and integrated states, through reiterative sequences comprising three steps. The first step, differentiation, consists of the *differentiation of a thesis and an antithesis*. A relationship of *thesis* and *antithesis* emerges whenever a new differentiation is created. The antithesis is that which is differentiated from the thesis. Although dialectical models can be applied to understanding change in all natural and social systems, within human activity, differentiations tend to emerge either (a) between an organized form of human physical and representational activity (thesis) and a novel experience of interaction with an external system (antithesis) that has not yet been assimilated to that form of activity (e.g., a child forms a global category of *doggie*, and then confronts for the first time an animal that is "not a doggie"), or (b) between two organized forms of activity (thesis and antithesis) that in some way can or do come into contact or conflict with each other (e.g., Piaget, 1952, has described infants developing sucking and grasping as separate forms of activity, which come into conflict when the infant encounters an object that simultaneously meets the criteria of "objects to be sucked" and "objects to be grasped").

We refer to the second step as *conflict*. In all dialectical processes, the relationship of thesis and antithesis remains unstable, conflictual, or in disequilibrium, until the differentiated elements or systems become organized into an integrated whole. In the case of development of the organization of human activity, simultaneous attention to the differentiated thesis and antithesis plays a crucial role in the process of developmental reorganization. Therefore in our analyses of psychotherapy processes, we use the term *conflict* to refer to the step in which attention is paid to both thesis and antithesis, but before an integrative relationship between them ("synthesis") has been established. Thus, "conflict" may be seen as generally referring to a wide variety of forms of unstable, opposing, or otherwise in some sense unacceptable relationships between differentiated elements. But in the context of human development (and psychotherapy more specifically), conflict that initially may be more *latent* tends to be *more fully experienced* when attention is paid simultaneously to the thesis and the antithesis that have been differentiated from each other.

The third step entails a *"synthesis" of thesis and antithesis*. In this step a novel synthesis is constructed in which the previously differentiated thesis and antithesis become integrated within some new form of organization. Piaget (1952) described the novel syntheses in individual human activity that result from conflict between an organized pattern of activity and novel experience as successful instances of "assimilation" and "accommodation." He described syntheses that resolve conflicts between two differentiated patterns of organized activity as examples of "reciprocal assimilation and integration."

Development then proceeds through successive reiterations of these three steps of the dialectic. Once a novel synthesis emerges, it can be further differentiated from something else, thus becoming the new thesis in relationship to a new antithesis for the next iteration of the dialectic process of development This process can be illustrated through a classic study performed by Inhelder, Sinclair, and Bovet (1974). These investigators analyzed the ways children's conception of conservation developed through the process of resolving conceptual conflict. In so doing, the researchers took advantage of the finding that many children gain an understanding of conservation of *number* (i.e., the understanding that the number of objects in a group remains the same despite a transformation in their appearance) before they develop an appreciation of conservation of *length* (i.e., the idea that the length of, say, a string remains the same despite a change in its arrangement). As indicated in Figure 2.1, children were presented with two straight lines of sticks that were attached to small houses. All children agreed at the outset that (a) the number of houses in the two rows was the same and that (b) the length of the two "roads" (juxtaposed sticks) in front of the houses was the same. Thereafter, as children watched, one of the "roads" was rearranged from a straight line to a crooked path (Row C). When this occurred, upon examination, some children indicated that although the number of houses on both roads remained the same, the length of the twisted road had become shorter.

Inhelder et al. (1974) were interested in how children became aware of and resolved the conflict between understanding conservation of number and length. Their study provided evidence of four steps in the developmental process. In the first step, children were unaware that a conflict

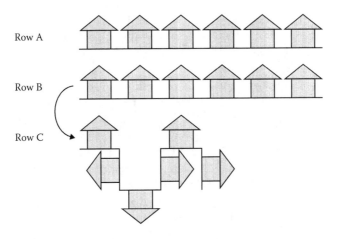

Row A

Row B

Row C

Figure 2.1 The induction of psychological conflict. Figures of houses like those used by Inhelder, Sinclair and Bovet (1974). When Row B is transformed to Row C, many 6-7 year-olds will conserve one dimension of the task (e.g., conservation of number) but not the other (conservation of length). This sets up a condition of conflict between two forms of conservation.

existed at all, responding with no signs of discomfort that the number of houses remained the same but that the road had become shorter. The dimensions of number and length were kept separate and distinct despite repeated questioning. In the next step, children began to notice a conflict. For example, a child may notice that although the straight and zigzagging roads appear to be of different lengths, they have the same number of sticks in them. During the next step, children attempted to resolve the conflict in inappropriate or ineffective ways. For example, a child may attempt to justify the conflict by saying that it would take longer to travel a twisting road than a straight road. Finally, during the fourth phase, children were able to coordinate their understanding of length and number into a higher-order synthesis, thus resolving the conflict. For example, a child might note that just as the realignment of the houses compensated for the apparent decrease in their number together, the length of the individual segments that compose the zigzagging road compensates for the apparent shortening of the length of the road.

These steps illustrate microdevelopmental transitions that occur from thesis and antithesis to conflict and then to synthesis. The first phase corresponds to the articulation of *thesis* (i.e., "There are the same number of houses and sticks in Rows A and C") and *antithesis* (i.e., "Row A is longer than Row C because it ends further to the right"). In the second phase, a child becomes aware of the conflict between thesis and antithesis (e.g., "How can Rows A and C have the same number of same-lengthed sticks, but be of different lengths?"). Thereafter, to resolve the conflict, in the third phase, the child engages in further constructive activity. In so doing, he or she attends to different aspects of the task and makes a series of novel differentiations. The child may focus attention on the contrast between length and arrangement. For example, through attentional activity, a child can make a variety of discriminations, such as "Although the houses in Row A are in a straight line, the houses in Row C are zigzagged"; "Row A ends farther to the right because the sticks are in a straight line"; "Row C doesn't go as far to the right because its sticks are zigzagged"; and so forth. In so doing, the child makes a series of finer differentiations in his or her experience and successively maps these various differentiations onto each other. In so doing, in the final phase, the child is able to coordinate the elements of these novel differentiations into a higher-order synthesis that resolves the conflict experienced in the second phase. In so doing, a child can create a synthesis such as "A is as long as C because the zigzags in C make up for the extra space to the right in Row A" (e.g., counting the number of sticks in each row, comparing the length of different rows with the number of sticks in each row, etc.) that eventually brings about awareness of a *conflict* between *thesis* and *antithesis*. Through continued coordinative activity (e.g., comparing the length of rows to the number of zigzags in each row, and noting how changes in length are compensated by changes in the number of zigzags), children are able to coordinate their understanding of thesis and antithesis to form a higher-order *synthesis* that resolves the contradiction.

Tracking the Structures and Processes of Development in Human Activity

To illustrate the orthogenetic and dialectical conceptions of development, we offer two examples. The first (nontherapeutic) example is the development of the capacity to dribble a basketball. Dribbling a basketball is a cultural activity. It is defined with reference to the rules and practices of basketball. As such, only certain forms of activity can properly be considered instances of dribbling. To dribble a ball, an individual must bounce the ball consistently as he or she is moving across space, typically a basketball court. In so doing, the dribbler typically must be able to keep the ball away from opponents, who will attempt to steal the ball. As a result, it is important that the dribbler be able to maneuver the ball deftly with both hands without looking at the ball. These skills specify the requirements for identifying any given act as a developed form of dribbling. To say that a person's dribbling skill is *developing* is to maintain that his or her actions are becoming more differentiated and integrated in a manner that more adaptively satisfies these requirements.

The capacity to dribble requires the coordination of multiple component activities—bouncing the ball with both hands, running up and down court, staving off attempts to steal the ball, and so on. Dribbling skills develop gradually and show orthogenetic change over time. Figure 2.2 provides an illustration of the types of orthogenetic changes that occur in the development of but one component of dribbling—the movements of a single arm and hand. When people first learn to dribble, dribbling actions are global and undifferentiated. A novice's arm and hand movements are rigid and jerky. As indicated in the left panel of Figure 2.2, the novice bounces a ball with an open and rigid palm. In so doing, the movements of the fingers, wrist, and forearm and upper arm are undifferentiated from each other. The novice slaps the ball to the ground in a single global movement. Further, the novice must look at the moving ball in order to monitor his or her bouncing activities. If the left panel of Figure 2.2 is understood as the undifferentiated thesis, we can begin to consider the dialectical process by which further differentiation, integration, and development may occur. As the individual extends this form of activity into new situations, he or she is likely to have the experiences of having the ball taken away by other players. This set of experiences, and the visual attention to the other players that will result, may be considered to be the differentiation of an "antithesis" that stimulates further development. Simultaneous attention to the hand and arm motions of dribbling and to the other players (conflict) will lead to the modifications ("novel synthesis") that integrate avoiding losing the ball to the other players while maintaining the process of bouncing the ball, and that constitute the more developed skill of the expert dribbler.

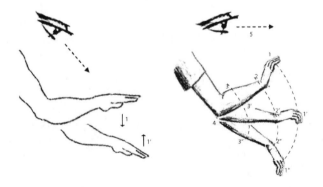

Figure 2.2 Structural transformations in the development of dribbling skills. The dribbling actions shown on the left are less differentiated and hierarchically integrated than those depicted on the right. The actions on the right involve greater differentiation in arm, wrist, finger and eye movements; greater coordination among these movements; as well as both greater integration of dribbling movements into a single seamless skill and integration of dribbling into the larger skill of *playing basketball*.

The right panel of Figure 2.2 illustrates the structure of dribbling in a more expert individual. The more expert individual's dribbling actions are more differentiated, integrated, and hierarchically integrated in a variety of ways. Unlike the novice's actions, the expert is able to cup her fingers over the ball (numbered *1* in the figure), move her wrist (numbered *2*) independently of her fingers and forearm (*3*), and modulate the movement of her upper arm (*4*) to keep her dribbling steady without looking at the ball (*5*). In this way, the movements of her fingers, wrist, arm, and eyes are *differentiated* from each other within the act of dribbling. At the same time, these various movements are *integrated* into the single fluid act of dribbling. Finally, the entire dribbling action is *hierarchically integrated* in that it functions in the service of the larger activity of playing basketball. This is indicated by the expert's ability to attend to other aspects of her playing while effortlessly dribbling the basketball (e.g., dribbling the ball without looking). This example illustrates the ways in which an apparently simple behavior such as dribbling a basketball undergoes massive structural transformation in development.

What does it mean to speak of psychotherapy as a process involving structural transformation? In the following example, we bring together our understandings of development as structural transformation and as dialectical process. We chart the structural changes that occur by tracing the sequences of differentiations, conflicts, and higher-order syntheses that take place over the course of a session of psychotherapy. We understand development, whether occurring primarily at the sensorimotor level as in dribbling a basketball or at the level of complex conceptual organizations of representations of activity, as occurring through the same dialectical process involving the prior development of the current thesis, the encounter with and/or differentiation of an antithesis (which poses a challenge to the functioning of the thesis in its previous form), the acknowledgment of a conflict between thesis and antithesis, and constructive efforts leading to a higher-order synthesis that resolves the conflict between thesis and antithesis.

Figure 2.3 depicts dialectical changes that occurred in the initial phases of a single (pivotal) session of short-term dynamic psychotherapy between a therapist and a 44-year-old woman experiencing depression and suicidal ideation (McCullough, 1999). This case will be the focus of our application of the method of developmental analysis in Chapter 8. In the session in question, the client described her feelings of (a) "not mattering." Thereafter, the client herself differentiated an antithesis and introduced a conflict: "(b) I matter onstage [at work, helping others] (c) but not offstage [by myself]." The client then offered a second antithesis conflicting with her own assertion of not mattering "offstage": (d) "It blows my mind to think that you and [my other therapist] would talk about me [showing

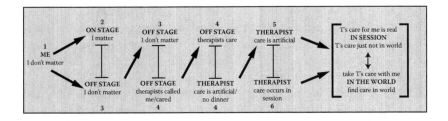

Figure 2.3 The role of conflict in psychological development. Microdevelopmental changes in a client's sense of *mattering to others* over the course of a psychotherapy segment. The outcome depicted represents a *synthesis* of that resolves a series of conflicts between and among several thesis-antithesis pairs over time.

care and implying that I matter] when I was home alone [offstage]." This statement yielded still another differentiation articulated by the client: (e) [Although you cared about me when I was offstage, being cared for by a therapist is] "artificial. I'm not going to invite you to dinner, and you're not going to invite me." In response to the therapist's suggestion that (f) "our experience will be here, in session," the client was then able to construct a higher-order synthesis that incorporated and resolved many of her earlier conflicts: (g) "Your care for me is real, not artificial; it's just not out in the world. My next step is to take your care with me and find other caring relationships in the world."

These brief examples illustrate both the assumptions and the methods of analysis that are central to this book. Development is understood as a process of both expression and extension of human activity within a social and natural environment. This process of expression and extension entails having new experiences, encountering new phenomena, and interacting with different people with different perspectives. These new experiences can be understood as differentiations, or antitheses, with respect to the prior pattern of activity that was expressed or extended. Differentiation entails both conflict and the opportunity for integration. In some cases the conflict may be intrapsychic—between two differentiated aspects of a person's activity or ways of organizing or making sense of that activity that are at first mutually incompatible, and that need to be in some way altered and/or coordinated in order for a synthesis, or integration, to be achieved. In some cases it may be conflict with the environment. A person (or group of people acting in coordinated fashion) may act in ways that cause unanticipated changes in the environment. Although the patterned activities that were extended into novel and changing environments represent theses, the discrepant events represent antitheses. The structure of the people's actions and anticipations must then be reorganized in order to achieve a synthesis that retains what was valuable in their prior organization of activity while allowing them to make sense of and be more prepared for the novel results. In still other cases, the conflict may be interpersonal or intergroup in nature. A person (or group of people acting in coordinated fashion) may act or express himself or herself in ways (theses) that contradict or disrupt the meaning making and related activity of other people (antitheses), who may then engage in responses that provide negative, unexpected, or problematic feedback to the original actors, making everyone aware that a conflict is present. Some combination of changes in the organization of all of the parties' activity and meaning making, which allows more effective coordination among the parties, then would be necessary to achieve a synthesis that resolves the conflict.

Applying these assumptions to psychotherapy, we assume that clients come to therapy facing "adaptive challenges." Such challenges consist of intra- and interpersonal conflicts for which clients have not yet been able to create novel syntheses. Clients may then encounter further adaptive challenges in the context of the therapy process. The adaptive challenges may include conflicts of any or all of the three types described above. Whatever the nature of the conflicts brought to therapy and encountered within therapy, when psychotherapy is successful, the therapist provides resources that the clients are able to use in creating novel syntheses that resolve conflict.

The Prescriptive Aspect of Developmental Models and Its Relevance to Psychotherapy Process and Outcome

The central explicit value entailed in approaching psychotherapy as a developmental process is placed upon the adaptive effort to resolve intrapersonal and interpersonal conflict through acts of organizing and reorganizing conflicting elements to form more differentiated, integrated, and adaptive wholes.[4] This central value, when understood in the context of

---

[4] Extensive epistemological justification for placing a fundamental value on conflict resolution of all three types may be found represented in philosophical traditions ranging from Hegelian idealism (Hegel, 1807/1977), to dialectical materialism (Wilde, 1989), to American pragmatism (Dewey, 1922, 1935/1999) as well as in Piagetian genetic epistemology (Piaget, 1970b). However, the reader is referred to the more recent work of Jürgen Habermas (Habermas, 1971) for the most comprehensive justification of the position that valuing human knowledge and truth entails valuing resolution of conflicts, within and between the organizations of activity of individuals and communities. Habermas' in-depth analysis of the nature of all forms of human knowledge suggests that to believe knowledge is possible presupposes the assumption that human knowledge and activity can become ever more adaptive, organized, and intersubjective, which in turn presupposes the possibility that conflict resolution of all types described above is a possibility. Furthermore, progress in the development of knowledge is inseparable from processes of resolution of emergent conflicts of the sorts described above. Thus, whether psychotherapy is understood as a form of inquiry aimed at discovering the truth, or as a context for the adaptive reorganization of human activity, conflict resolution can be understood as a reliable marker of success.

the coactive systems framework to be presented in Chapter 3, becomes the "comprehensive valuational framework" for guiding all psychotherapeutic practice that we alluded to in Chapter 1. Thus, we assume that when therapy is successful, the construction of novel syntheses can be observed. When therapy is unsuccessful, developmental processes of conflict resolution may be discovered to be stalled or blocked.

Within the context of this comprehensive valuational framework, there are many ways in which more specific developmental goals might inform, constrain, and shape psychotherapeutic practices and the developmental outcomes they promote. Different psychotherapies proceed with different types of goals in the minds of the participants. Figure 2.4 provides a schematic representation of the ways in which developmental goals and values might frame the developmental processes involved in different forms of psychotherapy. At the most general level, we suggest that (a) all successful psychotherapy functions by promoting developmental changes in patterns of acting, thinking, and feeling in order to meet adaptive challenges. This general psychotherapeutic goal can be actualized in a variety of different ways that can be understood as falling along a continuum. At one end of the continuum, some forms of developmental intervention are directed toward bringing about (b) preformulated outcomes using more or less prescribed pathways and developmental mechanisms. For example, some therapeutic approaches as well as types of presenting problems lend themselves to promoting particular types of therapeutic outcomes in clients. For example, the use of systematic desensitization as an intervention to overcome a phobia typically proceeds as a process of eliminating a particular fear through the development of skills in relaxation and emotional management that are then extended to the context of the feared object or situation. In such therapy, the anticipated developmental end point is clearly defined in advance, one can identify developmental change in the structure of the client's relaxation and regulation strategies over time, and one can evaluate the developing skill set with respect to the adaptive goals of managing or overcoming the phobia.

At the other end of the continuum, (c) developmental changes occur in a relatively open-ended fashion in the absence of prescribed or preformulated goals and pathways. For example, client-centered, constructivist, and other forms of collaborative psychotherapy often proceed in an open-ended fashion. In classic client-centered therapy (Rogers, 1951), the therapist adopts a "nondirective" stance, fashioning statements designed to bring the client's experience into greater awareness, with the assumption that the client will attend to experiences of conflict and create novel syntheses. In this way, although considerable development may take place during therapy, its outcomes and processes cannot be specified beforehand. In a different way, constructivist (Mahoney, 2003; Neimeyer,

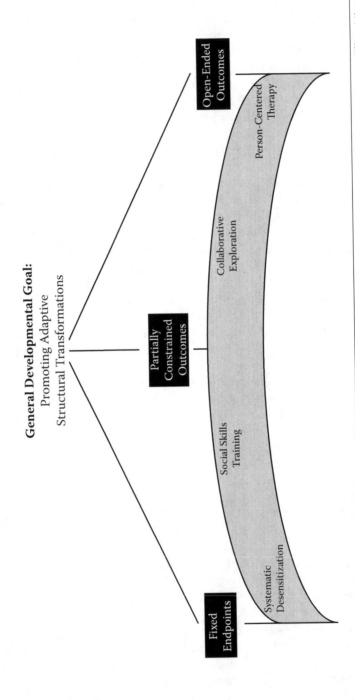

Figure 2.4 A continuum of developmental outcomes. Although all modes of therapy function to promote adaptive relations to a client's circumstances, different therapeutic encounters achieve this end in different ways. Figure 2.4 depicts a continuum of developmental goals from fixed developmental endpoints on the far left, through partially constrained endpoints, to open-ended outcomes whose structure and content cannot be determined prior to therapeutic intervention.

Herrero, & Botella, 2006), dialectical-constructivist (Basseches, 1997a, 1997b), and social-constructionist (McNamee & Gergen, 1992) therapeutic approaches proceed through dialogue where both representations of the clients' concerns and the construction of solution paths emerge jointly and cannot be specified beforehand. In such cases, one must wait until after the developmental process has been completed to identify the nature and the adaptive significance of the development that has occurred.

As is the case with developmental processes in all educational settings, a variety of approaches lies between these two divergent poles. Between these two extremes, developmental processes in psychotherapy vary in the extent to which their intended outcomes are specified beforehand. Further, such prespecification may constrain the manner in which the therapist responds to the client. For example, toward the more "constrained" end of the continuum, a therapist may set out to help a client remediate a social-skills deficit in order to be able to function effectively in a classroom. In contrast, toward the more open-ended end, a therapist may join with a client in an investigation into why all his intimate relationships seem to "end in disappointment." However, across this entire continuum, when psychotherapy is successful, the more developed outcome will be characterized by increased differentiation, integration, and hierarchical integration, with respect to the initial state.

The Value of Adopting a Developmental Perspective for Psychotherapy Research and Practice

Based on our understanding and valuing of development, we suggest that critical reflection on the effectiveness of psychotherapy may be greatly enhanced by going beyond the use of gross nomothetic measures of symptom reduction. It is as important to examine the process by which, in any given therapy, novel skills, meanings, and experiences take shape within psychotherapeutic exchanges. In adopting a developmental perspective for conducting such examination, one analyzes the changes that occur in successful psychotherapy in terms of the types of structural transformations that evolve over time through steps of differentiation and integration. As such, adopting a developmental approach to reflecting upon and analyzing psychotherapy provides a framework within which practitioners, theorists, and researchers can examine both the *structural changes* that occur in psychotherapy and the therapeutic *processes* through which those changes come about. The structures and processes involved in therapeutically induced change are not limited to what has traditionally been called *cognitive* processes. The structures that are transformed over the course of successful psychotherapy are structures of acting, thinking, and feeling; in everyday action, there are no "cognitive processes" that operate independently of action and feeling (Ackerman, Abe, & Izard, 1998; Freeman, 2000; Gallagher, 2005). Similarly, the social processes through which structural changes occur in psychotherapy are typically saturated with feeling and emotional meaning (Greenberg & Elliott, 2002; Plutchik, 2000). Emotion both organizes and is organized by psychotherapeutic encounters (Cozolino, 2002). Thus, adopting a holistic developmental perspective also helps us to understand more deeply what is going on when psychotherapy fails to succeed. It helps us to locate how progress is being blocked or thwarted in the interaction between client and therapist (see Basseches, 1997a, 1997b).

Further, the goal of promoting and analyzing psychological development directs the attention of practitioners, theorists, and researchers to the (positive) formation of novel structures of acting, thinking, and feeling as well as to the (negative) observations of symptom reductions that may result from such restructuring. By focusing upon *what develops* in psychotherapy in addition to *what goes away,* one is not only able to provide a richer analysis of the processes by which psychological "symptoms" are or are not mitigated, but also able to explore the ways in which psychotherapy and related social processes foster construction of more adequately organized forms of psychological and social functioning. Of course, the debate between those who view psychotherapy as a growth-oriented process and those who call for the rigorous analysis of the effectiveness of specific procedures in promoting symptom reduction is well-tread territory. However, in this book, in conceptualizing psychotherapy as a developmental process, we seek to move beyond such dichotomizing arguments. Instead, our intent is to provide a rigorous system of conceptual and empirical tools for analyzing with precision the nature and processes of developmental changes as they occur, or fail to occur, in any given course of psychotherapy.

CHAPTER 3

A Coactive Systems Model of Psychotherapy and Development

The central goal of this book is to articulate what it means to think of psychotherapy as a developmental process. Given the diversity among therapeutic approaches, there is a need for a theoretical framework that can integrate, as best as possible, conceptual and procedural insights from different schools of thought. Such a system would have to be a synthetic one that draws from different traditions in such a way as to resolve theoretical contradictions that separate those systems. We believe that contemporary systems approaches to human development have begun to provide ways to approximate this goal. Many of the tensions that separate traditional approaches to psychological development are based upon false dichotomies. These include strong distinctions such as inner/outer, nature/nurture, affect/cognition, thought/behavior, person/environment, self/other, subjective/objective, and many others.

Among the most basic insights of contemporary systems thinking is the idea that systems of thinking, feeling, and action emerge in development as a product of relations among processes rather than as the result of any single process or set of processes acting independently (Gottlieb, Wahlsten, & Lickliter, 2006; Kauffman, 1995; Lerner, 1991; Magnusson & Stattin, 2006; Van Geert, 1994). In this way, contemporary systems views embrace the idea of the lack of independence among the processes and systems that exist both within and between persons. Rather than pitting one or another "cause" of development against each other, systems thinking embraces the idea that developmental outcomes are products of how complex processes coact with each other over time. Thus, it is not helpful to ask whether genes or environment are more important in the development of an individual structure; the relationship between genes and the multiple environments in which they are embedded is a bidirectional one (Gottlieb & Lickliter, 2007; Oyama, 2000). It does not advance our knowledge to ask whether either cognition or affect is primary in human functioning; affect and cognition are inseparable as causal processes in the production of action, intentional or otherwise (Freeman, 2000; Lewis, 1995). Sharp distinctions between inner experience and outer behavior do more to obscure than clarify the nature of human action; there good reasons to argue that what we call the outer is a manifestation of the inner, and vice versa (Ekman, 1993; Mascolo, 2008a; ter Hark, 1990). By challenging the idea of the independence of causal processes, systems thinking provides a framework for understanding of how development occurs through relationships of mutual adaptation rather through the cumulative effect of independent influences.

In this chapter, we elaborate a coactive systems framework for understanding the production of meaning, experience, and action within social relations. The coactive systems approach builds upon three main traditions. These include Piagetian and neo-Piagetian constructivism (Basseches, 1984, 1997a; Fischer & Bidell, 2004; Mascolo & Fischer, 2006; Piaget, 1970a, 1970b, 1985), sociocultural and social-constructionist theory (Cole, 1996; Gergen, 2006; Rogoff, 1990; Shotter, 1997; Valsiner, 1998; Vygotsky, 1978; Wertsch, 1998), as well as contemporary systems theory that incorporates embodied conceptions of development (Bråten, 2007; Gottlieb et al., 2006; Lewis & Granic, 2000; Thompson, 2007).

Piagetian and Structuralist Foundations

As a genetic epistemologist, Piaget's (e.g., Piaget, 1970b) primary interest was in human beings as knowledge-constructing organisms. His work emphasized the biological similarities shared by humans with other organisms by (a) taking their *actions or activities* within their environments as a fundamental unit of analysis and (b) observing how such activity is organized and becomes reorganized over time. He emphasized what was unique about human activity by studying the role of intelligence in the reorganization of human activity. He thus viewed knowledge as a uniquely human, continuously developing organ that was used and shaped in the process of adaptation, parallel to the organs that play roles in the adaptive activity of other life-forms. For Piaget, knowledge was neither a more or less accurate copy of an independent external material universe nor a reflection of an *a priori* structure of the human mind imposed on the material world. Knowledge is an organization of human activity, formed and re-formed by the process of active adaptation in the course of interaction with the material. Its adequacy is to be judged by its capacity to provide equilibrium in that interaction. We take the implication of this view for psychotherapy to be that psychotherapy is a context in which new knowledge is created. The adequacy of the knowledge should be judged by its adaptive value, not only for the individual client but also for the ongoing, ever-expanding interaction of all members of the human species with each other and for their collective interaction with the material world.

The Piagetian focus on action or activity, which is simultaneously "experienced" by the individual and observed as "behavior" by others, also has many important implications for psychotherapy. All psychological processes are actions, organizations of action, or aspects of action. The role attributed to action implies directly that humans (including infants) are *active* beings who contribute directly to their own development. Although the initial organizations of action in the neonate may be in large part reflexive, the accompaniment and resultant integration of action with emotion quickly lead humans to become *goal directed* (Lewis, 1990; Mascolo, Fischer, & Neimeyer, 1999). They thus come to know their world by virtue of goal-directed manipulations of the world. The foundational modes of psychological functioning consist of sensorimotor actions, which involve the coordination of sensory and motor aspects of manipulating physical and social objects in the world (Piaget, 1952). This last point implies that our actions in the world are *embodied* (Thompson, 2007). They take place within the medium of the human body and within physical and social contexts. Action is organized around a continuous flow of sensory, motor, and affective experience in the physical and social world (Piaget, 1954, 1981).

Further, from this view, thinking is not a process that is separate from action; thinking is a form of *internalized action* (Piaget, 1952; Piaget & Inhelder, 1966/1971; Sarbin, 1972). For example, imagining—the process of constructing images in any given sense modality—is the product of abbreviated action. When a person constructs an image, his or her sensory and bodily systems—including brain activity—are put into states that are similar to but not identical with the states that occur when a person actually experiences the imagined scene (Annett, 1995; Nelson & Brooks, 1973). In this way, Piaget's conception of action is a holistic and integrative one. Because thinking is a form of internalized activity, there is no separate, independent mental sphere that lies behind and explains action. In this way, Piaget anticipated current conceptions of the embodiment of mind and thought (Clark, 1997; Glenberg, 1999; Thompson, 2007).

Piaget maintained that all action has *structure*. As such, the basic unit of psychological analysis is the *scheme* or *psychological structure*, which consists of an organized pattern of action, thought, or experience (Piaget, 1954/1970a). The most basic of schemes are biologically organized reflexes—innate elements of action that require direct stimulation for their evocation. Piaget's concept of reflex was not a mechanistic one. Piagetian reflexes are *molar* actions over which the neonate has a limited degree of active control. These include *looking* at an object placed in front of the eyes; actively *sucking* on a nipple placed in the mouth; *closing the fingers* around an object placed in the hand, and so forth. Within the Piagetian system, it is the *structure* of action that undergoes developmental change. In development, virtually any aspect of behavior undergoes a series of gradual changes in organization, which can be tracked. The innate sucking reflex undergoes structural change as it accommodates to the contours and resistances of the breast or nipple. The capacity to reach begins to develop very soon after birth and undergoes massive development over the first years of life. The uncontrolled swipe of a 1-month-old is not the same as the more controlled and directed reach of the 4-month-old, which differs considerably from the flexible capacity to reach around obstacles in the 8- or 9-month-old (Fischer & Hogan, 1989; Piaget, 1952). This principle applies to the development of virtually any class of psychological activity, including the complex structures of experience and action that emerge and develop in the context of psychotherapy.

Psychological structures, or *schemes*, operate through the dual processes of *assimilation* and *accommodation*. Drawn from the biological metaphor of digestion, *assimilation* refers to the process by which objects are broken down and incorporated into existing structures; *accommodation* reflects the complementary processes of modifying or adapting existing structures to accept or incorporate objects (Piaget, 1952, 1985). Any psychological act requires the assimilation of an object into an existing structure and the simultaneous accommodation of that structure to the incorporated object. For example, to perform the sensorimotor act of grasping a rattle, an infant incorporates (assimilates) the rattle into her grasping scheme. However, to grasp the rattle, the infant must modify her scheme to the particular contours of the incorporated object.

The concept of *equilibration* provides the backbone of Piaget's constructivist theory of development (Piaget, 1960, 1981, 1985). As mentioned in Chapter 2, Piaget elaborated upon several forms of equilibration. The first involves the detection of a conflict or discrepancy between an existing scheme and a novel object. Piaget (1985) held that a state of equilibrium results when an object is successfully incorporated into a given scheme, and thus when assimilation and accommodation are in a state of balance. A state of disequilibrium results when there is a failure to incorporate an object into a given scheme. A child who only has schemes for cats and dogs will have little difficulty identifying common instances of these two classes, but he might be in disequilibrium with his environment when first encountering a rabbit. Disequilibrium, in turn, is the starting point for equilibration—a series of successive acts of accommodation, differentiation, and reorganization that result in a significant modification of the existing schemes. Thus, new schemes emerge from the failure and modification of existing schemes. Where there were initially only schemes for cats and dogs, there were later schemes for cats, dogs, and bunnies. (The roles of words—for example, "bunnies"—and the social partners who may use the words in this differentiation of schemes are subjects of some controversy within the Piagetian tradition and will be discussed later in this chapter.) However, the main point here, which we incorporate into the coactive systems framework, is that developmental change is a process of equilibration. Thus the process of encountering and resolving disequilibrium brings about developmental change, and developmental change is reflected in the production of structures or organizations of activity that provide greater equilibrium. Developmental change is reflected in the increased differentiation, integration, and hierarchic integration of schemes, whether they are schemes of action or representational thought. Higher-level forms of organization of activity build on lower-level schemes through the process of coordinating increasingly differentiated schemes into higher-order structures.

Disequilibrium was alluded to in Chapter 2 by the use of the term *conflict* (Bearison & Dorval, 2001; Druyan, 2001; Inhelder, Sinclair, & Bovet, 1974). As we noted, conflict may be experienced as internal to a person's activity and thought, or between people and their physical and social environments. This book claims that the identification and resolution of intraindividual and interpersonal conflicts that may be identified at behavioral and/or epistemic levels are central aspects of all successful psychotherapy. We further claim that valuing development, as the identification and resolution of all these forms of conflict, provides an appropriate evaluative framework to guide all psychotherapy practice. Among the forms of disequilibrium or conflict discussed by Piaget (1985) were (a) scheme–object conflict (as in the example above, when a scheme or set of schemes fails to accommodate an object), (b) scheme–scheme conflict (e.g., as exemplified in Chapter 2, when conservation of length and conservation of number come into conflict; see Becker, 2004; Inhelder et al., 1974), (c) conflict between a subscheme and the system of which it is a part (e.g., an adult failing to conserve in a new conceptual domain—say, mass and energy—despite having already acquired an abstract and generalized concept of conservation), and (d) interpersonal conflict (i.e., when peers disagree over an interpersonal issue or about their explanation on a scientific or moral problem; Piaget, 1932, 1995).

Piaget also noted that disequilibrium is also sometimes an occasion for the production of affect (Piaget, 1981). Although Piaget is most notably known for his approach to cognitive development, for Piaget, cognition and affect do not function as independent systems. Emotion is a central aspect of all activity throughout ontogenesis. Piaget held that cognition and representational activity reflect the structural aspects of action, whereas affect provides the "energetics" of activity. Different forms of affectivity accompany and energize action in different ways depending upon the particular state of adaptation of an individual's psychological structures to the environment. The affective aspects of disequilibrium have been studied in research on the concept of *moderate discrepancy from a schema* (Kagan, 2002; Weiss, Zelazo, & Swain, 1988). A variety of studies performed in the 1970s (McCall, Applebaum, & Kennedy, 1977; Zelazo, Hopkins, Jacobson, & Kagan, 1973) suggested a curvilinear relation between infant attention and the degree of discrepancy from a familiar stimulus event. Events that are moderately discrepant from an individual's schemes evoke interest and curiosity. Nondiscrepant events engender boredom and underarousal; highly discrepant events may be so discrepant from existing schemes that they are not even noticed, or, if noticed, can precipitate signs of negative emotion (e.g., Hopkins, Zelazo, Jacobson, & Kagan, 1976; Kagan, 2002). The idea that discrepancy and disequilibrium generate emotion has obvious implications for the process of psychotherapy. Intra- and interpersonal conflicts that bring people to psychotherapy involve strong affect. The processes by which disequilibria and emotion are introduced, recognized, and managed within psychotherapy relationships play essential roles in the types of developmental changes that occur over the course of therapy.

Limitations of Piagetian Constructivism

Although we embrace both Piagetian models of psychological change and their organization into justifications of what constitutes epistemic progress (the development of more adequate knowledge), there are several aspects of Piagetian theory that we find limiting and attempt to transcend in our view of the nature of development. Most prominent among these are (a) the theory of global stages, (b) imprecision in identifying levels of psychological development, and (c) a lack of emphasis on social and cultural relations as constitutive of developmental change.

Regarding stages, throughout most of his career, Piaget was understood to be claiming that cognition and action develop over time through a series of broad-based and structurally homogeneous stages. Research conducted in the latter quarter of the 20th century is inconsistent with this assertion (Fischer, 1980; Fischer, Bullock, Rotenberg, & Raya, 1993; Flavell, 1982; Gelman & Baillargeon, 1983). Different skills, even those in the same conceptual domain (e.g., forms of conservation), develop at different rates—even in the same child! Variation in the developmental level of an individual's skills is the rule rather than the exception in development. Further, evidence suggests that psychological development is strongly tied to particular behavioral and conceptual domains, tasks, experiential history, sociocultural contexts, and other local conditions (Bidell & Fischer, 2006; Mascolo, 2008; Vygotsky, 1978). Such findings suggest that rather than thinking of development as a series of broad-based stages that change systematically over the course of childhood, it becomes possible to think of development in terms of structural changes that occur in *particular domains of acting, thinking, and feeling as they arise within particular sociocultural contexts*. It is the structure of particular classes of actions, thoughts, and feelings that develop as often as it is broad-based competences. Although the relevance of theories of global stages to psychotherapy has been explored by theorists such as Kegan (1982) and Ivey (Gonçalves & Ivey, 1993; Rigazio-DiGilio & Ivey, 1993),[1] the conception of development adopted within the coactive systems framework opens the door to thinking about the emergence of specific skills, experiences, and behavioral dispositions over the course of psychotherapy as developmental processes.

A second limitation concerns the level of precision afforded by structuralist theory in assessing levels and trajectories of developing skills. The four broad-based stages of logical understanding proposed by Piaget (sensorimotor, preoperational, concrete operations, and formal operations) provide too crude a yardstick to identify the contextualized and often fine-grained structural differentiations and integrations that occur as patterns of acting, thinking, and feeling develop over time (Bidell & Fischer, 1996). This is particularly the case in mapping out changes that occur in microdevelopmental time—that is, changes that occur in relatively short periods of time, such as hours, days, or months rather than years. To address these shortcomings, during the last 25 years, a series of neo-Piagetian thinkers have developed structural models of psychological development that allow researchers and practitioners to make major and fine-grained distinctions in the structure of specific skills over time (Case, 1992a, 1992b; Case & Okamoto, 1996; Demetriou, Shayer, & Efklides, 1992; Fischer, 1980; Fischer & Bidell, 2006; Mascolo & Fischer, 2004). Rejecting the doctrine of global stages (Dawson-Tunik, Fischer, & Stein, 2004), these theorists have developed powerful models of tracing with precision qualitative and quantitative changes in the structure of particular skills as they arise within particular contexts and domains. In this volume, we draw upon these models to chart changes in the structure of acting, thinking, and feeling across a variety of therapeutic interactions.

The third limitation is the lack of emphasis on social and cultural relations as constitutive of developmental change. A central problem for any

---

[1] See Basseches (1989, 2003), Fischer and Tunik-Dawson (2004), Mascolo (2008), and Mascolo and Fischer (2005) for discussions of both the value and limitations of "global stage" models.

developmental model is the question of how more powerful and highly developed structures can emerge from less powerful ones (Fodor, 1980). The concept of equilibration directs attention to the role of cognitive conflict or of unpredicted results of actions in development. However, cognitive conflict itself cannot explain the initial steps of cognitive development. For example, Inhelder et al. (1974) demonstrated four steps in the development of a child's capacity to incorporate and profit from cognitive conflict. Children only begin to notice a cognitive conflict after a long period of *failing* to notice a conflict. Thereafter, children begin to construct different types of solutions to resolve the conflict. As Becker (2004) and Fodor (1980) have cogently argued, cognitive conflict itself cannot explain the processes by which children move from failing to notice a conflict to noticing a conflict. If the experience of conflict is a necessary condition for development to occur, then how can development ever move beyond early levels in which individuals fail to notice a conflict?

To answer this question, it is necessary to postulate principles of developmental change in addition to the concept of equilibration. Piaget himself (1973) postulated four change processes that can instigate experience of conflict and thereby lead to developmental change: maturation, experiencing, social transmission, and equilibration. Local changes brought about by maturation, experience, and social transmission set the stage for the broader structural changes brought about by equilibration. For example, a 5-year-old who performs multiple acts of picking up and throwing different objects (e.g., blocks, rocks, and socks) will gain slightly different forms of knowledge from each such action. After multiple such acts, a child will gain sufficient knowledge to begin to compare and notice differences in his various experiences of throwing different objects (e.g., someone else or the child herself points out that she can't throw heavier objects as far as lighter objects). At this point, the child is able to begin to notice conflicts and discrepancies, and the process of equilibration ensues. This example shows that other change processes are necessary to support and activate the equilibratory process. A central mechanism of developmental change that is typically acknowledged but not analyzed in adequate detail in Piaget's accounts (see Piaget, 1996) is the role of social relations, language, and culture. In our efforts to track more closely the role of social relations in developmental change, we have built our coactive systems model of development in part on the contributions of sociocultural and social-constructionist thinkers.

Sociocultural and Social-Constructionist Foundations

Sociocultural theorists have articulated alternative developmental models that highlight the social and cultural origins of higher-order psychological processes (Cole, 1996; Kozulin, Gindis, Ageyev, & Miller, 2003; Lave & Wenger, 1991; Rogoff, 1990, 2002; Shweder, 1990; Valsiner, 1998; Wertsch, 1998, 2002). Although there are differences among sociocultural approaches, all generally share the assumption that action and meanings are constituted by processes that occur *between* rather than *within* individuals. Although they do not always address issues related to development, social-constructionist writers also maintain that meaning and action are joint products of discourse rather than properties of individual minds (Edwards & Potter, 2006; Gergen, 2006; Gergen & McNamee, 1991; Harre & Gillett, 1994; Shotter, 1997). Sociocultural and social-constructionist approaches have built upon Vygotsky's social-cultural-historical theory (Vygotsky, 1978, 1981, 1987). Vygotsky postulated that higher mental functions (e.g., voluntary attention, logical remembering, mathematical skills, and writing skills) are cultural-historical products rather than constructions of individual minds. All higher-order functions—such as mathematics, literature, art, and complex problem solving—are the *historical* and *cultural* products of communities of individuals working together within social contexts to solve social problems using particular social and cultural tools. Higher-order modes of thinking, feeling, and acting are represented within semiotic systems of tools, artifacts, and practices shared within specific linguistic communities (Rogoff, 2002). Different linguistic communities have created different semiotic tools, practices, and artifacts to mediate and regulate social life. Performing accounting operations using an abacus (Hatano & Amaiwa, 1987), counting using a 27-point system of locations on the body (Saxe, 1982), developing facility with algorithms, and using calculators and other modern technologies constitute different semiotically mediated systems for performing culturally embedded mathematical tasks.

Higher-order operations are produced and maintained through the use of language and other semiotic vehicles (Becker & Varelas, 1993; Rommetveit, 1985; Wertsch, 1998). Sign systems are particularly important in this process. *Signs* (e.g., words, or mathematical or musical notation) are one of several vehicles of *representation*—the capacity to make one thing stand for or refer to something else. Signs have special properties that make them particularly central vehicles of social interaction and the formation of culture. Signs exhibit at least three central properties that differentiate them from other forms of representation (McNeill, 1982). Signs are (a) *generative* systems that represent (b) *arbitrary* and (c) *shared* meanings. First, signs are *generative* in the sense that given a finite number of elements and rules of combination (e.g., phonemes, and letters), persons can generate an infinite number of meanings. For example, using the rules for combining the 26 letters of the English alphabet, one can construct an infinite number of possible meanings. The same, of course, applies to the infinite number of numerical expressions that can be created using numerals and their combinatory rules. Second, signs are *arbitrary* in the sense that the concepts and meanings to which they refer can be constructed in alternative ways based on purpose, history, and context. Words do not simply (or even primarily) refer to physical or concrete objects in the world. Instead, they refer to systems of *meanings*. Words do not gain their meaning through correspondence to fixed objects and entities in the world; words do not necessarily "carve nature at its joints." As a result, the meanings to which words and expressions refer are arbitrary in the sense that they *could be otherwise* depending upon the ways in which they are used (Mascolo, 2008a; Wittgenstein, 1954) to make social distinctions that serve human purposes. For example, the meaning of the term *democracy* does not come from its correspondence with an entity in the world, fixed or otherwise. In fact, as an abstraction, there is no tangible thing in the world to which one can point when speaking of democracy. Instead, democracy is a concept whose meaning has been shaped historically over time for human purposes. Still further, the various forms of government that can be considered to be democracies differ widely in their constitution and functioning. That which we call a democracy is made intelligible—and perhaps even comes into existence—through the ways in which the term *democracy* is used among persons within a linguistic community.

The third feature of signs is that they represent *shared* rather than *idiosyncratic* meanings. One way to appreciate this distinction is to compare the meanings of words to the meanings of images, pictures, and icons. What is the meaning of the symbol ☹? There are a wide variety of meanings that can be bestowed upon this symbol. It can refer to the concept of "sadness"; "a sad face"; "a frown"; "Joe, the guy who is always sad"; a poor grade on a student's paper; a warning to stay away from some dangerous area; and so forth. In this way, the meanings of a symbol, image, or picture are far more idiosyncratic than the meanings of a word. Although individual words and expressions can confer different meanings, there are far more degrees of freedom for interpreting the meaning of ☹ than there are in understanding the meaning of the sign (word) *sad*. Unlike the symbol ☹, the word *sad* represents a more or less *shared understanding* of the meaning to which this word refers. In this way, words are vehicles for constructing, representing, and conveying shared meanings. Further, because the meanings that words represent are both generative and more or less arbitrary, language operates as the quintessential vehicle for creating novel meanings between people within a given linguistic community. In this way, language can become a tool for thinking and for regulating action. To the extent that language represents socially shared meanings that have been historically shaped by social purposes over long periods of time, the process of thinking using language has social rather than personal origins.

Consciousness that is structured by language is thus simultaneously structured by meanings and practices that have their origins in the history of one's culture. From this view, that which we call the *mind* has social rather than personal origins (Wertsch, 1985). Thus, beyond the communicative functions of speech (Rommetveit, 1985), individuals use words and other semiotic vehicles to *think* with (Wertsch, 1985), to *regulate* their personal and social action (Diaz & Berk, 1992), and to *participate* in (Rogoff, 1993, 2002) social-cultural activities.

To the extent that persons use signs and other semiotic devices to think with, to regulate their actions, and even to mediate feelings, it follows that signs mediate psychological activity. Again, building upon Vygotsky (1978, 1986), Wertch (1998) suggested that what people call "mind" is a form of *mediated* action. From this view, signs and other cultural tools for acting function as *mediational means.* The idea that signs mediate individual and social activity is not to say that signs are simply an intermediate step between "stimulus" and "response." Signs exert what Vygotsky (1978) called *double action.* That is, signs exert regulatory control not only over stimulation from the environment but also over a person's actions toward the environment. Using signs, individuals are able to use cultural meanings not only to define the nature of environmental input but also to regulate thoughts, feelings, and actions in relation to such input. As such, signs *free* individuals from the constraints of the here and now. In so doing, signs function as emancipatory tools; using signs and other semiotic tools, individuals are able to fashion novel meanings to regulate their acting, thinking, and feeling in the world.

These ideas directly inform and reflect the sociocultural view that higher-order functions develop as a result of processes that occur *among* rather than *within* individuals (Gergen, 2001; Wertsch, 1985). In development, in interacting with other persons, an individual child steps into an already existing set of sociocultural processes mediated by sign activity. The process of developing higher forms of knowing involves the internalization of sign-mediated relations that occur between individual children and their socialization agents. This notion is cogently stated in Vygotsky's (1981) oft-quoted general genetic law of cultural development:

> Any function in children's cultural development occurs twice, or on two planes. First, it appears on the social plane and then on the psychological plane. First it appears between people as an interpsychological category and then within the individual child as an intrapsychological category. (p. 57)

The concept of internalization explains how sign-mediated activity that initially occurs between people comes to be produced within individuals in development. For example, to help his 6-year-old remember where she put her baseball mitt, a father may ask, "Where did you last play with it?" In so doing, the father and daughter use signs to regulate the mental retracing of the girl's actions. As the girl *internalizes* these sign-mediated interactions, she acquires a higher-order memory strategy—"retracing one's steps" (Wertsch, 1998). This vignette illustrates Vygotsky's (1978) notion of the *zone of proximal development* (ZPD). The ZPD refers to the distance between a child's level of functioning when working alone as compared to her developmental level when working with a more accomplished individual. In the above example, the father's questions raise his child's remembering to a level beyond that which she can sustain alone. The child's higher-order remembering strategy is *formed* as she internalizes the verbal strategy that originated in joint action. In this way, learning that occurs within a child's ZPD plays a leading role in "pulling" development forward.

Psychotherapy occurs largely through the medium of *talk*. Sociocultural and social-constructionist approaches highlight the special role of social interaction using cultural tools—most notably speech and language—in the *formation* of higher-order psychological processes. From this view, the developmental changes that occur in psychotherapy do not emanate from within the client; they occur as a product of processes that occur *between* the client and therapist. Through the use of language, development occurs as the client and therapist cofashion novel meanings that have the capability of transforming the structure of the client's thoughts, feelings, and actions. Thus, language is not simply a means of communicating thoughts and feelings that have their origins within the "separate and distinct" minds of the client and therapist; instead, analysis of the ways in which the client and therapist use language reveals the process of development itself. Further, to the extent that development occurs through sign-mediated interactions, it follows that the process of development within psychotherapy is not something that is necessarily hidden from the view of third-person observers (Shotter, 2000; ter Hark, 1990). The processes by which novel meanings, actions, and feelings are transformed are largely displayed within the language-based interactions themselves. Thus, analysis of how language is used in psychotherapy is central to understanding how psychotherapy operates as a developmental process.

Limitations of Sociocultural and Social-Constructionist Approaches

Unlike constructivist approaches, sociocultural and social-constructionist approaches attend to the central roles of language, culture, and social interaction in the construction of meaning and action. In so doing, they provide an important corrective to constructivist focus on the primacy of individuals in the construction of meaning. However, in appropriately highlighting the social and cultural origins of meaning, sociocultural and social-constructionist approaches tend to underrepresent the contributions of individual actors and their biological subsystems to the production of acting, thinking, and feeling (see Harré & Gillett, 1994; Valsiner, 1998, for important exceptions to this assertion). For example, Vygotsky (1978, 1981) and others (Gergen, 1991) have invoked the concept of *internalization* to explain the processes by which sign-mediated social activity prompts the formation of individual action. Sociocultural theorists have debated the utility of the concept of internalization for explaining the social origins of individual activity (Rogoff, 1993, 2002; Valsiner, 1998). Rogoff (1993) has suggested that the traditional notion of *internalization* implies that meanings must move from the "outside" to the "inside" of individuals. There are several problems with this view. First, the concept of internalization suggests a sharp distinction between the "internal" and the "external" (see Harré, 1983, for an extended critique of this distinction). In so doing, it treats meanings as if they were "objects" that must pass across a "barrier" en route to an inner world. To speak of the internalization of meanings implies that meanings-as-objects are untransformed as they pass from the external to the internal. However, individual actors transform the meanings that they gain from their social interactions (Mascolo, Pollack, & Fischer, 1997) as they assimilate them to their current purposes and the meaning system that structure their purpose. Therapists are well aware from the times clients tell them, "You said…" how much what they say is transformed into what the clients "hear." Similarly, the concept of internalization preserves a sharp distinction between *individual actors* and their *social worlds*. To say that a person internalizes meanings that are external to the self separates the individual actor from the social relations of which he is a part. However, individuals are active participants in their social interactions. They not only actively transform the meanings that they encounter but also influence the social process involved in the production of those meanings, and this is very evident in our observations of psychotherapy process.

To address this concern, in the course of elaborating her apprenticeship model of human development (Rogoff, 1990, 1993, 2003), Rogoff proposed the concept of *participatory appropriation* as an alternative to the notion of *internalization*. In guided social interaction (e.g., among students and teachers, or clients and therapists) among active participants, novel meanings and actions emerge *from the interaction among the parties*. Through *participation* in social activity, participants *appropriate—take and use for themselves*—meanings that arise from their guided participation in social exchanges with others. The concept of appropriation has several advantages over the traditional concept of internalization. First, it suggests that the individual is active in the process of learning and development.

Second, it suggests that the forms that arise in participatory interaction are not acquired wholesale. The individual is selective in that which he or she takes from the social interactions of which he or she is a part. In addition, individuals *transform* the meanings that they select and use in terms of their existing skills and understandings (Mascolo, Pollack, et al., 1997). A 4-year-old child may profit when her caregiver redirects her actions by saying, "If you don't share your blocks, your friends will think you are selfish!" However, it is unlikely that the child will be able to construct the same understanding of *share, friends*, and *selfish* as the caregiver. Given the child's developmental level, emotional state, and current motivations, the child might even transform the caregiver's complex meaning in terms of the much simpler "Mommy's mad!" Similarly, the developmental processes that occur within psychotherapy cannot be reduced to the mere internalization of external meanings. Any complete understanding of the processes involved in psychological development, whether or not they occur in a therapeutic context, requires detailed attention to the processes by which individual actors contribute to and construct meanings within social interactions of which they are a part.

Within sociocultural and social-constructionist accounts, development is seen as a process of internalizing sign activity (Vygotsky, 1978; Wertsch, 1985), developing private speech to regulate individual and social activity (Diaz & Berk, 1992), task mastery (Wertsch, 1998), or skill in collaborative problem solving (Wertsch, 2002). Although there has been much research devoted to studying the ways in which individual understanding emerges from culturally embedded social interactions, sociocultural approaches have not provided tools for analyzing the *structure* of developing skills, understandings, or actions. Any form of acting, thinking, and feeling exhibits structure. From our perspective, development involves the process by which any given system of acting, thinking, and feeling undergoes transformation (i.e., increased differentiation and integration) over time. There is no contradiction between a structural analysis of individual development and analyses of the social, cultural, and historical processes by which such structures arise and change over time. Indeed, an integration of structural-developmental and sociocultural approaches provides the core of the approach to understanding development and observing it in psychotherapy that we adopt. We ask, "How do novel structures of acting, thinking, and feeling emerge over the course of sign-mediated social interaction in various forms of psychotherapy?" "How do novel meanings emerge as a product of between-individual exchanges?" and "How do individual actors contribute to those changes?" Of course, in order to identify developmental changes in structure, there is a need for precise, contextually sensitive tools to identify the structure of acting, thinking, and feeling, as the well as the ways in which such structures undergo transformation both in moment-to-moment action and across longer periods of development. Such tools are available in the form of the neo-Piagetian approaches to development identified above, and particularly dynamic skill theory (Fischer & Bidell, 2006; Mascolo & Fischer, 2006). Such tools can be used to chart developmental changes in psychological structures as they emerge and change in the course of social interaction, including the varieties of psychotherapeutic exchanges.

The Embodied Coactive Systems Framework

Our approach to tracking and describing development brings together dimensions of the neo-Piagetian and sociocultural models of development to create a coactive systems framework for analyzing the dynamic organization and development of joint acting, thinking, and feeling. Our approach to the values embedded in the term *development*, and thus in the use of *developmental frameworks*, also brings together elements of these two models. We endorse the value from Piagetian genetic epistemology that increased differentiation and integration, and the ability that comes with it to maintain equilibrium (balance of assimilation and accommodation) across a wider range of human experience, can be equated with more adequate knowledge. At the same time, we extend the recognition from sociocultural models to claim that the development of more adequate knowledge is ultimately a social and cross-cultural process that occurs within and among communities. Rather than viewing knowledge as being extended and validated by individuals developing in parallel more complex understandings of a presumed stable world, we view knowledge as being extended and validated in the context of social interaction among changing individuals, and cross-cultural interaction among changing cultures, and that part of the adaptation–equilibration process in which knowledge is created and validated entails resolving not only cognitive conflict but also conflict at the intrapsychic, interpersonal, and intercultural levels.

The links that we use to bring these frameworks together include contemporary *systems* theory (Fischer & Bidell, 2006; Fogel, 1993; Gottlieb et al., 2006; Lerner, 1991; Lewis & Granic, 2000; Mascolo, Craig-Bray, & Neimeyer, 1997; Thelen & Smith, 2006; Van Geert, 1994) as well as *embodied* and *enactive* approaches to human development (Clark, 1997; Gallagher, 2005; Glenberg, 1999; Thompson, 2007; Zahavi, 2005). Thinking of human activity in terms of systems has a long history in psychology (Koestler & Smithies, 1969; Kuo, 1967; von Bertalanffy, 1968; Weiss, 1977) and psychotherapy (Guerin & Chabot, 1997). At its most basic level, from a coactive systems approach, instead of taking the individual person, the internal information-processing system, the dyad, or participation in sociocultural activity as a primary focus, the unit of analysis is the *person–environment system* (Bergman, Cairns, Nilsson, & Nystedt, 2000; Granott & Parziale, 2002; Mascolo, 2005; Wapner & Demick, 1998). From this view, a coactive systems conception maintains that action and experience are the emergent products of *coactions among subsystems* of the person–environment system, rather than from the independent operation of any single element or group of elements (Fischer & Bidell, 2006; Gottlieb, Wahlsten, & Lickliter, 2006; Oyama, 2000). The person–environment system is much like an organism. Although the subsystems of an organism are largely *distinct* from one another, they are *inseparable as causal processes* in each other's functioning, as well as in the operation of the organism as a whole. In this way, the coactive systems model rejects the privileging of any particular component of the person–environment system, whether it is individual action, social relationships, culture, particular classes of psychological processes (e.g., cognition or affect), or the biological substrata of psychological functioning. By focusing on relations among component subsystems of the person–environment system, important insights from constructivist and sociocultural approaches can be understood in relation to each other.

In addition, the coactive systems approach is informed by enactive and embodied approaches to human action and development. Human action is embodied in the sense that all human action takes place within and through the medium of the human body. As a result, although the meanings that people create in social interaction are mediated by signs and symbols that have their origins in social interaction and culture, the capacity for language and meaning making is founded upon the structure, functioning, and experience of the human body as it operates within physical and social space (Gallagher, 2005). Key among the embodied processes that ground the construction of meaning is emotion (Emde, 1983), and especially the experience of emotion in social interaction with others (Trevarthen & Aitken, 2000). In the past several decades, research on infant–caregiver interaction has highlighted the intensely emotional nature of infant–caregiver interactions. Researchers have also highlighted the ways in which sensorimotor experiences (Smith, 2005) and emotionally charged interactions with caregivers shape the development of meaning (Cowley, Moodley, & Fiori-Cowley, 2007) and even lay the foundations for cognitive and language development (Arbib, 2006; Tomasello, 2003; Zlatev, Brinck, & Andrén, 2008). Thus, in addition to understanding the ways in which structures of acting, thinking, and feeling are founded in language-mediated social interaction, it is also important to understand how bodily and emotional experience grounds and influences the direction of higher-order construction of meaning. Below, we examine how research on embodied action (Meltzoff & Brooks, 2007) and intersubjectivity (Trevarthen & Aitken) in infancy informs the coactive systems model.

We devote Chapter 9 to more detailed analyses of the role of emotion in development and psychotherapy.

The Person–Environment System

Figure 3.1 provides a schematic model of a coactive systems framework. As indicated in Figure 3.1, the person–environment system is composed of five basic classes of elements: Within a given *sociocultural context*, *individual action* is directed toward some physical or psychological *object*. In social interaction with other *persons*, individuals engage dialogically with other persons through the use of *mediational means*, which consist of culturally appropriated signs, symbols, and tools. Although each of these component processes can be *distinguished* from each other, none are independent or autonomous. Action in any given context is the emergent product of coaction among component processes, and is not a linear outcome of any single element (e.g., the individual child or the influence of others) or subelement (e.g., cognition or affect). As such, both within particular contexts and over the course of development, *control over the construction of action and meaning is distributed throughout the coacting elements of the person–environment system* (Granott, 1993; Salomon, 1993; Wertsch, 2002). Although elements of the person–environment system function as distinct units, they are nonetheless inseparable as causal processes in the construction of any given human action.

To illustrate the functioning of the person–environment system in individual activity, consider the simple act of drinking a cup of coffee. Any action is necessarily performed on some *object* (real or imaginal) within

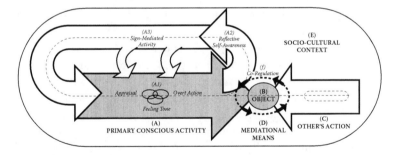

Figure 3.1 The person–environment system. The person-environment system is composed of five basic classes of elements. Typically, (A) primary conscious action is the result of the interplay among (A1) appraisal, affect and overt action; individual action (B) is intentional in the sense that it is directed toward objects (real or imagined), (C) takes place within socio-cultural contexts, most often (F) in co-regulated interactions involving (D) other people. Within social interaction, individual and joint action are (D) mediated by language and other cultural tools. Language thus functions as a form of (D) meditational means through which individuals (A3) reflect upon their actions and co-construct higher-order representations of (A2) self that drive thinking, feeling and social action.

a particular physical or social *context*. Actions are therefore *intentional* in the sense that they take objects; they either are performed *on* something or are *about* something (Merleau-Ponty, 1962; Searle, 1983; Vedeler, 1991). Like all action, the process of drinking a cup of coffee is a dynamic, situated, and intentional one. Drinking a cup of coffee involves coordinated acts of reaching, grasping, and moving that are performed *on* and *with* the cup. When drinking a cup of coffee, the physical structure of the cup plays a direct role in the coordination of the drinking action. An individual must adjust his or her reaching and grasping movements to the particular contours, weight, and structure of the cup. In this way, although actions are performed on objects, objects function as an actual part of ongoing behavior. Simultaneously, the *context* in which an action occurs also plays a central role in the emergence and execution of action. The actions involved when one drinks a cup of coffee at the breakfast table are different from those required to drink a similar cup of coffee in a moving car. These actions are different still from the actions utilized to drink coffee inconspicuously while sitting in the audience of a psychological conference. Further, the act of drinking a cup of coffee is as much a cultural action as it is a social and personal one. The act of drinking is *mediated* through the use of cultural tools. One may use a different type of cup in all three of the social contexts discussed above—one's favorite porcelain cup at breakfast, a plastic portable mug in the car, or a Styrofoam cup with a plastic lid at the conference. Each of these cultural tools provides a different means for mediating the act of drinking and plays a role in the actual organization of acts of drinking. Finally, other *people* figure prominently in acts of drinking. For example, when people mutually adjust their sips to fall into the breaks of conversational turns, they nonconsciously regulate each other's drinking actions.

The idea that objects, language, other people, and context simply "have an effect" on an individual's action is not a controversial one. However, the coactive systems view goes beyond the everyday idea that the social environment "has an effect" on individuals. The main point of the coactive systems view is that the elements of the person–environment system do not function independently of one another. This statement calls for a shift in the ways in which we often think about the analysis of causality in psychology. The various elements of the person–environment system are not "factors" that exert either individual or collective effects on an individual. Instead, the objects of a person's actions, the linguistic and nonlinguistic tools that mediate action, the actions of others, and the physical and representational aspects of the sociocultural context itself all function as a *part of the process* of an individual's ongoing action. Because control over action is distributed among elements of the person–environment system, at any given moment, even subtle shifts in relations among system elements can lead to significant transformation in an individual's action. A coactive systems analysis of psychotherapy processes requires ways to assess changes in the relations among coacting system elements as they operate in relation to each other over time.

Fleshing Out the Model: Co-Regulation and Intersubjectivity in Development

The concept of *coaction* (Gottlieb, Wahlsten, & Lickliter, 2006; Gottlieb & Lickliter, 2007) or *co-regulation* (Fogel, 1993; Lewis, 1996; Mascolo, Fischer, & Neimeyer, 1999) is central to a coactive systems approach. *Coaction* refers to the idea that although elements within a given system act according to their own principles of organization or structures, they nonetheless regulate or influence each other's functioning over time. The co-regulation of action in face-to-face social exchanges is indicated at point (f) in Figure 3.1. The concepts of coaction and co-regulation can be illuminated through an analysis of human communication systems. We often depict the process of communication mechanistically in terms of individual senders forwarding discrete and bounded messages back and forth to each other. Such a process is characteristic of discrete state communication systems (Fogel, 1993). From this view, a discrete message originates within a single individual and is encoded and then sent through a fixed communicational channel (e.g., as in a telegraph, mail, or e-mail). After the individual sends the message, it remains fixed and cannot be changed throughout the process of transmission. After the correspondent receives the message, she must decode it. Only *after* she has decoded the message can she switch roles from receiver to sender, and continue the exchange. This form of communication is typical of those that involve the use of letters sent through the mail, e-mail, telegraph, and related mechanical exchanges of information.

Face-to-face communication, however, does not proceed in this way. Face-to-face exchange provides an example of a continuous-process communication system (Fogel, 1993, 2006). In ordinary interaction, interlocutors are simultaneously active as both senders and receivers. As one person speaks, the other person provides *continuous feedback* in the form of verbal and nonverbal indicators (e.g., nodding of the head, changing of facial expression, direction of gaze, and even the time allowed to elapse before speaking). As a result, the "message" is not fixed and is free to change in the very process of communication. In social interaction, meanings are jointly constructed as social partners co-regulate each other's actions, thoughts, and feelings. In this sense, *co-regulation* refers to the process by which social partners simultaneously and continuously adjust their ongoing actions, thoughts, and feelings to each other (Fogel, 1993; Mascolo &

Fischer, 1998). It follows that within co-regulation, the actions of the other are part of the process of the self's actions, and vice versa.

The process of co-regulation is not restricted to social interactions that occur between people. Co-regulation occurs both within and between individuals. A case in point is the production and experience of emotion. Psychologists have long debated questions of the relationship between cognition, emotion, and behavior. Some psychologists have argued for the primacy of emotion as a central motivator of human action (Izard, 1977; Tomkins, 1962; Zajonc, 1984); others have argued that emotional feelings are dependent upon prior appraisals of the relationship between events and a person's motives and concerns (Frijda, 1986; Lazarus, 1991). Recent theory and research suggest that it is more helpful to view relations among affect, appraisal, and overt action as reciprocal ones. From this view, as indicated at point A1 in Figure 3.1, appraisal, affect, and overt action co-regulate each other over time. For example, at any given point in time, persons continuously and concurrently monitor information from thousands of sources. Most such processes necessarily occur without conscious awareness; it would not be possible to consciously appraise the thousands of classes of input available to a person at any given time. Notable changes in relations between events and a person's goals, motives, and concerns prompt affective changes. Affective changes, thereupon, *select, amplify, and organize these very same affect-generating appraisals for conscious awareness* (Lewis, 1995; Mascolo, Fischer, & Li, 2003). In this way, the experience of emotion both organizes and is organized by ongoing appraisals of one's circumstances. Emotion thus plays an organizing role in all forms of thinking and acting, intentional or otherwise (Freeman, 2000).

Emotion plays a central role in the co-regulation of action that occurs between people. The process of co-regulation between social partners begins at birth. This is an important idea that challenges long-held beliefs about the nature and origins of the capacity for intersubjective experience. Some traditions in psychology have held that infants enter the world as separate and independent beings. From these views, infants must "break into" social interactions through the process of perspective taking or by constructing an understanding or theory of the inner life of others (Kohlberg, 1969; Piaget, 1932). Another tradition holds that infants are initially fused with their caretakers and must develop the capacity to develop a sense of a distinct self through the process of separating or individuating from caregivers (Mahler, Pine, & Bergman, 1975). Contemporary research on the development of emotional intersubjectivity between infants and caregivers challenges both of these views. *Intersubjectivity* can be defined in terms of the capacity for shared or coordinated action or experience within episodes of joint action (Matusov, 1996; Rommetveit, 1979; Stern,

1985; Trevarthen, 1993).[2] Current research suggests that infants are capable of establishing *rudimentary* forms of intersubjectivity with caregivers from birth onward.

Support for this proposition comes from a variety of different research programs (Fogel, Garvey, Hsu, & West-Stromming, 2006; Legerstee, 2005; Zeedyk, 2006). For example, Trevarthen and his colleagues (Trevarthen, 1998; Trevarthen & Aitken, 2000; Trevarthen & Hubley, 1978) have traced the development of what they call *primary intersubjectivity* between infants and their caregivers. According to Trevarthen, the capacity for primary intersubjectivity emerges in the first months of life in the form of regularity in the timing of emotional facial actions and rudimentary forms of turn taking (Trevarthen, 1993). In face-to-face interaction, infants and their caregivers engage in a rich give-and-take of smiling, looking, cooing, and similar emotional behaviors. Through these richly co-regulated interchanges, infant and caregiver not only coordinate their facial and vocal actions *but also coordinate the emotional experiences that arise within the facial and vocal dance that occurs between them.* Gallagher and Hutto (2008) have suggested that these emotional exchanges suggest a capacity for immediate and prereflective forms of intersubjectivity and coordinated experience.

Such findings are bolstered by research that suggests that neonates are capable of imitating distinct facial actions modeled by others (Meltzoff & Moore, 1977, 1983).[3] In the case of facial imitation, the infant is unable to see her own facial movements. In order to imitate another person's facial action, an infant's processing systems must, in some way, integrate information obtained from observing another person's facial expression with proprioceptive experience of bodily movements that the infant cannot himself observe (namely, his own facial expression). This finding is inconsistent with Piaget's (1966) proposition that the capacity to imitate facial expressions must await a long period during which infants must gradually bring together separate visual and action schemes. Neonatal facial

---

[2] The concept of *intersubjectivity* is a somewhat elusive one. Perhaps the most common definition holds that intersubjectivity is a form of *shared experience* or *joint meaning*. One might ask, however, what does it mean to say that an experience is "shared"? Does it mean that one person has the same experience as another person? Or, at a higher level, does it mean that one person understands an event in the same way as another person? To what extent can very young infants be said to "have the same experience" as their caregivers? We prefer to think of intersubjectivity, at least in young infants, as a form of the *coordination* (see Matusov, 1996) rather than of (full) sharing of experience. When a mother's smile results in the elongation of an infant's smile, infant and maternal affect is clearly being *coordinated*; it is not as clear that their affect is *shared*.

[3] Claims of infant imitation remain controversial. Some evidence suggests that facial imitation disappears by 2 months of age (see Gouin-Decarie & Ricard, 1996; Müller & Runions, 2003).

imitation is an extraordinary finding, as it suggests infants are capable of perceiving cross-model correspondences between another person's actions and the actions and bodily experiences of the self.

The idea that infants enter the world capable of achieving primitive forms of intersubjectivity is bolstered by the recent discovery of "mirror neurons" (Gallese, Eagle, & Migone, 2007; Rizzolatti, 2005). Mirror neurons consist of neurons, initially discovered in the prefrontal lobes of monkeys, which become activated both when observing behavior in others and when executing the same action by the self. The existence of mirror neurons suggests that a common neurological system underlies both the observation and production of certain classes of motor behavior. The existence of such common neurological pathways provides a foundation for understanding how infants are capable of entering into emotionally mediated social interactions from the start of life. This proposition provides a framework for understanding not only the origins of neonatal imitation but also the broader capacity for intersubjectivity. It helps us to answer the question "How can humans—as separate and distinct individuals— come to appreciate the inner life of other such separate and distinct individuals?" The postulation of a mirror neuron or resonance system suggests an answer: Although individual persons are separate and distinct organisms, the mirror neuron system (or systems like it) provides the means for experiencing correspondences—however primitive at first—between the embodied action and experience of others and similar experiences within the self (Meltzoff & Brooks, 2007). This results in an *inversion* of traditional conceptions of the relation between social and cognitive development (Gallese, Eagle, & Migone, 2007; Hobson & Hobson, 2008; Rochat, 2008). Whereas traditional approaches maintain that intersubjectivity is a derivative product of cognitive development, the foregoing view suggests that psychological development builds upon a foundational capacity to establish intersubjective relations with others.

The Experiential and Discursive Construction of Self

How does the concept of self figure in the process of psychotherapy? We follow a long tradition of regarding self as a type of *experience* (Mead, 1934; Sarbin, 1952; Zahavi, 2005). To understand what it means to speak of *self* as a type of experience, it is helpful to differentiate two levels of conscious processes: *primary conscious activity* and *secondary acts of reflection.* Primary conscious activity is a form of prereflective awareness of aspects of the world. Primary conscious activity is represented in Figure 3.1 in terms of the gray base arrow (A). As indicated above, a key property of all action is *intentionality.* Intentionality refers to the *aboutness* of conscious experience—the idea that conscious activity is *about* something; it takes *objects.* A person cannot simply be conscious; a person must be conscious *of* the panorama in front of him, for example *awareness of* the *pain of his interlocutor,* or *experiencing a sense of not mattering to someone else.* In primary conscious activity, consciousness is externally directed toward some object of attention. The object of conscious action is represented in Figure 3.1 at point (B). In primary conscious activity, because one's full attention is focused on the object of one's activity, it is common for people to get "lost in the experience." One is primarily aware of the external object rather than of one's self. Despite the focus on an "external" object of consciousness, it is sensible to speak of an experience of self in primary conscious activity. Although we are primarily aware of the external object of attention (e.g., what our interlocutor is saying, the movie, or getting the ball in the basket), an implicit and prereflective experience of self is always available to use as a type of background. Looming in the background is an implicit and prereflective awareness of our body in space, an emotional feeling tone, and a sense of the agency of acting. It is likely that even very young infants experience a subjective sense of self in this way (Stern, 1985). At a more complex level, adults experience themselves in this way when they "lose themselves" in the flow of an engrossing activity (Csíkszentmihályi, 1991). Nonetheless, even when consciousness is engrossed in external objects, a background sense of self remains available (Gallagher, 2005; Zahavi, 2005). This implicit sense of self-in-action is represented in Figure 3.1 at point A1.

A second form of self-experience is the reflexive experience of self-consciousness. Self-consciousness occurs as a secondary act of self-reflection. Self-consciousness occurs as primary conscious activity loops reflexively back onto itself and *takes itself as its own object* (Mascolo & Fischer, 1998; Mead, 1934). The turning of consciousness back onto itself is represented in Figure 3.1 at point A2. As a higher-order process, secondary self-awareness begins to emerge in the middle of the second year of life with the capacity for symbol use. It is at this time that children begin to use signs and symbols to construct explicit representations of self. The construction of higher-order representations of self is a quintessentially social process. In development, socialization agents use language to draw individuals' attention to aspects of their own functioning. The parent who admonishes a child by saying, "Be a gentleman! We never hit!" not only has called a child's attention to himself but also has, through the use of language, encouraged the child to identify himself using a valued sociomoral category. Over time, children appropriate the language of their social community to identify their own experiential states, to regulate their own actions, and to form higher-order representations of self and identity. The use of language to mediate the higher-order construction of self is indicated in Figure 3.1 at point A3.

The distinction between primary conscious activity and secondary self-reflection is an important one for understanding the types of developmental processes that occur within psychotherapy. In any given instance of primary conscious activity, a person's consciousness is directed toward the most adaptively significant objects of action. All aspects of experience that are not the primary focus of a person's attention will occur in the background of consciousness. A person is not able to gain perspective on her experience during the time that she is immersed in it (Kegan, 1982). To gain a sense of the meaning of one's experience, it is necessary to engage in secondary acts of reflection. This follows for all types of experiences, including emotional experiences. Whereas the *experience* of emotion is direct, identifying the nature and meaning of one's emotional experience is not. The task of gaining insight into the nature of one's experience—emotional or otherwise—involves acts of reflection that are mediated by language. In psychotherapy, one of the key functions of a therapist's provision of attentional support is to orient the client's attention in such a way as to facilitate the client's attempt to articulate the nature and meaning of his experience. Similarly, when providing interpretations, a therapist attempts to frame the meaning of a client's experience in terms that arise from the therapist's own perspective. The use of language to represent the meaning of a client's experience is part of the process of co-constructing higher-order representations of the client's sense of self. Once constructed, higher-order representations of self play a central role in regulating thinking, feeling, and action (Carver & Scheier, 2002; Tangney, 2002). Thus, the transformation of representations of self plays a central role in many forms of psychotherapy.

The Process of Development: Individual Construction Within Joint Action

Whether it occurs in everyday life or in therapeutic contexts, development occurs as individuals construct higher-order structures of thinking, feeling, and action through the active coordination of lower-level actions and experiences. Although individuals are active contributors to their own development, individual actors are never the sole architects of their own development. In face-to-face interaction, social partners co-regulate each other's actions. An overwhelming body of research suggests that people are able to operate at higher levels of development when interacting under the guidance of a more accomplished other than when acting alone (Fischer et al., 1993; Vygotsky, 1978). These statements express a perennial tension in discussions about the nature of psychological development: On the one hand, individuals must play an active role in constructing higher-order meanings and skills; and, on the other hand, novel and higher-order actions and meanings arise in interactions with others. What is the relationship between individual actors and the social context in structuring development? How does the client contribute to her own development in the context of psychotherapy? How does the interaction between the therapist and client support the client's development? Drawing upon the coactive systems integration developed thus far, we suggest that *novel and higher-order forms of activity are jointly constructed in the therapy, but individually coordinated by each client.* Novel and higher-order forms of acting, meaning, and experience arise between people (or, more broadly, among elements of the person–environment system) within co-regulated interactions. However, in order for development to occur, individual actors must actively and effortfully coordinate and consolidate structures of action, thought, and feeling that have their origins in co-regulated interaction (Mascolo & Fischer, 2005; Mascolo, Pollack, et al., 1997).

How do individuals construct higher-order thoughts, feelings, and actions within co-regulated interaction? First, we begin with the assumption that *novelty* is a natural product of the types of co-regulated exchanges that occur in face-to-face interaction (Fogel et al., 2006). To the extent that partners jointly influence each other's actions in face-to-face exchanges, it is not possible to predict what meanings will emerge (Fogel, Lyra, & Valsiner, 1997). However, although novel meanings are created jointly in social interaction, the coactive production of novelty is not sufficient for development to occur. The production of novelty in face-to-face interaction provides a type of scaffolding within which individual actors construct and consolidate new skills and meanings (Mascolo, 2005). However, for development to occur, individuals must actively *do* something to construct stable and higher-order structures from the novel meanings that are jointly produced in social interaction. They must engage in acts that constitute the *transformation* of less developed meanings and skills into higher-order structures.

Fischer (1980) has proposed a series of transformation rules that describe how individual actors create higher-order structures from the coordination of lower-level skills and meanings. *Coordination* is the process of bringing into correspondence two or more previously unrelated meanings or actions. There are multiple forms of coordination. *Differentiation* refers to the process of articulating a new meaning in contradistinction to a previous or existing meaning. *Shift of focus* occurs when an individual changes the focus of his or her attention from one part of a task to another, without fully connecting the two parts. For example, when driving a car, learning to operate a manual stick shift requires the coordination of multiple actions at the same time. To reduce the attentional demands of learning to drive, the novice may first direct attention to one action (e.g., letting up the clutch with one foot) and then shift the focus of attention to another (e.g., stepping on the accelerator with the other foot). In this example, although shift of focus initially results in jerky stops and starts, it nonetheless allows the learner to begin to bring together two previously independent skills into an increasingly stable structure. *Generalization* (or *abstraction*) is also a form of coordination. Generalization occurs when an individual builds upon one or more concrete meanings or representations and coordinates them into a more general or abstract conceptualization. Finally, *full intercoordination* (*synthesis*) occurs when an individual brings together multiple lower-order actions or meanings in such a way as to produce a higher-order structure that resolves prior conflicts and contradictions. We view all forms of psychotherapy as providing contexts in which all of these processes *may* occur, and the therapist's effectiveness (mediated by his or her meaning systems derived from participating in psychotherapy cultures and broader cultures) in adapting to the client's action by supporting the right process at the right time, as central to successful psychotherapy.

Figure 3.2 provides a concrete example of how individuals coordinate novel forms of meaning within co-regulated interaction. This particular

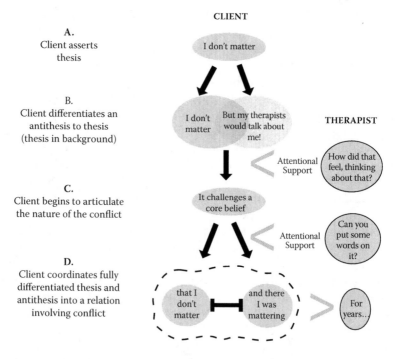

Figure 3.2 Differentiation and integration of novel meanings within joint action. In the context of attentional support resources offered by the therapist, the client engages in a series of cascading acts of differentiation and integration by (a) asserting a thesis; (b) differentiating an antithesis to the initial thesis, (c) coordinating the thesis and antithesis (d) into a relation of opposition indicating conflict.

interaction is taken from Chapter 8 (The Lady Cloaked in Fog). During this client–therapist exchange, the client begins by asserting her interpretation (thesis) of her major complaint, "I don't matter when I'm offstage [not at work]." Immediately, however, the client produces a concrete antithesis to this assertion: "It blows my mind to think that there were a lot of days like that when I'd go home and, my God, you and Carol [client's previous therapist] were talking on the phone. It blows me away." In this statement, the client performs an act of *differentiation*. Specifically, she articulates a representation of an event that provides a counterexample to her sense of not mattering. At this point, the full implications of this differentiation are not yet fully articulated. This is indicated in Figure 3.2 in terms of the overlap between the two representations that are undergoing differentiation. The phrase "It blows me away" is the only articulated part of the utterance that links the two evolving representations.

At this point, in responding to the client, the therapist provides attentional support by asking, "Now, how did that feel, thinking about that?" In response, in saying that "it … shakes something very deep … some real deep core belief," the client begins to perform a coordinative act of *generalization* or *abstraction*. Not yet articulating the belief that is being challenged, the client moves away from talking about the concrete events in which her therapists were talking about her. Instead, she begins the process of articulating the general implications of the differentiation that she is beginning to make. Sensing that the client has not yet articulated the nature of the "challenge," the therapist provides further attentional support by asking, "Can you put some words on it?" At this point, the client articulates the more fully differentiated meanings and identifies the conflicting relationship between them: "That I don't matter—and there I was mattering." This statement reflects an act of *coordinating* two meanings that have just been differentiated; in this case, the client coordinates her sense of "not mattering" and "there I was mattering" into a relationship indicating *conflict*. This conflict not only drives further co-constructive activity between the client and the therapist but also provides the core means by which the client will be able to deconstruct her sense of "not mattering." It will take emotionally charged co-constructive activity between the client and the therapist before the client is able to elaborate further and *actively experience* an emotional and embodied sense of truly mattering—in this case, to her therapist. But the seeds of the changes to come can be found in the very contradiction that the client articulated within the context of variations in attentional and emotional support provided by the therapist.

Moving Forward: Toward an Integrative Approach to Psychotherapy as a Developmental Process

Neither individual nor sociocultural approaches can adequately explain human activity or its development without reference to the other. Drawing upon systems theory and embodied approaches to development, the coactive systems framework brings these ideas together under a single umbrella. More importantly, it provides a set of conceptual and empirical tools for analyzing the ways in which psychological structures emerge and undergo developmental transformation within social interactions, and the role of individual and social and symbolic activity in bringing about such transformations. The developmental processes among coactive systems entailed by psychotherapy are clarified by locating the endeavor within the overall person–environment system as described above. Individual actors—clients as well as therapists—bring their backgrounds, meanings, experiences, and dispositions to the psychotherapy encounter. A focal question of this book is how we can understand how the personal resources and challenges that the participants bring, and the social interaction that transpires, coact to create novel syntheses or developmental transformations, understood as we described them in Chapter 2.

In the next chapter, we will focus both on the common resources that psychotherapists bring and on the common dialectical relational processes that occur, through which novel syntheses are created in psychotherapy. In Chapter 5, we relate these common relational processes to the specific languages and writings of theorists representing extant "schools" of psychotherapy. Finally, in Chapter 6, we will describe our system for charting developmental changes in the structure of acting, thinking, and feeling within the context of all psychotherapy, as well as the individual and joint change processes that promote such development. These conceptual and empirical tools will be used throughout the remainder of the book to analyze case studies of the course of psychological development in a variety of different psychotherapy encounters.

CHAPTER 4

How Psychotherapy Fosters Development

According to the developmental model presented in Chapter 3, assimilation and accommodation are aspects of every human activity. Cognitive conflict is ubiquitous, as multiple action-cum-experience schemes organize and are brought to bear on every novel encounter in life, and the novel aspects of those encounters challenge the schemes to accommodate to each other and to the environment. Furthermore, all this activity occurs in the context of social relations, social systems, and cultures that are simultaneously organizing, maintaining, and affecting each individual's activity. Social partners using culturally shared mediational tools evoke and direct one another's attention to (a) novel experiences that conflict with prior assumptions, (b) conflicting understandings of experience, and (c) unanswered questions. Whenever there is conflict, there are opportunities for the construction of novel syntheses, which represent development. So adaptive challenges, developmental opportunities, and developmental processes are ubiquitous too.

How do we understand what happens when a person enters psychotherapy? In the current cultural climate, as was stated before, clients' *entry* into psychotherapy can be understood as indicative of at least partially unsatisfactory results of clients' efforts to adapt to their environments by organizing and reorganizing their activity schemes, including their more conceptual meaning-making structures. The clients themselves, or whoever has referred them, have recognized some inadequacies in the clients' efforts to meet their current adaptive challenges. By entering therapy, the client is essentially recruiting from the therapist additional resources that potentially can be brought to bear on meeting those adaptive challenges present in the client's life. At the same time, the act of entering into therapeutic relationships creates its own set of adaptive challenges for therapist and client alike.

Because psychotherapy relationships entail social exchanges, the coactive systems model—our framework for understanding human development in the context of social exchanges—describes in the most general terms our understanding of the processes by which psychotherapy fosters development as well. However, in this chapter, we focus explicitly on the issue of the *kinds of additional resources* that the *psychotherapist may offer* that may be brought to bear on meeting the adaptive challenges present in the client's life. We also consider the questions of what needs to happen for the client to make effective use of the resources offered by the therapist, and how the therapist, to be effective, must adapt the resources he or she offers in recognition of what the client is or is not able to use. In understanding psychotherapy as essentially a context for social exchange that may foster development, we are inviting psychotherapists to conceptualize their role or contribution in a significantly different way from both the medical model, which views the therapist as providing a treatment that results in a cure, and the more behavioral "change agent" model, which views the therapist as implementing a technique that causes the client to change. Instead, we are saying that human development represents an ongoing struggle to adapt through reorganization of activity within social exchanges, and that therapists are in a position to offer resources that may increase clients' effectiveness in their processes of adaptation and reorganization.

Keeping in mind our view that development occurs when adaptive challenges are met through the *creation of novel syntheses*, we now ask, "What are the types of resources that therapists can offer that may ultimately lead to the creation of novel syntheses?" Our answer to this question is derived from our understanding of the roles of attention, representation, action, and reflection (as these processes occur within coactive systems) in developing persons' creations of novel syntheses. The role of attention in psychotherapy is well stated in a 1995 article by Greenberg and Pascual-Leone:

> Attentional allocation is the central processing activity determining people's awareness of themselves. What is important for therapeutic purposes is that attention is under both deliberate and automatic control. By using different types of interventions at different times, therapists can orient, direct, and monitor clients' deliberate and automatic attention (Greenberg et al, 1993). In this way, attention provides a medium for change. People can use attention to alter their focus of awareness and to symbolize their inner experience. Personal change then can be achieved in many ways, including the following: (a) by attending to and symbolizing the internal complexity generated by

automatic experience, (b) by bringing about a synthesis of new structures in therapy through coactivation of existing and newly formed schemes, (c) by generating vital explanations of currently symbolized experience, and (d) by restructuring emotional schemes by evoking them and exposing them to new input.

A dialectical constructivist perspective therefore yields a theory that recognizes the significance of the client's emotional experience as well as his or her capacity to construct meaning and develop concepts. This integration implies a view of human beings as multiple-level processors who use different types of propositional (symbolic-logical) information and affectively laden experiential (sensory, perceptual, imaginal, and representational) information. Human beings, in our view, construct representations of themselves and reality in a moment-by-moment fashion, all the while dynamically reacting to what they are attending to.

Thus, growth-promoting conscious experience derives from both deliberately controlled (often conscious, serial, and conceptual-representational) processing of information and automatic (often unconscious, parallel, and sensorimotor) processing of self-relevant information. Consequently, an adequate theory should recognize three major roots of experience: *(a) a conscious, deliberate, reflexive, and conceptual process …; (b) an automatic, direct emotional-experiential process …; and (c) the constructive, dialectical-dynamic interactions between the two* (Greenberg et al, 1993). Reflexive conceptual knowing processes provide explanations, whereas emotional schemes provide immediate reactions. The dialectical synthesis of these different sources of experience … ultimately leads the person to … psychological maturity.

In therapy, this dialectical constructive process often involves exploring differences between actual immediate experience and prior conceptually held views of how that experience should be. Contradictions between one's reflexive or acquired concepts (explanations) about how things are, or ought to be, and one's immediate experience of how things actually are constitute a great source of emotional distress, and these need to be focused on to produce new syntheses that can provide a greater sense of personal coherence. (pp. 183–184; emphasis added)

So some activity schemes and skills may function automatically, activated by elements of the situation, and some (often more reflective and abstract) meaning-making structures may be used deliberately by clients as they consciously work to make sense of their experience. And, according to Greenberg and Pascual-Leone (1995), simultaneous attention to the functioning of both sets of structures, as well as to contradictions among them, is needed "to produce the new syntheses that can provide a greater sense of personal coherence" (p. 184).

It is from this formulation that we derive our answer to the question regarding the types of resources that therapists can offer to clients.[1] When therapists assist, guide, direct, or participate in the creation of novel experience, in which clients' skill structures are activated, accommodate to new situations, and become objects of reflection, we view this as contributing resources to the dialectic of *enactment*. When therapists assist by offering conceptual-representational schemes and structures drawn from their own ways of making sense of experience, which then may be deliberately brought to bear on making sense of the client's experience, we view this as contributing resources to the dialectic of *interpretation*. When therapists assist clients in maintaining simultaneous attention to the full range of their experiences *and* ways of representing and making sense and meaning of their experiences, *and* the contradictions or conflicts among them, we view this as contributing resources to the dialectic of *attention*.

It is in the operation of these three dialectics, which we view as *co-occurring* in every psychotherapy, that the steps toward the development of novel syntheses can be detected and tracked. When psychotherapy is "successful," the *combination* of these processes—in which the therapist (a) provides attentional support, (b) offers interpretations, and (c) participates in the enactment of novel experiences—results in clients constructing more adaptive, differentiated, and integrated organizations of their own experience and action repertoires. Thus, the process of clients' development moves forward. We shall now consider these three dialectics in greater detail.[2]

---

[1] The description of resources that follows is based on an account first presented in Basseches, 1997a, pp.23–28, and included here with the kind permission of Springer Science and Business Media.

[2] In the following conceptualization of these three dialectics in which therapists offer resources that may be used in the service of clients' development, we are not attempting to make hard-and-fast distinctions among therapist interventions as being of one type or another. We have stated our belief that these three dialectics co-occur in every form of psychotherapy. Often, the very same utterance by the therapist may have the potential to contribute to more than one, or even all three, of the dialectics. Whether the utterance does in fact play any of these potential roles in fostering development depends on whether and in what way the client uses and responds to the therapist's act. Insofar as the therapist is aware of his or her intent in making a comment or taking an action, it may be possible to judge what sort of resource he or she is attempting to offer. But the actual role of the action in fostering development is evaluated by reference to what follows, rather than by reference to the intent. In Chapter 6, on the empirical analysis of psychotherapy as a developmental process, we will explain how we have chosen to deal with this challenge in tracking developmental processes within psychotherapy.

The Dialectic of Attention

Within the dialectic of attention, therapists can *support* clients in the process of holding conflicting experiences or meaning-making structures, or conflicts between immediate experience and prior conceptual understandings, together in their attentional fields. This process of holding together in attention a conflicting thesis and antithesis is what facilitates the construction of novel syntheses. Therapists, when intending to provide the resource of attentional support, may assist the client by making statements and asking questions that help the client to increase the scope and effectiveness of his or her attention and constructive activity. But their assumption is that it is the client's constructive activity that will be the source of novel meanings and content.

The forms of attentional support that therapists offer clients fall into two overarching categories. To clarify the distinction between these categories, let us start with our conceptualization of the client's entry into therapy as a response to at least partially unsatisfactory results in his or her other efforts to adapt to challenges to his or her evolving meaning-making structures (i.e., organization of action or experience schemes). For some clients, these unsatisfactory results may include extremely emotionally painful experience—acute distress or anguish. For some clients, the failure of one's meaning-making structures to function adaptively may itself be experienced as a crisis of personal integrity, respectability, or even viability.

One category of attentional support includes those ways in which the therapist directly assists the client in attending to the full range of the client's experiences. This facilitates the reorganization of those experiences in ways that help to resolve conflicts and meet adaptive challenges so that the client's development may continue. The second category includes ways in which the therapist shares or alleviates the client's burden of managing extremely painful, threatening, or disorganizing emotions, including the panic, anxiety, shame, or sense of isolation that may be brought on by the subjective experience of meaning-making failure and inability to maintain a coherent organization of activity and experience. The successful establishment of a therapeutic alliance often entails the client feeling less alone in the experience of disorganization, more hopeful regarding a successful resolution of the conflict, and assured that someone else can recognize and respect the integrity of his or her personhood, even when the client cannot recognize it himself or herself. This frees the client's attention from the sole management of the distress and the crisis of meaning-making failure and makes more attention available for renewed efforts to meet the adaptive challenges that precipitated the crisis.

The first category of forms of attentional support includes such varied therapist activities as asking clients questions, empathically acknowledging what one has understood clients to be expressing, drawing attention to aspects of clients' behavior and experience, and reminding clients of experiences that the clients previously described. Such activities represent some of the ways in which therapists from a wide range of therapeutic traditions guide and support their clients' attention to their own experience. Through such activities, therapists boost their clients' awareness of aspects of the clients' own experience that they might on their own tend to ignore. Therapists also assist their clients in simultaneously holding together in consciousness aspects of their own experience, behavior, and sense making that they might on their own tend to "split" (i.e., only experience sequentially in different times and/or contexts). Consider the following interchange (in the examples that follow, *T* indicates hypothetical comments a therapist might make, and *C* indicates hypothetical responses by a client):

T: How are you today?

C: Sick and tired of being told what to do by my mother.

T: Really had it with her meddling in your life?

C: Yeah, can you believe she called again today to check on whether I was doing my schoolwork?

T: She's just always right there.... Kinda like you really don't even get the chance to try facing it on your own?

C: Well, last semester she went about a month without calling me.

T: Is that sadness I hear in your voice?

C: (Starting to cry) Yes, dammit. I felt completely awful and ended up with two D's.

T: So you felt badly *and* you were disappointed with your grades?

C: I fell flat on my face! I just can't do it on my own, and I am so scared. (More crying)

T: So your mother's checking on you really infuriates you, *and* you are scared by what happened when she left you alone?

C: Yes. I really need to prove that I can succeed on my own.

T: Some kind of success is urgent.

C: I *did* succeed with my article on the hockey team's season! My roommate, my English teacher, and some guys from the team all said they really liked it!... And I never told my mother about that.... And I'm not going to....

The interchange above includes examples of empathically acknowledging named aspects of experience, highlighting under-attended-to aspects of experience, and bringing together in attention conflicting aspects of experience. Through such processes, conditions are created where clients can create novel synthetic transformations of their own experience. In the language of dialectics (Basseches, 1984), it is through the affirmation of theses, the discovery of antitheses, and the holding together of theses with their antitheses that the creation of syntheses occurs.

Often, but not always, finding the dialectical tension involves "exploring differences between actual immediate experience and prior conceptually held views of how that experience should be" (Greenberg & Pascual-Leone, 1995, p. 183). This may be accomplished by the therapist inviting, recalling and reporting, attending to, and symbolizing immediate experience and then holding it together with prior constructions. The interchange described above could easily lead to the client's acknowledging the belief that he or she should have achieved more sense of independence of mother than he or she frequently feels. In turn, accepting that conflict may lead the client to construct fuller, more complex, more adaptive representations of experiences of both independence and dependence.

The terminology of *guiding and supporting* attention, which allows the discovery of antitheses and the creation of syntheses in experience, is broad enough to describe a fair amount of what therapists who identify themselves as psychodynamic, cognitive-behavioral, or existential-humanistic, or in other ways (including "eclectic"), all do and to relate this activity to the fundamental developmental processes of the client. Each therapeutic tradition has its own language, and each therapist is guided by his or her own theories in guiding and supporting the client's attention. But in understanding psychotherapy as a developmental process, we view what the therapist does as only part of what makes psychotherapy a developmental process. Within the dialectic of attention, the clients may use therapists' guidance and support to increase the scope of their attention, to construct ways of holding conflicts together in attention, and ultimately to construct novel syntheses that resolve the conflicts. If the therapist, guided by his or her own theories, is directing the client's attention in ways that the client is unable to use, the therapy will only succeed if the therapist is able to adapt to support the process of the client in attending to those conflicts to which he or she is inclined and able to attend.

Our intention in using in this book a more generic developmental language for describing processes of attentional support is to help clarify the distinction between the appropriate and the inappropriate use of theory. Insofar as therapists' theories, by guiding the therapists' activity, play a role in creating conditions in which clients then create more complex and adaptive organizations of meaning, theory is being used appropriately. Insofar as therapists' preferred theories get in the way of clients' effective attention to their own experience (see Basseches, 1997b), they contribute to the difficulties in psychotherapy that we claim can be addressed through stepping back and adopting a more metatheoretical developmental understanding of psychotherapy processes.

The second category of forms of attentional support includes activities that are primarily reassuring rather than attention directive. They support the client's deployment of attention by freeing it rather than by assisting or guiding it. Instead of the therapist joining the client in holding the many aspects of the client's problems or conflicts in the attentional field, the therapist holds the client so that the client can more effectively hold the conflicts. If the client feels less alone in his or her experience, attending to even intensely painful feelings may be more manageable.

This type of activity was at the core of earlier formulations of "client-centered therapy" (e.g., Rogers, 1959). Rogers suggested that the therapist's primary job is to provide a climate in which the client experiences "unconditional positive regard," which Rogers believed would then free the client optimally to deploy his or her attention (or "awareness") in the service of his or her own development. It is questionable whether so-called nondirective responses merely echo the client's expression and communicate positive regard. Insofar as such responses inevitably *select* particular aspects of the client's communication to reflect, they must play a role in guiding the client's attention as well (Category 1). However, insofar as the principal effect is to reassure the client and to *encourage* the client's continued efforts to work toward growth, a nondirective empathic response may be said to fall into this second category.

Clearly, expressions of appreciation of the client's struggle made by therapists of all traditions also fall into this second category. When such appreciation is combined with therapist responses, which (in any theoretical or diagnostic language) implicitly or explicitly express the therapist's faith that this form of therapy can help this particular client, the client's panic may be relieved and a sense of hopefulness fostered. When this occurs, the client's attentional resources are clearly freed to address the task of creating novel syntheses of meaning-making schemes, and, therefore, such reassuring responses also fall into the second category of forms of attentional support. Attention-freeing responses may range from "Mm-hmm," to "I'm here," to "You've tried so hard to let him know how much you're hurting," to "You have a case of agoraphobia with panic attacks that can be treated successfully in any number of ways."

In sum, development can be understood as an attentional challenge. A wide range of emotion-laden action and experience schemes, constructed, organized, and reorganized throughout the client's entire history, and all in some way activated by various aspects of the client's current circumstances or deliberately employed by the client in response to that experience, must again be reorganized in novel and more adaptive ways to enable the client to function effectively and satisfactorily in these new circumstances. A client may be well aware of the functioning of many schemes; on the other hand, other schemes may be functioning with little or no conscious attention paid to them by the client except when their negative consequences are noticed. The construction of successful novel syntheses will require paying sufficient attention over time to all of the activated schemes and to their relationships with each other. Under conditions of crisis, the attentional challenge is even greater, as one's attention is inevitably drawn to those emotionally powerful schemes that are triggered by the experience of grave danger to the overall functioning of the entire organization of the self. Although the forms of attentional support provided in psychotherapy vary considerably, they all involve the therapist sharing some of the client's attentional burden.

The Dialectic of Interpretation

Within the dialectic of interpretation, therapists provide clients additional developmental resources by offering ways of making sense of experience *that are drawn* from the therapist's own representational schemes, structures, and processes. Offering potentially complementary or conflicting interpretations can be conceptually distinguished as a form of therapist activity from offering attentional support, although many therapists' comments in practice offer some of each. What distinguishes offering resources to the dialectic of interpretation is the awareness on the therapist's part that he or she is communicating an understanding of either a specific experience or human experience in general that is likely to be different from the clients' ways of understanding experience, and that is drawn from the therapist's own conceptual framework.[3] In attentional support, the therapist's effort is to increase or communicate understanding of the clients' own ways of making sense of experience.

Some approaches to therapy claim to rely almost entirely on processes of attentional support (e.g., Rogers, 1951). They support the client in mining the developmental possibilities inherent in the conflicts that the client experiences, through increasing awareness and holding together antithetical schemes and structures until novel syntheses are constructed. However, other approaches (e.g., traditional psychoanalysis) claim that offering the therapist's meaning-schemes (offering *interpretations*) to the client

---

[3] As used in this book, we distinguish the dialectic of interpretation from the more ubiquitous aspect of human meaning making in which clients as well as therapists are continually interpreting their own experience, and which therefore plays a central role in psychotherapy as a developmental process. In the case analysis chapters that follow, we will pay careful attention to tracking the steps that emerge as clients and therapists exchange with each other, accept, transform, and integrate interpretations of experiences. Here, we consider what happens in those moments when a therapist is deliberately offering a way of understanding experience that he or she expects may differ from the client's typical ways of making sense of his or her experience.

represents an essential ingredient of the developmental process. Doing so may facilitate development in a variety of ways.

The therapist may offer schemes that are useful to the client in explaining or reorganizing conflicting activated schemes of the client. For example, consider the following exchange:

T: It is quite common to long to be close to someone *and yet also* to very much fear closeness.

C: Well, you know, now that you mention it, I think that is exactly what I feel when I have been going out with someone for quite some time. How do other people deal with that situation?

Or the following:

T: My guess is that wanting to hide your feelings of how much you like her *has something to do with* fear of conflict with other men.

C: I did have this really awful dream where I got beat up last night ... and in the afternoon I had had this thought about buying flowers for Sandy.

We view the therapist's offering of an interpretation drawn from his or her ways of making meaning as constituting one way in which a *therapist* may offer a resource that may contribute to development within psychotherapy. However, we view such an act as representing only one step within the dialectic of interpretation as a developmental process. It is extremely important to recognize the role of clients' interpretive activity, as well as the dialogue between therapists and clients, within the dialectic of interpretation. The client may accept, reject, fail to understand, transform, or modify the content of an interpretation that the therapist offers. The client may also offer alternative interpretations. The value of the therapist's interpretation is realized only once the client is able to make use of it in his or her own organization of experience. It is essential for the therapist, once having offered the interpretation, to go on to collaborate with the client in discovering whether or not it is useful and relevant to the client, and, if it is useful, how. This perspective follows from our coactive systems model, in which developmental aliment is recognized as coming from others, in the form of culturally and linguistically mediated representations. However, as was stated in Chapter 3, it is only when the individual offered the aliment actively uses it to reorganize his or her own meaning making that the developmental potential is achieved.

Alternatively, the therapist's schemes may function as the antitheses to the meaning-making schemes of the client so that it is in integrating the client's schemes with those of the therapist that development may occur. For example:

T: You told me that you concluded you were powerless to influence things at your daughter's school, *but* in the situation you just described, it sounds to me like you came across as pretty powerful, maybe even scary, to your daughter's teacher.

C: Really? I seemed scary? I've never thought about myself that way.

Or the following:

T: I can see why you might take his offering to do the presentation with you as reflecting a lack of confidence in you, *but* it occurs to me that he may actually see it as an opportunity to learn something from you, or maybe to get to know you better.

C: Well, maybe, but you always have a more optimistic view about these things than I do.

T: Why do you suppose that is?

Again, it is essential to recognize the therapist's offering an interpretation as representing only one step within the dialectic of interpretation as a developmental process. It is through the *clients'* interpretive activity, as well as the dialogue between therapists and clients, that the developmental value of offering this resource is realized. In the case of a therapist's interpretation that conflicts with that of the client, the developmental potential lies in the conflict, and the developmental achievement lies in the construction of a novel synthesis that integrates the parties' perspectives. Therefore, it is crucial that therapists go on from this point of offering their perspectives to collaborate in discovering whether or not, and how, therapists' and clients' perspectives can be integrated. Furthermore, if it is clear from clients' responses that they are unable to make use of interpretations offered by therapists, reasserting those interpretations is likely to stall developmental progress, whereas responding to the meanings that clients are making and to the conflicts that clients are now experiencing is likely to foster effective psychotherapy.

We use the term *interpretation* in a very broad way, and not simply in the particularly psychoanalytic sense of an account of unconscious dynamics that may underlie conscious experience. *Interpretation* describes any situation in which therapists offer clients their own ways of understanding phenomena—ways of understanding that differ from or extend beyond the clients' understanding. Because therapists may differ tremendously among themselves in the theories they use and in the idiosyncratic ways that they understand human experience, human suffering, the sources of human difficulties, and how they can be ameliorated, interpretations can take very many specific forms. From a dialectical-constructivist perspective, the therapeutic value of such interpretations lies in the role they play within the dialectic of holding these interpretations in relation to other aspects of the clients' meaning making, and constructing novel syntheses that contribute to the evolving organization of clients' lives.[4]

Dialogue is a rich source of individual learning and development, and it is the fact that the therapist has different ways of making meaning from the client that creates the potential for movement inherent in the dialectic of interpretation. Therapists' formal theories represent part of the therapists' different ways of meaning making, and insofar as they contribute to the generation of interpretations that are useful to the client, they may play an important contributory role to effective psychotherapy.

The Dialectic of Enactment

A client's past and present experience—and existing ways of organizing that experience—necessarily constitute the bulk of the ingredients out of which novel, more adaptive syntheses are created in therapy. The therapist's attentional support contributes to this creative work. At times, as we have seen in the previous section on interpretations, therapists communicate their understandings, and these understandings also contribute to the creative work. The interpretations supplement the mix, serving as additional ingredients that facilitate the creation of new syntheses. However, what are needed most often in the mix of ingredients to increase the likelihood of clients creating novel, more adaptive syntheses are not only new understandings but also new experiences. It is through the dialectic of enactment that the therapist directly and actively participates in or influences the creation of new experiences.

Consider the following example:

A woman, Marla, who was sexually abused as a child, operates on schemes developed out of that experience, and repeatedly participates in new situations in which she is abused, devalued, or exploited. She withdraws from relationships, becomes desperately lonely, and then, motivated by her desperation, enters new exploitative relationships. She

---

[4] This dialectical-constructivist coactive systems view of therapeutic value contrasts with the tendency of objectivist (see Neimeyer, 1995, for the distinction between objectivism and constructivism) perspectives to derive the therapeutic value of therapists' interpretation from some notion of accuracy of either the interpretation itself or the framework from which the interpretation is derived. It also contrasts with the dialectical-constructivist coactive systems view of the *epistemological* value of both interpretations and frameworks, which lies in the role they play in providing equilibration within the full set of nested individual and social systems that human activity comprises. Within that broader context, developing systems of individuals' meaning making are interacting components out of which larger processes of epistemological validation derive, whereas for the objectivist, therapeutic value derives from prior epistemological validity.

views such exploitation as an inevitable aspect of intimate relationships, and has well-developed schemes for both creating and escaping from relationships. She describes her experiences in therapy. Her therapist formulates and offers interpretations of how she may have come to limiting beliefs that abuse and exploitation are inevitable aspects of close relationships. These interpretations may be useful to her, and she may become more aware of and able to conceptualize how her behaviors may contribute to cycles of abuse. She may even be able to entertain intellectually the possibility of escaping such cycles. However, she is likely to lack a repertoire of schemes or skills for creating and participating in trusting and trustworthy relationships. Without these schemes, such relationships would likely remain in the realm of abstract possibility for her. As Herman (1992), in her work *Trauma and Recovery*, articulated, it is often through the creation and constant testing of a trusting relationship with the therapist that victims of repeated exploitative relationships establish an initial experiential basis for alternative relational possibilities. It is through the therapist continually proving himself or herself as trustworthy to not exploit the client, in the face of a variety of tests and challenges, that recovery is facilitated.

The process described in this example is one form of enactment in that novel activity generated in the context of the therapy relationship itself becomes the basis of the development of new schemes that then become key ingredients in novel syntheses.

There is a very wide range of other forms that enactment and the inducement of novel actions and experiences may take. These include, for example: (a) enactment of transference patterns in psychodynamic therapy, creating the opportunity to transform the relationship and alter the patterns through interpretation of the transference; (b) systematic desensitization in behavior therapy; (c) experiments in relational expression in gestalt therapy; (d) homework assignments in cognitive-behavioral therapy and other out-of-session experimentation (e.g., in family therapy), planned and reviewed within the therapy sessions; (e) developing new supportive relationships in group therapy; (f) enacting a new ending to an unresolved past relationship in psychodrama; and (g) suggesting novel experiences in hypnotherapy, guided meditation, or progressive relaxation. In all of these techniques, new experiences are produced, attended to, conceptualized, and ultimately conceptually and behaviorally integrated with the rest of the client's experience.

Again, the diversity of forms of therapy suggests that there are a wide variety of theoretical frameworks that may guide therapists in creating novel experiences with their clients. There is also variation in the importance that particular theories of therapy and particular therapists may give to the enactment of novel experience and the creation of new activity schemes (relative to the offering of new interpretations and of support in attending to existing coactivated activity schemes in novel combinatorial ways). However, every course of psychotherapy will inevitably involve novel experiences, and everything that a therapist does that helps induce, structure, or guide the creation of novel skills may be understood as contributing resources to the dialectic of enactment.

But in understanding psychotherapy as a developmental process, what is most important from our dialectical-constructivist perspective is what all parties do to organize and make sense of novel experiences once they have occurred. A novel experience may be made sense of as irrelevant or harmful, or at worst experienced as traumatic. If therapists and clients can collaborate in the process of creating transformative novel syntheses that integrate the novel experience and skills with clients' prior repertoires and ways of making meaning, novel experience has the potential to function as one of the ways in which psychotherapy has the potential to foster development. However, if the therapist fails to recognize and be responsive to the novel experience and its meaning to the client, the negative and disorganizing potential of novel experience is as likely to be realized.

Summary of the Three Dialectics Within Psychotherapeutic Process

Attentional support, interpretation, and *enactment* are seen as representing three fundamentally different ways in which a therapist may offer resources within the context of psychotherapy—a potentially developmental process of social exchange that is somewhat unique in that clients' lives and experiences remain the primary focus of all parties' attention. In each of these three ways, a different sort of relational dialectic is occurring. In attentional support, conflicts emerge within the client's life and representational activity, and the therapist's intent is to assist the client in attending fully and effectively to those conflicts, which in turn facilitates the client's construction of novel syntheses. In interpretation, the therapist's intent is to introduce alternative ways of representing, organizing, and construing the client's experience, based on the therapist's own frame of reference. The therapist's interpretations then function as antitheses to the clients' habitual forms of organizing activity, creating dialectics in which the novel syntheses created represent integrations of both parties' perspectives. In enactment, the therapist's intent is to collaborate in the creation of novel experiences in the client's life, which then represent the antitheses to the client's prior experiences. The dialectics created involve the construction of syntheses that integrate these newly differentiated possibilities for the client within the client's life as a whole.

Diverse therapists' approaches may differ in the specific ways in which they (a) support and guide their clients' attention, (b) generate interpretations and offer them to their clients, and (c) contribute to clients' enactment of novel experiences. Therapists may also differ in the relative importance that they place on each of these kinds of processes and in how they conceptualize their integration. Some of these differences will be considered at length in Chapter 5. However, regardless of the extent to which the conceptual schemes and the immediate experiences reflected upon in therapy are those the client brings from life outside the therapeutic context, or are generated by the therapeutic context, the interactions of the levels of abstract conceptualization and immediate experience are crucial in psychotherapy.

The terms *attentional support, interpretation,* and *enactment,* because of their history within different psychotherapeutic traditions, may carry various connotations for various readers. We wish to address this issue here. Our choice to use these terms can be understood as a decision not to discard these connotations as irrelevant. However in our "common factors" pan-theoretical approach, we are equally hoping *to free these terms from their more narrow meanings* within specific theoretical traditions and to understand these developmental processes much more broadly. So, for example, the category *attentional support* may include the kind of "non-directive" empathic acknowledgment that Rogers (1951) argued creates conditions that expand clients' awareness of their experiences. But it may also include very directive questions, inviting clients to direct their attention to previously undisclosed aspects of their experience, as might often occur in an initial intake, or diagnostic interview. The category *interpretation* may include a traditional psychodynamic "depth interpretation," which reformulates a client's experiences in terms of anxiety-provoking hidden motives or feelings and protective defenses. But interpretation may also include any offering of the therapist's own thoughts or attitudes regarding a set of events that the client has related. *Enactment* may include activities as diverse as direct coaching of clients by therapists regarding new ways of handling situations, role-playing of challenging interactions in the office in an effort to discover new ways of responding, exploring possibilities for new ways of relating in group or family therapy, and homework assignments that explicitly involve attempting new behaviors outside the therapy office; however, enactment also includes the "reenactment" of clients' patterns of emotional and interpersonal conflicts within the relationship with the therapist, with either party looking for the opportunity to create novel endings or variations to the typical pattern.

These three core processes of psychotherapy sometimes function quite smoothly in promoting the client's development. Various elements of the therapist's organizations of activity, including those shaped by the therapist's professional training, may contribute to the smooth functioning of these processes. These may include the therapist's theories of psychology and psychotherapy. However, the occurrence of these processes does not depend on the therapist holding any *particular* theory. In fact, it is quite possible that any person (a) sufficiently empathic to attend to the client's experience (to facilitate the process of supporting the client's more effective deployment of attention), and/or (b) sufficiently thoughtful about human experience (to facilitate the process of offering the client dialectically relevant new meaning-making schemes), and/or (c) sufficiently self-reflective to be able to collaboratively reflect with the client on novel experiences arising from therapy (to facilitate the process of the client integrating such novel experiences into his or her own organizations of meaning) can function as an effective therapist in some cases.[5]

As we stated in Chapter 1, our goal in this book is not to prescribe a different therapeutic approach or set of techniques, or to prescribe that therapists abandon what they have learned to do effectively in the course of their training. What we are trying to do, in addressing the questions of how psychotherapy fosters development and what role in these processes therapists' contributions play, is to *describe* the fundamental processes that *all* cases of successful therapy have in common. However, what we are *prescribing* is that the developmental effectiveness of the resources that the therapist is offering be examined. Our further prescriptions relate to those situations in which the theories and practices that therapists have learned over the course of their training and experience are not in fact leading to interactions that foster developmental movement within these three dialectics. (See Basseches, 1997b, for a discussion of how the therapist's theoretical and technical commitments may at times actually obstruct the three dialectics.) In these cases, we invite therapists to take a step back from their accustomed theories and practices and to examine in much more general terms what may be blocking developmental movement within any of the

---

[5] Dawes (1994) (a) summarized the evidence that psychotherapy's effectiveness for the most part does not depend on any particular theoretical training, (b) derived from that evidence the advice to would-be clients that they seek out "any empathic person" to provide psychotherapy, and (c) concluded by casting doubt on the whole idea of expertise in psychotherapy. Although recognizing the same evidence base as Dawes, in this book we follow a different line of reasoning with respect to the issue of expertise. From our coactive systems model, we derive that all social exchanges, including psychotherapy, have the potential to foster development or to pose challenges to which participants are unable to successfully adapt. We conclude that expertise in psychotherapy relates not to particular theories that a therapist holds, but to the capacity to reflect on and recognize whether clients are able to use the particular resources that therapists are offering, and to adapt the resources one offers to what one's clients are able to use. We believe that the use of the methods of analysis that we offer in the next part of this book can make an important contribution to the development of this type of psychotherapeutic expertise.

three dialectics. We also invite them to consider what alternative psychotherapeutic resources to the ones they are offering might be of greater use to their clients.

For each type of resource that a therapist might offer that we have described in this chapter, we have described the ensuing movements—actions on the part of both client and therapist—that would need to occur for the psychotherapy process to successfully foster clients' development. In Chapter 6, we will describe methods for tracking the ensuing movement that does in fact occur, and for observing whether and how developmental novel syntheses are co-constructed in psychotherapy. In Chapters 7 through 9, we will use two psychotherapy cases to illustrate the intertwined processes of therapists offering resources to the dialectics of attention, interpretation, and enactment. We will explore how these resources, taken together, may foster development within Greenberg et al.'s (1993) "conscious, deliberate, reflexive, and conceptual process ... automatic, direct emotional-experiential process ... and ... the constructive, dialectical-dynamic interactions between the two." We will also use these cases to illustrate the developmental tracking methods described in Chapter 6, and their use to reveal whether the necessary processes of mutual adaptation occur in which clients learn to use the resources that therapists offer, and therapists learn to offer the resources that clients can use.

CHAPTER 5

Multiple Traditions, Multiple Paths
How Different Therapeutic Approaches Foster Development

Different schools of therapy foster developmental change in different ways. Different approaches to psychotherapy are organized around different principles for understanding the core processes by which psychotherapy produces changes in individuals. A central goal of this book is to provide a *common* framework and method for understanding how different approaches to therapy promote developmental change. We have argued that the core psychotherapeutic processes employed across different approaches to therapy can be understood in terms of three basic kinds of resources offered by therapists—attentional support, interpretation, and enactment—and the dialectical processes that can ensue. Furthermore, we have argued that these three processes, in some combination, are responsible for fostering developmental change in all forms of therapy. These basic categories are not meant to replace the theoretical systems upon which different approaches to therapy are based. Instead, they provide a set of meta-analytic tools for understanding how different approaches to psychotherapy promote development.

To illustrate application of these meta-analytic tools and the recognition of processes of attentional support, interpretation, and enactment—in varying forms and combinations—within all therapy, we have chosen four diverse approaches to psychotherapy to examine. These include Malan's psychodynamic approach (Malan, 2001), Rogers' (1942, 1951, 1961/1995) client-centered psychotherapy, Linehan's (1993a, 1993b) dialectical behavior therapy, and Yalom's (1980, 1995, 2005) existential group therapy. These

73

therapeutic traditions foster developmental change in clients in different ways. Although it is not reasonable to claim that any subset of approaches is "representative" of all of psychotherapy, we believe that every psychotherapeutic tradition and set of techniques is susceptible to this type of examination.

Malan's Psychodynamic Approach to Psychotherapy

Malan (2001) described the global process of therapeutic change as a movement from maladaptive to adaptive behaviors and from symptoms to symptomatic relief. This occurs because unconscious feelings are brought to consciousness, resulting in insight, and thus the feelings no longer need to be expressed through symptoms and maladaptive behavior. From this we can discern the idea that changes in clients' self-understanding supported by therapy will bring about concurrent positive behavioral changes within the client's life. Malan (2001) asserted that in this process, interpretation is "one of the therapist's most essential tools" (p. 3). In Malan's view, the therapist makes available to the client information that the client has defended against, and this presentation of repressed material allows the client (a) to realize how he or she "really feels," (b) to discover that these feelings and thoughts are not as painful or as dangerous as feared, and (c) to "work through" this material in the context of the therapeutic relationship. Finally, not only should the changes in therapy generalize beyond therapy and into the client's life, but also, according to Malan, these changes should remain stable over time.

The Primacy of Interpretation in Malan's Psychodynamic Approach

Though Malan listed interpretation as "one" of the therapist's most essential tools, it is clear from his focus upon it that to him, like many psychodynamic therapists, it is the most essential tool. This is not to say that Malan has not discussed other theoretical constructs. He has described and espoused a number of classically psychodynamic constructions that will be described below. But these concepts are about understanding the maladaptive nature of the client's symptoms. These concepts are interrelated around understanding why the client is in therapy. For Malan, interpretation is the key to the client gaining insight into his or her own condition that allows the interrelation of these phenomena to be interrupted and for the client to achieve positive life changes.

Malan elaborated upon the concepts of the unconscious, defense mechanisms, and transference in great detail. He presented unconsciously repressed "material" as being causally significant to the process of symptom expression and the development of maladaptive behaviors. He noted that this necessitates a process of discovery of unconscious material through such means as free association, dream interpretation, and observation of behaviors such as the development of transference. These provide the therapist with the clues necessary to formulate an interpretation with which to attempt to assist the client in becoming aware of his or her unconscious processes. It is interesting to note that Malan also approached his cases from a developmental approach in that he espoused interpreting Oedipus complexes—though less dogmatically than some—while questioning the ubiquitous significance of them that some other dynamic theorists have suggested. Furthermore, Malan's writing exhibits the concern with childhood experiences and the belief that these childhood experiences play a significant role in clients' contemporary lives.

Building upon the concept of the unconscious, again in the classical psychodynamic tradition, Malan has described how various defense mechanisms are used—without conscious awareness by their users—to protect clients' egos from assault. By bringing these patterns of behavior into the client's awareness, again usually via interpretation, the therapist assists the client in developing more sophisticated and adaptive defense mechanisms that result in reduced symptoms and maladaptive behaviors. Again, much of this theoretical construction is in effect giving meaning to and adding significance to the importance of the use of interpretation in psychotherapy.

It could be argued that there are both benefits and risks of such a sharp focus on the one therapeutic dialectic of interpretation. A benefit is a clearly articulated understanding of what is "one" of a therapist's "essential tools." Malan's (2001) *triangle of conflict* depicts the interrelation of defenses, anxiety, and hidden feelings. Malan joined this conceptualization with Menninger's (1958) *triangle of person* (originally referred to by Menninger as the *triangle of insight*) that depicts the interrelationship of transferences involving a parent (or sibling; P), an other (O), and/or the therapist (T). Together these "two triangles" provide a cogent model for analyzing cases, formulating interpretations, and categorizing them as well. To illustrate these categorizations, interpretations noting the parallel between a client's past feelings toward a parent (or sibling) and his or her current transference toward the therapist are termed *T/P interpretations*. Interpretations are assumed to have a cumulative and eventually permanent effect upon the nature of the *triangle of conflict* through a process of making unconscious processes conscious. One risk of overemphasizing interpretation is that the potential of the other dialectics to foster development may be systematically overlooked by therapists following Malan's approach. Another is that suggesting that the curative power of an interpretation derives from its *accuracy* in representing the client's triangle of conflict (a theoretical construction), rather than its usefulness as socially mediated *aliment* in the client's process of self-construction, can lead to overlooking the client's agency within the meaning-making process.

The Roles of Attentional Support and Enactment in Malan's Therapy

Although Malan emphasized and systematically developed a model to follow for the process of interpretation, he also discussed the necessity of building rapport with clients as an essential aspect of the psychotherapeutic process. Malan (2001) introduced the Law of Increased Disturbance, which states, "Under the impact of uncovering psychotherapy a patient always has the potential to become as disturbed as they have ever been in the past, or more so" (p. 244). Malan stated that this can be aggravated or mitigated by the actions of the therapist both positively and negatively. The latter occurs when anxiety-producing techniques are used inflexibly by the therapist. And he noted,

> The factors relieving anxiety that can appropriately be used to mitigate the dangers of uncovering psychotherapy consist essentially of *being both flexible and human*, of which we may mention: explaining what is required of the patient and why, answering legitimate questions, offering support and encouragement, and … genuineness and non-possessive warmth. (2001, p. 244)

The provision of support and encouragement reflect different forms of attentional support. The therapist's supporting/holding utterances function to modulate a client's affective state in order to maintain developmental challenges within client's attentional field. The provision of techniques to manage a client's anxiety and a genuine and non-possessive human relationship, in which the client's questions are answered and the expectations of the psychotherapy relationship are explained, constitute forms of enactment.

Figure 5.1 represents the relations among interpretation, attentional support, and enactment within Malan's psychodynamic approach to therapy. As indicated in Figure 5.1, interpretation functions as the primary vehicle of therapeutic change. Despite the primacy of interpretation, attentional support and enactment are not absent. Instead, they function in the service of interpretation. Attentional support is necessary to support the client's attempts to articulate the material upon which the therapist's interpretations can be based. Further, enactment of genuine and nonpossessive warmth

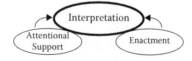

Figure 5.1 Structure of therapeutic resources in Malan's psychodynamic approach to therapy. In Malan's psychodynamic approach, interpretation is understood as the primary therapeutic resource supporting development. However,; attentional support and enactment play essential roles in the service of the dialectic of interpretation.

bolsters the client–therapist relationship, and provides the socioemotional foundation necessary to articulate emotional meanings. Thus, in Malan's psychodynamic approach, although attentional support and enactment operate as important components of the therapeutic process, they function through the contributions they make to the interpretative process.

We now examine the roles of interpretation, attentional support, and enactment in segments of Malan's (1994) "The Case of the Secretary With the Violent Father":

> The client is a twenty-seven-year-old single secretary who came to the psychiatric clinic subsequent to a crisis. Her boyfriend had attempted suicide and was admitted to the psychiatric service of a hospital. She complained of having been depressed since age thirteen and also of problems in interpersonal relationships. She felt that her depressions were caused by the fact that she had led a very restricted life at home and that this had been imposed on her by her father. As a child, she would sit at the window and watch the other children going out and enjoying themselves while she could not. She talked about her father being a rather strange man who drank heavily and who had frequent violent behavior. She indicated that her depressions tend to get worse in February and March. She said there were a lot of things to do in the summer but she didn't find things to do in the winter, and this caused her depression. (p. 129)

T: I notice you don't mention the thing that has apparently precipitated your coming here, which is something to do with your boyfriend having attempted suicide. Now, where does that fit into this story?

C: Well, it was the last straw. It's what made me decide to stop wasting time and go talk to somebody. I think I would have eventually done it. I think that this has caused me to do it at this particular time. Also, it's a very bad time for me to be depressed because I don't think that's what he needs right now, to see me depressed, it would make him a lot worse because he would be seeing himself as the cause.

T: You've managed to keep this from him, have you?

C: Yes, although I've told him that I was seeing a psychiatrist because I would like to talk to somebody and that I'm not feeling that great. But he doesn't understand that I felt this way before and that I get depressed. I didn't feel that this was the time to talk to him about it.

T: All right. Can we talk a little bit about the relation with him, then? Let's start with how long ago you met him.

C: Almost two years ago.

T: Can you tell me how your relationship developed?
C: Yes. It was very sudden. We met, and it took us about a week to establish the fact that we liked each other, and we were not separated very much after that. He stayed at my place all the time and went home for extra shirts. We've been very close, and we're now living together. He's been really good for me because he's mature, very logical and steady-headed. He doesn't express his emotions very much, but he's been much more open as we've gotten to know each other. What I really liked about him was his stability. That's very unusual, I think, for people not to have a hang-up somewhere. It was very confusing when he got depressed like that. (p. 129–130)

Although Malan emphasized the role of interpretation in the process of psychodynamic therapy, the quest for interpretation is supported by the *attentional support* questions asked in order to bring the client's experiential field into the shared space of therapy. Attentional support facilitates the creation of an experiential foundation upon which further therapeutic action—including the provision of interpretations—will be built. It also provides the therapist (and client) with information about the nature of the client's relationships with others, how the client responds to the therapist, and about the client's *triangle of conflict*.

Later in this session, Malan (1994) combined attentional support—in the form of giving feedback to the client—with some interpretation drawn from his own meaning-making framework, in the choice of the words "hiding," implying intentionality, and "tea-party conversation."

T: But you're hiding from me how much it must affect you. You're telling me that the boy you live with suddenly gets depressed out of the blue, saying he wants to kill himself and finally makes a suicide attempt. You're telling me as if it were just a tea-party conversation. (p. 131)

Malan's commitment to recording and analyzing the entirety of his sessions is expressed in his practice as well as his advocacy of the use of recorded sessions as the focus of empirical inquiry. This provides us with a rich picture of how his work transcends his own theoretical constructions. What Malan chose to focus upon (i.e., interpretations) ignores the importance of his own skillful use of *attentional support* techniques in therapy and their general importance and usefulness in the therapeutic endeavor.

At the end of this session, the following sequence of utterances takes place:

T: Something which I felt rather strange about, knowing something of the story, you know, that your boyfriend had got near to suicide and had to be admitted to the hospital … I expected you to come saying that you're desperately depressed because of what's happened to him. But you've never really said that. You said that you've been depressed since the age of thirteen and it happens every February and March and, of course, we're in February and March now. Do you feel that this is what you're asking for help for? (Malan, 1994, p. 140)

Here Malan offered the resource of an opportunity for *enactment* by articulating a personal reaction to the client in the session. He then shifted to *attentional support*: first by bringing up what the client had said earlier in the session (i.e., directing her attention to an aspect of her experiential field), and second, by asking her to bring her attention to another aspect of her experiential field by way of a question. In effect, we see the adept use of a number of varied techniques that we would expect to see in the work of a master therapist, such as Malan, that demonstrate the usefulness and importance of not just interpretation but other modalities of offering resources to a client as well.

This was an initial session that Malan presented in which the vast majority of Malan's efforts were in gathering information about the client's life circumstances, her relationship with her boyfriend and parents, her sexual experiences and responses over the course of her life, and other specific details about her. Much of the interpretative work (and, by our way of thinking, *enactment* as well when involving novel experiences within the therapist–client relationship) that Malan espoused cannot easily take place until the therapist has had an opportunity to gather much more information than is typically possible in a first session. Our intent here is not to suggest that Malan's constructs around interpretation are incorrect. Our intent is to broaden the focus beyond Malan's analysis of interpretation and demonstrate the usefulness of identifying and understanding other aspects of therapy as well, and ultimately the richness of looking at their interaction. The developmental analysis of psychotherapy process (DAPP) method presents both the opportunity to look at what Malan described as interpretation in a way more generalizable to the ways all therapists share their ways of understanding human activity, and the opportunity to use Malan's elegant construction of interpretation in conjunction with DAPP to provide a more organismic (vs. mechanistic; see Pepper, 1961) conceptualization of the processes within therapy that support the use of *interpretation* and play potentially equally valuable roles in not only the relief of symptoms but also the development of clients toward greater adaptation to their environments.

Rogers' Client-Centered Therapy

Carl Rogers has exerted a profound influence on the theory and practice of psychotherapy through his articulation of *client-centered therapy* (Rogers, 1942, 1951, 1957). In his view, clients bring with them their own intrinsic capacities for growth and development; the task of the therapist is largely one of providing and facilitating attention to the client's internal frame of reference, so that these capacities may be unleashed in the service of growth. Rogers is commonly understood as suggesting that the therapist's primary contribution is made through the offering of *unconditional positive regard*—a form of attentional support. The idea that individuals possess the constructive resources needed to foster their own development provides the underpinnings for Rogers' approach to clients. It influenced Rogers' understanding of what brought clients to therapy, the goal of treatment, and the necessary and sufficient conditions for therapeutic change.

Arising as it did in the early 1940s, client-centered therapy—which Rogers initially termed "non-directive counseling"—contrasted sharply with the diagnostic and prescriptive methods employed by psychoanalysis, and the medical model from which it had emerged. Extant psychoanalytic approaches typically framed the therapist as the omnipotent, omniscient "expert in the room" (Farber, 1996, p. 4). To Rogers (1942), by demanding that they submit themselves to processes in which "the more able could effectively guide the less able" (Bowen, 1996b, p. 84), psychoanalytic methods required clients to sacrifice their individuality in favor of social conformity. The methods also appeared to assume that psychoanalytic training and frameworks could ably equip a therapist to formulate inferences and interpretations that would somehow be more useful to the client than could be the client's own understandings and experiences. Further reinforcing the privileged position of the analyst and analytic technique was the customary requirement that clients postpone making decisions on major life choices while in therapy. For Rogers, psychoanalysis was based in part on the idea that one person in the treatment room had the answers—and that that person was the therapist (Farber).

Client-centered therapy represents more than Rogers' negation of psychoanalysis. The development of the approach was also heavily informed by his own early clinical experiences, in which he observed that he was more helpful to clients when he simply listened to them than when he conducted structured interviews, made diagnoses, or offered advice (Bowen, 1996b). Perhaps just as significant was the influence of John Dewey (1916), who believed that children's own inclinations would direct them toward the learning experiences that would be of greatest developmental value to them. Rogers extended Dewey's argument by affirming that this tendency remains throughout life, and by claiming that this fact is as important to recognize in psychotherapeutic practice as it is in other educational endeavors.

But if that is true, then what is it that interferes with the natural process of development? What brings clients to therapy? And what does this mean for the goal of the therapy, and the approach and tasks of the therapist? For Rogers, a key developmental obstacle lay in the difficulty individuals have in freely attending to all aspects of their experience, and incorporating these aspects into their own self-concepts. He believed that rather than openly accepting and coming to terms with all parts of themselves, clients were often inclined to attend to only those experiences that supported or reinforced the images they sought to portray to themselves and/or others. Constrained by the specter of the "conditions of worth" imposed upon them by important social others, individuals censored themselves, both in their interpersonal dealings and, to a more harmful degree, internally. Thoughts and feelings that were "unacceptable," or that did not "fit," were transformed, if possible, into elements that *would* fit; those that could not be made to fit were withheld from awareness altogether.

Given this distortion between experience and awareness, Rogers described an overall goal of therapy as follows:

In therapy the person adds to ordinary experience the full and undistorted awareness of his experiencing—of his sensory and visceral reactions. He ceases, or at least decreases, the distortions of experience in awareness. He can be aware of what he is actually experiencing, not simply what he can permit himself to experience after a thorough screening through a conceptual filter. In this sense the person becomes for the first time the full potential of the human organism, with the enriching element of awareness freely added to the basic aspect of sensory and visceral reaction. The person comes to *be* who he *is*, as clients frequently say in therapy. What this seems to mean is that the individual comes to *be*—in awareness—what he *is*—in experience. He is, in other words, a complete and fully functioning human organism. (Rogers, 1961, pp. 76–77)

How is such a goal to be achieved? As noted in Chapters 1 and 4 and the earlier section of the present one, different theoretical traditions typically use their own unique languages in describing the general approaches and specific "active ingredients" incorporated within their therapies. Rogers considered three aspects of therapist attitude and behavior to comprise the *necessary and sufficient conditions* for effective client-centered treatment. These were that the therapist is *transparent and genuine* in her dealings with the client, that the therapist demonstrates *empathy,* and that the therapist interacts with the client with an attitude of *unconditional positive regard* (Rogers, 1957, 1961). On the surface, all three of these conditions can be seen as constituting and bolstering the provision of attentional support. Yet more broadly, these conditions encompass enactment and carefully crafted interpretation as well. Our reframing translation of Rogers' overall approach in general, and of the necessary and sufficient conditions in particular, is described below.

The Primacy of Attentional Support and Enactment in Client-Centered Therapy

For Rogers, the view that clients possess the resources needed for their own development was more than just a theoretical tenet; it was a stance that directly affected the conduct of the session itself:

> It is hardly necessary to say that the person-centered view drastically alters the therapist-client relationship, as previously conceived. The therapist becomes the 'midwife' of change, not its originator. He or she places the final authority in the hands of the client, whether in small things such as the correctness of a therapist response, or large decisions like the course of one's life direction. The locus of evaluation, of decision, rests clearly in the client's hands. (Rogers, 1977, p. 15)

Figure 5.2 depicts the relations among attentional support, interpretation, and enactment in Rogers' client-centered therapy. In Rogers' approach, attentional support functions as a primary vehicle for therapeutic change through enactment. The goal of therapy is to foster the client's awareness of his or her own organismic valuing process within the context of deep empathy, therapeutic understanding, and unconditional positive regard. The therapist communicates empathy and unconditional positive regard by adequately representing the client's own experience to the client. In this way, attentional support functions as the vehicle of the enactment of novel experiences within the client–therapist relationship. It is through the enactment—through attentional support—of an empathic client–therapist relationship that the client is able to develop a felt awareness of his or her own organismic valuing process, which constitutes the movement toward

Figure 5.2 Structure of therapeutic resources in Rogers' person-centered therapy. Rogers' person-centered therapy is understood as relying on the therapeutic resource of attentional support. However, enactment and interpretation, while understood as carrying risks to which the conceptual framework is attentive, can nevertheless be seen as playing essential roles in guiding and enhancing the impact of the attentional support offered.

therapeutic development. The dialectic of interpretation is not neglected in Rogers' approach. However, the process of interpretation is subordinated to the primary processes of attentional support and enactment. According to Rogers (1942, p. 205), interpretations can be useful, as long as they are framed in ways that reflect the client's representation of experience and that acknowledge the primacy of the client's role in judging the value of the interpretation provided by the therapist.

In this way, the client-centered practitioner seeks to conduct a therapy in which the client holds primary responsibility for the course that the treatment—as well as his or her own life—would take. More emphasis is placed on the client's own resources than on the therapist's; freed from the dictates of psychoanalytic approaches, client-centered therapy typically focuses on the present, rather than on the past. Rogers' focus on growth and development also positioned the therapy as emphasizing potential, rather than pathology. As Farber (1996) stated, Rogers also focused more on "the ability of the therapeutic relationship to provide a positive human experience than an intellectually meaningful one" (p. 5). In all of these ways, Rogers' therapy presented clients with a novel experience, at least in relation to the major therapies in existence at the time of its origination. It was a therapy and a set of experiences very closely aligned with his views regarding clients' potentials, possibilities, and responsibilities. In addition to this general approach to therapy, the necessary and sufficient conditions can be seen both singly and particularly in combination as the means by which the client-centered therapist offers the client the resources of attentional support, enactment, and interpretation.

Transparent and Genuine

These two attributes, often classified under the overall heading of *congruence*, constitute the first of Rogers' necessary and sufficient conditions. By demonstrating them to the client on a faithful and repeated basis, the therapist seeks to accomplish two things. The first is to provide a gentle illustration that fuller awareness of undistorted experience is *possible*. By "being his own experience" in the therapy setting, Rogers hoped to serve as a subtle exemplar of the very kind of integration he believed his clients would be able to achieve on their own account. As such, the therapist's transparent and genuine behaviors serve the client as a form of enactment, in the way they provide the (potentially) novel experience of observing and relating to a more "fully functioning" human being. By interacting with a client in such a manner, the therapist may also have the effect of implicitly suggesting, *this is a way that you can be, too.*

The therapist's transparent and genuine approach also is intended as a means of establishing safety within the therapeutic relationship—again, often a novel experience. Perhaps particularly among those clients whose previous treatments had been psychoanalytic in nature, Rogers' interpersonal stance helped establish him as a full, engaged, and engaging human being, rather than simply as an expert playing out a preconceived therapeutic role (Farber, 1996). Over time, as the client gained experience in observing the therapist's candid reactions, the client could in turn gain assurance that the therapist possessed no hidden agendas or motives in the therapy, and no undisclosed opinions about either the client's situation or the therapeutic relationship (Zimring, 1996). In this way, the transparent, genuine approach served less as an "active ingredient" in its own right, than as an essential and confirmatory means of bolstering the import of the empathy and unconditional positive regard offered concurrently. Put differently, if the other necessary and sufficient conditions were designed to convey that the therapist was not overtly judging the client according to his or her own "conditions of worth," transparency and genuineness were assumed to counteract the fear that the therapist might be covertly judging the client according to hidden conditions of worth.

Empathy

Brief accounts of client-centered therapy often focus on the means by which Rogers sought to convey an empathic stance, and as a result pay relatively little attention to the theoretical and practical importance of empathy itself. As a result, the therapy was frequently mischaracterized as consisting mainly of a technique for reflecting feelings back to the client (Brink, 1987). Rogers (1986) objected to the notion that "reflecting feelings" was his goal:

> I'm not trying to 'reflect feelings.' I am trying to determine whether my understanding of the client's inner world is correct—whether I am seeing it as he or she is experiencing it at this moment. I suggest that these therapist responses be labeled not 'Reflection of Feelings' but 'Testing Understandings' or 'Checking Perceptions.' (p. 376)

Thus the goal of client-centered empathy is, as the term itself suggests, to see the world through the client's own eyes, and to adopt the client's *internal* frame of reference. One reason for doing this, in Rogers' view, was for the effect it had in directing the client's own attention to his or her own experience. As Zimring (1996) noted,

> Many clients enter therapy concerned with the objective world and with the problems and standards of that world. If we focus on the client's objective world and problems, we succeed in reinforcing the importance of that world for them. Rogers' framework for therapy was to focus on and trust the person's subjective framework. By doing this the importance of the objective world for the person is lessened,

and, hopefully, the importance of the subjective world increased for them. (p. 71)

In seeking to view the world from the client's perspective, Rogers attends to the client's internal experience. As importantly, he issues a subtle but powerful invitation to the client to do the same. From our developmental perspective, both constitute forms of attentional support. In his detailed analysis of Rogers' work in the case of Gloria, Zimring observed that when the therapist attended to the client's own internal frame of reference, she in turn spoke from, or about, it. In contrast, when Rogers commented instead upon the social expectations that Gloria faced, she too turned her attention outward, and away from her own personal experience and the meanings she attached to it. In short, in his focus on clients' subjective experience, the therapist implicitly holds that up as an object utterly worthy of consideration and understanding, for both therapist and client alike. Thus, the attentional support provided by Rogers is not entirely nondirective. Rogerian therapists must continuously make choices about what in a client's experience to attend to, and when therapists selectively direct their own attention, they direct their clients' attention as well. The choice to selectively support attention to internal experience, rather than to social expectations and meanings, is an acknowledged aspect of Rogerian therapy. We believe that this selective directing of attention, in addition to supporting attention, is an inevitable aspect of all the many forms of attentional support characteristic of various approaches to psychotherapy.

As Farber (1996) suggested, Rogerian empathy provides not only an invitation for the client to attend to his or her own experience, but also a *new* experience in the way that the therapist—another human being—is providing a similar level of attention:

> Perhaps because so many individuals grow up feeling alienated from their 'true selves,' the experience of having another human being trying his or her best to listen—constantly checking the accuracy of his or her understanding in a caring, gentle style—can be a profound and moving experience. The therapist's openness, availability, expressiveness, and faith may all serve to validate a person's sense of worth. For some, this means of interaction can break through long-standing barriers of isolation to start a process of self-reorganization. (p. 9)

Thus empathic responses, although providing support for development through the dialectic of attention to complex experience, may also contribute novel experiences to development through the dialectic of *enactment*.

Benefit derives not only through the novel experiencing of the therapist's attention but also through the client's own richer, fuller, and undistorted experiencing of the self. This aspect of empathy permits a kind of unfolding that Rogers (1961) described as follows:

> Here, it seems to me, is an important and often overlooked truth about the therapeutic process. It works in the direction of permitting the person to experience fully, and in awareness, all of his reactions including his feelings and emotions. As this occurs, the individual feels a positive liking for himself, a genuine appreciation of himself as a total functioning unit, which is one of the important endpoints of therapy. (p. 67)

The variety of forms by which Rogers strived to deepen and convey his understanding of clients helped to further substantiate his stance that although empathy was a goal to pursue, it was not to be achieved by the rote application of "technique." Client-centered therapy requires a flexible application of principles, not a rigid reliance on scripts or interventions. Farber (1996) observed that in his work with Jim Brown, Rogers patiently tolerated long silences, engaged in self-disclosure, and verbalized his caring toward the client openly. Such therapist behaviors can not only demonstrate that a degree of empathy is already in place but also simultaneously raise the possibility that the client will be increasingly inclined to allow himself to be understood by the therapist. In this way, conveyance of an empathic attitude holds the promise of becoming a virtuous cycle. Far more than just "reflecting feelings," Rogers' flexible approach toward conveying empathic understanding illustrated, in the case of Jim Brown, that "being truly person-centered meant not losing the flexibility demanded by the uniqueness of individuals" (Farber, p. 11).

Though the practice of obscuring the key distinction between "reflecting feelings" as a method and "empathic understanding" as a goal is perhaps the most common mischaracterization of client-centered therapy, it is assuredly not the only one. Despite popular misconceptions that client-centered therapists strenuously avoid offering interpretations, the ability of the therapist to view the world through the client's personal lens provides a unique vantage point for doing just that. Although Rogers (1942), in an early critique of psychoanalysis, stated clear views in opposition to intellectualized interpretations focusing on childhood experiences and the underlying meanings of symptoms, as mentioned above he also held open the possibility that interpretations attuned to the client's current experience may indeed be useful. Rather than rejecting interpretation outright, Rogers (1942, p. 205) actually provided readers with a list of "Cautions" regarding the practice. These included the suggestions to (a) avoid interpretation "when the counselor feels unsure of himself," (b) offer interpretations phrased exclusively in the client's own terms and symbols, and (c) interpret only those client attitudes that have already been openly expressed. In his review of Rogers' work with Jill, Bowen (1996b) illustrated how an accurate, empathic understanding of the client can foster the formulation of meaningful interpretations, providing that they are kept near to the client's immediate experience, and offered tentatively, always subject to the client's acceptance or correction.

Unconditional Positive Regard

Minimally, Rogers' practice of offering unconditional positive regard was a direct means of countering the socially imposed conditions of worth that he believed his clients had typically fashioned into constrained, distorted, and limiting self-concepts. More broadly, and particularly when coupled with the therapist's offerings of transparency and genuineness, unconditional positive regard increases the safety of the therapeutic relationship, permitting the client to pay heightened attention to his or her experience. As Rogers put it,

> In the security of the relationship with a client-centered therapist, the client can let himself examine various aspects of his experience as they actually feel to him, as they are apprehended through his sensory and visceral equipment, without distorting them to fit the existing concept of self. Many of these prove to be in extreme contradiction to the concept of self, and could not ordinarily be experienced in their fullness, but in this safe relationship they can be permitted to seep through into awareness without distortion. (Rogers, 1961/2001, p. 76)

This quote reinforces the compatibility of Rogers' understanding of "unconditional positive regard" as a form of attentional support with the DAPP framework. Our idea that the dialectic of attention fosters development by bringing *conflict* into the attentional field and, with the therapist's support of the client in holding it there, allows novel syntheses to be constructed is mirrored in Rogers' statement that "many of these (felt experiences) prove to be in extreme contradiction to the concept of self" (1961, p. 81). Rogers' theoretical writings and case materials imply that unconditional positive regard was a means of facilitating the opening of attention among all clients. But evidence also exists to suggest that the warmth Rogers conveyed constituted uniquely novel experiences for some clients. In the case of Mrs. Oak, "This letting the counselor and his warm interest into her life was undoubtedly one of the deepest features of therapy" (Rogers, 1961, p. 86). As such, provision of unconditional positive regard often goes beyond a means of providing attentional support. For Mrs. Oak, who had had difficulty accepting warm feelings from others, it provided a transformative opportunity within the dialectic of enactment:

Perhaps one of the reasons why this is so difficult is that it essentially involves the feeling that 'I am worthy of being liked' … this aspect of therapy is a free and full experiencing of an affectional relationship which may be put in generalized terms as follows: 'I can permit someone to care about me, and can fully accept that caring within myself. This permits me to recognize that I care, and care deeply, for and about others.' (Rogers, 1961, p. 86)

At least in Mrs. Oak's case, Rogers perceived that the novel experience was occurring not just between the two people in the room but also within Mrs. Oak herself. In part on the strength of the warm feelings that emanated from him, she was able to experience herself as a healthy person: "This experience occurs when she does not reject her feelings but lives them" (Rogers, 1961, p. 90). As such, unconditional positive regard served as a means of facilitating Mrs. Oak's attending to her own experience (attentional support), her receipt of the therapist's feelings toward her (enactment), and the development of new feelings for herself (perhaps a novel synthesis evolving through both dialectics).

In sum, Rogers' efforts to attend to his clients with empathy and care were designed to transform their tendencies toward distorting or ignoring those aspects of themselves that they found to be unacceptable. Yet, as the case of Gloria reveals, Rogers *selectively* attended to the client's reports on her *own* internal experience, greatly privileging them in relation to her concerns about social or other external expectations. Thus, the colloquial label *nondirective therapy* notwithstanding, Rogers' attentional support does indeed play the attention-directing function that we have conceptualized as a central aspect of the dialectic of attention in all forms of psychotherapy. Furthermore, in providing such rich attention generally, as well as differential attention in favor of the client's internal frame of reference, Rogers also provided the client with novel experiences: the warm, unquestioning acceptance of another human being, and an implicit invitation for the client to apply a similar warm acceptance to the self. Although client-centered therapy is commonly mischaracterized as strictly avoiding interpretation, Rogers recognized that interpretations can have a role as long as they are delivered in ways that express the client's attitude in terms he or she understands, and in which the therapist's own sense of confidence is balanced by the belief that only the client can judge the value of the offering.

Linehan's Dialectical Behavior Therapy

Although we chose Linehan's (1993a, 1993b) dialectical behavior therapy (DBT) for examination for a number of reasons, including its unique structure and conceptual underpinnings, it also exemplifies many aspects of the cognitive and behavioral traditions in psychotherapy, integrations of which are often referred to as *cognitive-behavioral therapy* (CBT). DBT represents a body of techniques and procedures that have been successfully empirically supported through the type of rigorous outcome research methods that is common for therapeutic approaches in the behavioral tradition. Linehan has developed a complex theoretical structure that combines applied dialectics, Buddhist teachings, and a transactional awareness that goes beyond the behavioral tradition's focus on environmental contingencies. Although DBT was developed as an approach for treating individuals with borderline personality disorder, it has also been extended in the treatment of a wide range of psychological conditions.

Dialectical behavior therapy is a highly structured therapeutic program. It is organized with reference to a series of therapeutic priorities; contracts and agreements between the client and therapist; a specific sequence of therapeutic stages or activities; specified techniques; and a formal model for the combining of individual DBT therapy, psychoeducational group activity, and collaboration within a consultation team for the therapists involved. The team operates as an administrative body for monitoring treatment, providing peer supervision, and addressing the treaters' needs (Miller, Rathus, & Linehan, 2007). The consultation team enforces rules about client participation in the program (e.g., determining if clients or therapists have violated their contracts), ensuring that the priorities and bounds of DBT are being maintained by each practitioner, and ultimately validating each practitioner and supporting his or her efforts around doing what is intrinsically difficult work.

Individual DBT Therapy

Individual DBT sessions occur when therapists work in detail with clients using common cognitive and behavioral techniques that are engaged in the context of Linehan's (1993a) applied dialectics. For instance, one of Linehan's (1993a, p. 98) foundational dialectics combines therapists' validation of clients with assisting clients in changing. The CBT techniques that are used include homework, diary cards and data collection methods, assessments, fixed hierarchical priorities for the therapist to attend to, operational definitions of target behaviors, contracts, handouts and educational materials, problem solving, exposure techniques, skills training and practice, contingency management, cognitive modification, positive reinforcement, extinction, aversive contingencies, shaping, modeling, behavioral rehearsal, coaching, behavioral chain analyses, and in vivo consultation. Individual DBT is organized around four stages of treatment. The first stage is the *pretreatment stage*. Pretreatment involves several sessions in which the client is provided with information regarding the nature and course of DBT therapy. During this time, the therapist also performs intake and diagnostic and assessment activities. Part of the pretreatment phase involves assessing the client's understanding of the nature and course of psychotherapy. The therapist works to frame DBT as a "psychoeducational" process that requires a commitment on the part of the client in order to be effective. The pretreatment process provides an opportunity for the therapist and client to determine if they are willing and able to work together. Through these activities, the pretreatment phase functions to enhance client commitment and decrease the number of "client dropouts."

Stage 1 involves *attaining basic capacities* and is the first formal stage of treatment. This stage focuses on facilitating behavior change and skill acquisition. The specific focus of the first phase is guided by Linehan's hierarchy of therapeutic priorities. In approaching intervention, the first order of priority is the treatment of suicidal behaviors, then therapy-interfering behaviors, and then major quality-of-life-interfering behaviors. As the client and therapist work on these priorities in individual therapy, the client attends a psychoeducational skills group. An important aspect of DBT is establishing close relations between skills taught in the psychoeducational group and work within and between individual sessions. Although groups are organized around a one-year commitment, Stage 1 has no set length. Given mutual agreement between client and therapist, clients may continue to participate in psychoeducational groups. Stage 2 is organized around the goal of *reducing posttraumatic stress*. During this stage, treatment involves the use of desensitization techniques to manage the effects of posttraumatic stress–related cues and triggers. Linehan maintained that successfully mastering Stage 1 skills and establishing strong social support networks are essential in order to buffer clients against regression to the maladaptive behaviors used in the past. Clients sometimes find progress difficult in Stage 2; when this occurs, there is the option of returning to Stage 1 to continue to build and consolidate basic emotion management skills and/or a social support system. Stage 3 is organized around the goals of *increasing self-respect and achieving individual goals*. Many of the skills acquired in Stage 3 overlap with those under development in the first two stages. However, Stage 3 places greater focus upon the client using his or her mastery of the DBT skills to make progress toward goals identified by the client. There is also movement toward greater generalization of the use of skills and adaptive learned behaviors to new aspects of the client's environment.

The Psychoeducational Group

The psychoeducational group provides a format in which skills and concepts can be taught from four modules: *core mindfulness, interpersonal effectiveness, emotion regulation,* and *distress tolerance.* In the *core mindfulness* module, group members are introduced to dialectics through the Buddhist concept of the *wise mind*. The group focuses on the development of two types of mindfulness skills: *what skills* and *how skills*. What skills consist of the ability to observe and describe experiences in a nondistortive fashion. How skills reflect particular ways of approaching one's actions and experiences in the world. They include skills for adopting a *nonjudgmental stance* toward one's experience; acting with *one-mindfulness*, that is, devoting the entirety of one's attention or awareness to the task at hand; and effective action. The development of what and how skills facilitates the departure from learned schemas and patterns of behavior, and the progression toward effective interactions outside of group interaction and individual therapy sessions.

The *interpersonal effectiveness* module seeks to modify the maladaptive forms of interpersonal interaction exhibited by people diagnosed with borderline personality disorder. It is composed of a number of classic assertiveness training techniques, including *challenging interpersonal myths*, *analyzing interpersonal situations in order to determine priorities*, and *challenging maladaptive interpersonal schemas*. It is also in this module that Linehan introduced the first of the acronyms that are used throughout the rest of the modules. These provide a mnemonic device for remembering the individual components for step-by-step heuristics around how to effectively accomplish tasks. For example, the acronym DEAR refers to *describe, express, assert,* and *reinforce*. The DEAR sequence is one of many procedures that can be used to regulate effective interpersonal interaction. Using the DEAR sequence, one *describes* one's situation to another person, *expresses* one's feelings and opinions about the situation, *asserts* what one is asking for, and makes clear that there are *reinforcing* consequences (positive or negative) to how the other person responds. Such skills are intended to build upon the what and how skills developed in the mindfulness module.

The third module contains instruction on a variety of skills necessary to promote *emotional regulation*. The goal of this module is to help the client to develop ways to regulate emotion through the development of greater understanding of emotions themselves and how they can be affected. Building upon the mindfulness skills developed in the first module, this module begins with instruction on how to use emotion words to identify and describe phenomenal experience. The capacity to use emotion words to identify emotional states is seen as a prerequisite for being able to manage those experiences. The module also involves instruction on the nature of emotions, how everyday events affect emotion, and strategies for controlling emotion.

Linehan (1993a, p. 462) noted that many of the suicidal and parasuicidal behaviors exhibited by people diagnosed with borderline personality disorder appear to be tied to difficulty in tolerating distress. The *distress tolerance* module is designed specifically to provide skills and self-interventions directed toward tolerating distress in new adaptive ways, thus obviating the need for the more maladaptive techniques (e.g., cutting and burning oneself). Group members are introduced to distraction and self-soothing techniques, ways of "improving the moment" (e.g., imagery and prayer), and analyzing the use of various skills (adaptive and maladaptive) using pros and cons. It is also in this module that the client is introduced to more meditative techniques (e.g., half-smile, observation of one's breath, and awareness exercises) as well as the concept of radical acceptance (a process of negating distress through choosing to accept difficult realities).

The Primacy of Enactment in DBT

As indicated in Figure 5.3, as with many varieties of CBT, DBT is organized around the dialectic of *enactment*. Linehan's whole program is designed to help clients develop skills that are unique and novel to their experience: to tolerate distress in new and adaptive ways, to observe and label one's emotions as was not possible before, to relate to others in a masterful way that had never been previously experienced, and ultimately to gain a level of effectiveness in regulating one's affective relationship to the world in a way novel to the client. Most of Linehan's explicitly identified *techniques* (as with much CBT) do fall under the rubric of *enactment*. They represent the therapist and client engaging in an experience novel to the client or, in the case of homework or in vivo consultation, sending the client out into the world with the specific intent that she obtain novel experiences that will provide the means to stretch her awareness of her interacting with that world and ultimately interface with that world more adaptively through the use of the skills gained in the psychoeducational parts of the treatment.

Further, Linehan provided a great deal of direction for the therapist new to DBT. Her workbook (1993b) provides lesson-by-lesson outlines for the psychoeducational skills group, and she provided advice for dealing with many situations that occur in therapy. The high level of structure and instruction provided by Linehan attests to the importance of therapeutic

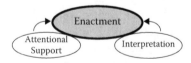

Figure 5.3 Structure of therapeutic resources in Linehan's dialectical behavior therapy. To the extent that DBT is directed toward promoting skill development under the guidance of therapists familiar with the target skills, it relies on the dialectic of enactment. However attentional support and interpretation can be observed to play important roles in DBT in the service of the dialectic of enactment.

direction in the promotion of target skills. The importance of therapeutic direction reflects the dual assumptions that (a) guidance in the development of novel skills comprises experiences that are key to therapeutic change, and (b) clients are often not in the position to initiate such changes for themselves. The massive support and direction provided by the therapist to the client—and from Linehan's manuals and support team to the therapist—underscore the importance of enactment within her approach to psychotherapy.

Consistent with the primacy of enactment in DBT, but inconsistent with traditional forms of behavior therapy, Linehan maintained that the relationship between the therapist and client is central for the success of treatment. Linehan (1993a) wrote,

> The therapist must work to establish a strong, positive interpersonal relationship with the patient right from the beginning. This is essential because the relationship with the therapist is frequently the only reinforcer that works for a borderline individual in managing and changing behavior. With a highly suicidal patient, the relationship with the therapist is at times what keeps her alive when all else fails.… Not much in DBT can be done before this relationship is developed. (p. 98)

Linehan's emphasis on the importance of the client–therapist relationship reflects an important difference between DBT and more traditional forms of behavior therapy. The focus on the client–therapist relationship remains consistent with the primacy of enactment as the major vehicle of therapeutic change, as is clear in her reference to it as a "reinforcer." The client–therapist relationship is founded in exchanges in which the client and therapist treat each other directly as social partners. In this way, the client–therapist relationship is founded upon and is carried forward within the dialectic of enactment. At the same time, we can only assume that once this relationship is established, it allows the therapists to provide attentional support to clients as they articulate their experience of pursuing subsequent treatment goals.

Although enactment functions as the primary therapeutic mode in DBT, the dialectics of interpretation and attentional support are also represented. However, as indicated in Figure 5.3, both attentional support and interpretation processes are viewed as subordinate to the primary process of producing novel skills and experiences through enactment, and then synthesizing those skills and experiences with the rest of a client's repertoire. With regard to the process of interpretation, Linehan (1993a) held,

> The goal of insight strategies, as the label suggests, is to help the client notice patterns and achieve insight into functional interrelationships.

Although this is a fundamental goal of behavioral analysis as described above, the therapist may also offer his or her own "insights" at many other points in therapy, independently of a formal behavioral analysis. Offering therapeutic insights (typically labeled "interpretations" in more traditional psychotherapies) can be very powerful in both a positive and a negative sense. Thus, it is essential that they be offered as hypotheses to be tested rather than as immutable facts. Furthermore, the therapist should be careful to recognize that the insights offered are products of his or her own cognitive processes, and thus are not necessarily accurate representations of events external to the therapist. (pp. 265–266)

In this passage, Linehan demonstrated an appreciation for interpretive insights that arise in psychotherapy. However, her appreciation is tempered by an awareness of the harm that can come from an overly rigid approach to interpretation. Further, she explicitly shared with us the view that it is important that therapists recognize the epistemological status of interpretations as products of the therapist's cognitive processes, whose value to the client's adaptation processes is yet to be determined.

Yalom's Existential Approach to Psychotherapy

Since the death in 1994 of his former therapist, Rollo May, Irvin Yalom has emerged as the primary spokesperson for existential psychotherapy (Wedding & Corsini, 2001). The Freudian legacy maintains that conflicts between the id, ego, and superego are at the core of psychological suffering. Rogers pointed to clients' difficulty in attending fully to the totality of their experience; the traditions of behavior therapy make reference to patterns of maladaptive behavior that arise from maladaptive exchanges with the environment. For Yalom (1980), the root of psychic pain is "the dilemma of being a meaning-making creature who is thrown into a universe that has no meaning" (p. 9).

Yalom is also a leading theorist and practitioner of the modality of group psychotherapy, which makes possible a wide range of opportunities for providing resources for the common developmental processes of attentional support, enactment, and interpretation. A recent work (Yalom & Leszcz, 2005) reviews the expanding array of interventions encompassed under the "group therapy" umbrella. These range from traditional "process" groups operated by clinicians, to peer-led self-help groups such as Alcoholics Anonymous; groups operating on acute inpatient wards, and in the comfortable private offices of practitioners; and groups organized to operate for a brief, predefined period to address specific symptoms, and others lasting for many years. Yalom (1995) reviewed significant empirical evidence suggesting that group treatment can comprise an effective (and cost-efficient) treatment modality for those grappling with a wide array of difficulties.

If the human being's central dilemma involves being a meaning-making creature in a meaningless world, what, in particular, brings certain of those humans to therapy? What is the therapist to do in response? Most broadly, Yalom (1995) suggested that individuals generally seek therapy because "neurotic obstacles have stunted the development of the patient's own resources" (p. 104). Given this formulation, and following Horney (1950), Yalom (2002) responded that a key task of the therapist is to engage in a process of *obstruction removal*:

> My task was to remove obstacles blocking my patient's path. I did not have to do the entire job; I did not have to inspirit the patient with the desire to grow, with curiosity, will, zest for life, caring, loyalty, or any of the myriad of characteristics that make us fully human. No, what I had to do was to identify and remove obstacles. The rest would follow automatically, fueled by the self-actualizing forces within the patient. (p. 1)

This stance acknowledges that the client's true capacities, although often underestimated, are never fully knowable; it also has the effect of relieving the therapist from what may seem an overwhelming, personal, and unilateral obligation to provide "cure."

Yalom (1995) viewed all forms of therapy as "basically a form of learning" (p. 58), in which the curriculum centers on clients' understanding and alteration of their inner worlds, so that resources can be developed and applied to a fuller, self-transcendent, and authentic way of living. This framing maps readily with our common developmental processes approach, as the aspect of Yalom's "curriculum" focused on "understanding" can be translated as the client creating novel syntheses of conflicts in their experience—a process to which the therapist (and other members of therapy groups) can contribute resources through attentional support and interpretation. The "alteration" aspect of the curriculum can be understood as occurring through enactment processes, in which novel experiences occur in the relational context of the therapy group. Over the course of group enactments, the focus of change is the "inner world" of individual clients. In elaborating this notion, Yalom (1995) stated that a meaningful life arises not from "an obsessive introspection or a teeth-grinding effort to actualize oneself" but from a process of becoming absorbed in someone (or something) "beyond the self" (p. 13). Though Yalom has been clear in his view that self-understanding is an essential goal on this path, it is of limited value in its own right. Instead, much of its value derives through its use in the service of change.

> When we focus on change rather than on self-understanding as our ultimate goal, we cannot but conclude that an explanation is correct if it leads to change. Each clarifying, explanatory, or interpretive act of the therapist is ultimately designed to exert leverage on the patient's will to change. (Yalom, 1995, p. 85)

Thus, within Yalom's approach, therapeutic change occurs through the distribution of attentional support and interpretation as it occurs within the context of social enactments within the group.

The 11 Therapeutic Factors

How does the therapist facilitate the processes by which obstructions are removed? How does Yalom's existential group therapy promote self-understanding, change, and development? What does the therapist *do*? Yalom (1995) answered these questions in terms of *11 therapeutic factors*. These factors are (a) *instillation of hope*, (b) *universality*, (c) *imparting information*, (d) *altruism*, (e) *the corrective recapitulation of the primary family group*, (f) *development of socializing techniques*, (g) *imitative behavior*, (h) *interpersonal learning*, (i) *group cohesiveness*, (j) *catharsis*, and (k) *existential factors*. The therapist's core role is to create the conditions in which these factors can operate. In individual therapy, it is the therapist who brings these factors to bear, more or less directly; by contrast, in group therapy, the task instead is "to create the machinery of therapy, to set it in motion, and to keep it operating with maximum effectiveness" (Yalom, 1995, p. 106). Thus, in comparison to individual therapy, the group therapist's role is relatively indirect: "If it is the group members who, in their interaction, set into motion the many therapeutic factors, then it is the group therapist's task to create a group culture maximally conducive to effective group interaction" (Yalom, 1995, p. 109).

Yalom (1995) regarded the 11 therapeutic factors as "transtheoretical" elements that arise from "an intricate interplay of human experiences" (p. 1). They operate as a framework within which the group therapist "may base tactics and strategy" (Yalom, 1995, p. 1). Yalom suggested that after formulating the goals of a newly established group, the next task is to identify those of the factors that are most likely to be useful in meeting those goals. However, although important, the factors merely provide "provisional guidelines to be tested and deepened" (Yalom, 1995, p. 4). The factors vary in importance from group to group, within a group at different times, and even within the members of a given group at a particular point in time (Yalom, 2005). In addition, retrospective analyses indicate that upon the conclusion of therapy, patients and their clinicians differ—sometimes

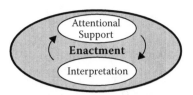

Figure 5.4 Structure of therapeutic resources in Yalom's existential group therapy. In Yalom's understanding of group therapy novel interactions among group members, including the therapist are the essence of the context in which therapy occurs. However, within this context, attentional support and interpretation play essential roles within the varied processes that are enacted among individuals within group therapy.

quite dramatically—in the relative value they place on the various factors involved in the treatment.

In what follows, we provide a brief description of each of the 11 factors along with an analysis of how they represent examples of attentional support, interpretation, and enactment as therapeutic processes. As depicted in Figure 5.4, because therapeutic change occurs through direct relations that occur between group members, the dialectic of enactment provides the central backdrop of Yalom's existential approach. Within the context of enactment, the therapist and group members alike support each other's development by participating in the dialectics of attentional support and enactment. Thus, against the backdrop of enactment among members of the group, all three therapeutic modes jointly constitute Yalom's existential group therapy. A summary of the specific ways in which these therapeutic resources are represented in the 11 factors is provided in Table 5.1. As the factors often work in combination, points of intersection and overlap are noted.

1. Instillation of Hope   Of the 11 factors, the instillation of hope is the only factor introduced prior to the client's actual experience within the group. During the therapist's pre–group orientation with a prospective member, the therapist seeks to reinforce positive expectations about the benefit that can be derived within the group setting, to remove negative expectations, and to "provide a lucid explanation of the healing properties of the group" (Yalom, 1995, p. 4). Effective instillation of hope is often required to "keep" a client in a group, before the other therapeutic factors have had a chance to exert an effect, and before any symptom relief is felt. This instillation of hope can be seen as an indirect form of attentional support, in that it frees the client from the burden of solely managing fears about his or her situation. Through contact with more senior group members who have already derived benefit, the novice member is presented with a powerful interpretation that may support the enactment of a novel experience that *improvement is possible.* For example, Yalom cited leaders of Alcoholics

Table 5.1 Key Intersections of Yalom's 11 Therapeutic Factors With the Common Developmental Processes Approach

Therapeutic Factor	Attentional Support	Interpretation	Enactment
1. Instillation of hope	To effectively instill hope, the therapist must join the client in attending to his or her concerns.		Receipt of the therapist's hopeful message, and contact with senior members who have already obtained relief through the group experience, may convey the novel information that *improvement is possible.*
2. Universality	Attention is drawn to the client's "unique" circumstances.	Those circumstances are reinterpreted as being less unique than previously thought.	Clients undergo the novel experience of stepping away from the prior notion of being "unique in their wretchedness" (Yalom, 1995, p. 5).
3. Imparting information	Conveyance of information intended to be useful to the client involves attending to the client's particular concerns.	Information delivered by the therapist is delivered from the therapist's structures of understanding.	Receipt of information from the therapist and fellow group members may constitute the unique experience of also receiving interest and caring.
4. Altruism			By organizing a group such that members are able to behave altruistically to others, the therapist provides these members a potentially (and regrettably) novel experience.
5. The corrective recapitulation of the primary family group		Therapy groups, which are often seen as being populated with "siblings," provide a means of interpreting commonalities between a client's past and present circumstances.	*Corrective* recapitulation provides the client with a novel experience.

6. Development of socializing techniques			Within a supportive group environment, members feel relatively free to experiment with new and novel interpersonal behaviors.
7. Imitative behavior	Imitating others' behavior (or, alternatively, choosing *not* to imitate it) presupposes that that behavior is being attended to.	Similarly, the choice of whether or not to imitate another's behavior presupposes some degree of interpretation that perhaps might be offered by the therapist or other group members as to whether that behavior would be a helpful addition to the client's own repertoire.	As with socializing techniques more generally, the group provides a safe, supportive context for behavioral experimentation, thereby promoting novelty in experience.
8. Interpersonal learning	Attention to and resolution of parataxic distortions is a key aspect of this learning process.	Generalization of novel interpersonal behaviors from the group to the social world requires interpretations (which may be offered by the therapist or other group members) in which the suitability of such extensions is evaluated.	Again, the client has an opportunity, within the safety of the therapy group, to enact novel behaviors, including (but not at all limited to) participation in consensual validation.

Table 5.1 Key Intersections of Yalom's 11 Therapeutic Factors With the Common Developmental Processes Approach (Continued)

Therapeutic Factor	Attentional Support	Interpretation	Enactment
9. Group cohesiveness	In a cohesive group, members are better able to attend to their own thoughts and feelings.	A client's ability to participate in a cohesive group may be supported by interpretations by the therapist and other members that he or she is not "horribly unique."	The sense of belonging to a loyal and supportive group is likely a novel experience for certain members, as is the process of working through disputes with those one feels close to.
10. Catharsis	Cathartic expressions involve the application of attention by the client to his or her own concerns, and by other members to the client's affective discharge.	Catharsis alone is insufficient; therapeutic catharsis requires interpretation.	The acts of catharsis in general, and reflecting upon and interpreting catharsis in particular, are likely novel for many group members.
11. Existential factors	Attention is focused on the "ultimate concerns of existence" (Yalom, 1995, p. 91).		

Anonymous and other self-help groups as performing this "instillation of hope" function by serving as "living inspirations to others" (1995, p. 5). In instilling hope, the therapist's role involves attending to the prospective client's experience to the degree necessary that an effective, hopeful message can be formed and conveyed. The fact that receipt of such a message may constitute a novel experience serves, in a poignant way, as a marker of the pessimism and hopelessness with which so many clients struggle.

2. *Universality* This factor works to counter the reality that "many patients enter therapy with the disquieting thought that they are unique in their wretchedness, that they alone have certain frightening or unacceptable problems, thoughts, and fantasies" (Yalom, 1995, p. 5). By being exposed to the issues faced by others, disconfirmation of one's sense of horrid uniqueness can provide a powerful sense of relief, sparking feelings such as "Welcome to the human race," "We're all in the same boat," or even "Misery loves company" (Yalom, 1995, p. 6). Yalom also noted that universality appears to have particularly strong benefit in groups where members share struggles regarding experiences that they are keeping "secret" (e.g., disordered eating or sexual assault). Illustrating one of the many ways in which the therapeutic factors work together, Yalom observed that "as patients perceive their similarity to others and share their deepest concerns, they benefit from the accompanying catharsis and from ultimate acceptance by other members" (1995, p. 7). Universality relies upon all three dialectics within our common developmental processes approach. *Attention* is drawn to the client's unique circumstances, which, in a context populated by others suffering similarly, are then *reinterpreted* as being less unique than previously thought. This finding in turn gives way to the client's novel experience of stepping away from the prior self-label of *horrid uniqueness* and experiencing mutual support with others facing similar struggles.

3. *Imparting Information* In the group therapy setting, information is conveyed to members through both formal didactic programs and participants sharing information about themselves or things they have learned, that they believe might be useful to others, or that others may find useful. The information may at times be presented in the context of direct advice. Didactics have a long history in the recovery group tradition, though they are considerably less common in traditional psychotherapy groups oriented toward interaction and process. Like instillation of hope, this factor can serve as an initial "binding force" to structure a group, and keep it intact, until other factors have a greater opportunity to take effect. Yalom observed that information can also help mitigate anxiety, in that the explanation of a phenomenon can serve as an initial step in its

control (1995, p. 10). Although therapists can actively control whether or not to include formal didactics in a group, direct advice giving will occur inevitably, whether the therapist wants it to or not. Yalom has observed (1995, p. 10) that by counting the number of times direct advice is given, he can estimate the maturity (or extent of regression) of a group; members of advanced groups offer much less advice than do those in relatively immature ones.

Information can help members correct their own misinterpretations of symptoms (e.g., when members of a panic disorder group are taught about adrenaline) or help them direct their attention more skillfully to future symptoms (e.g., information about the effects of anniversaries for members of a bereavement group). Within our common developmental processes approach, "imparting information" represents a form of interpretation, in that it is derived from the therapist's or other group members' structures of understanding. To the extent that advice giving functions to guide the construction of novel experience, it can also function within the dialectic of enactment. As a form of enactment, Yalom (2005) noted the subtle yet important benefits of advice giving:

> It is rare that a specific suggestion for some problem will directly benefit the client. *Indirectly,* however, advice giving serves a purpose; the *process,* rather than the *content,* of the advice, may be beneficial, implying and conveying as it does mutual interest and caring. (p. 11, italics in original)

4. Altruism   In describing this factor, Yalom pointed to the benefits a suffering person can receive by performing a useful act for someone else. Among others, he cited Warden Duffy of San Quentin Prison, who "claimed that the best way to help a man is to let him help you" (Yalom, 1995, p. 13). For many, this act of giving may represent a very novel experience:

> In therapy groups too, patients receive through giving, not only as a part of the reciprocal giving-receiving sequence but also from the intrinsic act of giving. Psychiatric patients beginning therapy are demoralized and possess a deep sense of having nothing of value to offer others. They have long considered themselves as burdens, and the experience of finding that they can be of importance to others is refreshing and boosts self-esteem. (Yalom, 1995, p. 12)

From the perspective of existential therapy, altruistic acts help to overcome the morbid self-absorption of those plagued by meaninglessness, and represent an act on the path toward self-transcendence. Taking the perspective of the member receiving the altruistic act, Yalom (1995) noted that many clients will accept from other group members, who represent "the real world," what they will not accept from the therapist, whom they view as "the paid professional" (p. 13).

Because it provides the opportunity for group members to experience the giving and receiving of helpful acts, altruism within the group environment operates as a strong example of the dialectic of enactment.

5. The Corrective Recapitulation of the Primary Family Group   According to Yalom, the therapy groups organize themselves in ways that are reminiscent of a family. In group work, similarities arise that are comparable to sibling rivalry. For example, group members often compete for the therapist's attention and support. Yalom suggested that it is often helpful to have male and female group co-leaders—in part to help evoke early family issues. Yalom observed that regardless of members' endorsement (or even awareness) of structural similarities between the primary family group and the therapy group, early family conflicts often appear in session. When they do appear, at least in the awareness of the therapist or other group members, communicating that awareness can function within the dialectic of interpretation. But it is clear that Yalom (1995) viewed this factor as more than an opportunity for interpretation:

> What is important, though, is not only that early familial conflicts are relived but that they are relived *correctively.* Growth-inhibiting relationships must not be permitted to freeze into the rigid, impenetrable system that characterizes many family structures. Instead, fixed roles must be constantly explored and challenged, and ground rules for investigating relationships and testing new behavior must be constantly encouraged. For many clients, then, working out problems with other members is also working through unfinished business from long ago. (p. 14, italics in original)

In discussing his views on the relative importance of this factor, Yalom stated that he generally prefers to work in the "here and now." Yet part of the power of this factor seems to lie in the way that it brings to the here and now the traces of prior, unresolved family conflicts. When this occurs, the client has an opportunity to "try on" new ways of being, as well as to consider the common features between current conflicts and those from long ago. As such, this factor operates within the dialectic of enactment.

6. Development of Socializing Techniques   Like the recapitulation of primary family issues, development of social skills is a therapeutic factor much more amenable to group than to individual therapy. Yalom touched only briefly on this factor, mainly noting that over time, group members can acquire an array of highly sophisticated social skills. These include becoming attuned to interpersonal process, being helpfully responsive to others, resolving conflicts skillfully, being less judgmental, and growing more capable of experiencing and expressing accurate empathy. It is within the supportive group context that members feel the safety and freedom necessary to experiment with, receive feedback on, and ultimately incorporate novel behaviors such as these. They also are exposed to the behaviors of other participants, who thereby serve as role models. In both these ways, the therapy group provides a venue for enactment.

7. Imitative Behavior   Yalom (1995) described this factor as a form of "vicarious therapy" or "spectator therapy," in which clients derive benefit from observing the work and improvement of other group members. More conceptually, Yalom suggested that imitative behavior can be seen as a combination of the factor of universality and Bandura's (Bandura, Blanchard, & Ritter, 1969; Bandura, Ross, & Ross, 1963) notion of social learning, which holds that direct reinforcement is not sufficient to explain all behavior change. In short, as a form of enactment that occurs between social partners, group members have a particular opportunity to observe and "try on" bits of the behavioral repertoires displayed by others. Although opportunities for imitative behavior are especially rich in the group setting, Yalom also cited evidence suggesting that even in individual therapy, imitative behavior (using the therapist as model) takes place.

8. Interpersonal Learning   Yalom (2005) characterized interpersonal learning as "the group therapy analogue of important therapeutic factors in individual therapy, such as insight, working through the transference, and the corrective emotional experience" (p. 19). He described interpersonal learning in terms of three interrelated elements—the *importance of interpersonal relationships*, the *corrective emotional experience*, and the group as a *social microcosm*. Each reflects the primacy of enactment as a mode of therapeutic change. In elaborating upon the *importance of interpersonal relationships*, Yalom drew particularly upon the writings of Harry Stack Sullivan, especially in relation to the notion of *parataxic distortion*. This term describes a person's tendency to maintain distorted perceptions of others, and "occurs when one person relates to another not on the basis of the realistic attributes of the other, but on the basis of a personification existing chiefly in the former's own fantasy" (Yalom, 1995, p. 17). In comparison to transference, parataxic distortion provides more grist for the therapeutic mill in at least two ways: It extends to the client's perceptions of *all* others, not just the therapist; and it functions to meet *current* intrapersonal needs, rather than simply representing the carrying of past objects to the present. In its extension beyond the therapist, and into everyday life, parataxic distortions can have widespread negative effects, in part because they tend to be perpetuated through self-fulfilling prophecies (Yalom, 1995, p. 20).

Yalom (1995, p. 20) called further upon Harry Stack Sullivan's legacy in framing the therapeutic (and *human*) importance of interpersonal relationships. Yalom drew upon a series of assertions originally advocated by Sullivan (1940): (a) "Mental disorder" refers to interpersonal processes that either are inadequate to the social situation or are excessively complex because of the introduction of illusory persons into situations, (b) treatment should be directed toward the correction of interpersonal distortions, (c) "one achieves mental health to the extent that one becomes aware of one's interpersonal relationships" (p. 207), and (d) psychiatric cure consists of the "expanding of the self to such final effect that the patient as known to himself is much the same person as the patient behaving to others" (p. 237). If individuals come to therapy as a result of problems brought about by interpersonal distortion, how is it helpful for them to join a group populated by others with similar distortions? Sullivan's—and Yalom's—answer lies in the process of *consensual validation*, or the comparison of one's own interpersonal evaluations to those of others.

In describing *the corrective emotional experience*, Yalom drew upon Franz Alexander, who "insisted that intellectual insight alone [into parataxic distortion] is insufficient: there must be an emotional component and systematic reality testing as well" (1995, p. 24). The therapy group can serve as an excellent venue for such experiences, as there is typically no shortage of interpersonal distortion and tension. Yalom (1995, p. 26) listed the typical components of corrective emotional experience in a therapy group as follows: (a) a strong expression of emotion, which is interpersonally directed and is a risk taken by the client; (b) a group supportive enough to permit this risk taking; (c) reality testing, which allows the client to examine the incident with the aid of consensual validation from other members; (d) a recognition of the inappropriateness of certain interpersonal feelings and behavior or of the appropriateness of certain avoided interpersonal behavior; and (e) the ultimate facilitation of the individual's ability to interact with others more deeply and honestly.

Given all of the above, Yalom (1995) maintained that *group functions as a social microcosm*: to the extent that a group can be structured so that members behave in an unguarded way, "there [will be] no need for them to describe or give a detailed history of their pathology: *they will sooner or later enact it before the group members' eyes*" (p. 28; italics in original). Symptoms emerge (at least in part) from disturbances in interpersonal relationships. The well-constructed therapy group functions as a social microcosm, making each member's patterns of interaction available for display. Group members use feedback from others, as well as attention directed at themselves, to comprehend all aspects of their social behavior more clearly and fully:

> The patient, who will often have had a series of disastrous relation-ships and subsequently suffered rejection, has failed to learn from these experiences because others, sensing the person's general inse-curity and abiding by the rules of social etiquette governing normal social interaction, have not communicated the reasons for rejection. Therefore, and this is important, *patients have never learned to dis-criminate between objectionable aspects of their behavior and a self-concept as a totally unacceptable person.* The therapy group, with its encouragement of accurate feedback, makes such discrimination possible. (Yalom, 1995, p. 43)

Feedback and self-observation enable the member to develop heightened skills as a witness to his or her own behavior. They also help members to understand the impact of their behavior on the feelings of others, *and* on the opinions others hold of them. With a nod to his existentialist roots, Yalom also observed that "the patient who has become fully aware of this sequence also becomes aware of personal responsibility for it: each indi-vidual is the author of his or her own interpersonal world" (1995, p. 43). Once individuals come to understand their interpersonal worlds as things they have created, they can in turn see them as worlds within their power to *change*.

Harking back to Alexander, Yalom suggested that the power of these processes varies in depth and meaning in direct relation to the amount of *affect* associated with them. The more "real" and the more emotional an experience, the more potent its impact; experiences that are more distant and/or intellectual in character result in interpersonal learning that is less effective. Interpersonal sequences of this sort encourage group members to risk new ways of being with others. Yalom suggested that the likelihood of such risk taking is a function of each member's motivation to change, or dissatisfaction with the status quo; the extent to which each member lets the group *matter*; and the rigidity (or flexibility) of the member's char-acter structure and interpersonal style. As the member continues to take the risk of interpersonal behavior change, he or she ultimately realizes that whatever fears—"such as death, destruction, abandonment, derision, and engulfment" (Yalom, 1995, p. 44)—that previously stood in the way of change were irrational. And Yalom stated that the changes first seen within the safety and security of the treatment room inevitably seep into members' broader social environments. The conclusion of this sequence has been described by Yalom (1995) as follows:

Gradually an *adaptive spiral* is set in motion, at first inside and then outside the group. As a patient's interpersonal distortions diminish, his or her ability to form rewarding relationships is enhanced. Social anxiety decreases; self-esteem rises; the need for self-concealment diminishes. *Others respond positively to this behavior and show more approval and acceptance of the patient*, which further increases self-esteem and encourages further change. Eventually the adaptive spiral achieves such autonomy and efficacy that professional therapy is no longer necessary. (p. 44)

How can these complex, interrelated, interpersonal learning processes be viewed from within our common developmental processes framework? Clearly, the enactment of novel interpersonal behavior is at the core of Yalom's account of interpersonal learning. However, awareness of parataxic distortions is also an attentional task in which the group supports the member. In giving the member feedback or information from their own perspectives, others are providing interpretations which represent antitheses to the distortions. Attending to one's own perceptions, the ways in which they differ from the perceptions of others, and the resolution of these differences via reality testing is a process that clearly integrates the dialectics of attentional support and interpretation.

The ability to engage in corrective emotional experiences requires a member's ability to attend to internal affects, and the group's ability to bear them. Yalom suggested that the kind of intense affective discharges most likely to have therapeutic value *gain* such value in part through their very novelty, again emphasizing enactment. However, increased engagement in the new behavioral sequences and hypothesizing that initial sequences can be extended first to subsequent sequences within the safety of the group, and then later generalized to the social world more broadly, also imply the likelihood of interpretational processes in which group members jointly participate.

9. Group Cohesiveness   Just as interpersonal learning is the group therapy analogue of individual treatment elements such as insight and transference work, cohesiveness is the group form of the relationship between the individual therapist and client. Cohesiveness is defined more precisely as

the attractiveness of a group for its members ... it refers to the condition of members feeling warmth and comfort in the group, feeling they belong, valuing the group and feeling, in turn, that they are valued and unconditionally supported and accepted by other members. (Yalom, 1995, p. 48)

Yalom identified the mechanisms of action underlying group cohesiveness quite specifically. For many clients, the acceptance found within a cohesive group marks an experience that is unusual outside of the group; the very rarity of the experience makes cohesion a powerfully novel and therapeutic experience in its own right. More importantly, cohesiveness "is a necessary precondition for the other therapeutic factors to function optimally" (Yalom, 1995, p. 49). Only in a group that feels sufficiently safe and supportive will members be emboldened to express their feelings, solicit viewpoints from others, and try on new ways of being. Yalom also cited the importance that Rogers placed upon group atmosphere; a member is more likely to take seriously the feedback of a group held in high regard, than that of a group to which he or she feels less committed and attached.

The tensions that inevitably arise within any group are more likely to be of special therapeutic effect when the group does cohere:

> The group and the members must mean enough to each other to be willing to bear the discomfort of working through a conflict. Cohesive groups are, in a sense, like families with much internecine warfare but a powerful sense of loyalty.... Cohesiveness is not synonymous with love or with a continuous stream of supportive, positive statements. Cohesive groups are groups that are able to embrace conflict and to derive constructive benefit from it. (Yalom, 1995, p. 64)

As seen from the common developmental processes framework, a cohesive group is one in which members are attended to in a warm and supportive environment; as such, members are in turn freed to attend to their own, previously unexpressed thoughts and feelings. Thus, such a group provides attentional support. At the same time, the simple fact of membership in such a group can serve as a powerfully novel event for members, especially those with long histories of relational difficulty, and represents yet another example of the enactment dialectic in group therapy. As such, for some members, the act of belonging to a cohesive group may be interpreted as evidence that stands in opposition to prior self-appraisals of being "horribly unique"; when such interpretations are offered and/or supported by the therapist or other group members, the effect may be more powerful still.

10. Catharsis   Although Yalom presented research findings suggesting that moments of catharsis are typically cited by those who have completed group therapy as being particularly memorable and decisive points in their treatment, he has been clear in his own view that *"catharsis is not enough"* (1995, p. 73; italics in original). As he observed, it is not uncommon for individuals—in and out of therapy—to have emotional experiences, yet these experiences alone infrequently lead to lasting change. In contrast, Yalom (1995) defined therapy as "the dual process consisting of emotional experience and of *reflection upon* that experience" (p. 78; italics added).

Here, Yalom's words seem to echo those of Greenberg and Pascual-Leone (1995), cited in Chapter 4, emphasizing the complementarity of enactment, attentional support, and interpretation within successful group therapy. Catharsis is of most therapeutic value when the novel act and its content are subject to shared interpretation. The act of catharsis may be a novel one for some group members, and the process of actively reflecting upon and interpreting it is likely novel for many more. In addition, cathartic expressions imply the presence of a sufficient level of attention—both by the self and by the group—so that affects can flow freely.

11. Existential Factors   The last of Yalom's (1995) *11 therapeutic factors*, this focuses on what he termed the givens, the ultimate concerns of existence: death, isolation, freedom, and meaninglessness. Anxiety arises from basic conflicts in each of these realms: We wish to continue to be and yet are aware of inevitable death; we crave ground and structure and yet must confront groundlessness; each of us desires contact, protection, and to be part of a larger whole, yet experiences the unbridgeable gap between self and others; and we are meaning-making creatures thrown into a world that has no meaning (Yalom, 1995, p. 91). Consideration of such factors within the group context has been shown to provide "existential lessons" (p. 91) to members. These include the ideas that despite close relations with others, basic aloneness remains, and that the ultimate responsibility for one's life cannot be shifted or delegated. In short, the therapeutic intent is to help participants shift from Heidegger's (1962) stance of *forgetfulness of being*, to the alternative *mindfulness of being*.

From our common developmental processes perspective, the therapist's assumptions regarding the importance of existential givens play a role in his or her directing the group's attention to those "ultimate concerns of existence" (Yalom, 1995, p. 91). Although perhaps different in content from the schools of thought with which existential psychotherapy defines itself in contrast, most therapists hold parallel assumptions that play central roles both in how they direct clients' attention and in the nature of the interpretations they offer. Our perspective leads us to evaluate the effectiveness of both the attention directing and the interpretations based on whether they lead to the clients' construction of adaptive, differentiated, and integrated novel syntheses.

Different Therapies, Common Processes: Representing Diverse Approaches to Therapeutic Change

Together, the categories of attentional support, interpretation, and enactment provide a conceptual system for understanding and analyzing the change processes that occur within psychotherapy. As is indicated throughout the analyses above, these categories do not constitute a theory of psychotherapy. Instead, they name categories of therapeutic processes that we believe operate in all approaches to psychotherapy.

Different approaches to psychotherapy make use of these therapeutic processes in different ways. For example, in Rogers' client-centered therapy, the practice of restating and representing a client's understanding of experience acts as a form of attentional support. However, as will be illustrated in later chapters, other forms of attentional support exist. For example, asking questions is a form of attentional support. Questions function to support the construction of a client's understanding of events and experiences. The form of the question asked orients a client's attention in a particular direction. In this way, the question both supports and constrains the client's constructive activity. Other forms of attentional support involve modulating emotions and providing "holding" statements—statements that reduce the emotional burden on a client in order to help the client to make developmental challenges more manageable.

Similarly, different approaches to therapy invoke the dialectics of interpretation and enactment in different ways. Both psychodynamic and Rogerian approaches to therapy employ interpretation. However, psychodynamic approaches tend to privilege interpretations made from the therapist's perspective; when using client-centered techniques, interpretations arise as the therapist attempts to frame the meaning of the client's utterances for the client. Further, the dialectic of enactment is employed in different ways by different therapists. For example, although attempts to induce novel experiences through the therapeutic relationship and through the use of behavioral techniques are both forms of enactment, they differ markedly in the ways in which they produce those novel experiences.

Different approaches to therapy invoke different forms of attentional support, interpretation, and enactment. More importantly, different therapeutic traditions define the therapeutic process in terms of different *relations* among these basic therapeutic modes. By identifying different relations among attentional support, interpretation, and enactment, it is possible to identify differences in the *structure* of different approaches to psychotherapy. Figures 5.1 through 5.4 provide four such representations of the structure of different approaches to psychotherapy. Thus, different forms of psychotherapy are defined not simply in terms of the forms of attentional support, interpretation, or enactment that they espouse; they are defined in terms of the particular ways in which these processes function in relation to each other.

To use interpretation as the primary mode of psychotherapeutic change (as in Malan's psychodynamic therapy) is different from using interpretation as a vehicle of attentional support (as in Rogers' client-centered therapy). Using attentional support as the primary vehicle for mediating the enactment of novel experience between a client and therapist (as in Rogers' approach) is different from invoking attentional support as but one of many modes of communication that occur in the emergent enactments that arise in existential group therapy.

In analyzing the structure of different approaches to psychotherapy, we regard no single set of relations among attentional support, interpretation, and enactment as optimal or correct. We expect that many therapy cases entail therapists shifting approaches as they learn from experience what resources they are most able to offer and their clients are most able to use in the service of their development. Probably the practitioners who attempt to practice faithfully a single approach, and the relations among attentional support, interpretation, and enactment implicitly or explicitly espoused by that approach, are in the minority. However, as analytic tools, examining the espoused relationship among the three dialectics provides a means for understanding *how* the different approaches to therapy operate.

The question of the effectiveness of any espoused or practiced way of providing therapeutic resources in promoting development for any particular client is an open and empirical one. We turn now to an articulation of methods for tracking the ways in which various resources are offered to clients, and whether they are being effectively used to make developmental progress.

PART **III**
Method

CHAPTER 6

The Developmental Analysis of Psychotherapy Process (DAPP) Method

The DAPP method entails several ways of reviewing a psychotherapy session or series of sessions. Such review can occur in the context of reflecting on what just happened in a session or on what may have been happening over time. However, the more formal use of the coding process described below requires working from audiotapes or videotapes, or ideally transcribed sections of tapes. The three principal ways of examining the material include (a) examining what kinds of resources were offered by the therapist and whether and how they were used by the client (this includes analysis of the kinds of resources the client may have been looking for and whether they were offered by the therapist); (b) examining what developmental movement, if any, may have occurred through this process of offering and use of developmental and therapeutic resources; and (c) representing both the novel developmental structures that may have been co-constructed over the course of the session(s) and the roles and actions of the parties through which these co-constructions occurred.

There are a variety of methods that are relevant to tracking the structures and processes of developmental change as they occur within psychotherapy. These analyses may be useful for a variety of practical, research, and teaching purposes, including reflecting on the work of one therapist with one or more clients, comparing different therapeutic approaches, or comparing psychotherapy to other kinds of relationships in which human development occurs. As a result, we organize our presentation around *primary* and *secondary* tools for tracking developmental change. The *primary* tools consist of methods for identifying the forms of therapeutic resources provided by the therapist (i.e., attentional support, interpretation, and enactment) and for tracking developmental changes in the construction and hierarchical coordination of meaning structures (i.e., thesis → antithesis → conflict → synthesis) over the course of psychotherapy. The *secondary* tools provide additional methods for performing fine-grained moment-by-moment analyses of the social processes involved in the joint construction and personal coordination of meaning and action. Thus, whereas the primary tools provide ways of tracking main developmental movements fostered and supported by particular classes of therapeutic actions, secondary tools allow more subtle analysis of the ways in which therapist and client influence each other in the joint construction of novel forms of meaning. Practitioners, researchers, or individuals involved in clinical supervision may find some techniques more appropriate than others to their work. Thus, depending upon their purposes and interests, different readers might prefer to focus on different sections and analytic tools.

Primary Analytic Tools: Analyzing How Psychotherapy Fosters Developmental Change

As indicated in Chapter 4, we have suggested that psychotherapists promote developmental change in clients by offering three basic categories of resources. These include *attentional support, interpretation,* and *enactment.* In Chapter 4, we presented conceptual descriptions of the dialectical processes to which these three classes of resources contribute. In this section, in order to facilitate the empirical and/or reflective analysis of how development occurs in psychotherapy, we attempt to identify more precise definitions of these processes. Table 6.1 identifies three dimensions that are useful in discriminating the processes of attentional support, interpretation, and enactment. Although these modes of engaging clients are often overlapping (and a single utterance can simultaneously engage a client in more than one way), the provision and use of therapeutic resources differ with respect to the nature and source of the meanings constructed and the particular roles of the therapist and client in the process.

When providing attentional support, a therapist's actions are directed (a) toward bringing together and maintaining within the client's attentional field as full a range of the client's experience and understandings as possible, and (b) toward supporting the client's efforts to further represent or understand his or her experience. In using attentional support, the client *attends to* and *reflects upon* past or present experiences and events and his or her own ways of making meaning. In attentional support, it is the client who is the primary source of novel meanings; the therapist functions to direct and maintain the client's focus of attention in an attempt to facilitate

Table 6.1 Three Categories of Therapeutic Resources

	Source and Nature of Novel Meaning	Role of Therapist	Role of Client
Attentional Support	Clients' own reflections on past and present experience and the meaning made of such experience.	Assists client by helping to simultaneously focus client's attention on various aspects of client's actions, experiences, and reflections.	Client engages in attention and reflection in order to make sense out of present or past experience. Focus is on the client's constructive processes.
Interpretation	Therapists' interpretations of the meaning of actions, experiences, or reflections.	Offers interpretive content drawn from the therapist's own meaning system.	Client may appropriate, use, transform, reject, and so on the therapist's interpretive content, in a process of integrating the therapist's interpretation with the client's own interpretations. Client also plays a role in stimulating therapist's interpretive activity.
Enactment	In-session novel interactions among clients and therapists, or out-of-session novel activity by clients that is influenced by direct instruction, suggestion, or induction by interactions occurring within sessions. Through interactions, guided novel experience, and reflection on such experience (rather than reflection on existing patterns of experience), the dyad creates novel skills, meanings, or experiences that may then be further generalized within the client's daily experience and integrated with the client's prior repertoire.	(a) Actively directs, induces, or provides opportunities for the formation of novel experiences, actions, or skills; or (b) treats C as a direct relational partner and attempts to co-create novel experiences that occur in the relationship between the client and therapist and that function as opportunities for skill building.	Using the direction or support of the therapist, or in interactions with the therapist and/or other clients, the client actively participates in the production of novel actions, experiences, and skills.

the *client's* process of representing, interpreting, or making sense of issues at hand. The therapist does not offer novel or alternative meanings.

In contrast, when the therapist contributes resources to the dialectic of *interpretation*, it is the *therapist* who is the initial source of novel meanings. The therapist offers interpretations drawn from his or her own interpretive system. The therapist may offer interpretations of the client's statements or experiences, or may offer broader or more generic interpretations of events and aspects of the human condition or the client's particular circumstances. In the dialectic of interpretation, the client is free to use, modify, qualify, or reject the interpretive content provided by the therapist. To speak of the therapist as the source of novel meanings in the dialectic of interpretation is not meant to imply that the client does not engage in interpretive activity. To the contrary, the client offers his or her own interpretations at all points during the therapeutic process. Although a client may appropriate and use interpretations offered by the therapist, it is also the case that therapists appropriate and use elements of their clients' interpretations in the formulation of their own interpretations. Ultimately, the novel synthesis that the client achieves in the dialectic of interpretation results from the active transformation and synthesis of the interpretation offered by the therapist with the client's meaning-making structures. In this way, both parties contribute to the co-construction of a novel synthesis, in a dialectic in which the therapist offers an interpretation.

Our statement that the therapist is the source of novel meanings in the dialectic of interpretation arises from our primary focus on the role of the therapist in offering therapeutic resources to the client. In contrast to attentional support, in which the therapist offers the resource of supporting the client's own constructive efforts, in interpretation the therapist takes a more active role in offering interpretive content to the client.

In the dialectic of enactment, the therapist (or the therapeutic relationship, or the therapeutic setting, as in group or family therapy) plays an active role in the production of novel actions, experiences, and skills in areas of therapeutic concern. Enactment differs from attentional support and interpretation in several ways. First, in attentional support and interpretation, the client or therapist acts by *reflecting upon* and making sense *of* past or present experiences, events, and issues. In enactment, novel actions, skills, and experiences are jointly constructed and made sense of by acting jointly. In such joint constructions through enactment processes, the therapist participates in the planning, production, or assessment of the significance of novel actions, experiences, or skills, or assists the client in putting novel meanings into practice. Thus, rather than devoting therapeutic resources toward reflecting upon the meaning of conflicts and events, resources are directed at the production of the novel actions, experiences, and skills. The therapist may participate in enactments in many ways, including direct instruction, coaching, modeling, role playing, the induction of novel emotions, guiding clients through novel activity, making suggestions for novel actions, or accepting and performing the role of relational partner to clients.

Tracking Action and Meaning Elements and Their Relations

The first step to tracking developmental change in the activity and meaning structures constructed between client and therapist is to divide any given segment of interaction into a series of *action or meaning elements.* In the case of most adult psychotherapy, verbal discourse is the major medium of interaction, and what is exchanged are utterances that simultaneously create and communicate meaning. However, actions, as occur in play therapy, may also be the medium of interaction in which dialectical movement is tracked.[1] What we call a *meaning element* consists of a single basic idea or representation of action, experience, or interaction. Each meaning unit may be defined as roughly corresponding to a single declarative sentence (e.g., "I feel that I do not matter" or "I am always apologizing to people"). Complex and run-on sentences may be composed of many phrases, sentence fragments, or sentences, each of which may contain one or more meaning elements. For example, the sentence "I am always apologizing to people because I'm afraid I am going to hurt their feelings, but they get the message that I'm not confident in myself" is composed of three basic meaning elements, (a) "I am always apologizing to people," (b) "I am afraid to hurt their feelings," and (c) "They get the message that I'm not confident in myself," as well as ways of relating those meaning elements to each other.

Each meaning or activity element is identified as a *thesis, antithesis,* or *synthesis* (for a discussion of syntheses, see the section on relations of meaning elements below). As indicated in Table 6.2, a *thesis* simply consists of an action or meaning that is initiated or put forth and that stands on its own in relation to previous actions or utterances. Any "positive" statement or assertion constitutes a thesis. A thesis is "positive" not because it is regarded as good, but instead because it *affirms* something; it "puts forth" or brings into psychological awareness some state of affairs. Such a statement can introduce an idea or an interpretation of events, describe a state of affairs, refer back to and/or reintroduce a previous statement, or the like. In contrast, an *antithesis* consists of any action or idea that expresses a differentiation in relation to a prior thesis. An antithesis affirms something by distinguishing it from, or in juxtaposition to, something else (i.e., a thesis).

---

[1] In the following discussion of elements of meaning and activity, it may be helpful for the reader to keep in mind our view, explained in detail in Chapter 3, that all meaning, including that represented in language, comprises representations of activity and interaction within an environment, using representational tools participatorily appropriated from social and cultural contexts.

Table 6.2 Microdevelopmental Elements

Microdevelopmental Element	Example
Thesis (T). A thesis consists of any ("positive") statement or assertion about the issues under discussion. A thesis is "positive" not because it has value (is good), but instead because it puts forth a statement of some type. A statement can introduce an idea, describe a state of affairs, refer back to and/or reintroduce a previous statement, and so on.	Thesis: "I matter when I'm at work."
Antithesis (A). An antithesis consists of a statement that makes a differentiation in relation to a thesis. It affirms something by distinguishing it from something else (i.e., a thesis), or it may simply negate the thesis. A therapist or client can offer an antithesis by negating or by stating a contrary, opposing, or alternative view in relation to a present or prior statement made by either interlocutor. An antithesis is "negative" only in the sense that it is defined in contradistinction to a present or prior thesis.	Thesis: "I matter when I'm at work." Antithesis: "I don't matter when I'm home alone."
Conflict (C). Conflict occurs when a differentiated thesis and antithesis are brought together in attention, but with no statement regarding the relationship between them or a statement that the relationship between them is unstable or inadequate.	"I matter when I'm at work, but I don't matter when I'm home alone."
Synthesis (S). Synthesis occurs when a relationship between thesis and antithesis is articulated. In synthesis, the conflict between thesis and antithesis is resolved in terms of a higher-order representation or meaning.	"I matter to you [the therapist] whether I'm with you or not with you. Your caring for me is real, not artificial. My next step is to find places I matter outside of our sessions."

It is the exception, rather than the rule, that the antithesis simply negates the thesis. An antithesis is "negative" only in the sense that it is defined in contradistinction to a present or prior thesis. An antithesis can elaborate a thesis further, extend it in a different direction, specify a contrasting meaning, articulate a finer or more general meaning in relation to the thesis, or articulate an opposing or conflicting meaning.

In tracking the dialectical changes in the production of novel meaning throughout a psychotherapy session, we have found it useful to identify theses and antitheses and to assign each a number. We have found it to serve as a helpful notation to number these meaning elements using a **T.AAA** format. In this format, the number to the left of the decimal point indicates the *thesis number* for the meaning element in question. When a thesis is introduced, it is identified in the form of *Tx*. Thus, the first thesis is indicated as *T1*, the second as *T2*, and so on. Antitheses are indicated in the places to the right of the decimal point. Any given thesis can generate a number of different antitheses. Each antithesis to a given thesis is assigned a different number. For example "1.1" indicates the first antithesis to the first thesis, "1.2" identifies the second antithesis to the first thesis, and so forth. Antitheses themselves, of course, can give rise to still further antitheses. We refer to an antithesis to an antithesis as a *nested antithesis*. Each embedded series of nested antitheses is indicated using the number position to the right of the antithesis to which it is related. Thus, utterance 1.11 indicates the first antithesis to utterance 1.1 (which itself is the first antithesis to thesis 1.0), utterance 2.32 identifies the second antithesis to the third antithesis to utterance 2.0, and so forth. This notion can accommodate any number of theses and antitheses. In our analyses, however, nested antitheses rarely move beyond the third decimal place.

Tracking the Development of Meaning and Activity Structures

There are a variety of ways in which meaning or activity elements can be related and intercoordinated over time. We differentiate three basic relations among elements: (a) *differentiation*, (b) *conflict*, and (c) the *synthesis* of two or more elements into a higher-order coordinative structure. One way that elements can be related is through *differentiation*. Elements that are differentiated are defined in terms of contrast—they are antitheses and are tracked using the numerical identification system described above. Any elements identified by numbers that occupy any place to the right of the decimal point are defined in terms of some sort of contrast or differentiation with respect to elements indicated by numbers identified in places to their immediate left. Thus, Thesis 2 and Antithesis 2.1 are defined in contrast or contradistinction to each other; but no such direct relation exists between, say, elements 4.2 and 2.1.

A second way in which elements can be related is through *conflict*. Elements that are differentiated are not necessarily in conflict. Some antitheses simply mark distinctions relative to their thesis. For example, in the utterance "I think you must be as human as anyone else. Some topics are going to be more interesting to you than others," the first complete thought (i.e., "You must be as human as anyone else") may function as a thesis. The second complete thought (i.e., "Some topics are going to be more interesting to you …") marks a differentiation or contrast in relation to the thesis, and thus constitutes an antithesis. In this case, although the antithesis marks a contrast, the differentiation clarifies, elaborates, or refines what is communicated in the thesis. There is no conflict between thesis and antithesis. As indicated in Table 6.2, conflicts arise when a thesis and antithesis are brought together in attention in the context of an indication that the relationship between them is unstable, incompatible, or inadequate in some way. For example, the statement "I matter onstage, but I don't matter offstage" is composed of a thesis, an antithesis that exists in tension with the related thesis, and a relational term indicating this tension (i.e., "but"). It is also possible that statements can communicate conflict when a thesis and an antithesis are brought into attention without a direct statement about the instability or unsuitability of their relationship. In such cases, the incompatibility of thesis and antithesis may be implied rather than explicitly indicated. Conflict among meaning elements is indicated as $(A.B <C> X.Y)$. For example, $(T4 <C> 4.1)$ or, in alternative equivalent notation, $(4.0 <C> 4.1)$ indicates that Thesis 4 conflicts with Antithesis 4.1. Similarly, $(4.2 <C> 4.21)$ would indicate a conflict between Antithesis 4.2 and Antithesis 4.21.

A *synthesis* occurs when one or more theses, antitheses, or conflicts are intercoordinated in such a way as to produce a higher-order coordinating structure that organizes activity or meaning in a novel way. The process of synthesizing previously differentiated elements is the primary process by which development occurs. Syntheses can occur in a variety of different ways. The most important form of synthesis occurs when previously conflicting elements are coordinated in such a way to produce a higher-order structure that *resolves or transcends conflict* among theses and antitheses. Such a synthesis generally occurs in psychotherapy after additional elements are constructed in the context of interactions among therapists and clients, and attention has been given to one or more conflicts. The novel synthesis thus stands in a relation of coordination or transcendence to the conflicts it addresses. Over time, elements are coordinated in such a way as to transform and resolve the previously conflicting thesis–antithesis relations. A second form of synthesis occurs through the process of generalization. Generalizing syntheses occur when a client or therapist abstracts across a variety of particular meaning elements in order to form a more generalized meaning structure. Because it proceeds through the intercoordination of multiple meaning elements to form a higher-order structure, generalization is a form of synthesizing activity. The construction of higher-order syntheses is an iterative process. A synthesis emerges from the intercoordination of lower-evel theses, antitheses, and conflicts. Once this happens, the emergent synthesis essentially functions as a new thesis. It can itself become the object of focus, discussion, and action; can generate antitheses and new conflicts; and eventually become part of still higher order syntheses.

It is possible to track the process of thesis–antithesis–conflict–synthesis movement over the course of a therapy excerpt, an extended therapy episode, an entire therapy session, or a full course of therapy illustrated by episodes from different sessions. In order to use DAPP for all of these purposes, we have adopted the convention of identifying syntheses using the following notation:

$$S_x/T_y[\text{Element}_i \leftrightarrow \text{Element}_j \leftrightarrow \text{Element}_k \ldots]$$

S_x refers to the synthesis number. We call the first synthesis in the case material we are subjecting to DAPP analysis *S1*. The next synthesis is named *S2*, and so on. T_y refers to the new thesis number assigned to the synthesis in question. All new theses have been numbered sequentially, and because a novel synthesis, once created, becomes a new thesis, it is given the next highest thesis number to the most recent thesis. Thus, when analyzing backward, the novel coordinating structure is more likely to be referred to by its synthesis number, but when tracking forward, it is more likely to be identified by its thesis number in **T.XXX** notation. The items specified within the square brackets consist of the numbers assigned to the particular elements that have undergone intercoordination to produce the novel synthesis in question. Intercoordination of elements that produce novel syntheses is indicated using a double arrow ($\leftrightarrow$). An example of synthesis through generalization involves the following. Consider the following exchange that occurred between the client described in Figure 2.3 and her therapist:

C1: My vote matters (**T1**), but *I don't* … (**1.1**) the things I can do (**1.2**), and um, changes I can make (**1.3**) and uh stuff I do to make the world a better place (**1.4**).

T1: Your actions matter. (**S₁/T2[1.0 ↔ 1.2 ←THROUGH→ 1.4]**)

The client begins her statement by articulating a thesis (i.e., "My vote matters" (**T1**)) and an antithesis to that thesis (i.e., "but *I don't* (**1.1**)"). Thereafter, the client lists various ways in which her "vote matters," including "the things I can do (**1.2**)," "changes I can make (**1.3**)," and "stuff I do to make the world a better place (**1.4**)." Thereafter, in an attempt to place the client's statements in a larger framework, through an act of generalization, the therapist offers the interpretation "Your actions matter." In so doing, the therapist abstracted across the various descriptions (i.e., 1.0, 1.2, 1.3, and 1.4) and generalized them into a single interpretative category. In so doing, the therapist also coordinated the instances provided by the client into a novel interpretive synthesis. This transformation can be represented as (**S₁/T2[1.0 ↔ 1.2 ← THROUGH → 1.4]**). It is notable that antithesis **1.1** was not integrated into **S1/T2**. In the therapist's next response, she acknowledges this by saying in contrast to **S1/T2**, "But there is a part of you that doesn't." Because this utterance is now presented in distinction to the synthesis (S1) that has become thesis 2, it is represented in our notation as (2.1). By tracking the ways in which therapists and clients differentiate and coordinate elements into novel syntheses, one can identify the structures and processes of development as they occur in psychotherapeutic exchanges.

It is important to note that the process of identifying and tracking changes in meaning and activity structures depends upon one's purposes and interests. For some purposes, it might be necessary to identify each element produced in any given psychotherapeutic exchange; for other purposes, it might be appropriate to track changes among elements that are considered to be primary or otherwise important within a particular developmental sequence, ignoring elements that are peripheral to that sequence. A complete analysis of elements can lead to insights about the nature and course of the meanings and actions that might be missed or obscured if one focuses only on larger themes and transitions. However, such an analysis may be both labor-intensive and time-consuming, may be too complicated to present to a reader without the forest becoming lost in the trees, and may be unnecessary for some purposes. The selective analysis of developmental transitions in main meaning elements or themes may be most helpful in reviewing and evaluating recorded psychotherapy sessions as well as in contexts of clinical supervision and training.

Secondary Analytic Tools: Analyzing the Structure and Processes of Joint Action

The coactive systems framework proceeds from the premise that, in any given face-to-face encounter, social partners co-regulate each other's actions (Fogel, 1993; Mascolo & Margolis, 2004). Within co-regulated social interaction, individual participants continuously adjust their actions, thoughts, and feelings to the ongoing and anticipated actions of their interlocutors. In this way, the actions of one's social partner are part of the process of an individual's activity. Development arises not from processes that occur within individuals, or even as a result of external social forces that impinge upon individuals, but instead as a product of processes that occur between individuals. A second set of analytic tools enables moment-by-moment analyses of the ways in which discursive processes that operate between individuals lead to the production of novel meanings and actions, often in unanticipated and nonobvious ways. These tools include (a) identification of different *forms of co-regulation and coactive scaffolding* that occur between individuals, (b) tracing the origins of novel meanings and actions to particular sequences of *discursive acts* that occur between client and therapist over time, and (c) identifying and tracking changes in the *structure of joint action* as it occurs over time, and the ways in which such changes prompt the formation of novelty and higher-order action over the course of psychotherapy. The task of identifying the structure of joint action in psychotherapy builds upon the previous two methods (i.e., identifying forms of co-regulation and sequences of discursive action), and culminates in what we call a *relational activity analysis*.

Levels of Coactive Scaffolding Within Therapeutic Discourse

In the developmental literature, the concept of scaffolding refers to the ways in which more expert partners assist less expert individuals in the development of novel skills and meanings (Mascolo, 2005; Rogoff, 1990; Stone, 1998; Wood & Middleton, 1975). The scaffolding metaphor likens the social support for individual development to the scaffolding placed around a building as it is in the process of construction. A physical scaffold is built around a building to support the individuals who act to construct the structure in question; it provides a support structure for the construction of a building. In so doing, it not only supports the process of construction but also anticipates the structure of the building. A scaffold often takes the shape of the emerging building before its final structure is in place. Once a structure is constructed, the scaffolding is no longer needed and can be discarded.

There are many ways in which adults and more accomplished peers can scaffold the development of children and/or less expert individuals. A more expert individual can break down a task; direct the more novice individual's attention toward particular features of a task; cue the novice to perform acts already in his or her repertoire; perform one part of the task while the novice performs the other; manage emotion and frustration that occur during task completion; and so on. In this way, when one person scaffolds the development of another person, she often takes on part of the burden of the task itself (Fischer, Bullock, Rotenberg, & Raya, 1993), gradually turning over the full burden of the task to the novice once the requisite skills and meanings have been acquired. However, at this point, the expert may "up the ante" and set in motion developmental processes to promote the development of still higher order skills for reflecting upon and improving task performance (Rogoff, 1990). Athletic coaches for mature athletes typically play such roles. At this point, the level of scaffolded support may return, but in a different form that functions to support the production of still higher level action and reflection. The scaffolding metaphor has been useful in highlighting the ways in which social agents structure individual development. It provides a useful metaphor for representing the role of therapists in promoting development in clients. Implicit in the notion of scaffolding, however, is the idea that the outcomes and directions of development are preconceived by the more expert individual. It is important to keep in mind the open-ended nature of development. As indicated in Figure 2.4, the goals and outcomes of development—both within and outside the context of psychotherapy—cannot necessarily be specified beforehand. One reason why this is the case is that the individual who receives scaffolding support plays an active role in the developmental process. This is especially the case in many forms of psychotherapy. Mascolo (2005) has introduced the concept of coactive scaffolding to account for the dynamic and often open-ended nature of the scaffolding process.

Table 6.4 identifies nine levels of coactive scaffolding or support that therapists often offer throughout the course of psychotherapy and the codes that we use to represent them. The levels differ in the amount or degree of support provided by the leading partner (usually the therapist) in promoting constructive activity in the guided partner. Higher levels indicate that the guiding partner is providing more support or direction than in lower levels. No assumption is made that higher levels of scaffolded support are better or more preferred modes of functioning than lower levels. We suggest that a successful psychotherapist is one who is able to adapt and adjust his or her level of support to the particular needs of his or her client at any given point in time. Further, if the purpose of psychotherapy is to promote adaptive psychosocial functioning in clients, one might argue that the ultimate goal is to foster sufficient development so that clients can function effectively independent of the therapist. In successful psychotherapy, we assume that therapists adjust the level and form of the support they provide to the current developmental needs of their clients.

The first five levels of scaffolding[2] described in Table 6.4 involve different forms of *attentional support* that one partner (usually the therapist) provides for the other. As indicated above, when offering attentional support, the therapist helps direct and maintain clients' attention to clients' own experience and ways of expressing and making meaning of their experience. The therapist does not offer novel or alternative meanings. The first and lowest level of scaffolding—Scaffolding Level 1 (Scl)—occurs when one partner **PROMPTS** (PROMPT) or **CUES** (CUE) another partner to execute an already existing "skill" (in parentheses, we indicate the codes we use for each type of act in which therapist or client engages). In so doing, a client has already acquired a particular meaning structure, skill, or way of acting as part of his or her repertoire. The therapist scaffolds

---

[2] In describing the levels of scaffolding we refer to "discursive acts." Table 6.3 describes the abbreviations we use for discursive acts and how they are integrated with the numerical codes discussed above in the section on "Tracking Action and Meaning Elements and Their Relations." This integration will be further explained below under the heading "Tracking the Offering and Use of Therapeutic Resources."

Table 6.3 Types of Discursive Acts

Initiator	Example	Respondent	Example
Offer [O(1.1)].[1] A initiates a new statement not directly tied to a prior statement.	C: My vote matters, but I don't matter (initiating a new thread of discussion).	**Affirm** [AFF].[4] A indicates agreement with B's utterance.	"Yes, that's it" or "Absolutely!"
Request [REQ(1.1)].[3] A asks B to perform a physical or symbolic act.	T: Can you jump onto the mat for me? C: Can you say that again?	**Acknowledge** [ACK].[4] A indicates understanding of B's utterance or uses utterances to encourage B's ongoing constructive action.	"Mm-hm" or "Uh-huh." "I see." "Now I understand what you mean."
Encourage [ENC(1.1)].[3] A offers a positive evaluation to foster B's continued activity.	T: You can do this. T: That's good—just keep doing what you're doing.	**Reject** [RJ(1.1)].[2] A disagrees with B's utterance.	"That's not right" or "No, that's incorrect."
Prompt [PROMPT(1.1)].[3] A cues action or utterance in B that is under B's full control.	T: Tell me the story that you told me last time. T: When you meet someone, first you say, what?	**Qualify** [Q(1.1)].[2] A agrees with B's utterance, but limits agreement in some way.	"That's not quite right." "Yeah, but ..."
Restate [RS(1.1)].[2] A restates or clarifies B's utterance in modified or condensed form.	C: You seemed bored when I said that. T: Uh-huh, you thought that I felt bored.	**Appropriate** [APP(1.1)].[2] A takes B's utterance and uses it in his or her own utterance.	T: "You feel your actions matter." C: *"My actions do matter."*
Question [QUES(1.1); PROBE(1.1)].[3] A asks a question that requires B to provide novel information; the question or probe produces a demand for novel constructive action in the other.	T: Is there a difference between "I want" and "I demand"? T: Can you put some more words on that?	**Elaborate** [E(1.1)].[1] A continues to construct novel meanings linked to previous statement made by A or B. A appropriates B's utterance and adds additional meaning.	T: "You feel that your actions matter." C: *"My actions matter, especially when I'm at work. It's like when I'm onstage, I matter."*

Table 6.3 Types of Discursive Acts (Continued)

Initiator	Example	Respondent	Example
Expansion [EXP(1.1→1.2)]. A restates or builds on B's statement (1.1) and extends its meaning further (1.2).	C: I spoke, and nothing happened. T: You spoke and then hoped something would happen *between us?*	**Transform** [TRANS(1.1→1.2)]. A appropriates B's statement (1.1) and transforms it (1.2) in a novel way.	T: "Your actions matter, but your feelings don't." C: *"I matter onstage but not offstage."*
Hold [HOLD, SUPP].[4] A communicates intention to share the burden of intense feelings with B (emotional holding).	T: Don't worry; I'm here to help you through these painful feelings.	**Follow** [FOLLOW (1.1)].[2] A actively follows B's directives.	T: "Now, count to 10 calmly and slowly." C: "1, 2, 3, 4..."
Interpret [INT].[1] A offers B a different way of understanding, based on A's making meaning.	T: There is this part of you that is like Eleanor Roosevelt.	**Imitate** [IMITATE(1.1)].[2] A actively copies B's actions.	T: "Go ahead, say, 'Hello, my name is Fred.'" C: *"Hello, my name is Fred."*
Direct [DIR(1.1)].[1] A directs, instructs, or explains.	T: Now, imagine that you are talking with your mom.	**Yield** [YIELD]. B follows A's physical lead.	T takes C's hand and moves it into a position to shake another person's hand; C yields to T's lead.
Model [MODEL(1.1)].[1] A models desired actions.	T: This is the way you shake hands (models act).	**Act** [ACT]. A executes symbolic or physical action.	T (to child): "Fly off to Russia!" (Child pretends to fly and jumps on deep pressure mat.)
Role Play [RP(1.1)].[1] A and B assume roles and role-play.	T: I'll be your mother and you be yourself....		

Note: Acts in "Response" column may follow any act indicated in "Initiator" column. Entries are not exhaustive.
1 Number in parentheses refers to the code for the *new* element produced through the act in question.
2 Number in parentheses refers to the code for the *earlier* element to which the discursive act refers.
3 Identification of element number is optional only when the discursive act clearly refers to an *earlier* element to which an interlocutor is expected to respond.
4 No element number is required.

the client's action by cueing, reminding, or suggesting that the client perform or deploy the skill or action in question. Cuing can take both verbal (e.g., "Do you remember what you said last time?" or "Now jump on the mat!") and nonverbal forms (e.g., pointing or gesturing). Therapists often use prompts as a way to keep a client's attention on a task, or to help a client move from one idea or action to another. For example, in contexts involving social skills training, a therapist may prompt the next step of a given course of action (e.g., "You've said hello ... now shake hands!"). Given this level of support, the client is performing an independent action, but requires being helped by acknowledgment, reassurance, or emotional encouragement to support ongoing action.

As was the case in Level 1, the client constructs a meaning or action structure for himself or herself. However, the therapist provides support by acknowledging attention to or understanding or appreciation of the client's activity, or by modulating negative emotion or providing encouragement. Emotional support (Sc2) can take verbal (e.g., "You can do it," or "Don't worry—it makes sense that you'd be self-conscious"), vocalic (e.g., "Mmm-hmmm" or "Uh-huh" to acknowledge and encourage further activity in the client), or nonverbal forms (e.g., nodding the head while smiling to encourage further activity). Sc2 differs from the form of indirect attentional support we call *emotional holding* (see Sc5, below), in which the therapist holds the client by sharing the burden of managing intense disorganizing feelings, so that the client's attention is freed to attend to the conflicts he or she faces.

The third level of scaffolding (Sc3) involves **RESTATING** (RS) a partner's (or one's own) utterance. Although many forms of attentional support play central roles within client-centered psychotherapy (Rogers, 1951), as discussed in Chapter 5 this approach is often associated with restatement. Restatement maintains a client's attention to his or her own meaning making, while also providing an opportunity to confirm whether the client's meaning has been adequately understood by the therapist. Restatement differs from higher levels of coactive support in that the therapist is not intending to add interpretative meaning to the client's utterance from the therapist's frame of reference, but only to check if the therapist is able to assimilate to and accommodate the client's intended meaning. The restatement or reframing of the client's utterance may also function in a selective and directive role, directing the client's attention to what the therapist considers to be more important aspects of the client's felt experience and/ or reflective meaning making.

The fourth level of support (Sc4) consists of the use of **DISTANCING** statements (Cocking & Renninger, 1993; Sigel, Stinson, & Kim, 1993). *Distancing* refers to a range of statements in which one social partner invites reflection by the other, which may result in novel constructions.

Table 6.4 Forms and Levels of Coactive Scaffolding Within Psychotherapeutic Discourse

FORM AND LEVEL OF SCAFFOLDED SUPPORT	EXAMPLES	SYMBOL Client	Therapist
ATTENTIONAL SUPPORT[1]			
Sc1. Cue/Prompt (CUE, PROMPT). A cues or prompts an already existing skill in B. B deploys full skilled action by him or herself without further support or direction throughout process.	(1) C: "I don't know how to ask for what I want! T: Remember we talked about "I -Statements" or "How about an "I - Statement"? (2) C: "Hello, Bob..." T: "and?" C: "Oh yeah, I shake hands"		AS1: Cue
Sc2. Encouragement/Acknowledgment/Affirm (ENC, ACK, AFF). A reassures, encourages or modulates B's self - evaluative emotional reactions to support ongoing activity, or acknowledges B's statement so to motivate continued action	(1) As C speaks, T affirms by saying "mm hm", "uh huh", "yeah," or something similar. (2) T supports B by saying "that's a horrible way to feel" or "it's okay to feel that way", etc.		AS2: Ack/Enc
Sc3. Restatement (RS). A restates B's utterance to clarify or consolidate B's meaning. In so doing, A does not transform B's meaning or add significantly beyond what B has said.	(1) C: It's sort of a, um, it's sort of a strong, sort of a self, kind of place. T: A strong self, kind of place. (2) C: I'm off to Spain (child jumps on mat). T: Off to Spain!		AS3: Ack/Enc
Sc4. Distancing (DIST, QUES, EXP, PROBE). Partner creates cognitive demand on interlocutor, motivating constructive action. Distancing motivates that, but does not specify the interlocutor's activity (as in Direction). Examples include open-ended questions; probes; expansions; requests for evaluation, inference, comparison, etc.	(1) T: "What did you hope would happen?" (2) T: "How does it feel to think about her having the same feeling for you that you have toward others? (3) C: I thought that you were bored by this. T: So I did something to make you feel I'm bored and this made you feel that something wasn't quite right?		AS4:Dist
Sc5. Emotional Holding (HOLD/SUPP). A communicates (with empathic acknowledgment of feeling or sometimes with explicit reassurance) a willingness to share the burden of managing intense feelings that result from B's attending to painful experience. A expresses confidence that therapeutic relations can hold, contain, or manage such feelings.	(1) C: "I am afraid to talk about how my father raped me" T: "I will be here to help you through it " (2) C: "I'm really embarrassed to tell you this." T: "Don't worry, I'm here for you ." (3) T:" I'm here to help you through the process when bad things come up."		AS5:Hold
INTERPRETATION[1]			
Sc6. Interpretation (INT) A offers explicit explanation or way to understand the meaning of a given issue or event Interpretations go beyond a concrete descriptions of an particular event or state.	(1) C: "She was off duty and didn't have to answer the phone for me." T : "That's a way of not taking in that she did call." (2) T: "You've been in the shadows so long... with your mother. You were 'out there', then I say "Let's shine the light on you" and it's glaring..."		I6:Interpret

DIRECTED ENACTMENTS

Sc7. Direction (DIR). A goes beyond merely providing an interpretation to directing B's symbolic, physical or emotional activity in area of intervention (but without modeling). A instructs B on how to representation or interpret a past, present or future event, or directs/coaches B on how to perform a particular task.	(1) T: "Okay, first look him in the eye and say 'hello'…now shake hands…ask your question…" (2) T: " Let's just think about it this way. Is there somebody who you work with….that y ou know is…in pain…and really want to see feel better or feel sad about their pain?"	E7:Direction
Sc8. Guided Enactment (MODEL, RP). (a) A models (most often with direction) an activity that B performs in the therapeutic context (e.g., B imitates A's modeled action); (b) treating B as a relational partner in domain under development, A induces experiences or (c) models or leads role enactments in role playing context.	(1) T models how to "shake hands" for a child. (2) T induces experience in C by expressing genuine feelings: T: "How much are you going to allow yourself to savor these [feelings from others]?" (3) T: "I'll be your mother and you be you. Say how you feel"	E8:Model
Sc9. Physical Guidance (PHYS). A uses *physical direction* or other types of supports that directly modulate or organize B's actions or experiences (e.g., hand-over-hand guidance; touching to regulate calming; providing physical pressure to foster sensory-integration; biofeedback, etc).	(1) T puts hand on C's shoulder to calm C before an act of public speaking. (2) T uses hand-over-hand guidance to show child how to swing a baseball bat.	E9: Physical Guidance

[1] There are two ways that scaffolding activities by the therapist can qualify as contributions to the dialectic of enactment. The first involves higher-order acts of direction, guidance, and physical guidance (Levels Sc7, Sc8, and Sc9). However, at lower levels of support, when discursive activity is focused upon novel activity in which the client has engaged (e.g., interactions with the therapist or other clients within sessions, "homework" that the client has completed outside of sessions, or ways in which the client has translated ideas developed in session into suggestions for out-of-session practices), acts of attentional support or interpretation may also contribute to the dialectic involved in the discursive act. For example, RS (Sc3/e) refers to a restatement (i.e., attentional support at Scaffolding Level 3) that occurs within the context of discussing novel activity.

A distancing statement promotes psychological development by creating "distance" between an individual's current representations, actions, or expressions and novel, alternative, or more abstract possible representations of what has been previously expressed. Distancing statements include **QUESTIONS** (QUES) (e.g., "What did it feel like to think that Carol cared about you in that way?"), **PROBES** (PROBE) (e.g., "Can you put some words on that?"), and **REQUESTS** (REQ) for comparisons (e.g., "Do you think that she loved you any less than she loved your brother?" or "Which happened first? Was it his nasty comment or your feelings of anger?"), higher-order causal analyses (e.g., "What do you think was the cause of that?"), generalizations (e.g., "Now, can you think of other solutions that are similar to the one that you just described?"), and a variety of other statements. Another form of distancing involves the use of **EXPANSIONS** (EXP). Expansions occur when one partner restates but extends the meaning of the other partner's utterance in a significant way. Unlike Scaffolding Level 3, which involves restating or bringing together different aspects of what one's social partner has already stated, expansions extend the meaning of what is said beyond the initial utterance. For example, in response to a client's statement "I approached my mother, and she had little to say to me," a therapist might say, "So, you talked with your mother and felt disappointed in her response." In this statement, the therapist goes beyond the client's statement "and she had little to say to me" and infers or offers additional meaning for the client (i.e., "You felt disappointed"). Distancing utterances present different degrees of discrepancy or cognitive conflict that a client may be invited to resolve. A distancing strategy prompts the client's attention to the ways in which his or her existing ideas or meanings can be elaborated or developed to a more abstract level. For example, not all *questions* invite distancing. Many teachers, for example, ask questions the answers to which the student already knows (Wells, 1999). In order for a question to qualify as a genuine act of distancing, it must prompt novel constructive activity. A distancing question introduces a gap (i.e., distance) between a client's current level of thinking and a future level of understanding. The client's attention is directed toward constructive action intended to fill this gap.

The fifth level of scaffolded support (Sc5) consists of the provision of **EMOTIONAL HOLDING** (HOLD) by the therapist. Emotional holding occurs when the therapist communicates, often with deep empathic acknowledgment of feeling but sometimes with explicit reassurance, a willingness to share the burden of managing intense feelings that result from the client attending to painful experience. *Emotional holding* refers to the second, more indirect form of attentional support that was discussed in Chapter 4 and contrasted with therapist responses that direct or maintain attention to conflicts that may represent developmental opportunities. The therapist may express confidence that the therapeutic relationship can hold, contain, or manage intense feelings over time. Emotional holding is different from the type of encouragement typical of Scaffolding Level 2. In Sc2, the acknowledgment or affirmation is with respect to particular elements of experience or meaning that the client has shared. A therapist might say, "Yes, I understand how frustrating that was"; "That seems important; are you able to continue with the story?" or "Mm-hmm, I see," as examples of Level 2 emotional support. Such utterances occur at the level of the momentary act or utterance. Emotional holding, on the other hand, occurs at the level of the therapeutic relationship itself. When a therapist extends the resource of emotional holding, it is with the knowledge that the client needs someone else to help carry the burden of painful feelings, either in the moment or extended over longer periods of time, in order to proceed with the disclosure or constructive activity that occurs in the context of painful feelings. In so doing, the therapist offers the resource of the therapeutic relationship itself as a way of helping the client move through painful emotional processes. Emotional holding can take a variety of different forms. For example, a client may express fear about her ability to talk about events that raise strong emotion. A therapist might say, "I will be here to help you through this"; "Don't worry, I'll be here for you"; or even "It will be important for you to feel that you can share your burden with me. You won't be alone; I'll help you through it" or something similar.

The first five levels indicated in Table 6.4 describe forms of attentional support. At Level 6, the therapist takes a still more active role in attempting to influence the client by offering **INTERPRETATIONS** (INT) of the client's actions, utterances, or situation from the perspective of the therapist's own conceptual system. Using interpretation, a social partner derives from his or her meaning-making system ways of understanding, explaining, or representing the meaning of the other's experiences and/ or the social and physical contexts. An interpretation consists of a representation offered by the therapist that goes beyond concrete description of a given experience or event. Instead, an interpretation represents the meaning of an event, experience, or set of larger processes. Interpretation occurs when a therapist or a client draws upon his or her own conceptual framework in an attempt to provide an explanation or representation for whatever events are under discussion. An interpretation may be differentiated from a description. An interpretation occurs when a social partner attempts to go beyond simply reporting or describing the concrete details of an event (e.g., "Yesterday, I talked with my mother about the situation that occurred last week"). Instead, an individual attempts to explain the event or situation. For example, a therapist might say, "I think your son has ADHD," "That's a way of not accepting the fact that she does care for you," or "I think you tend to avoid conflict in your interpersonal encounters."

As discussed above, enactments consist of fostering (and reflecting upon) novel activity and experience (that may occur in the moment between the therapist and the client, or in the client's life in between therapy sessions). When development occurs through the dialectic of enactment, the therapist's communications foster the production of and reflection upon novel meanings, experiences, or actions in the client that the client might not produce or sustain alone. This may occur through the therapist engaging in directing, coaching, role-playing, modeling, training the client to develop a novel skill, and giving instructions for doing activities outside of the therapeutic context. In these contexts, because the therapist provides increasing levels of support to the client, each of these forms of enactment occurs at scaffolding levels that are higher than those described thus far. These levels will be described further below.

However, development through the dialectic of enactment may also occur (a) *when a therapist engages a client as a direct relational partner and interacts directly with the client in ways that create novel experiences or have the potential to promote the development of novel skills*; (b) when, during a session, two or more clients interact in new ways with the support of the therapist in acknowledging, mediating, or reflecting upon the interaction; and (c) when a therapist, by providing attentional support and/or interpretation, helps the client to reflect upon the ways in which he or she has put into practice between sessions new ways of thinking, feeling, or acting. Such interactions, regardless of the level of scaffolding provided by the therapist, function within the dialectic of enactment. As a result, depending upon the focus of discourse, the *process of enactment can occur at any level of coactive support*. Thus, we differentiate between lower-level (Sc1 through Sc6) and higher-level (Sc7 through Sc9) forms of offering resources to the dialectic of enactment. Although lower levels of scaffolding typically involve the provision of attentional support or interpretation by the therapist, these levels of scaffolding *also* can be considered to be offers of resources to the dialectic of enactment, *when the object of attention is novel activity of any of the types described above*. Furthermore, reflections upon the possibilities for applying ideas and skills developed through therapy to future interactions either in or outside of therapy sessions may also be considered to be aspects of the dialectic of enactment. These possible interactions may take place within relationships among clients and therapists or may be extrapolated from novel meanings that are co-constructed during therapy sessions.

For example, a distancing question that probes the client's sense of the ongoing relationship (e.g., "How does it feel to hear me say that to you?") between the client and therapist can be considered a form of both attentional support and enactment. We use the convention /e to differentiate lower-level enactments from corresponding levels of pure attentional support or interpretation. For example, *Sc4/e* may refer to an act of distancing (attentional support) that occurs within the context of acknowledgment of a novel activity, or reflection on interactions between the client and therapist.

Levels 7 through 9 consist of higher-level forms of enactment. In these levels of scaffolding, the therapist plays still more active roles in structuring the production of novel meanings and experiences for the client. We have distinguished three forms of higher-order enactment that differ with respect to the degree of support provided by the therapist in scaffolding action. At Level 7, a therapist can use **DIRECTION** (DIR) to structure the formation of a client's actions, thoughts, and experiences. Direction involves providing specific instructions about how to perform a given activity or how to organize a particular of set of representations or concepts. When providing direction, the therapist acts as a kind of teacher or coach, identifying a particular course of action that the client may choose to follow. In this way, the therapist assists the client in building specific actions or meanings that are expected to be put into practice either in or outside of the therapy session. Sometimes, direction using verbalizations is not sufficient to evoke a novel skill. In such circumstances, the therapist may engage in a still higher level of structuring (Sc8) involving **GUIDED ENACTMENT**. At this level, the therapist moves beyond mere symbolic direction and provides additional support by enacting target thoughts, feelings, and actions *for* and/or *with* the client. For example, the therapist may **MODEL** (MOD) a series of actions or action strategies for the client (e.g., model a strategy for resolving a conflict with another person). The client is generally expected to **IMITATE** (IMITATE) the modeled actions. The therapist may treat the client as a mock relational partner and engage in **ROLE-PLAYING** (RP) as a way of either jointly constructing a way of relating or putting into practice a set of strategies that were discussed previously (e.g., assuming the role of the client interacting with his or her mother).

The highest level of enacted support consists of **PHYSICAL GUIDANCE** (Sc9). Using physical guidance, a therapist supports the client using any of the scaffolding processes discussed above (especially those identified in Level 8), but with the added provision of physical or physically mediated guidance. For example, at this level, if a therapist were showing an autistic child how to play with a doll, he or she might use hand-over-hand guidance to physically move the child's hands and arms in the desired ways. Physical guidance would include any form of physical contact that is intended to support the production of desired actions, thoughts, and feelings. This may include simply laying a hand on a client's shoulder in an attempt to induce calm in the presence of a feared object through the use of biofeedback.

Tracking the Offering and Use of Therapeutic Resources

There are many ways to track the offering and use of therapeutic resources over the course of psychotherapy. In what follows, we offer a system (and related notation) for analyzing the course of psychotherapy in terms of how clients use or do not use the various resources offered by the therapist. Our approach to tracking the offering and use of therapeutic resources has been to think of psychotherapy as a form of discursive activity. As a discursive activity, on any given conversational turn, the client or therapist engages in one or more *discursive acts* (Perinbanayagam, 1991; Wells, 1999; Wood & Kroger, 2000). A *discursive act* refers to an action that serves a particular function within any given unit of social discourse. A discursive act generally contains two parts. The first part is the act itself—what the therapist and client *do* in relation to each other with the meanings, actions, and experiences under discussion. For example, each of the levels of scaffolding and support identified in Table 6.4 is defined with reference to different types of discursive acts. That is, when providing attentional support, a therapist may perform acts of *cueing* or *prompting* (Level 1); *acknowledging, affirming,* or *encouraging* (Level 2); *restating* (Level 3); *questioning* and *probing* (Level 4); or *offering emotional support* (Level 5). When providing interpretation, a therapist may *offer* an interpretation (Level 6). When engaging in higher-order enactments, a therapist may engage in acts of *directing* (Level 7), *modeling* or *role-playing* (Level 8), or *physically guiding* (Level 9). The second element of a discursive act consists of the meaning, experience, or movement in the broader process of meaning construction that is the object of a given discursive action. It may be either the meaning that is offered by the acting partner, or a prior meaning that the discursive act is performed *upon.*

We have identified a series of discursive acts typically produced by clients and therapists throughout psychotherapeutic exchanges. A nonexhaustive list of these acts is provided in the top two panels of Table 6.3. The left half of the table identifies discursive acts typically exhibited by the initiator or leader of a given conversational turn. The right half indicates discursive acts performed by the respondent. To track the offering and use of therapeutic resources throughout a psychotherapeutic session, for each conversational turn we classify the nature of the discursive acts exhibited by the client or therapist as well as the operative content of any given act. For purposes of notation, we have represented these acts and their operative content using the following basic syntax:

DISCURSIVE ACT (OPERATIVE CONTENT)

Thus, to use the DAPP method, for any given conversational turn one first draws upon Table 6.3 to identify the type of discursive act expressed by the social partner in question (e.g., **OFFER, REQUEST,** or **ENCOURAGE**). Then one identifies the *operative content*, which refers to the particular meaning or action elements (thesis, antithesis, conflict, or synthesis) that are being produced, as a result of the discursive act in question.

Any given discursive act exhibits a type of double action. It is both a response to a prior discursive act and the creative source of a novel meaning that extends the ongoing discourse. In identifying discursive acts, an observer must identify the relation between any relevant prior acts and the novel content provided by the speaker in question. In practice, it is possible to identify a discursive act for each meaning element produced by an interlocutor on any given conversational turn. Any given discursive act may be identified by asking two basic questions: (a) What is the speaker *doing* to produce the novel content in question? And (b) how does the current act relate to *prior* discursive acts (produced by either the speaker or her interlocutor) that the current act is intended to extend? Thus, when an actor initiates a novel topic of conversation, he or she performs an act of *offering*. A social partner taking for one's own and using the meaning produced by another social partner performs a discursive act of *appropriation*. A partner continuing to produce novel meanings as part of a connected stream of discourse produced by either oneself or one's partner performs an act of *elaboration*. Table 6.3 provides a list of (a) different types of discursive acts that we have found to recur in psychotherapeutic dialogue, (b) the syntax that we have adopted for coding and recording each type of act, and (c) examples of discursive acts in different psychotherapeutic contexts. The following provides examples of possible codes, their notation, and their meaning.

1. **O(1.0)**   OFFER THESIS 1.
2. **E(1.1)**   ELABORATE AN ANTITHESIS TO THESIS 1.
3. **APP(3.1)**   APPROPRIATE ANTITHESIS 1 TO THESIS IS 3.1.
4. **TRANS(4.0 → 5.0)**   TRANSFORM PRIOR MEANING (4.0) INTO THESIS 5.0.
5. **QUES(3.1)**   ASK A QUESTION ABOUT ANTITHESIS 3.1.
6. **RJ(4.1)**   REJECT ANTITHESIS 4.1.
7. **Q(3.1)**   QUALIFY THE FIRST ANTITHESIS TO THESIS 3.
8. **EXP(4.1 → 4.2)**   EXPAND ELEMENT 4.1 TO PRODUCE ELEMENT 4.2.

The tracking of *discursive acts* differs somewhat from the tracking of changes in the *operative content* of meaning elements. The analysis of operative content focuses on the status of particular *meaning elements* or groups of meaning elements as theses, antitheses, conflicts, or higher-order syntheses. The operative content of one meaning element is defined with reference to one or more other meaning elements. In this way, the operative content (i.e., the thesis, antithesis, etc.) of any given meaning element is defined with reference to its relations to previous *content*. For example, Antithesis 2.1 is defined in contradistinction to Thesis 2.0. In contrast, discursive acts are defined with reference to their *function within ongoing interaction*. A discursive act is defined with reference to its function within *discourse or coordinated activity* and thus in terms of its relation to prior or future acts. The act of offering invites a subsequent response, elaboration implies adding to a thread produced by prior discursive acts, appropriation implies the taking in and use of content produced by a prior act, a question calls forth a particular type of future act on the part of one's interlocutor, and so forth.

Tracking the Construction of Novelty Within Joint Action: The Relational Activity Analysis

If the patterns of acting, thinking, and feeling produced in face-to-face therapeutic interactions are co-regulated, it is not possible to understand the developmental course of therapeutic action by focusing only on individual actors. Instead, it becomes necessary to develop methods to analyze the ways in which meanings arise and are distributed *between* individuals within discursive exchanges. Such a goal requires a shift in the unit of psychological analysis from the individual to the *joint activity* (Rogoff, 1990) or *social ensemble* (Granott, 1998, 2005). Mascolo (Mascolo & Margolis, 2004) has developed a method for analyzing the *structure of joint action*, meaning, and feeling in development. One can analyze the structure of joint action using a procedure called the *relational activity analysis*. The basic principles for performing a relational activity analysis are as follows. For any given unit of social interaction, a researcher proceeds by (a) identifying the structure of acting, thinking, and feeling produced by each social partner; (b) identifying the form of co-regulated social interaction that occurs *between* the two individuals; and (c) tracking changes in the structure of action that arises as a product of co-regulated exchanges that occur over time. Using these procedures, for any given unit of social interaction, it is possible to identify and chart changes in the *structure of joint action* and how novel forms of thinking, feeling, and acting arise as a product of joint action as it unfolds over time.

The process of analyzing the structure of joint action proceeds by identifying *relational activity structures*. Relational activity structures can be represented visually in the form of a relational activity diagram. Figure 6.1 represents a relational activity diagram. A relational activity diagram is

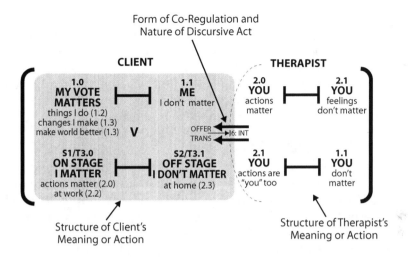

Figure 6.1 The relational activity diagram. Relational activity diagrams are composed of three basic elements. The left and right side of the diagram depict the structure of the client's and therapist's actions respectively. The symbol between the diagrams indicates the form of co-regulation that occurs between the client and therapist. The text within and outside of the symbol indicates the form of discursive acts produced by the client and therapist. The I—I symbol indicates that two meaning elements are in conflict. The V symbol indicates a shift-of-focus from one meaning element to another. The ↔ symbol indicates non-conflictual connections among two or more meaning elements. Many of these connections represent novel syntheses.

composed of three basic elements. First, as indicated in the top diagram of Figure 6.1, the left and right sides of the diagram depict the specific *structure of the meaning or action* produced by each social partner in a given episode of social interaction. Second, the *co-regulation symbol* located in between the partners' meaning structure identifies the form of co-regulation that occurs between the two social partners. Third, the terms identified within and around the co-regulation symbol identify the specific form of scaffolding and the form of discursive actions exhibited by social partners in the interactive episode. The relational activity diagram depicted in the top panel of Figure 6.1 provides a visual representation of the joint construction of meaning as it occurred at a single point during a psychotherapy session involving the Lady Cloaked in Fog (see Chapter 8). During this episode, the client and therapist discuss the client's sense of mattering and not mattering to other people. In an act of interpretation, the client begins the episode by drawing a contrast between her "vote" and her "self"—"My vote matters … but I don't matter." The diagram depicted represents the activity that occurred immediately *after* this statement was made by the client. Building upon the client's utterance, the therapist tries to put the conflict into her own words, drawing on her own meaning-making categories in offering this interpretation. She draws a contrast (conflict between thesis and antithesis) between acting and feeling: "Your actions matter ... but your feelings don't matter." The structure of this contrast is depicted in the *right*-hand side of the diagram. The client continues by elaborating on the therapist's interpretation, making a distinction between being "onstage" and "offstage": "I matter onstage, but offstage [I don't]." The structure of this contrast (conflict) is indicated on the *right*-hand side of the diagram. The symbol between these two structures indicates the form of coactive scaffolding (co-regulation) that occurs between the therapist and client in this context. Table 6.4 specifies a series of symbols corresponding to different patterns of coactive scaffolding. The co-regulation symbol is supplemented with a code indicating the level and form of coactive scaffolding provided by the therapist. This is indicated as **LEVEL: FORM OF SCAFFOLDING**. In Figure 6.1, the therapist's utterance provided a novel interpretation that extended the client's previously articulated utterance in a new way. Because interpretation functions at Scaffolding Level 5, the therapist's act is represented as **I6: INT**. (As forms of attentional support **(AS)**, Scaffolding Levels 1 through 5 are indicated by **AS*n*: FORM OF SCAFFOLDING** (e.g., **AS3: RS**); as higher-order forms of enactment **(E)**, Scaffolding Levels 7 through 9 are indicated as **E*n*: FORM OF SCAFFOLDING** (e.g., **E8: RP**)).

The relational activity analysis is based upon the coactive systems principle that *control over acting, thinking, and feeling is distributed throughout the therapeutic dyad*. From the coactive systems perspective, although individuals exert control over their actions, they do not do so autonomously. Action, thought, and feeling are co-regulated between social partners within any given face-to-face interaction. Further, in social interaction, social partners often perform at levels that are higher than they could otherwise sustain while acting alone. This is especially the case for guiding, teaching, or therapeutic interactions in which one person plays a guiding role. It follows that the production of novel meanings and experiences cannot be attributed to the activity of individual persons. In the production of many forms of novel behavior, *individual actors are often not capable of producing or sustaining emergent forms of action, thought, or feeling in the absence of their social partners*. The other person is a part of the process of producing the novel action, meaning, or experience. As a representation of joint activity, the relational activity diagram depicts the structure of action as it is distributed throughout the dyad. In many (but by no means all) social interactions involving the production of novelty, individual actors are able to produce the particular psychological structures that are observed within the interaction itself as it takes place within the history of a given set of dialogical interactions. To the extent that this is so, the relational activity analysis provides a means for identifying the emergent structure of acting, thinking, and feeling *as it is embedded within* ongoing social interaction. By representing the ways in which the client's and the therapist's actions are constituted in relation to each other, a relational activity diagram provides a visual snapshot of how novel structures have their origins in co-regulated social interaction.

By tracking changes in the relational activity structures over time, one can construct a visual model of the developmental changes that take place in the joint construction of meaning and action over the course of psychotherapy. Figure 8.2 describes the meaning system constructed by the client in Episode 9 of the same psychotherapy session. Chapter 8 is devoted to explaining the pathways and processes by which the dyad moved from the structure depicted in Figure 6.1 (Episode 1) to that indicated in Figure 8.2. For now, it suffices to say that the joint meaning structures created in Episode 9 are dramatically different from those created in Episode 1. In comparison to Episode 1, the client's meaning structure in Episode 9 not only is more differentiated and hierarchically integrated, but also resolves the conflict between mattering and not mattering that forms the core emotional focus of the client's attention. Further, in Episode 9, the client is able to construct her complex meaning structure with little if any support or scaffolding from the therapist. In Episode 1, the client's meaning structure arises as a product of a series of successive revisions that occur within the context of higher-level scaffolding provided by the therapist. The latter structure is dominated by the client; the former structure is co-regulated with high levels of support provided by the therapist. In this way, the use of relational activity diagrams can provide a holistic yet precise visual analysis of shifts in the organization of dyadic activity as they occur over time.

Illustrations of the Use of the DAPP Method

In this section, we illustrate the ways in which the foregoing tools can be used to track the processes of microdevelopment that occur in psychotherapy. As is the case with any empirical analysis, it is important to distinguish between the ways in which quantitative or qualitative data are *analyzed* and the ways in which the results of such analyses are *presented*. In the following section, we present a series of fully coded transcriptions of brief excerpts culled from the actual psychotherapy sessions that will be discussed later in the book. These analyses are intended to illustrate the ways in which one can use the foregoing tools to track element-by-element changes in the development of meaning and action in any given section of therapeutic discourse. It is upon such detailed element-by-element analyses of the course of psychotherapy sessions that our presentation of case material in Chapters 7 and 8 will be based. To promote clarity of understanding, we refrain from presenting the coding of every element of discourse. Instead, we focus our presentation on analyses of those elements that play central roles in the developmental changes that occur over the course of the therapeutic sessions, or from which we believe important lessons regarding therapeutic process can be derived.

In the present section, we present full illustrative analyses of brief excerpts from two psychotherapy sessions. The cases involve a 21-year-old student who struggled to express her feelings and desires in interpersonal relationships, and a 44-year-old depressed woman who struggled with issues of "mattering" and "not mattering." In addition to providing detailed coded analyses of sample transcripts, we will also illustrate different ways of representing the structures and processes of development in a visual format.

Eva Interprets Her Patterns of Communication

The first excerpt involves the case of Eva, a 21-year-old student at an Ivy League college. When Eva began therapy, she was feeling overwhelmed by choices she was facing at college, in realms ranging from value commitments, to career directions, to personal relationships, to daily issues of time management and "how much is the right amount of time to spend studying." She said she kept comparing herself to others and finding herself wanting. The initial segment of a session identified as a "critical incident" by her therapist (Basseches, 1993) follows:

C1: I know that I'm always apologizing and things too **O(1.0)**, because I'm afraid it's gonna hurt the other people **E(1.1)** {**S₁/T2[1.0↔1.1]**} like we said ... because maybe things would hurt me **E(1.11)**. Like I'm so concerned it might hurt other people, that I bring about this whole apologizing [T: Uh-huh, uh-huh **ACK**] atmosphere **RS(2.0)**. And what people interpret is more that I don't feel very comfortable in what I'm saying **E(2.1)** {**2.0 <C > 2.1**}. Whereas, I mean, I feel it is my right to be saying whatever I'm saying **E(2.11)** but I just don't want to hurt them **RS(1.1)** {**2.11<C>1.1**} so I try to make it ... and it really doesn't get.... It's a different [T: Mm-hm, mm-hm **ACK**] message that comes across **RS(2.1)**. And that also brings me to get into what I think is pretty related, which is, as I was telling you before, that when I have conversations with people about topics I'll say, "Well, I don't know very much about this, but I think that da da da"—instead of ... **E(T3)** And other people would just say, "Oh this is what happens." **E(3.1)**. Even if they know as much as I know **E(3.11)** {**3.0 <C> 3.1**}. So all those three things together, I've sort of been thinking about lately. And I think they're all a part of the same thing.... **E(S₂/T4[1.0←THROUGH→3.11]**)) I don't know [T: Uh-huh **ACK**] what you think [T: Uh-huh **ACK**] about that **REQ(4.0)**.

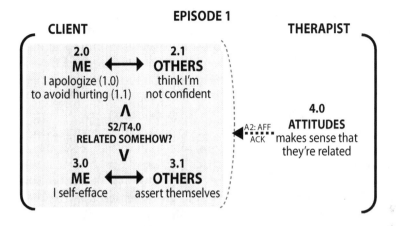

Figure 6.2 Relational activity diagram representing the initial state of Eva's conception of her communicative dynamics. The left hand portion of the Figure 6.2 depicts the structure of Eva's initial representation of her adaptive challenge, which was organized in terms of a series of conflicts between representations of her own actions and the ways in which she experience the responses of others to those behaviors. At this point on the session, the therapist offered attentional support at the relatively low level of Acknowledgement and Affirmation (Scaffolding Level 2).

T1: Makes sense that they're connected **A, AFF(4.0).**

A relational action diagram depicting the structure of this interaction is provided in Figure 6.2. The client begins by offering a thesis: "I am always apologizing" **(1.0)**. Her actions come from her fear of "hurting other people" **(1.1)**. The intercoordination of these two statements results in the first synthesis of this session **(S₁/T2[1.0↔1.1])**. The client's apologizing brings about undesirable consequences: "[W]hat people interpret is more that I don't feel very comfortable in what I'm saying" **(2.1)**. The first antithesis **(1.1)** differs from the thesis **(1.0)** only in that it marks a differentiation of the reasons why the client feels she "apologizes." In contrast, the antithesis **(2.1)** to her understanding of why she apologizes **(2.0)** recognizes a conflict between the client's apologizing and its unintended consequences **(2.0<C>2.1)**. The client later shifts to the articulation of a related but distinct thesis: "[W]hen I have conversations with people about topics I'll say, 'Well, I don't know very much about this, but …'" **(3.0)**. The client indicates that her self-effacing behavior also brings about conflict, namely, that "other people would just say, 'Oh this is what happens'" **(3.1)**. Thus, although the client engages in self-effacing behavior in order to avoid hurting others, she acknowledges a conflict with the recognition that others assert their positions without regard for whom they might hurt **(3.0<C>3.1)**. The client indicates that she sees a relationship between these two relational dynamics: "I think they're all a part of the same thing." Although the client is unable to articulate the particular ways in which the two dynamics are related, in indicating that they are "part of the same thing," the client has begun the task of synthesizing a higher-order representation of the presenting issue. We regard her statement that "they're all a part of the same thing" as a weak synthesis of the interactive dynamics that she has described (S_2/T4[1.0←THROUGH→3.11]). Throughout the client's elaboration, the therapist has remained silent, providing attentional support in the form of verbal and nonverbal acknowledgment (**ACK**) (Sc2). In response to the client's request for the therapist's interpretation of her remarks (**REQ(4.0)**), the therapist responds with attentional support in the form of an affirmation (**AFF(4.0)**) (Sc2) of the client's incipient synthesizing activity.

In the relational action diagram depicted in Figure 6.1, the left portion of the diagram represents the structure of the client's activity. As discussed above, the client constructs a weak synthesis (i.e., S_2/T4, "they're all a part of the same thing") of two pairs of conflicting representations (i.e., (**2.0<C>2.1**) and (**3.0<C>3.1**)). The right portion of Figure 6.1 displays the structure of the therapist's activity. The therapist response, "Makes sense that they're related," functions to *affirm* the construction produced by the client. Viewing this client–therapist exchange as a single unit, we are able to see that the client was able to construct her representation of the problem in the context of a relatively low level of scaffolded support from the therapist (Sc2). As we will see in the full analysis of Eva's case in Chapter 7, this demonstrated ability of the client is just one part of the reason why the therapist responds to the client's probable request at the end of C1 for interpretation (or possibly enactment) with more attentional support in T1. However, in this particular exchange, the novel meanings constructed are largely the product of the *client's* constructive activity. A full analysis of the development of Eva's representation of her communicative dynamics is provided in Chapter 7.

Mattering Versus Not Mattering

The second excerpt is culled from the pivotal session between a 44-year-old depressed woman, described by her therapist as "The Lady Cloaked in Fog," and her therapist (McCullough, 1999). The session from which this transcript is excerpted will be the primary focus of the analysis presented in Chapter 8.

C1: Essentially me, my vote matters **O(1.0)**, but *I don't matter....* **E(1.1)** the things I can do **E(1.2)**, and um, changes I can make **E(1.3)** and uh stuff I do to make the world a better place **E(1.4)** (**1.0<C>1.1**).

T1: Your actions matter. **O(S_1/T2.0[1.0↔1.2 ←THROUGH→1.4])**

C2: My actions matter and stuff but … **APP, Q(2.0)**

T2: I know, uh-huh **ACK**. But there is a part of you that doesn't [feel you matter] **E(2.1)**. It's important … because your actions are you too E(1.11) {2.1<C>1.11}. But something you were saying, the core of you, the feeling of like of you, your feelings don't matter TRANS(1.1→2.1) {2.0<C>2.1}. I'm just trying to narrow it down.

C3: Yeah. I guess that's it. AFF It's like I, it's like when I'm at work, I matter TRANS(2.0→2.2), and when I go home, am by myself, I don't matter TRANS(2.1→2.3). It sort of on or off. Um, onstage E(S$_2$/T3.0[1.0 ↔ 2.0 ↔ 2.2]) or offstage. E(S$_3$/T3.1[1.1 ↔ 2.1 ↔ 2.3]) {3.0<C>3.1}

This excerpt is coded with an analysis of the ways in which developmental changes in meaning structures are discursively produced in interactions between therapist and client over time. A relational action diagram of this therapeutic episode is provided in Figure 6.1. Even in these few conversational turns, one can track the role of client and therapist in the joint construction of meaning. The key meaning structure that is co-constructed in this dialogue is articulated in Conversational Turn C3. Here, the client elaborates a conflict between two representations: "Onstage, I matter, but offstage, I don't matter." The client sets the stage for the development of this key meaning in conversational turn C1, when she offers an initial representation of the problem. In so doing, she articulates an initial thesis (i.e., "My vote matters" (1.0)) and antithesis (i.e., "but I don't" (1.1)). She then proceeds to discriminate among several examples of how her vote matters (Antitheses 1.2, 1.3, and 1.4). As such, in her first conversational turn, the client *offers* and *elaborates* a conflict between "My vote matters" and "I don't [matter]" (1.0<C>1.1). In T1, the therapist performs an act of generalization, resulting in a new synthesis. In so doing, she generalizes across the three examples of "mattering" provided by the client. In so doing, she *transforms* the client's initial meaning into the interpretation "Your actions matter." This novel synthesis (S$_1$) is thus created through the intercoordination (↔) of Thesis 1.0 and Antitheses 1.2, 1.3, and 1.4. This new synthesis produces a new thesis, namely, Thesis 2.0, and is indicated as (S$_1$/T2.0[1.0 ↔ 1.2 ←THROUGH→1.4]). During this conversational turn, the therapist supports the client mainly by the provision of *interpretative* resources (i.e., the interpretation "Your actions matter"). In turn C2, the client *appropriates* (i.e., "My actions matter and stuff") but *qualifies* (i.e., "but") the interpretation provided by the therapist in T2. The therapist then continues to elaborate the interpretation that she provided in T2 and that the client appropriated in C3 (i.e., 2.0). In so doing, she states that "the core of you, the feeling of like of you, [you feel that] your feelings don't matter" (2.1). In articulating the distinction between "you feel that your actions matter, but your feelings don't," the therapist continues to *elaborate* an interpretation of the client's stated problem. In so doing, the therapist articulates a second version of the conflict reported by the client (2.0<C>2.1).

The key change in this episode occurs in conversational turn C3, where the client synthesizes a new way of representing the conflict between "mattering" and "not mattering." She begins by appearing to *appropriate* the therapist's interpretive distinction (i.e., "Yeah. I guess that's it"). However, the client immediately *transforms* (appropriates and changes) the interpretive distinction offered by the therapist from "My actions matter, but my feelings don't matter" to "I matter onstage, but I don't matter offstage." This transformation occurs as the client constructs two novel syntheses—namely, "onstage," which arises from the coordination of previous elements 1.0, 2.0, and 2.2 ($S_2/T3[1.0 \leftrightarrow 2.0 \leftrightarrow 2.2]$), and its antithesis "offstage," which is the emergent synthesis of elements 1.1, 2.1, and 2.3 ($S_3/T3.1[1.1 \leftrightarrow 2.1 \leftrightarrow 2.13]$). These two novel syntheses thus redefine the nature of the conflict at a higher, more integrated level, namely, "I matter onstage, but I don't matter offstage" (3.0 <C> 3.1). Again, in this exchange, the therapist primarily provides the resources of *interpretation* (Sc6: INT) and, to a lesser extent, the provision of attentional support through the acts of affirmation and acknowledgment (Sc2: AFF, ACK). The remainder of the psychotherapy session builds upon the fundamental distinction between *mattering onstage* versus *not mattering offstage*. The full course of the changes that occur in this therapy session are discussed in Chapter 8.

Quantitative Representations of Developmental Change

The analytic methods described above provide tools for analyzing developmental changes in the organization of meanings and action as they occur in psychotherapy. The diagrams displayed in Figures 6.1 and 6.2 provide qualitative representations of the structures and processes of developmental change that contain a high degree of precision. The tools described above also lend themselves quite easily to quantitative analysis. They do so in a variety of different ways. The first involves tracking micro- and macrodevelopmental changes in the complexity of action and meaning structures over time. Although there are a variety of ways to identify the developmental level of hierarchical complexity of any given action within particular contexts (see Case, 1992a; Commons et al., 1995; Fischer, 1980), a simple yet powerful way to quantify developmental changes over time is to tabulate the number of outcome-related meaning elements or actions produced by any given actor on any given conversational turn and to track changes in the number of intercoordinated elements produced over time. Such a method can be used only *after* a specific developmental outcome has occurred. In psychotherapy as in development, it is often not possible to predict developmental outcomes before they occur. Novel forms of psychological activity emerge in development. It is only after a novel developmental outcome has emerged that it is possible to identify the steps leading that outcome. Once the steps leading to the outcome are identified the next step is to perform a *task analysis* of the outcome in question (Berger & Wilde, 1987; Zhang & Norman, 1994). A task analysis consists of identifying the particular pattern of actions, thoughts, and feelings that compose the outcome in question (Gagne, 1974). One asks, "What are the various things a person has to do, know, or feel in order to exhibit the particular outcome in question?" Following the task analysis, one can track quantitatively the number of coordinated elements, and qualitatively, the particular subset of target actions, thoughts, and feelings exhibited by each actor. Using this method, it is possible to view the ways in which component parts "come together" in the construction of any given skill or developmental outcome. In Chapter 7 and 8, we use this basic method to track micro- and macdevelopmental changes in patterns of acting, thinking, and feeling over the course of psychotherapy.

It is common to think of developmental changes in terms of increases in level of skill or capacity over time. To be sure, to the extent that any given psychological process can be said to undergo growth or *development*, measures of development should exhibit some form of increase over time. However, as illustrated in Chapters 7 and 8, curves that track developmental changes in real time (moment by moment) rarely show a simple increase in developmental complexity over time. As will be discussed further in Chapters 7 and 8, although the developmental complexity level of the meaning structures produced by each actor increases over time, growth curves are rarely linear (Van Geert, 1991). Instead, in the development of any given skill or system of meanings, moment-to-moment changes are profoundly nonlinear. Development generally occurs in fits and starts, showing patterns of increasing and decreasing complexity in the form of any given psychological structure at any given time. In such cases, movements involving a decrease in complexity can be as illuminating as those that show developmental progress. Granott, Fischer, and Parziale (2002) have noted the importance of what they call *backward transitions* in the process of developmental change. Backward transitions occur when actors return to lower levels of functioning after having attained progress in the development of any given psychological structure. Granott et al. (2002) demonstrated the ways in which a transition to lower levels of functioning often plays a functional role in the developmental process. Backward transitions are often necessary in order to begin to consolidate gains, to refine unstable elements of a development skill, or to build novel subskills that will eventually be coordinated with previously constructed higher-order skills. Thus, shifts in the trajectory of any developing skill often signal important periods in which developmental processes are especially operative. Quantitative measures of development are necessary to identify upward or downward shifts in growth and development. However, to fully understand the nature of the developmental processes operative during such fluctuations, one must also examine the specific and often unique actions and change processes that occur during those shifts. Such goals are often facilitated through the use of qualitative methodology. In this way, qualitative and quantitative methods should not be understood as incompatible with each other. Qualitative and quantitative methods are needed to supplement each other in any full assessment of the structures and processes of developmental change (Dawson, Fischer, & Stein, 2006).

In addition to changes in the client's (or therapist's) level of developmental complexity over time, it is also possible to provide quantitative analysis of the form and level of social support provided by the therapist. Table 6.4 quantifies the nine different levels and forms of scaffolded support that a therapist can provide to a client on any given conversational turn. The quantification of levels of scaffolding allows an investigator to track (a) the ways in which the level of therapeutic scaffolding varies over the course of a session or sessions, (b) how therapists adjust their level of scaffolding to the needs of particular clients over time, and (c) individual differences in the level of support provided by therapists in the context of different presenting issues, clients, or contexts, or therapeutic approaches.

Applications of the DAPP Methodology

The DAPP approach provides a suite of qualitative and quantitative methods for analyzing the structures and processes of developmental change as they occur over the course of psychotherapeutic discourse and action. Using these various analytic tools, a practitioner or investigator can (a) identify and chart changes in the structure of particular skills and experiences as they occur over time, (b) identify the particular dialectical movements through which development occurs as well as the modes of scaffolding that therapists use in order to foster developmental changes, (c) identify the particular contributions of both client and therapist to the particular skills and experiences that develop, and (d) provide qualitative and quantitative representations of the structures and processes of developmental changes observed. Depending upon one's purposes, the methods described above can be used either in isolation or in conjunction with each other. These tools can be used by psychotherapy researchers to make precise analyses of the types of developmental changes that occur as a result of particular interventions as well as of courses of therapy as a whole. These methods can be used by practitioners and students as tools for reflecting upon the nature and course of their therapeutic practices with particular clients.

The methods described above lend themselves to developmental analyses at different levels of bandwidth or generality. For some purposes, analyzing therapeutic interaction in terms of the primary dialectics of attentional support, interpretation, and enactment can aid reflection upon one's therapeutic practice; for others, a full analysis of the particular types of developmental movements over the course of one or more psychotherapy transcripts may be useful. In using these tools, practitioners and students engaged in clinical training can identify and reflect upon the types of therapeutic processes that promote or do not promote development in particular clients. Further, researchers interested in analyzing psychotherapeutic processes and outcomes can use these tools to analyze the course of psychological development within and between particular types of psychotherapeutic work. Such analyses can function as a primary form of inquiry, or can complement and supplement more traditional outcome analyses of psychotherapeutic effectiveness. In either case, the use of these methodological tools carries two central advantages. First, they allow identification of *what develops* as a result of psychotherapy, rather than simply measure the extent to which unwanted psychological activity (symptoms) is eliminated. Second, they recognize that precisely what develops in any particular psychotherapeutic inquiry (or "treatment," for those who prefer a more traditional term) may be *unique*, and may depend on the client's (and therapist's) particular circumstances, challenges, and contexts.

PART IV

Case Analyses

CHAPTER 7

From Isolation to Intimacy

The Transformation of Eva's Communicative Repertoire

The first case that we will consider is that of "Eva," a 21-year-old college senior from a Latin American country, studying in the United States. The case of Eva is similar to the case of the "Lady Cloaked in Fog," to be discussed in Chapter 8, in that both contain a "critical incident" identified by the therapist. Using the DAPP framework and methods to track in detail the developmental processes that occurred over the course of the critical incident, as it is reflected in verbatim transcripts, is the central focus of each chapter. However, in each case we also will examine how the sessions earlier in the course of therapy set the stage for the events that occur in the critical incident.[1]

In this chapter, we first provide a DAPP analysis of the therapist's narrative accounting of the full course of Eva's psychotherapy. In most cases, narrative accounts of therapy sessions, whether they are reconstructed from notes taken during a session or from a therapist's recollections, are all that a therapist and colleagues have available when reflecting upon and evaluating the course of any given session or course of therapy. In the first section of this chapter, we treat the therapist's narrative as a form of descriptive data that lends itself to reflection and interpretive analysis

---

[1] This case was initially written up by the first author for a project looking at "critical incidents in psychotherapy" (Lipson, 1993). The project entailed therapists identifying critical incidents that seemed to significantly affect the course of therapy. Then, along with their colleagues who played the role of commentators, the contributors attempted to conceptualize why these incidents were important, what choices the therapists had to make and how they made them, and finally how the choices influenced the therapeutic process and outcome.

using the dialectical categories proposed in the DAPP model (i.e., attentional support, interpretation, and enactment). Our basic strategy will be to read the therapist's narrative with several questions in mind: What resources does the therapist offer? Does the client use these resources? If so, how? If not, why not? How does the therapist adjust the provision of therapeutic resources to the client's needs? In interpreting the therapist's narrative accounting of the course of psychotherapy, we illustrate the ways in which the concepts of the dialectics of attentional support, interpretation, and enactment can serve as tools for reflecting upon the effectiveness or ineffectiveness of psychotherapy processes.

After this initial interpretive analysis of the overall course of Eva's psychotherapy, we use DAPP methods described in Chapter 6 to provide a detailed episode-by-episode analysis of the developmental transformations and therapeutic change processes that occur within a single session in Eva's therapy. We analyze in detail a transcribed segment of Eva's 15th psychotherapy session—a segment offered by the therapist as a "critical incident" in psychotherapy. In analyzing this segment, we use qualitative and quantitative analytic tools to (a) track microdevelopmental changes in the structure of the client's thinking, feeling, and action; (b) trace the ways such changes arise through the process of resolving intra- and interpersonal conflicts that become articulated over the course of the session; (c) examine how the therapist scaffolds the client's development through the responsive provision of therapeutic resources; and (d) track the specific contributions of the client and therapist to the production of novel forms of meaning and experience at important "developmental moments." Such analyses demonstrate how researchers can use the DAPP framework to make precise assessments of the ways in which psychotherapy fosters developmental change.

One goal of the DAPP approach is to provide a common framework for understanding the processes by which psychotherapy promotes development regardless of the theoretical perspective of the practitioner. In the last section of the chapter, we describe some of the conclusions that can be drawn from the application of the DAPP analysis to the case of Eva. In particular, we focus on how the DAPP analysis provides a way of describing how the therapist's theoretical framework functions as a strand in the therapeutic-developmental process.

Analyzing the Therapist's Account of Eva's Therapy

The therapist's narrative regarding his work with Eva begins with their initial meeting. (All case material quoted below is culled from Basseches, 1993.) To expand our shared understanding of the context of the critical incident that we will go on to interpret using the DAPP method, we will intersperse excerpts from the 1993 narrative with our current understanding of the therapist's choices and struggles regarding what therapeutic resources to offer to the client.

In our first session [Eva] told me that she was an only child whose parents had divorced when she was 2 or 3. She and her mother had moved many times, living in many countries around the world. Through the process of having to adapt together to new surroundings many times, they had become very close. Eva relied on her mother for advice, and for positive feedback about how Eva was handling the various challenging situations which she had faced, and in the face of which she had often felt inadequate. She was feeling overwhelmed by choices she was facing at college, in realms ranging from value commitments, to career directions, to personal relationships, to daily issues of time management and "how much is the right amount of time to spend studying". She said she kept comparing herself to others and finding herself wanting. I acknowledged the loneliness in being so far from her mother that I thought I heard in her story, and the heaviness of the burden of having to make so many choices on her own.

The therapist understood his primary offering in the first session as one of attentional support, which apparently helped foster a therapeutic alliance based on the shared understanding of the burden of choices and the loneliness that the client is experiencing.

We agreed to meet weekly, and in our second session, the topic of what our relationship would be like came up a couple of times. She expressed hopefulness about our work. She said at one point, "I hope you'll tell me what I'm doing wrong but you probably have a policy of making people guess for themselves". Near the end, she asked what I thought of her, and we agreed to explore her question and what was behind it in the next session.

The therapist understood the client's comments in Session 2 in two ways. First, he saw them as constituting a somewhat ambivalent and self-deprecatory request regarding the role that interpretations by the therapist would play in the therapeutic process. Second, he saw them as an expression of both hope and anxiety regarding her relationship with the therapist—about how the therapist experienced her, and about what kind of personal feedback she could expect from the relationship.

In our third session, she was framing her concern in terms of whether I would "give her insight," or if she would be required to figure things out for herself. I said that I would try to share what I saw, but I also wondered out loud if she was wanting something from me in the way of reassurance or a pat on the back. When she confirmed that she had felt that way, I suggested that we might treat the moments when that feeling comes up as opportunities to work on ways of giving that reassurance to herself. Her association was that she had written in notes after our previous session that "I want you to play the role of my mother, to evaluate me and to praise me". I affirmed her longing for that, and invited her to continue to recognize it when it comes up, but I also said that if I played her mother's role, we would be doing a dance that was familiar to her, instead of helping her to expand her repertoire. I felt we ended the session with a shared understanding that there was something to be gained by my not playing her mother's role, and she acknowledged that she had felt a kind of support that allowed her to feel more independent in our sessions thus far.

The therapist conceptualized what occurred in Session 3 not only as a continued negotiation of shared understanding regarding the role that interpretation would play in the therapeutic relationship, but also as an opportunity to offer the possibility of learning from the enactment of novel interaction patterns within their relationship. The therapist experienced and the client acknowledged her relational longings for reassurance and praise, as tied in with her wish for interpretations. Although the therapist agreed to "share what he saw," he somewhat downplayed the role of "insight" he could "give," in comparison to the opportunity to support the client in her own decision-making and self-reassuring processes. This response seemed to foster the client's differentiating the sort of support she experienced from her mother from the sort of support she experienced in therapy, and recognizing the feelings of independence associated with the latter.

Over the course of our work, at moments when Eva felt this sense of support especially keenly, she would begin to speak of her relationship with her father. She felt tremendous guilt at not having had as close a relationship with him as she had with her mother. Her father had on occasion spoken to her of his great and enduring sadness at not having been as big a part of her childhood as he would have liked. However, he also made clear that he (a) understood how it had happened, (b) in no way saw it as Eva's fault, and (c) saw it not as a problem to be solved, but rather a sadness to be endured. Eva acknowledged to me that she felt unable to really assimilate this communication from him.

The therapist has learned that unlike Eva's mother, her father evidently expresses negative feelings more directly and that Eva finds this communication difficult. The therapist also associates Eva's readiness to discuss her father with her previous experiences of support of her independent capacities within the therapeutic relationship. However, during this period of the therapy, he chose to offer Eva attentional support for attending to her feelings about her father, rather than an interpretation of the connection he saw between her talking about her father and what was occurring in the therapeutic relationship. Although he saw that Eva was using the attentional support to articulate the conflicts she felt in her relationship with her father (he felt sadness, whereas she felt guilt; she could repeat his words but could not assimilate his meaning), the therapist did not see sufficient developmental value to offering his interpretation at this time.

The therapist described Sessions 4 through 13 as follows:

Eva used our time very productively to explore for herself and to share with me 1) her feelings, 2) her constructions of the world and herself, 3) her history, with emphasis on her relationships with parents, boyfriends, and cultures, and 4) the sorts of emotional and relational difficulties which she felt she had repeatedly encountered. (Eva's relational difficulties seemed to involve managing the expectations of others. In the course of her travels, she had lived in many places. As a result, at the time of this therapy she had boyfriends on three different continents. Each of these three boyfriends expected that Eva would marry him after she graduated. She attributed the development of these expectations to the care she had taken not to say anything hurtful to any of them, but a consequence was that she dreaded the life decisions she would need to make after graduating. Aside from the issue of her boyfriends, Eva faced difficulty with decision-making within many domains and time frames. She was able to connect these difficulties to the sense that within her various personal relationships and cultural environments, she had co-constructed with others images of herself, and that not living up to any of these images felt like a kind of betrayal of those relationships. At the same time that she felt constrained by all her relationships, she also felt dissatisfied. She was lonely, and longed for a kind of intimacy that she was not experiencing.)

Eva went on to make connections across her discoveries in all four of these categories, and out of these connections she began to build a theory of herself. With her theory-building she also seemed to develop more courage in facing life. I felt I had for the most part remained in the stance I had established in the first three sessions: Interest in her, the bulk of my attention going to acknowledging what she seemed to be feeling, appreciation of her courage in doing this work, and occasionally contributing an elaborating thought to a connection that she had made. We seemed to have a very good rapport. Eva seemed to find in my stance safety and support that helped her to work productively. She made frequent allusions to how much she valued our sessions and that she looked forward to coming. She continued to bring a notebook full of between session thoughts to sessions, and she often used her notes as a starting point for sessions. However, she occasionally expressed some frustration and questions regarding where this process was going.

In a number of these sessions, Eva made comments on the theme of needing hugs. The associated feelings were usually ones of loneliness and the intellectual context was usually the difference between Latin American and New England culture, and how much more common physical contact is in the former culture. The first time this theme came up was in session five, when Eva said, in regard to visiting her Latin American cousin nearby, "I know intellectually that I'm OK, but I need a hug. I need filling up, just a bit". On this occasion, as subsequent ones when she brought up this theme, I tried my best to acknowledge what she was feeling. I also noticed that I began offering her a handshake each time she left the office.

The narrative of Sessions 4–13 recognizes the client's use of the attentional support that the therapist offered and describes it as effective theory building, accompanied by an affective shift in attitude described as developing "more courage in facing life." At the same time, the therapist acknowledges a process of emergence of some conflictual feelings within what appears to be an otherwise developmentally supportive therapy relationship. He juxtaposes Eva's allusions to how much she values the sessions with her occasional frustration with the ambiguity regarding the direction in which the therapy was headed. He goes on to note Eva's expressions of loneliness and longing for physical contact, and suggests that along with responding to these expressions with attentional support, his beginning to offer handshakes at the end of sessions represented a response to her expressions of frustration and longing.

In his 1993 introduction to his theoretical perspective and this case, the therapist stated,

> I see critical incidents in psychotherapy as involving transformations. The most powerful ones in my experience involve a transformation of the relationship (between client and therapist in individual therapy), and a concomitant transformation in the client's understanding of what is possible.

The therapist's attention to conflictual feelings within the therapy relationship is consistent with this theoretical perspective. At the same time, this recognition becomes a more explicit source of concern for the therapist after the 14th session, which he describes in his write-up of the case as follows.

> I believe that our 14th session set the stage for the critical incident of the 15th. I wrote in my notes after the session "I surprise myself in being very advising—interpretive. It seemed to work. It felt good. I was doing more of what Eva had wanted at the outset. Perhaps I had resisted more when her wanting that went with presenting herself as inadequate and now that has changed. Perhaps I am compensating for the feeling I'm being depriving regarding the 'wanting hugs' which she has expressed".... Eva had told me about Steve, who had invited her to a dance, but she was very troubled about whether to expect it to be "romantic"—a decision she seemed to feel she had to make in advance. She seemed to see the only two options as either counting on it being romantic and thereby risking great disappointment and hurt, or else maintaining a solely platonic perspective on the evening.

This time, when Eva presented a decision-making difficulty, in which her main concern seemed to be managing feelings in such a way as to avoid disappointment, the therapist chose to respond by offering an interpretation from his frame of reference, described below. His account above speculates on the reasons for his shift, but his allusion to "surprise" indicates that it was not entirely a conscious choice.

> The main interpretation which I had offered (rather enthusiastically) was to make an analogy between her feelings, as she saw them, and a spring-loaded knob which she either had to wind up fully in advance or on which she had to place a lock so that it wouldn't operate. My advice, however implicit or explicit, was to consider the possibility of keeping the lock off the knob but not winding it up, and allowing it to be turned or not turned (her role and Steve's in turning it was left unclear) as the evening progressed. Eva seemed very grateful for my interpretation, but I was concerned enough about the meaning of my shift in stance to discuss it in peer supervision. I entered the next session with some concern that I not get carried away by forces that I didn't fully understand, just because it felt good. I also recognized that as sound as my advice may have been vis-a-vis Steve, I might have given an inadequate message if in some way, however unconsciously, Eva was trying to address questions regarding our relationship.

Here, the therapist makes an association in his mind between Eva's occasionally expressed discomfort with ambiguity regarding where the therapy was going, and the parallel content in Session 14—a discomfort with the ambiguity regarding where Steve's inviting her to a dance might lead. Whereas Eva feels responsible for the outcome of the date, and sees herself as facing a choice between only two possibilities, the interpretation the therapist offers suggests a greater range of possibilities, and challenges Eva's assumptions regarding both the need to decide in advance, and her sole responsibility for what happens. Not only does Eva seem to find the interpretation useful for approaching her date with Steve (we can speculate that the metaphor of her feelings being a spring-loaded knob that she could allow to turn during the date represented a novel synthesis for her, integrating the possibilities of the relationship being romantic or platonic), but also the therapist further notes that she seemed to find his shift in stance to be a satisfying shift (as did he).

Thus, on the one hand, offering the resource of interpretation appears to be a developmentally effective approach, because the client uses it to create a more adaptive, differentiated understanding of her options for approaching the "date." On the other hand, in recognizing that his offering this interpretation seems to have resulted in the therapy relationship feeling gratifying in a new way, the therapist is recognizing that simultaneously with the movement through the dialectic of interpretation, movement may also be occurring in the enactment dialectic through an experienced difference in the therapist–client relationship. He leaves the session feeling concerned that inherent in Eva's discomfort with where the therapy relationship is going were wishes that may now be gratified or encouraged, at the expense of being understood. Mindful of the possibility that material discussed in therapy is often reflective of the client's feelings about the therapeutic relationship itself, the therapist wondered about the extent to which the drama between the client and Steve was also being played out in the client's mind with reference to the therapeutic relationship itself. If this were the case, the therapist's advice about the relationship between the client and Steve (to allow the question of a platonic versus romantic relationship to be settled over time) would not be appropriate when applied to the therapeutic relationship. The therapist felt the need to communicate, however indirectly, the bounded nature of the therapeutic relationship.

As we will see in the discussion of the "critical incident" in the 15th session, this shift in emphasis to offering the therapeutic resource of interpretation in the 14th session (which can be understood as an "antithesis" within the enactment process to his primarily offering attentional support in prior sessions) does appear to have been experienced by the client as a gratifying form of mutual engagement. Thus, when the therapist returns in the 15th session to something closer to the previous stance, the relationship of contrast between the two antithetical stances appears to have been experienced by the client as "boredom" on the part of the therapist. It was this dynamic between the client and therapist that we view as the relational context for the critical incident that the therapist identified in the 15th session, which he introduces as follows:

> Eva came into the 15th session with a set of notes on topics she wanted to discuss this session. This was not unprecedented. In her notes she had observed some patterns in the behaviors and feelings she experienced interacting with others in social and academic contexts.

A DAPP Analysis of the Critical Incident in Eva's Therapy

In what follows, we first provide an overview of the developmental changes that occurred in what the therapist (Basseches, 1993) identified as a "critical incident in psychotherapy." We identify the major theses, antitheses, conflicts, and syntheses that Eva and the therapist co-constructed over the course of the critical incident. Thereafter, we present a more detailed episode-by-episode analysis of how these changes occurred over time. In this more detailed analysis, we track changes in the structure of the discursive activity that occurs between the client and therapist over time. In so doing, we demonstrate the ways in which the precise changes in the structure of the client's thinking, feeling, and action develop over time through the dialectics of attention, interpretation, and enactment. Following this qualitative analysis, we provide a quantitative analysis of the shapes that that development took over the course of the critical incident.

Overview of Major Developmental Changes in the Critical Session

Figure 7.1 provides an overview of the major developmental changes that occurred during the critical incident. The incident is divided into 10 episodes. In Episode 1 (C1–T1),[2] the client offers a series of reflections upon her own behaviors and others' reactions to them. In so doing, she offers a series of thesis–antithesis conflicts describing difficulties in communication with others. Specifically, she indicates that in an attempt to avoid hurting others, she is always "apologizing," which makes others feel that she is "not confident." Similarly, to facilitate smooth interactions, she engages in deferential and self-effacing speech, whereas others simply "say what they think." Eva indicates that these dynamics are "related somehow."

In Episode 2 (C2–C5), after the therapist acknowledges and affirms the client's initial descriptions, the client asks the therapist whether or not she should "think about why I could have these attitudes … or just, like, practice not having these attitudes?" The therapist responds by saying that his

---

[2] Numbers in parentheses refer to those conversational turns taken by the Client (Cn) and Therapist (Tn) in the transcript that is presented and analyzed below, which are comprised by the episode being discussed.

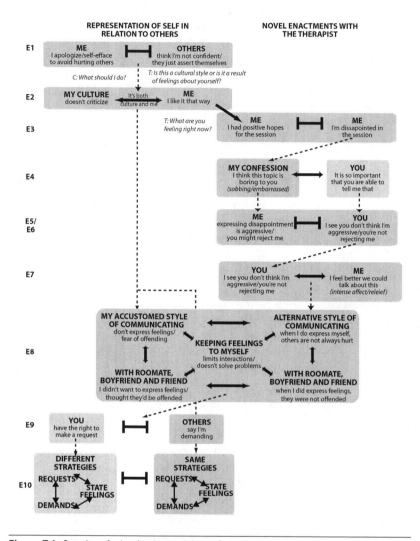

Figure 7.1 Overview of microdevelopmental transformations en route to the construction of Eva's representation of her conflicting communicative styles. Figure tracks patterns of differentiation and integration within and among three lines of development -- representations of self, others and novel interactions with therapist. Dark boxes indicate meaning structures coordinated by the client; light boxes indicate structures produced by the therapist. The I—I symbol indiciates conflicts among meaning elements; the ↔ symbol indicates non-conflictual connections among meaning elements, many of which represent novel syntheses.

advice would depend upon whether or not the client's attitudes reflect, on the one hand, a style of speaking that has its origins in her unique cultural experiences, or, on the other hand, more deeply held beliefs that the client holds about herself. In response, the client develops a complex synthesis that incorporates but extends beyond the therapist's dichotomy. She describes the origins of her communicative difficulties in what may be called a "culture–self cycle," a process whereby cultural practices become internalized to form beliefs about the self and styles of communication.

In Episode 3 (C5–T12), the client interrupts the flow of the discussion, criticizes her own verbal presentation during the session, and wonders about how the therapist has been hearing her. Because the client's self-criticism seemed incongruent with what the therapist had experienced thus far, he asks, "What are you feeling right now?" In response, the client begins to talk about the conflict between her hopes for the session (i.e., that she would present a list of her problems and discuss them with the therapist) and her disappointment that the discussion had not yet focused upon any single issue. Episode 3 continues as the therapist invites the client to explore the nature of her disappointment within this conflict.

The client's continued participation in this exploration proved to be extremely painful. In the therapist's narrative, he recounted the entire process that we trace over Episodes 3–7 as follows:

This led sequentially to her expression of a) some disappointment in how the session felt to her thus far, b) disappointment in my response to her, c) a concern that I was bored, d) being overwhelmed by embarrassment and pain at acknowledging this feeling to me, e) the sense that she was being demanding, and in fact aggressive toward me, and f) the fear that she was hurting me and that I would shut off to her and not want to deal with her if she treated me thus. She seemed to be dissolving deeper into tears as she went through this sequence. During this time, I think I was communicating with my face and non-verbal sounds an appreciation of the pain she was in, while with my words I was somewhat relentlessly asking her to help me understand the nature of her disappointment, as well as her embarrassment and fear. Somehow, this combination seemed to counteract what I felt was her desire to extricate herself from the situation, and as we stayed in the situation longer, a sense of relief seemed to grow on her part.

In Episode 4 (C13–C17), the client's acknowledgment of her impression that the therapist was "bored" by the conversation thus far takes the form of a "confession." In an attempt to provide a safe environment for the client to disclose her feelings, with deep empathy, the therapist says, "I think it is so important that you are able to tell me that." The client continues by expressing feelings antithetical to the content of the confession: "[T]his is the kind of thing which is very hard for me to tell you because I sort of feel like I'm insulting you." After the therapist explicitly affirms the value of working with the enactment opportunity presented by the client's in-session experience, the client begins to sob. Then, as the crying becomes more intense, the client expresses confusion and embarrassment. The therapist combines various forms of attentional support including acknowledgment and emotional modulation, as well as distancing when he asks the client to articulate what feels embarrassing. This episode ends with the client's articulation that, for her, it is inappropriate for her to expect or demand the therapist's (or anyone's) attention, and that in any conversation, it is her responsibility to accommodate what the other person finds interesting.

In Episodes 5 through 7, the therapist offers a combination of interpretation and attentional support, as therapist and client explore their experience as well as the interpersonal and affective implications of what is occurring within the enactment between them. In these episodes, the client comes to be able to express her fear that if she were to express her disappointment in the session or place any demands on the therapist's attention, the therapist might experience her as aggressive and reject her. In contrast to the client's fears, the therapist responds with empathic acknowledgment of the client's statements. Episode 5 (T17–C24) begins with the therapist offering the interpretation that an alternative to either demanding attention or accommodating another person's interest is to simply "talk about what you're feeling ... in the moment." It ends with the client's articulation of how a novel experience has been enacted in the session with the therapist, in which expressing her feelings was not experienced in the way in which she feared. Despite this conceptual acknowledgment on the part of the client, the therapist senses that Eva's fears are so intense and deeply rooted that they are likely to overpower her single articulated novel experience. Therefore, he begins Episode 6 (T24–C27) by empathizing with those fears, thus inviting further exploration of the depth of the fears and their underlying assumptions.

Throughout Episodes 5 through 7, in the context of continuous acknowledgment, acceptance, and emotional support, the therapist communicates his appreciation of the intensity of the client's *fear* of being perceived as aggressive. Episode 7 (T27–C28) begins with the therapist stating explicitly that he does not feel offended by the client's remarks, and sharing his own emotional response of *curiosity* to learn more from the client's disclosure. He further locates this learning process within a more general articulation of the nature of the therapeutic work. Building upon what she has heard from the therapist and experienced with him, the client goes on to articulate a novel synthesis that stands in contrast to her characteristic way of communicating with others (including the therapist). Seeing that she was able to express her feelings to the therapist without being seen as aggressive, she begins to appreciate the value of being able to talk about the feelings that she disclosed. This realization (synthesis) resolves the conflict that the client expressed in Episode 4 between wanting to disclose feelings yet fearing being seen as aggressive. The resolution marks a profound shift in affect as the client experiences deep relief from intense pain and embarrassment experienced prior in the session. It also provides the experiential basis for the articulation of an alternative to the client's customary style of communication, and for the client's application of this insight to the task of understanding her relationships and interactions with others. This articulation occurs in Episode 8.

In Episode 8 (C28–T30), with minimal support from the therapist, the client is able to construct a powerful synthesis that marks the main developmental achievement of the session. As indicated in Figure 7.1, in Episode 8, the client is able to represent her customary style of communication (i.e., "I don't express my feelings out of fear of offending others") and to identify this as a problem that limits her interactions in relationships. In contradistinction to her customary style, the client is able to form a generalized representation of the alternative style of communication that she had enacted with the therapist (e.g., "When I do express my feelings, others are not necessarily hurt"). She is also able to apply this generalization and identify specific interactions in the past (with her ex-boyfriend and roommate) in which her spontaneous use of the alternative communication style had indeed produced positive results. In Episode 8, the client once again turns back to the details of what was occurring in the novel enactment that took place in immediately preceding episodes. However, this time she is no longer in the grip of her fears of a rupture in her relationship with the therapist. Rather, she is happy and laughing with the therapist as they engage together in an analytic reconstruction of the events of the sessions and the lessons learned. Each, at times, finishes the other's sentences as they co-construct a fuller shared understanding of both the enactment and the novel synthesis, and how this novel synthesis transcends the "limitation" that the client has previously identified.

In Episode 9 (C31–C35), in commenting upon the novel insight that the client constructed in Episode 8, the therapist provides more of the resource of interpretation. He begins with the assertion that the client has a right to make requests of others (e.g., that her roommate make less noise). The client counters the interpretation, indicating that others have experienced her as "very demanding," which leads her to question if she indeed has that right. But the client immediately generates the new differentiation and antithetical question: "Am I very demanding, or is it just that I've been told I'm very demanding?" This, in turn, leads the therapist to inquire into the formative experiences that constituted her self-image as "very demanding." Multiple sources of the client's self-image, but most saliently the client's relationship with her father, are revealed by the client in the course of this exploration. The exploration results in a shared appreciation of the toll that these formative experiences have taken, but leaves quite open Eva's question about what meaning she should make of these experiences, especially regarding the acceptability of her feelings and wishes.

In the final episode, Episode 10 (T35–C50), the dialogue in the session comes full circle. In this attempt to assist Eva in constructing novel ways to articulate her needs and desires to others without appearing demanding, the therapist distinguishes among three possible communicative strategies: "expressing feeling," "requesting," and "demanding." However, Eva articulates two reasons why she experiences these three communication strategies as "all the same." One relates to cultural norms—if it is rude to say "no" to a request, then requests become demands. The other relates to her fear that expressing her feelings might be experienced as aggressive. The therapist then identifies Eva's reasons as reflecting the same communicative distinctions that she had articulated in Episodes 1 and 2, namely, the hazards of cross-cultural miscommunication and the feeling she does not have a right to express what she feels. The therapist brings these earlier issues into juxtaposition with the current issue of "being demanding."

The session ends as the client is able to articulate the nature of the disappointment that she initially experienced between herself and the therapist in Episodes 1 and 2. Eva states that "you weren't excited … you were … leaning back and passively listening." Immediately, the client qualified this statement by restating a previously articulated antithesis: "I can't demand [to] always … have all your attention." In reaffirming the novel experience that he has previously enacted with the client, the therapist says, "[B]ut you can notice if you feel a difference … and we'd both (come to better) understand."

Analyzing the Structures and Processes of Development in the Critical Session

The foregoing overview provides a summary of the major structural changes that occurred over the course of the critical incident. In the following section, we track *in detail* the ways in which the client's representation of self and other undergo microdevelopment over the course of the conversational turns of the "critical incident."

In so doing, we combine several of the tools in the DAPP method (see Chapter 6) that we have claimed permits methodologically rigorous documentation of developmental movement that occurs in *a single case of psychotherapy*, and makes DAPP an equally appropriate method for documenting psychotherapy effectiveness to the demonstration of symptom reduction outcomes in randomized controlled trials of manualized treatment approaches. Although we see DAPP process research and psychotherapy outcome research as complementary, our hope is that DAPP offers the opportunity to document the success of individual practitioners' work, which may be varied and eclectic with respect to psychotherapy approaches employed. We invite readers who wish to examine the rigor of the method to review our analyses very closely, and invite others to use the analyses for utterance-by-utterance insights into exactly how psychotherapy functions as a developmental process. However, we recognize that there may be some readers for whom the overview above felt like an adequate communication of how psychotherapy fostered Eva's development, and may find the detailed analysis to be repetitive. There may be others who are more interested in reading the raw transcribed data of the dialogue in which critical therapeutic gains were made, and reflecting on their own interpretations of that dialogue, than in the codes that we have inserted into the transcripts for our detailed DAPP analysis. We welcome each reader to examine what follows as closely or broadly as suits his or her interest in DAPP.

In what follows, we will track how particular elements of meaning and action undergo successive differentiation and hierarchic integration (synthesis). We will also examine specific changes in the structure of *joint* action that occurs between the client and the therapist. By tracking episode-by-episode changes in relational activity structures over time, we identify specific ways in which the client's and therapist's contributions to patterns of joint activity result in successive transformations in the structure of the client's representation of novel modes of communication and intimate exchange.

Episode 1: Representing the Client's Communicative Conflict
In the first episode of the transcribed material, with minimal attentional support provided by the therapist in comparison to previous sessions, the client is able to move forward in articulating a representation of a problem that she has planned to discuss during the session. In so doing, she shares her observations and thoughts about her customary style of communication in her interpersonal relationships:

C1: I know that I'm always apologizing and things too $O(T1 \equiv 1.0)$, because I'm afraid it's gonna hurt the other people $E(1.1)$; $\{S_1/T2[1.0 \leftrightarrow 1.1\}$[3] like we said ... because maybe things would hurt me. Like I'm so concerned it might hurt other people, that I bring about

---

[3] As a clarification of our use of codes in the context of our method of coding, the code (1.1) refers to the element "I'm afraid it's gonna hurt the other people," which is a further differentiation of the initial thesis, "I'm always apologizing" (element 1.0). The relationship between the two elements that is articulated by the client, reflected in the use of the term *because*, is expressed in the code $(S_1/T2 (1.0 \leftrightarrow 1.1)$. Thus, this coding reflects the articulation of a thesis, an antithesis (an element differentiated from the thesis), and a synthesis (a statement of the relationship between thesis and antithesis). The client's words that follow, "like we said ... because maybe things would hurt me," are an example of an element that we are *choosing*, for presentation purposes, *not to recognize and number*. We make this choice, as well as many similar choices in presenting the material that follows, because the subsequent developmental movement in the session does not build significantly on the element that we choose to ignore.

this whole apologizing [T: Uh-huh, uh-huh **ACK**] atmosphere **RS(2.0)**. And what people interpret is more that I don't feel very comfortable in what I'm saying **E(2.1)** {2.0<C>2.1}. Whereas, I mean, I feel it is my right to be saying whatever I'm saying **E(2.11)** but I just don't want to hurt them **E(1.1)** {2.11<C>1.1} so I try to make it … and it really doesn't get…. It's a different [T: Mm-hm, mm-hm **ACK**] message that comes across **E(2.1)**. And that also brings me to get into what I think is pretty related, which is, as I was telling you before, that when I have conversations with people about topics I'll say, "Well, I don't know very much about this but, I think that da da da"—instead of … **E(3.0)** And other people would just say, "Oh this is what happens." **E(3.1)** Even if they know as much as I know **E(3.11)** {E(3.0 <C> 3.1)}. So all those three things together, I've sort of been thinking about lately. And I think they're all a part of the same thing. **O(S₂/ T4[1.0←THROUGH→3.11])** I don't know [T: Uh-huh **ACK**] what you think [T: Uh-huh **ACK**] about that.] **REQ(4.0)**.

T1: Makes sense that they're connected **AFF(4.0)**.

The basic structure of this episode is depicted in Figure 7.2. In this episode, the client identifies two central thesis–antithesis pairs, which she then coordinates into a weak initial synthesis. She begins by articulating her first thesis, itself a synthesis of her observations of her apologizing behavior and the associated motivation. She states that "I'm always apologizing … because I'm afraid it's gonna hurt the other people" [S₁/ T2 [1.0 ↔ 1.1]]. She then elaborates the antithetical interpretation of the meaning of her behavior that she's discovered other people make: "What other people interpret is more that I don't feel comfortable with what I'm

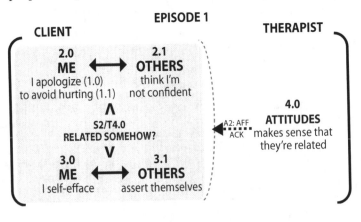

Figure 7.2 Episode 1.

saying" (2.1). Thereafter, in the context of minimal levels of attentional support (Scaffolding Level A2), the client describes a parallel pattern of social interaction. In so doing, she articulates her second central thesis (T3), stating she acts in self-effacing ways (i.e., saying, "Well, I don't know very much about this"). In contrast (3.1), other people simply tend to assert themselves (i.e., they say, "Oh, this is what happens"). In reflecting upon these two relations, the client is able to indicate her awareness that these two patterns are related. Although she cannot yet articulate *how* they are related, by specifying that a relation exists, the client is engaging in synthesizing activity. We may regard her statement (i.e., "I think they're all a part of the same thing") as a weak synthesis [S_2/T4[1.0←through→3.11]] of the client's observations and representations of her customary patterns of social interaction. At this point, the client requests that the therapist react to her description of her experience (i.e., "I don't know what you think about that"). Refraining from offering any interpretation, the therapist relies on attentional support (Sc A2) to *affirm* the client's initial synthesis (i.e., "Makes sense that they're connected").

We learn later in the session (Episode 3) that the preceding interaction may have been experienced in conflicting ways by the therapist and the client. The therapist's experience was that the client was actively and successfully engaging in constructive meaning-making activity, as indicated by her articulation of syntheses, and that Scaffolding Level A2 was providing appropriate encouragement for her to continue. However, the client may have felt that it was her task to engage the therapist in dialogue, and may have taken the therapist's response as indicative that she would have to work harder to succeed at this task.

Episode 2: Reflecting on the Origins of Communicative Conflict (the Culture–Self Cycle)

In Episode 2, the client becomes more explicit in trying to engage the therapist by soliciting direction about what to do about her dissatisfaction with her interpersonal style (see utterance C2, below). Feeling that he did not understand Eva's experience well enough to offer advice, the therapist attempts to gain a more complete understanding. In so doing, the therapist shares his uncertainty about the extent to which the client's self-observed interpersonal style reflects a cultural style of communication that has its origins in her ethnic heritage, or whether the style arises from the client's sense of herself. In offering his own question, the therapist redirects the client's attention. This provides attentional support intended to foster additional constructive activity on the part of the client (Scaffolding Level A4). In addition, he also offered a novel interpretation—a question drawn from his own ways of understanding the presented material—to help frame and direct the client's continued constructive activity (Level I6). Given these resources, the client proceeds to create a series of syntheses (thesis–antithesis relations) that transcend the distinction offered by the therapist.

C2: So I guess. I guess. Do you think it's good for me to think about why I could have these attitudes? **REQ(4.1)** Or should I just, like, practice not having these attitudes? **REQ(4.2) REQ(4.1 <C> 4.2)** (Pause)

T2: I guess I find myself wondering about how much what you're talking about **REDIR(5.0)** is a kind of style of talking **O(5.1)**—how much it's a reflection of attitudes and beliefs that you have about yourself **E(5.2)**, how much it's a style **RS(5.1)**. You know, I mean we've talked about the cultural, uh, kind of history. It seems to me that … if you're just saying, you know, this is a style, and you want to evaluate what's good about the style—what its strengths **E(5.11)** and what its weaknesses **E(5.12)** are, then we could look at it that way **E(5.1)**. But if it's not just a style, if it reflects more deeply held beliefs about yourself … **E(5.2) {5.1<C>5.2}**

C3: Well, I think it's both **E(S₃/T6(5.1 ↔ 5.2)**. It definitely is part of a cultural thing, I mean I can totally see, it's like so obvious that (Ethnic Group, hereafter EG) aren't straightforward when they have to criticize. Actually (EG)—you can't ask a (EG) to criticize something. Cause they just can't, you know. [T: Uh-huh, uh-huh **ACK**] We can't say something bad about something you've created or something like that. And we'll always … **E(5.13)** So, I know that part of it is that. I just think that you know they talk about sexist language, like what, the way you speak, also has significance on the way you think so I think that, for me, there's like this … [T: Mm-hm **ACK**] Yeah obviously it is partly cultural, and that doesn't really bother me that much…. I'm quite happy to be that way…. **E(6.0), TRANS(5.11→6.11)** I don't think it's the best thing in the world **E(6.1), TRANS(5.12→6.12)**, but then you know each culture has its [T: Mm-hm **ACK**] pros **APP(5.11)** and cons **APP(5.12)**. Sometimes it's … so it's good yeah, to have like straightforward Americans who'll always say what they think **E(5.111)** but then sometimes they're a little, they're a little um [T: Obnoxious?] obnoxious, or like socially inept, and not diplomatic **E(5.121)** … [T: Mm-hm **ACK**] enough in certain situations [T: Mm-hm **ACK**] where you would require some diplomacy, or whatever **E(5.121)**. So I mean every style will have its [T: Mm-hm **ACK**] problems and its good things. But I guess … **(S₄/T7[5.11←THROUGH→6.12])**

T3: So, it really, what I'm hearing is what really matters to you is not … you can think about the pros and cons of a style **RS(7.0)** [C:

Yeah (stretched out) **ACK**] but what really matters is how you feel about yourself **ACK, EXP(6.0, 6.11→7.1)**.

Following this offer of attentional support in utterance T3, the client goes on to expand both (a) on how her unique cross-cultural experience may have influenced the way in which her ethnic group's cultural style shaped her own thinking about herself and (b) about the difficulties that she reports in her communications with others. Figure 7.3 depicts the dialectical sequence of the microdevelopmental movements that constitute this episode. Building upon a synthesis [S$_2$/T4] that she constructed in the first episode, the client asks a question in which she differentiates between "think[ing] about why I could have these attitudes" [4.1] and trying to "practice not having these attitudes" [4.2]. In utterance T2, the therapist transforms the client's question by sharing *his* question about the meaning of Eva's observations. He thereby guides or redirects her attention with an alternative question (Scaffolding Level A4) while simultaneously drawing upon his own frame of reference in framing the question (Interpretation—Scaffolding Level I6). In so doing, he differentiates between whether her attitudes reflect a style influenced by culture [5.1] or "more deeply held beliefs about yourself" [5.2].

The client then articulates a series of thesis–antithesis distinctions that culminates in a synthesis describing her sense of the origins of her interpersonal style as a product of both culture and attitudes about herself. Specifically, the client states that her difficulty in asserting herself has its origins in a cultural practice of refraining from criticizing others [**E(5.1)**]. In linking this cultural practice to attitudes about herself, the client notes that just as people internalize cultural forms of sexist language, she has internalized the cultural practice of refraining from criticizing others [**E(S$_3$/T6[5.1 ↔ 5.2])**]. The client acknowledges that there are "pros and cons" of different cultural practices (which she then goes on to illustrate in the case of "Americans") [**S$_4$/T7[5.11←THROUGH→6.12]**]. Nonetheless,

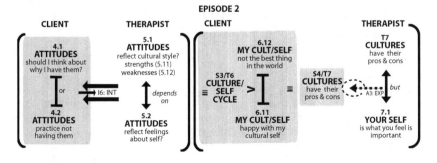

EPISODE 2

Figure 7.3 Episode 2.

she is happy to have internalized this aspect of her own cultural heritage [**E(6.0, TRANS(5.11→6.11)**]. The client synthesizes these relations into a general representation of the importance of self in what may be called a "self–culture cycle" [**S6/T7**]. In so doing, she successfully transcends the distinction offered by the therapist between culture and attitudes toward self as explanations of the origins of the client's difficulty with self-assertion. Thereafter, offering attentional support, the therapist attempts to restate (Sc A3) and expand (Sc A4) the core aspects of the client's synthesis: "you can think about the pros and cons of a style [**RS(7.0)**] but what really matters is how you feel about yourself" [**EXP(6.0, 6.11→7.1)**]. The client then goes on to use this restatement and the therapist's continued attentional support to further develop her theories about how her cross-cultural experience influenced the self–culture cycle, as well as to consider other influences on her feelings about herself.

Eva has succeeded in engaging the therapist, to the extent that he has *transformed* the descriptions and interpretations she offered in Episode 1 into a new question. Then she is in fact able to use the question to construct a higher-level synthesis (elaborating and transforming the construction he offered). However, evidently, as we only learn later in Episode 3, she still feels concerned about what the therapist is experiencing and she feels disappointed in his reaction. It is worth considering whether this is because he chose not to answer her question by taking the lead in telling her what to do (e.g., providing a higher level of guidance than she may have been hoping for in her request), and instead "answered a question with a question," therefore putting the leadership back in her court. Analysis of these developmental movements suggests that (a) a therapist can offer aliment that a client successfully uses developmentally, while still frustrating her wish for a different form of interaction; and, further, (b) the therapist might be aware or unaware that this is going on until such time as it may become an explicit focus of discussion.[4] It is important to note that from an observer's perspective, Eva's disappointment is not revealed in the microdevelopmental movements that occur in Episode 2. These experiences only begin to move into the sphere of shared discourse during Episode 3.

---

[4] In this particular case, we know from the therapist's narrative of the case that he had left the previous session with concerns about the ways in which the emotional intensity of the dialogue, although apparently mutually gratifying, might need to be further observed and understood to appreciate its therapeutic and developmental significance. So he may well have been aware that in his renewed focus on observation, he was "holding himself back" from that level of engagement. Although he thought this "holding back" might be helpful in understanding the emotional dynamics being enacted in the client–therapist dialogue, he was not aware that the client was experiencing disappointment in the moment, and he also felt that the client was making effective use of the resources that he was offering.

Episode 3: Expressing Disappointment and Explicitly
Entering the Dialectic of Enactment

After Eva uses the therapist's continued attentional support to further develop her theories about how her cross-cultural experience influenced her experience of what we've dubbed the *self–culture cycle*, as well as to consider other influences on her feelings about herself, she interrupts her entire line of discussion as follows:

C5: ... (Pause) I don't know if you're getting like any message ... I mean I sort of feel like this whole ... like all of what I've been saying has been very like not organized, or anything ... and sort of like jumping from one thing to another **O, REQ (8.0)**, but ...

T5: What are you feeling right now? **QUES/e[5] (8.1)**

C6: Well, I guess I'm feeling that I wanted to like present to you, like, specific topics for today, or something or, or, or, or a case or whatever, and then we would talk about that **O(8.11)**. But I find myself ... like now this is sort of like the third thing I'm talking about, and we haven't really like talked about one thing **E(8.111)** {8.11<C> 8.111} which is probably fine too I guess **E(8.1111)**.

T6: But there, there was this hope that you could come in with a topic and you could [C: Yeah (drawn out)] something would happen [C: Yeah (drawn out) **ACK**] between us around that topic, that would ... **RS/e (8.11<C> 8.111)** [C: Yeeah (high pitched, almost childlike) **ACK**]

C7: Yeah **AFF**, cause I usually, I mean I always feel like I think that I've understood something when I leave here, you know? **E,O(9.0)**

T7: You feel that last time? **QUES/e (9.1)**

C8: Yeah, **AFF** I think I always do. **O(9.2)** {S_5/10.0[9.0 ↔ 9.1]}

T8: Mm-hm, and you say you want to have that sense each time that ... **RS/e, TRANS/e (8.1, 10.0→10.1)**

C9: Yeah **AFF**, just, maybe I, I guess, um, let's see, so I don't, when I, when I leave here I always feel like, um, I understand this (emphatically)! **E(10.1)** You know maybe I forget it the next day when I leave you know **E(10.11)** [T: Mm-hm **ACK**], after I leave here

---

[5] As indicated in Table 6.3, enactments can occur at any level of scaffolding. Scaffolding Levels 7 through 9 consist of enactments at the highest levels of scaffolding. However, enactments also occur at lower levels of scaffolding when therapeutic discourse focuses on relations between the therapist and the client (i.e., when the therapist and client treat each other directly as relational partners) or when the discussions refer to enactments in which the client engages outside of therapy (e.g., "homework," trying out suggested courses of action, etc.). To indicate the presence of enactment at lower levels of scaffolding, we add the suffix "/e" to the code for the discursive acts in question. For example, the code "QUES/e" identifies a particular QUESTION (Scaffolding Level 4) that functions as a form of attentional support and enactment.

I feel that I've understood something about something and I guess **E(10.1)**, maybe I've just like been, um, looking forward so much to coming this week [T: Uh-hm **ACK**] that I ... **E(10.1)** **E(10.1 <C > 8.111)**

T9: Hoping that, as you were looking forward to coming, what was your hope or fantasy about what, what would happen? [C: What might happen? **CLAR, QUES**] T: What would be good about it to ...? **QUES/e**

C10: Uhm, I g-uess maybe it's what, what I wrote here about this whole, like underestimating myself and stuff. **O(10.2)** (Pause) OK. I think I know what happened. I presented this and then we, sort of like nothing happened, like we didn't [T: Mm-hm **ACK**] talk it was like there was nothing to say about it. **O(10.3), RS(8.11<C> 8.111)**

T10: What were you hoping would happen? **QUES/e**

C11: (Laughs) I guess I was hoping, that we would find some kind of solution or something (beginning to sound very sad) or some kind of, um, or, or just maybe like talk about why, why I'm so insecure. **O(10.11)** But then I also feel that we've already talked about that but now I can't remember exactly what we said about it. **E(10.111)** [T: (very quietly) Uh-hm **ACK**] C: (very quietly) and then ... (inaudible) I think maybe that's what I'm feeling. **E(10.11<C>8.111)**

T11: Hm-hm (pause) so we'd talk about 'why you're so insecure **RS/e(10.11)** and how would that leave you feeling'? **E, QUES/e (10.112)** [C: and what] T: That kind of talk? Say we said "OK, you know you are so insecure? You've brought these different observations that all reflect your insecurity and ... **EXP/e (S_6/T11 [10.1 ↔ 10.11 ↔ 4.0)**

C12: Yeah (long pause) **AFF** I mean yeah [T: so that], that's what I guess I basically thought we'd talk about. **AFF(11.0), RJ(10.112)** (*Eva affirms that T gets it about what the hope was for the discussion, but ignores T's question about the feeling.*)

T12: Hm hm, and you hoped that would feel good, for us to talk about why you're insecure? **RS, E, INT/e (10.112)**

Figure 7.4 depicts Eva's interruption of the line of reasoning that she was developing after her syntheses of Episode 2 were affirmed by the therapist. She first expresses her concern with how the therapist has been experiencing the session thus far, and then seems to go on to criticize her own communication in the session as not very organized. This is where the therapist first becomes aware of disequilibrium within the therapy relationship, when he experiences this client, who has been making perfect sense to him, questioning her own communication style. He responds by

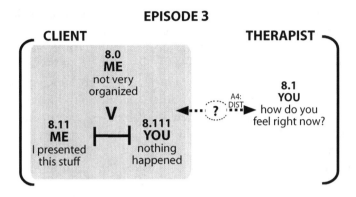

Figure 7.4 Episode 3.

trying to understand: "What are you feeling right now?" This is a form of attentional support (Sc A4), in that it represents a shifting of attention from the effectiveness of Eva's communication as well as the therapist's response to it to what Eva is experiencing in the moment. It also represents an offer of attention to the dialectic of enactment (Sc E4) as its content is directed at processes that are occurring within the therapeutic relationship itself. The therapist believed that Eva's interruption of her meaning-constructive activity with self-criticism and concern about her impact on her relational partner reflected an emergent disequilibrium in the therapy relationship, and thus an important opportunity for novel experience in the moment.

We also can see Eva's self-effacement in the face of potential conflict as an expression, with the therapist, of the interpersonal style that she was describing in general in Episodes 1 and 2. Eva hints at her disappointment in the session by saying, "Well, I guess I'm feeling that I wanted to like present to you, like, specific topics for today, or something or, or, or a case or whatever, and then we would talk about that. But I find myself … like now this is sort of like the third thing I'm talking about, and we haven't really like talked about one thing" [O(8.111) (8.11<C> 8.111)]. Although Eva immediately tries to move away from the disappointment with "which is probably fine too I guess" [8.1111], the therapist chooses to keep his attention on the disappointment that is being experienced in the moment. Devoting attentional support to what is being enacted between them, he remains intent on getting a handle on what the client was hoping for in the session, and why she is experiencing what has occurred as disappointing. This turns out to be a very challenging task, as the process of talking about her disappointment ultimately makes the client very uncomfortable. For a while (through C10), Eva tries to discuss the disappointing element of her experience while maintaining her composure. But as the therapist presses to fully understand the nature of the disappointment, Eva's affect becomes more intense, and in C11, this intensity is reflected first in laughter, followed immediately with extreme sadness.

As indicated in Figure 7.4, the content of the discussion remains the elaboration of Eva's hopes in presenting her thoughts [**8.11–10.111**], and the disappointment in their not being realized [**8.111**]. However, as noted in the excerpt of the therapist's account of the critical incident, quoted in the context of the foregoing overview, the subsequent exploration process was very painful for the client, and was facilitated by a variety of forms of attentional support on the part of the therapist. Within the context of the ongoing enactment between the client and the therapist, these included encouragement, emotional modulation, restatement, distancing, and emotional support (Scaffolding Levels A2/E2 through A5/E5). One can observe in the dialogue above the therapist's relentlessness in asking her with words to explain the thoughts, hopes, wishes, and ultimately feelings behind her disappointment, while being supportive and empathic (with facial expression, tone, and sounds) in acknowledging the degree of painful effort she was making. As the client becomes more aware of the nature of her pain and disappointment stemming from the unexpected result of her interaction with the therapist, the therapist, by restating the discrepancy, continues to invite her to attend to the novelty of the situation as an enactment opportunity (Scaffolding Levels A2/E2 through A4/E4), in which the client has an opportunity to acknowledge the pain to which she is vulnerable in interpersonal interactions, and to discover new ways of handling interactions that evoke such pain. When in utterance C12, the client indicates that the therapist has understood what she hoped would happen, but chooses to not respond to his invitation to speculate on how the realization of her hopes would have left her *feeling*, the therapist responds in utterance T12 by offering an interpretation for her to reflect on (Sc I6), "and you hoped that would *feel good*, for us to talk about why you're insecure."

Episode 4: The Confession

The client at this point accepts the invitation to explore the novel possibilities in the situation. She answers the therapist's question by offering a "confession"—thus bringing into the open an aspect of her inner experience that she would typically be unwilling or unable (without the resources of the therapist's scaffolding) to admit.

C13: (Laughs) Well the truth is [T: yes **ACK/e**] I'll tell you the truth, this is a *confession* [T: OK **ACK/e**] wait … and I … like this idea's passed through my mind twice, and now I say, O.K. I guess I should just say "I had the impression that this topic just bored you, so that you didn't feel like talking about it." **E(12.0)** [T:

(empathically) Uh-hmm **ACK/e**] and so I didn't want to talk about something that you'd be bored about.

T13: So somewhere in the midst of bringing up this topic you picked up some signals of "this was boring" and **ACK, RS/e, (12.0)** [C: Yes! I think so. **AFF**]

C14: (chuckles) It's sort of hard, see. **E(12.1)** This is the kind of thing which is very hard for me to tell **E(12.2)** you because (short pause) I sort of feel like I'm insulting you **E(12.21)** or something or something by telling you that I perceive that this might be boring for you or whatever **E(12.0)** {12.0<C>12.2 <C>12.21}

T14: I feel this is so important for you to … to be able to say that. **SUPP/e 13.0)** {13.0<C>12.2}

C15: It, it's so hard for me, that I have to cry! **E(12.2)** [T: Oh (sympathetically **SUPP/e**)] C: (said through sobbing) It's like very hard for me to say this to you, you know? (short pause) …. I don't know why (emphatically) **E(12.22)**

T15: You noticed something that felt a little like I was bored **RS/e (12.0)** … or like, is it hard because it's like something that isn't quite right in our relationship **QUES, INT/e (12.221)**?

C16: (Laughter) Umm … No, **RJ(12.221)** I mean I think I, think that, that um, that you're um as human being as anybody else and there must be topics that interest you more than others **E(12.2211)** … and, and that obviously, um, (voice cracking) some days … (crying) … and I'm still like very embarrassed about this. **E(12.23)**

T16: Embarrassed—about what? **ACK, QUES/e**

C17: I don't know, I can't … Do you want me to think exactly about why it's like this … [T: what you feel, what feels?…] this whole situation [T: what feels embarrassing?] **QUES/e** Well, OK I know what feels embarrassing **E(12.231)**. Like I feel like can't like really make, like it's not my right to make any demands with you, you know like of attention **E(S₇/T14(12.0←THROUGH→12.231)** [T: Yeah (very soft) or of um, um **ACK**] … yeah (definitive tone). So, like, so I sort of feel like, it's like with any person that you interact, if you see that the person doesn't want to talk about something **(E12.0)**, I mean you can't just like impose, um … a topic. You just sort of like have to find out what, like I guess I sort of feel that that's the way that it is when you talk, when you have a conversation with people is that, you talk about something that interests you both **E(12.22111)**) {S₈/T15 (14.0 ↔ 12.22111)} [T: Mm-hm **ACK**] Right? Um. **REQ**

As illustrated in Figure 7.5, the client's "confession" includes a set of related painful feelings about what she observed, about how embarrassing

EPISODE 4

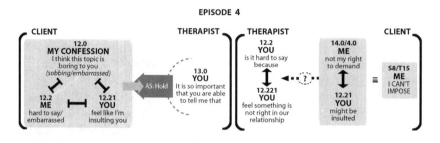

Figure 7.5 Episode 4.

it feels to reveal the observation, and why. Expressing all of these feelings represents novel behavior. After the "confession," the next tension expressed in the session is between the client saying (T14) that this process (the novel behavior) is very difficult and the therapist saying, with deep affect, "I feel it is so important for you to be able to say that." So at this point, both parties' attention is on the enactment process. Assuming the role of relational partner, the therapist asserts his view that the client's disclosure is important (an interpretation based on his view of therapy), even though the client finds it hard. By offering his presence, participation, and care to the client, the therapist supports the client at Scaffolding Level 5 (emotional support) *in order to* help the client manage and invest in what he is acknowledging is a very painful process for the client. Simultaneously, the therapist operates at Scaffolding Level 6 (interpretation) by asserting his view of what is valuable in the therapy process.

The client responds to this level of support by further crying, expressing the difficulty she feels in making this confession, though she doesn't know why she has this difficulty. The therapist continues his interpretive activity (Sc I6) suggesting that the client might find it difficult because she feels that something's not quite right in their relationship. Although the client rejects the therapist's interpretation, she joins in the effort to understand her experience by beginning to place her interaction with the therapist in the context of her approach to interactions in general. She thereby begins to connect her novel experience in the enactment with her account of her accustomed interpersonal style that she described earlier in the session. As she starts this process, she says (almost pleading for help) that she is still very embarrassed by what she is doing.

Instead of helping to extricate her from the situation, the therapist responds, "Embarrassed—about what?" first acknowledging the feeling, but then continuing to probe the discomfort. It may not be unambiguously evident from the transcript, but to the therapist in this case (the first author) it seemed that she was at first a bit surprised by the therapist's reaction—which perhaps for her represented a novel experience of a response to her plea for help. But once she was able to reframe the therapist's request in terms of the idea *that he wants her to* think about why it's embarrassing, she's able to comply with his wish. She constructs the explanation that it is an inappropriate imposition for her to expect or demand the therapist's (or anyone's) attention, and that in conversation it is her responsibility to accommodate to what the other person finds interesting (**12.22111**). *In so doing, she identified within her relationship with the therapist the conflict that she had previously articulated in her efforts to characterize her interpersonal approach in general (4.0)—between denying, disregarding, or devaluing her own feelings, and hurting another person by expressing them.*

Episode 5: The Enactment of Novel Experience With the Therapist I

In Episode 5, the conflicts related to the client's fear of hurting another person are explored in greater depth. Over the course of the episode, the client finds that, contrary to her fears and expectations, her earlier "confession" was not seen as an insulting or aggressive act by the therapist. This realization results in great emotional relief in the client. This enactment between the client and the therapist provided a context for the client to experience a direct counterexample to the fear that the client expressed in connecting the enactment to her accustomed communication style—namely, that her interlocutor might reject her if she were to express her feelings openly. The exploration begins with the therapist explicitly formulating an approach to interpersonal situations that represents a novel, third alternative (antithesis) to both (a) the approach that the client has described of accommodating at the expense of self-devaluing or self-denying, and (b) the approach the client fears of imposing, demanding, and hurting. This is the idea, "But the other thing you can do is talk about what you're feeling … in the moment." This formulation represents an offer of an interpretation, in that it is drawn from the therapist's ways of making meaning, but it also offers an enactment opportunity, in that it could be (and is being) put into practice in the current interaction. The client acknowledges the therapist's proposed alternative. However, the client evidently experiences the need to further elaborate the meanings behind her approach of accommodating (which in turn leads to further elaboration of her fear of imposing). She also needs to experience the affirmation of having these meanings appreciated and understood. Finally, she needs to further review what she has in fact done in interacting with the therapist. As will be seen below, it is only after the enacting of the novel alternative of talking about feelings and fears has been practiced to the extent that it leads to a sufficient novel experience of reassurance that the client is able to recognize that she feels better, that the client is able to affirm the value of this proposed novel alternative.

T17: But the other thing you can do is talk about what you're feeling … in the moment. **E,INT/e(15.1) {15.1<C>15.0}**

C18: Yeah, yeah, you can do that too **AFF**, but I guess, um, I think it's sort of funny because obviously every time I come in I always like to review some problem of mine, right? … **E(15.11)** *(The client then goes on to place the therapy relationship in the context of other relationships in which reciprocity is achieved by taking turns discussing each other's problems, then says,)* So I sort of feel that I can't like come and impose you with my problems **E(15.0)** I mean I should ask.… **E(15.2)** Maybe if we had different things we could talk about myself **E(15.21)** and if some things are more interesting to you **E(15.211)**. Other than in my perception—maybe you were not bored **E(12.4)**, we're assuming that. You know, we don't know if you were bored or not. **S₉/T16(12.0 ↔ 12.4)** But I perceived that you or … or I thought that maybe you were **E(16.1)** like you know me thinking about what other people were thinking or whatever **S₁₀/T17(16.1 ↔ 4.0)**. So I just felt that … so, so I just don't feel comfortable like coming and imposing something that might be bor—boring for you, you know? **ES₁₁/T18(15.0←THROUGH→15.211 ↔ 17.0)** … *(After the therapist's response leads to a brief digression, the client returns to reviewing what occurred in her interaction with the therapist.)*

C20: OK (very strong), so I wanted to talk about something **RS(8.11)** and then I thought, well maybe he thinks this is really boring, **RS(8.111)** so I'm not going to talk about it anymore. **E(15.2)** But then …

T20: But yet it was the thing you had hoped to talk about. **RS/e(8.11) {15.2 <C> 8.11}**

C21: Yeah, even, yeah that's the thing I tried to talk about **AFF(8.11)**, but then I said well you know if it's boring him, I'm not going to talk about it. **E(15.3)** So I said well I might as well just tell him. **E(15.31)** [T: Mm-hm, mm-hm **ACK**] and so I told you **E(15.31) {S₁₂/T19(8.11 ↔ 8.111 ↔ 15.31)** but it was just like very hard **E(12.2)** 'cause at the beginning, I mean now that we talked more I feel [differently].… **E(12.24) {S₁₃/T20(12.0 ↔ 14.0 ↔ 15.1 ↔ 12.24)}** I mean what really was hard for me … is to say … that you felt I was being aggressive toward you, right? Like by telling you oh, you're bored, you're bored about what I'm saying. **E(15.12)**

T21: That that would be aggressive? **CLAR/e(15.12)**

C22: Yeah. Because that would mean that I wasn't perceiving the attention you were giving me, or that I was demanding like, some kind of like expression of your attention that you didn't give me. TRANS(14.0→15.11) You know like, "oh," you know like, I don't know [T: Mm-hm **ACK**], and that would be sort of like aggressive towards you because I was telling you that you hadn't shown to me what I was expecting **E(15.12)**.

T22: You were feeling disappointed in my reaction **INT,EXP/e** **(8.11<C>8.111→15.121)**.

C23: Yeah **AFF**, so that would be hurtful to you **E(15.121) E(15.12 ↔ 15.121<C>1.1)**.

T23: Why ... (interrupts self) ... Mm-hm, mm-hm **ACK/e**.

C24: So, but of course now after we've talked more, I feel comfortable that you don't think I'm being aggressive **E(15.122)**, so it doesn't bother me that much anymore **E, RS(20.0)** {S₁₅/T21(12.2 ↔ 20.0 ↔ 15.122 ↔ 1.11)} [T: Mm-hm Mm-hm **ACK**] C: But I couldn't even bring myself to say it **RS (12.2)**.

As indicated in Figure 7.6, the therapist proposed the possible response **(12.3/15.1)** to the client's observations of the therapist's possible boredom **(12.0)**—"saying what you feel in the moment" **(15.1)**. This was proposed as an alternative **(15.1)** to accommodating to the "other" **(15.0)**. This proposal both represents an interpretation (the therapist's idea) and also contributes to the enactment dialectic in that it is an idea that can be, and in fact has been in the session, put into practice by the client. The therapist's proposing this alternative leads ultimately to a deeper expression of the client's fears of being experienced as hurtful—the topic that the client introduced as a concern in Episode 1. The client's initial response takes the form of "yes, but ..." which she uses to indicate how important the therapy is to her **(15.11)**, and that she feared that the therapist would experience her as aggressive **(15.12)**. The therapist's acknowledgment and empathizing with these feelings is important, but because Eva is no longer as terrified as she was in Episode 4, these acts represent therapeutic support at Scaffolding Level A2 (i.e., encouragement) rather than A5 (i.e., emotional holding). However, equally important in utterances T21 through

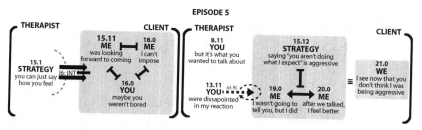

EPISODE 5

Figure 7.6 Episode 5.

T22, in acts of interpretation (Sc I6), the therapist implicitly suggests that what he felt was not what she feared. He does this when he questions her thought that she was being aggressive and when he restates what happened in his own terms. (He becomes more explicit in discussing his experience in later episodes.) However, even while explaining her fears, Eva has signaled some awareness that something new has happened that challenges her meaning making when she says. "Maybe you were not bored, we're not, we're assuming that. You know, we don't know if you were bored or not. [S_{10}/T16[12.0 $\leftrightarrow$ 12.4]] But I perceived that you or I, or I thought that maybe you were, like you know me thinking about what other people were thinking or whatever." But by the end of Episode 5, once she feels reassured that the therapist did not experience her as aggressive [S_{15}/T21(12.2 $\leftrightarrow$ 20.0 $\leftrightarrow$ 15.122 $\leftrightarrow$ 1.11)], she is able to acknowledge what was novel in the enactment. She did in fact say what she was feeling in the moment [S_{13}/T19[8.11 $\leftrightarrow$ 8.111 $\leftrightarrow$ 15.31]] and the response was not what she feared—the therapist did not experience her as aggressive.

The key moments in this episode occur when the client is able to acknowledge that she has enacted a novel experience with unexpected positive results. This occurs (a) when the client states in utterance C21, "and so I told you [that I thought you were bored]" (19.0), thus expressing the client's sense of disappointment in the session; and (b) when she acknowledges in utterance C24 that "but of course now after we've talked more, I feel comfortable that you don't think I'm being aggressive so it doesn't bother me that much anymore" [E(20.0) {S_{15}/T21[12.2 $\leftrightarrow$ 20.0 $\leftrightarrow$ 15.122 $\leftrightarrow$ 1.11]}].

Episode 6: Further Exploration of the Fear of Hurting Others

Even though over the course of Episode 5, the client was able to express that she has had a novel experience that was antithetical to or discrepant from what she feared, the therapist senses that the power of this new experience is vulnerable to being dwarfed by the intensity of her fears. Thus, he initiates Episode 6 in utterance T24 by empathizing with those fears, and expanding on them with the emotional expression "so scary." He thus invites further exploration of those terrifying fears and their underlying assumptions, and he offers his support in embarking on that exploration. The client's response is to use the support to elaborate on the fears.

T24: It was so scary at that moment that I might feel it as aggressive
     SUPP, EXP/e(21.0→21.1).
C25: Yeah, and obviously, and I think obviously the fear is that if you felt that I was being aggressive then what you would do maybe is just like shut yourself off and like never **E(21.2)** [T: Protect myself **ACK**] **E(21.3)**] never be like interested in any of like, whatever

I talked about again. You can say, "oh well, you know, if she's going to be like this, you know, I don't want to have to deal with her," kind of E(21.2).

T25: That in order for me to feel OK dealing with you, you have to be a certain way, you have to be ... **ACK, EXP/e(21.2→21.21) {S₁₆/ T22(21.2 ↔ 15.121)}**

C26: Well I have to be, um, like careful with your feelings **E(22.1)** ... maybe I'm exaggerating to think that it's going to hurt your feelings so much that I tell you that I think something is boring you. **E(22.11)** ... also, I mean the other reason I thought that it might, like bother you or something is I guess, um, and this is also something that's hard for me to say **E(12.21)**, is that um, because it's sort of like your profession, I guess, to listen to, to other people's problems and then that would be (sighs as she says this word ... unintelligible) **E(22.12) E(S₁₇/T23[21.12 ↔ 22.0])**.

T26: It feels like saying I'm not doing such a good job? **SUPP, EXP/e(23.1)**

C27: Um, yeah! **AFF** But that's not what I want to say, you know, **E(23.11)** [T: Mm-hm **ACK**] and so I'm like so afraid of like **E(12.2)**, like making you think that, that I'm saying that [T: Mm-hm, mm-hm **ACK**] that I won't say it, or if I say it it's just like so painfully embarrassing **E(12.23)** [T: Mm-hm, mm-hm **ACK**] ... like it sort of is, you know, right now, and so (pause, sad tone of voice), so that's how **E(23.1<C>23.11)** ...

As indicated in Figure 7.7, the central novel elements introduced by this more in-depth exploration of fears and assumptions are (a) that acknowledging feeling that the therapist was bored would be tantamount to challenging his professional competence (**23.0→23.1**), and (b) that the

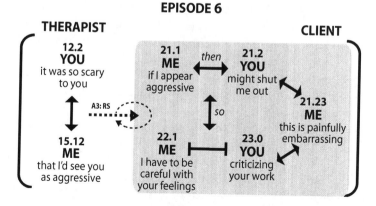

EPISODE 6

THERAPIST

CLIENT

12.2 YOU
it was so scary to you

A3: RS

15.12 ME
that I'd see you as aggressive

21.1 ME
if I appear aggressive

then

21.2 YOU
might shut me out

so

21.23 ME
this is painfully embarrassing

22.1 ME
I have to be careful with your feelings

23.0 YOU
criticizing your work

Figure 7.7 Episode 6.

risk of doing so is that the therapist would "shut yourself off" to her and would "never be like interested in any of like, whatever I talked about again" (**21.1**). When the therapist puts the former assumption into words, picking up on the client's introduction of the issue of it being the therapist's "profession" to listen, the embarrassment returns and feels overwhelming to the client. Thus, though the client has affirmed at the end of Episode 5 that she has "learned" and seen the value of the novel behavior of talking about what she is feeling, when the therapist assists in directly bringing this activity in juxtaposition to the discomfort involved, the challenges in practicing it become clear as the client dissolves into the grip of her fears once again.

Episode 7: The Enactment of Novel Experience With the Therapist II

The therapist responds to the client's falling back into the grip of her fears by this time offering interpretation (Sc I6), including his own understanding of what happened between them, and locating it in the context of "our work" in therapy. This response in effect also carries forth the dialectic of enactment, in offering his naming of what they just did as relational partners. In so doing, the therapist also provides the client with emotional holding (Sc A5) in order to support the client's continued efforts to explore the novel behavior and meanings constructed. By identifying what is occurring between the client and the therapist as "our work" in therapy, he implicitly offers to share the burden of the intense discomfort that the work entails. The client ultimately responds to this support by reinforcing her discovery of novel experience and the novel synthesis that she created at the end of Episode 5.

T27: I mean, I don't, I don't feel like I'm not doing a good job **E/e(23.12)**. I feel like you picked up on something that made you feel I wasn't paying attention **EXP(12.0)**, and I'm really curious about what that was **O(21.3)**. To me, part of our work is being honest with each other and learning from that, and I think we can both learn from your noticing your reaction. "Oh," you know, "I feel he's not paying attention" and bringing that up, and then we can both understand what's going on **SUPP, E/e(S$_{18}$/T24[23.12 ↔ 12.0 ↔ 4.0 ↔ 12.1])**.

C28: I mean, like (voice is still a little choked), just the way, um, like things are turning out right now. **RS(21.0)** It's so much better to talk about it **E(15.1)**, because you're not being offended at all **TRANS(21.0→21.2)**. But I thought that you might be offended, right? **E(21.21)** And so I feel a lot better that we could talk about something **E(10.112)** {(S$_{19}$/T25[23.0 ↔ 21.0 ↔ 15.1 ↔ 21.2 ↔ 21.21 ↔ 10.112])}.

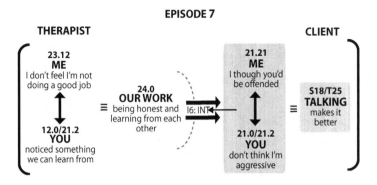

Figure 7.8 Episode 7.

In Figure 7.8, the left side represents the key elements of the therapist's naming of the shared experience (**S18/T24**) and providing emotional holding (Sc A5), Scaffolding Level 5, by placing the difficulty in the context of shared work. The right side represents the elements of the client's appropriation, transformation, and articulation of her version of the synthesis (S19/T25), restating the lessons that she has learned and ending with the idea "I feel a lot better that we could talk about something [this difficult]."

Episode 8: Identifying Alternative Modes of Self-Assertion Within Intimate Relationships

In Episode 8, the client brings together a variety of meaning elements constructed in earlier episodes and synthesizes them into the central insight of the entire psychotherapy session. In this episode, the client creates a grand synthesis that resolves many (but not all) of the conflicts that arose in earlier episodes. Among others, there were two extremely important developments that we tracked in Episode 8. First, the client begins the process of generalizing the synthesis that she appropriated and articulated at the end of Episode 7—using it as a framework for understanding her other relationships. Second, in doing so she goes back to her "accustomed pattern" that she discussed in Episodes 1 and 2, and she articulates that this is a "limitation to my interaction with people that I'm so concerned about how they're going to react to something that I don't say things." It's another step that she explains in a generalized way why her accustomed pattern doesn't work: "And then they affect me more, because I'm thinking … if they knew what I'm thinking … if, you know, I want to tell this, I want to tell them this, but they might think this, and so something I don't tell them it still is on my mind, right?"

As can be seen below, she then moves back to the enactment sphere in the service of using what was enacted with the therapist to illustrate her point. And that is when therapist and client join together in articulating their shared understanding of what happened in the enactment, and of how it illustrates the problems with Eva's accustomed pattern, as well as their shared relief to have made it through to a more satisfying interaction with each other.

C28: And so I just like, I just like uh making a parallel like some of my problems with [my ex-boyfriend] O(26.0) that I wouldn't mention something because E(26.1) I was really afraid that he would be offended or he would feel rejected, or feel really bad E(26.11), so I wouldn't bring them up RS(26.1) and in fact, like the days when I got really courageous and said OK now I'm gonna tell you E(26.12)—he really took them as like normal things E(26.111) as maybe you're taking this now RS(25.0). And I was like, thinking like before like I, I spent like months never telling him something RS(26.1) because like I was really afraid that it was gonna hurt him RS(26.11) and it turned out that (laughter—unintelligible) [T: Mm-hm, mm-hm ACK] it didn't hurt him at all RS(26.111) {S_{20}/T27[25 ↔ 26.0←THROUGH→26.12]}.

And so, and like, just like when I brought, when this thing that's happened a couple of days ago with my friend that was potentially a complicated situation O(28.0), and I brought it up E(28.1), and I was also saying, you know I'm really embarrassed to tell you this E(28.11), or I'm really, but I think that um, that that situation was uncomfortable or whatever RS(28.0). And, and but he didn't feel bad, E(28.111) {S_{21}/T29[27.0←THROUGH→28.111]} but I'm always like, and I think that's sort of like a limitation to my interaction with people O(29.1) that I'm so concerned, about how they're going to react to something that I don't say things E,RS(4.0) {S_{22}/T30[29 ↔ 29.1 ↔ 4.0]}. And then they affect me more E(30.1), because I'm thinking [T: Mm-hm, if you're trying ACK] … if they knew what I'm thinking … E(30.11) [T: To think … you're trying to … well, OK, right ACK, RS] if, you know, I want to tell this, I want to tell them this but they might think this and something I don't tell them it still is on my mind, right? {S_{23}/T31[30←THROUGH→30.11]} [T: Mm-hm, mm-hm ACK] And that's when I picked it up or something, cause it came out on the second time. {S_{24}/T32[31.0 ↔ 14.0]} [T: yeah ACK/e] … It was still on my mind E(32.1) [T: Yeah, and it won't go away by not … ACK, EXP/e(32.1→32.11)] … and it won't go away by not talking about it EXP(32.11), and so it's affecting the way I feel E(32.111) about the person (language shifts from specific event to the more general "the person") {S$_{24}$/T33[32.0←THROUGH→32.111]} [T: Mm, hm **ACK**] because obviously if I feel a person is bored and I don't tell them and then they go ... then I, I start feeling resentful **EXP(33.0→33.1)** because I'm like, because, because then I start believing yeah they're bored, they're bored, and **E(33.11)** {S$_{25}$/T34[33.0←THROUGH→33.11]}.

T28: And (short pause) and it's like you were trying to solve the problem of my being bored **TRANS/e(34.0→34.1)**. You assumed I was bored and it was your responsibility to solve that problem, and to come up with something interesting **E/e(34.11)** {S$_{26}$/T35[34.11 ↔ 14.0)}. So you were working very hard **EXP/e(34.11→34.12)** [C: On solving problems **E(S$_{27}$/T36[35.0 ↔ 34.1])**] on solving the problem that **APP/e(36.0)**

C29: That didn't even exist **E(36.1)** {S$_{28}$/T37[36.0 ↔ 36.1 ↔ 12.4])}.

T29: Exactly, exactly **AFF/e** [C: Yeah, yeah **AFF**] and I was trying to understand what was going on with you **E/e (37.1)** [C laughing] and not knowing that [C: Yeah, yeah (happy and excited tone) **AFF/e**] what you were trying to do was solve the problem of my being bored **E/e(37.0<C>37.1)**.

C30: Yeah **AFF**, and then ... and then maybe if you're, if there's like this one thing that was making me think you were being bored and you're doing the same thing **E(37.2)**, then I think, this isn't working! **E(S$_{29}$/T38[37.0←THROUGH→37.2])** This is (laughter, unintelligible)

T30: This isn't working **ACK/e**—right, right **AFF/e**.

As indicated in Figure 7.9a, in this dialogue, the client, with minimal attentional support provided by the therapist, is able (a) to construct a representation of her customary interactive style and (b) to contrast this with a representation of the alternative communication style that she constructed in her enactment with the therapist. In so doing, (c) the client is able to identify multiple specific concrete examples of how she has, in the past, already had success with the alternative interaction style. Specifically, as indicated in Figure 7.9a, having constructed a synthesis of the alternative communication style in (S18/T25), in successive acts of coordination, she shows how she used this novel communication style with her ex-boyfriend (S20/T27) and her friend (S21/T29). She then contrasts these syntheses with a representation of her customary communication style (S22/T30), indicating the specific ways in which her customary style limits her interactions (S23/T31). Finally, she identifies the ways in which her customary communication style manifested itself in the enactments that occurred

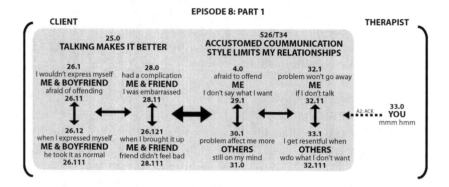

Figure 7.9a Episode 8.

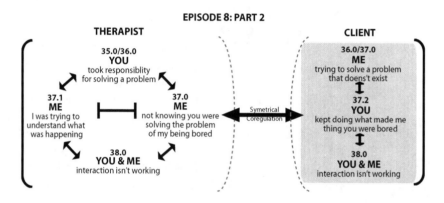

Figure 7.9b Episode 8.

between her and the therapist (S25/T34). Eva coordinates all of these meaning structures into a grand synthesis.

Equally notable is the way in which Eva and the therapist collaborate in the process of reflecting upon Eva's grand synthesis. In so doing, they complete each other's sentences and appropriate, expand upon, and transform each other's points. This structure of these latter interactions is depicted in Figure 7.9b. Overall, this process reflects not only a very effective process of collaboration and shared meaning making but also the emotional relief that both parties feel in having transformed the very painful emotional responses that were enacted within the therapeutic relationship.

Episode 9: Identifying the Conflict Between
Expressing Feelings and Being Demanding

Episode 9 begins with the client taking the novel syntheses that have been co-constructed in Episode 8 and attempting to generalize their implications still further to her relationship with her roommate. The therapist tries to support and reinforce this generalization by stating what is clearly an interpretation (drawn from his ways of making meaning): "You have every right to make a request." The client responds with another "Yes, but"; in so doing, she questions if she indeed has this right. But in doing so, she introduces a new and very important differentiation related to her self-image. She states that she's confused as to whether she is a "very demanding" person, or if it is just that people have told her she's very demanding. This leads to a shared exploration of the formative experiences giving rise to Eva's self-image as demanding. The exploration is scaffolded by the therapist's attention-supporting invitation for more specifics, when he reflects back, "Someone's told you you're demanding?"

C31: And the same thing, I mean now, it just occurred to me that the same thing happens like with my roommate **O(39.0)**. It's so hard for me to tell her, like if there's something that bothers me like in the morning if she makes noise or anything **E(39.1)**. It's just so hard for me to tell her, you know, please, just try and be more quiet in the morning or whatever, I just can't bring myself to tell her because I'm afraid that she's, that she's gonna get upset or something **E(39.11)**, and then like the couple times that I have brought myself to say **E(39.12)**, she takes it like very natural, sort of like, "oh yeah, sure" **E(39.121)** {S_{29}/T40[38.0 ↔ 39.0←THROUGH→39.131]}.

T31: You have every right to make a request **O(40.1)**.

C32: Yeah … **AFF** So, so I …

T32: To say, "It disturbs me when you wake me up in the morning" it's saying something about you **E(40.11)** [C: yeah **AFF**] Right, it's giving, saying you know, "I worry that you're not interested when you such and such …" you're giving me information about your feelings **E/e{S_{30}/T41[40.0 ↔ 40.11 ↔ 12.3 ↔ 14.1]**}.

C33: Yeah but, **AFF, Q(41.0)** I guess the reason I feel that some, that I, I don't know if I have the right to is because, **RJ(40.1)** I don't … see now I'm getting confused, because I don't know if it's that I am very demanding **E(40.12)** or it's just that people have told me I'm very demanding **E(40.121)** {40.12<C>40.121}.

T33: Someone's told you you're demanding? **QUES, TRANS(40.121→ 40.1211)**

C34: Yeah **AFF**, and so, I mean but the thing is I, it is quite a generalized thing (laughs) **RS(40.121)**, I mean in my family **O(42.0)** they all know that I … well everybody just talks about how I'm so demanding about so many things **E(42.1)**.… So in that sense, sometimes I don't, I don't feel I have the right to ask things because, because it's just like maybe too oppressive to people **E(42.11)** {**42.11<C>40.1**} {**S₃₁/T43[42.0←THROUGH→42.11 ↔ 40.12 ↔ 40.121]**}, and I'll tell you like examples of what I mean, um, not so much with my mother because I grew up with her **E(44.0)** and so we you know, we, we know each other so well **E(44.1)**, that she's not going to say, "you're so demanding" **E(44.11)**. I mean it's like whatever way I am **E(44.2)** and whatever way she is **E(44.21)** it's just understood and we don't like verbalize it, ever **E(44.3)**. Cause there's no point or anything {**S₃₂/T45[44.0←THROUGH→44.3]**} {**45.0<C>43.0**}.

But like when I was living with my dad, um, in high school for a couple years **E(46.0)**, and like every time that I go on vacation with him and his wife and stuff (sighs) um, oh, well they'll like laugh at me or whatever, "Oh remember when you were with us and you told us to turn the TV down at night when you went to sleep, and stuff" **E(46.1)** and uh, and I (unintelligible) and then like my cousin will tell me, like he told me the other day, um, like he's asking if he can come over and visit me **E(47.0)** and I said, "Well yeah but, I have to study, so you can bring a book or something so you can work, or whatever"—or, "I only have like an hour like to (unclear) and then we can study or do whatever" **E(47.1)** and he said, "you don't have to be like so organized, just be a little more spontaneous" or whatever ... **E(47.11)** (Barely audible sigh) {**(47.1<C>47.11)**} {**(S₂₃/T48[43.0 ↔ 46.0 ↔ 46.1←THROUGH→47.11])**} And, so I don't know if it's just that I take them too seriously, **E(48.1)** maybe they're just like joking, you know, or maybe they're just saying oh, come on, don't be that way **E(48.11)**. {**48.1<C>48.11**}. And I take it like really seriously, meaning it's like, you know **E(48.1)**. [T: There's something wrong **ACK, EXP(48.1→47.2)**] Yeah **AFF**.

As represented in Figure 7.10, the exploration in response to "Someone's told you you're demanding?" entails discussion of the messages that she's received from different members of her family, and the contexts in which she's received these messages. In the course of the discussion, Eva differentiates the responses of her mother and her father. The salience of the memory of one particular triangular situation, in which Eva (perhaps in high school) is trying to sleep and her father "and his wife" are watching TV, and she asks them to "turn it down," has evidently been coded not only in Eva's mind but also in family lore as paradigmatic evidence that Eva is demanding. Eva also mentions her negotiations over time spent with her cousin, and his responses to her efforts to assert her needs. Having reviewed

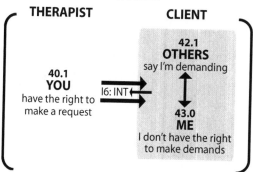

Figure 7.10 Episode 9.

these incidents, she then formulates a synthetic question of whether these family members are engaging in friendly joking, and whether she may be taking it "too seriously." The episode ends with the therapist stating what he thinks is the underlying fear that Eva's expressing in this discussion of her self-image—that "There's something wrong" with her.

Episode 10: Differentiating Requests, Demands, and Sharing Information About Feelings

Eva continues after Episode 9 to try to trace and understand her sense of being too demanding, both by speculating on how much attention she received as an only child, and by describing feedback from at least one boyfriend when she expressed her wishes for his attention. But Episode 10 begins when the therapist again draws on his interpretive framework to try to engage Eva in co-constructing what he sees as an important distinction. This is the distinction between appropriate expressions of feelings and wishes (as he believes may have occurred in her relationship with both father and boyfriend, as well as what occurred with him when Eva expressed the concern that he was bored) and behavior that is "too demanding."

T35: Is there a difference, though, between "I want" **QUES (48.3)** and "I demand"? **QUES (48.31)**

C36: (Blows nose) Well, I think so, **AFF** because, um, you could want ... I think I demand because I don't, I don't want to be talking to someone who isn't interested in what I'm saying, or ... **E(48.32)**

T36: T—To me, to me it would have been demanding if you'd said, "Unless you pay closer attention to me, I'm getting up and leaving." **E/e(48.311)**

C37: (Lots of laughter) See that is something that I could—never do. **O(48.3111)**

T37: That would be demanding **RS(48.311)**

C38: —ever.

T38: Um, if you said, "I would really like for you to pay closer attention to me," that would be a request, you know that would be very reasonable. **E(48.33)** {48.33<C>48.311} It, you have every right to make a request {(S$_{33}$/T49(48.33 ↔ 40.1 ↔ 22.1 ↔ 8.1 ←THROUGH→8.111 ↔ 10.1 ↔ 10.11 ↔ 14.0), you know, and I have every right to say either I can do that, **E(49.1)** or I can't do that **E(49.11)**. Or it's easy for me to do that **E(49.2)** or it's hard for me to do that **E(49.21)** {(S$_{34}$/T50(49.0←THROUGH→49.21)}. And then a step that isn't even making a request is to say, "Gee, I notice I feel bad **E(50.1)** you know, when you look away," if that's what I did **E,TRANS/e(21.22→50.11)**.

C39: No … (very definite tone) **RJ(50.11)**

T39: I still don't know what I, what **REQ/e(50.11)** [C: I'll tell you **AFF**] did OK (laughing good-naturedly) **ACK** cause I'd still like to know that **RS/e(50.11)**. But what, you know, if you say "I feel bad when you do that" **RS/e(50.1)** it isn't saying, "You know that's your problem, you should change" **E(50.111)**. It's just reporting a piece of information that we can then say, "OK, you know, what are we going to do about that?" **E(50.1111)** {50.111<C>50.1111}

C40: Mm, hm. Well, there's two reasons why I …

T40: So that's … so, so reporting information or feelings **E(50.1)** is different from making a request **TRANS/e(48.33→50.2)**.

C41: And different from making a demand **E(48.31→50.3)**.

T41: And making a request **E(50.2)** is different from making a demand **E(50.3)** {E(S$_{35}$/T51[50.1←THROUGH→50.3])}.

C42: The reason why I think that they're all making a demand … (under breath)—or there're two reasons. **RJ(51.0) O(51.1)** One might be because in (EG) people don't say "no" **E(51.11)**.

T42: Don't say "no" **RS(51.11)**, and so if people can't say no to requests, then any request is, is [a demand]…. **RS (51.1)** {S$_{36}$/T52[51.1 ↔ 51.11]}

C43: Is, is … Do you understand? **REQ(ACK)** So like, no, I mean I don't think it would be very, I mean it, I think it's virtually impossible for a (EG) … I mean I'm not saying all (EG's) are the same, but the way I … To get up, "if you don't pay more attention I'll leave," **RS(48.311)** I mean that's like something that just doesn't even cross our minds **E(48.3111)**. So, so, just the fact of like [T: Mm-hm **ACK**] telling you, "oh would you please pay attention to me," **RS(50.2)** means … Or I don't know, since things are not clear you never [T: Mm-hm, mm-hm **ACK**] know exactly, but it could mean, potentially could mean, that look, I think you're not paying attention to me, and (pause) (under breath)—so that's like really bad or whatever. **E(50.21)** And I think that's a demand. And then, and then, I also think that just me mentioning that I'm not satisfied with your reaction **E(50.3)** is also a demand you know {**S₃₇/T53[52 ↔ 50.1←THROUGH→50.3]**}. [T: Mm **ACK**] So, if I don't know if it's culture **TRANS(5.1→53.1)** or person **TRANS(5.2→53.11)** or whatever, but I, I would say that any one of them would be a demand ... (very softly) ... you know {**S₃₈/T54[53.0 ←THROUGH→53.11]**)}.

T43: Well, if it's the culture, you know ... **RS(53.1)**

C44: (Interrupting) When it, it wasn't, when it really wasn't a demand, because the truth is that I—just felt that, and I really wouldn't demand ... I mean, I mean, I really wouldn't demand that. [T: unintelligible] Well I don't know, I ... I guess I'm confused, now. But I mean my intention is not aggressive **RS(12.2, 23.11)**. And I'm always worried [T: Mm-hm **ACK**] that people are gonna think it's aggressive **RS, E(1.1, 2.0)** [T: Mm, hm **ACK**] just because it could be interpreted as being aggressive {**S₃₉/T55[2.0 ↔ 12.2 ↔ 23.11]**}. So, I'm always like saying, "I'm not being aggressive you know, but this.... **E(55.1)** So I'm really sorry about what I'm going to say **E,RS(2.0)**, but this...." and so people (laughter) **RS(2.1)**.

T44: So this is, I mean this is like the original.... This is the original issue we were talking about, {**E(S₄₀/56[55.0 ↔ 55.1 ↔ 4.0)**} and if this is just a cultural ... **E,TRANS(53.1→56.1)** insofar as this is an issue of cultural style that in (EG) one would never make a request, unless it was a demand, so a request translates as a demand **E(52.0→56.11)** [C: I don't know if you can say that generally **Q(52.0)**] and saying "no" is not an option **RS(51.11)**. But if it's something like that, and what you're afraid of is miscommunicating {**E(S₄₁/57[56.0 ←THROUGH→56.11)**}—that you would say, "uh, I want such and such," **E/e(57.1)** and then I would interpret it as a demand when you don't mean to be demanding **E(57.11)** then that's a problem in learning to communicate across the cultures. **E/e(57.111)** {**E(S₄₂/58[57.0 ←THROUGH→57.111)**} But if what you're feeling is that you don't have a right to want ... that you're bad if you want **E(49.3)**, that's more independent than how we communicate **E/e(58.1)** {**S₄₃/59[49.3 ↔ 56.0 ↔ 58.1]**}.

C45: Again I think it's both things. You know, I think one part is maybe a miscommunication problem and another part is that I think ... that I'm not sure that I have the right to demand, you know? {**S₄₄/60[59.0 ↔ 58.0]**} So I'll tell exactly what happened, and

why ... **RESP(50.11)** [T: (very softly) Yeah **ACK**] C: And, and
this is also very embarrassing for me so it's hard for me to tell
RS(12.23, 12.2). Because I think it's a natural thing that ... Uh
oh, I'm feeling very embarrassed about having to tell you this
RS(12.23) (laughter and a small scream/sigh).

T45: That's okay, I'm with you. **SUPP/e**

C46: Um, I guess the only thing that I noticed was that you weren't excited
O(12.4) [T: Mm-hm **ACK**] about what I was sorta like ... yeah.
[T: Mm-hm **ACK**]. I mean like, you were looking into my eyes
and stuff **E(12.41)**, but sort of like leaning back and just passively listening. I think, I guess I sensed some kind of pass ...
p ... p ... passivity? Or ...? Instead of like active listening which
I guess is something that you can't really explain, but it's something like, something. I guess it's expression, or something
E(12.4<C>12.41). And then I was thinking, you, well ... maybe
he's tired you know. 3:00 in the afternoon, is sort of like tired. I
know I do, I go to class sometimes at 3:00, and I'm like ... you
know, I'm listening to what they're saying but, I don't really
feel like dealing with it, because, whatever, just cause I'm tired
{S_{45}/61[12.4 ↔ 12.41]}. So as I was saying, you know, he has all
the right to be tired **E(61.1)**. And that's why I feel, that I can't
demand that you always like you know have all your attention,
and like always be totally active in our conversations **RS(14.0)**
and stuff. {S_{46}/62[61.0 ↔ 61.1 ↔ 14.0])}

T46: But, but you can notice if you feel a difference. **O(RS/e(50.1)**
{62.0<C>50.1})

C47: Well yeah **AFF**, but I think that, that you have the right to **E(62.1)**.
And I feel very bad to tell you know, "Well I think you're fall-
ing asleep or whatever," you know. Not exactly that but ...
TRANS(12.23→62.11) So ...

T47: You can say, you can say, "Hey, I feel a difference today"
EXP/e(50.1→62.111) and I could say, "Yeah, I'm a little tired
today" **E/e(62.1111)** and we'd both understand what's going on
E/e (62.2) {S_{47}/63[62.0←THROUGH→62.2]}).

The dialogue in Episode 10 moves through three basic themes, each of
which is represented in Figure 7.11. In the first, in an act of interpretation (Sc I6), the therapist offers a synthesis (**S36/T51.0**) by differentiating
and comparing three communicative strategies: demands (**48.31, 48.311**),
requests (**48.33**), and statements of feeling (**50.1**). The therapist offers these
strategies with the hope that the client would be able to appropriate (at
least) the last one—stating feelings—as a nonintrusive way to express
her wishes and desires. Restating her prior assertion that members of her

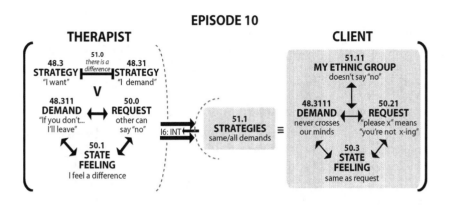

Figure 7.11 Episode 10.

ethnic group "do not say no," in a parallel act of synthesis (**S37/T53**), Eva rejects the therapist's differentiations with the statement that "they're all a demand" (**51.1**). She follows this with the statement "I don't know if it's culture or person or whatever, but I, I would say that any one of them would be a demand" (**S38/T54**).

The client follows up her invocation of the culture–person distinction by saying that "my intention is not aggressive. And I'm always worried … that people are gonna think it's aggressive" (**S39/T55**). This statement prompts a shift in the focus of the discussion. The therapist links the ongoing conversation back to the issues that started the session: "This is the original issue we were talking about.…" (**S40/T56**). In response, the client reiterates and reframes the position that she articulated in C3: "I think one part is maybe a miscommunication problem and another part is that I think … that I'm not sure that I have the right to demand, you know?" (**S44/T60**). The session ends as the client finally discloses what the therapist did to make her feel as if he were bored. In the context of a high level of emotional support (Sc A5), the client indicated, "You weren't excited" (**12.4**). She immediately tempered this statement by asserting the conflicting view that "I can't demand that you always like you know have all your attention" (**S46/T62, 62.0<C>12.4**). The therapist ends the session with an attempt to transcend the conflict by saying, "You can say … 'Hey, I feel a difference today' … and we'd both understand what's going on" (**S47/T63.0**).

The therapist's final comment, "we'd both understand what's going on," represents an important synthesis with respect to the entire session, and not only a concluding of his hypothetical playing out of what could have happened if Eva had expressed her feelings of disappointment as soon as she observed them. This synthesis is important because it simultaneously (1) names what *has indeed occurred* over the course of this very painful critical incident, (2) asserts the potential *value of the client's adding to her repertoire* the alternative response to her accustomed interpersonal style (which the therapist has articulated as an alternative and which the client and therapist have enacted together), and (3) indicates how this *alternative transcends the "limitation" to her own interpersonal style*, which the client herself has identified in Episode 8, Utterance C28, Element 29.1.

Quantifying Developmental Changes Across the Session

Figure 7.12 provides a structural representation of the major developmental transformations that occur over the course of the "critical incident" psychotherapy session. Figure 7.12 displays a quantitative analysis of changes in the structural complexity of the client's representations over the course of the psychotherapy session. It also tracks changes in the level of scaffolding provided by the therapist over the course of the session. The bottom panel shows changes in the *number of meaning elements coordinated* by the client across conversational turns. As is typical in analyses of developmental change, Figure 7.12 indicates that developmental changes that occurred across the session were nonlinear and dynamic. The curve rises and falls throughout the session, reaching its highest peak in Episode 8. Analysis of the meaning of these dynamic changes is aided by identifying how developmental complexity changes over the course of specific episodes.

The session begins productively. During the first two episodes, the client is able to construct meaning structures composed of between 8 and 10 elements. The size of the meaning structures diminishes abruptly; this shift co-occurs with the client interrupting the flow of dialogue and expressing her concern regarding the experience (hers and the therapist's) of the therapy session. The drop in structural complexity marks a transition to a lower level of structural complexity as the client redirects her attention from building novel meanings to the enactment that is occurring between the client and therapist. As such, the drop in complexity reflects a shift from one task to a second task. The developmental trajectory that accompanied activity on the first task was interrupted as the dyad turned their attention to a different task. At this point, constructive activity began anew at a lower developmental level. The complexity of the client's meaning structures begins to rise again only at the end of Episode 3, after a period during which the client and therapist made a series of differentiations that culminated in the meaning structure constructed in C11.

During Episode 4, with much emotion, the client discloses her confession (i.e., "I thought you were bored"). During this period of time, the therapist supports the client in articulating elements of her fear about appearing aggressive. After making a series of differentiations in the client's experience, in Episode 5 (C17), with minimal support of the therapist, the level of complexity of the client's meaning structure rises as she coordinates a series of previously constructed meaning elements into a synthesis

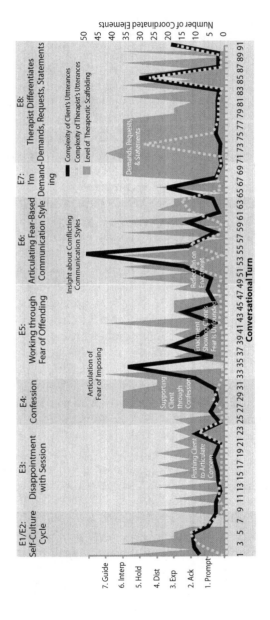

Figure 7.12 Quantitative analysis of the development of Eva's representation of her communicative style.

communicating her fear of imposing and appearing aggressive to the therapist. The level of complexity rises and falls throughout Episodes 5, 6, and 7 as the dyad explores different aspects of the client's fear of offending others.

The developmental curve reaches its peak in Episode 8 (in C28). This is the point at which the client constructs her grand synthesis—a representation of the limitations of her customary communication style and its contrast to the novel style enacted with the therapist (see Figures 7.9a and 7.9b). This achievement was accomplished through the intercoordination of several previously constructed differentiations and syntheses and the application of her new insight to understanding both successful and unsuccessful interactions in the present and past. After the construction of this core novel synthesis, the developmental level of the client's representations again drops precipitously. Once the core synthesis is constructed, the elements of this insight become the focus of attention. This process begins to occur in Episode 9. In this episode, the therapist attempts to strengthen the client's novel sense of being able to "express feelings" in difficult interactions by saying, "You have the right to make a request."

In rejecting this remark, the developmental level of the client's meaning making rises as she articulates an antithesis to the grand synthesis that she had just constructed. Her antithesis was organized around the idea that others in her family have a generalized sense that she is demanding. Thereupon, the dialogue shifts toward efforts to articulate the foundations of this belief. The shift in attention resulted in another decline in the level of complexity of the client's meaning structures as the therapist and client work together in making a series of differentiations to explore the foundations of this belief. The developmental level rises again as the client synthesizes a complex representation of why requests, demands, and expressions of feelings are all demands. Thereafter, the level of complexity fell again as the conversation shifted to the question of what the therapist did to make the client feel he was bored. In this way, after having successfully constructed a higher-order synthesis that worked to incorporate and resolve multiple conflicts articulated throughout the session, the client's insight itself became a focus of discussion. As a result, the level of complexity of the client's meaning making fell as new conflicts (or new versions of existing conflicts) were identified and explored, preparing a new foundation for the construction and coordination of still higher order meaning structures in subsequent sessions.

Figure 7.12 also tracks changes in the highest level of scaffolding (support) provided by the therapist in any given conversational turn over the course of the critical incident. The therapist's level of support ranged from Level 2 (i.e., acknowledgment and encouragement) through Level 6 (i.e., interpretation). During the first half of the session, the modal level of scaffolding that the therapist provided was Level 4 (i.e., distancing); during the second half of the session, the modal level of scaffolding was Level 6 (i.e., interpretation). In addition, Figure 7.12 tracks changes in the complexity of the therapist's utterances. As indicated in Figure 7.12, with exceptions, the level of complexity of the therapist's utterances does not generally rise above the client's complexity. This is especially the case for the first half of the session in which the therapist primarily used various forms of attentional support to scaffold the development of the client's thinking. The level of complexity of the therapist's utterances increased during the second half of the session, when the therapist took a more active role in offering his interpretations of issues raised by the client and of the extended enactment that occurred in the middle portion of the session.

The Impact of the "Critical Incident"

According to the therapist, the critical incident functioned as a turning point for the client. The client was able to extend the insights and novel skills that she developed in the session to situations in her other relationships. Much of her work in subsequent months continued along these lines. For example, in her interactions with her father, there was a significant change. Eva reported that her relationship with her father improved over the months that followed. Rather than fearing and avoiding discussions because of her difficulty in responding to his expressions of feeling, she was able to actively participate in such discussions by sharing heartfelt feelings of her own. Whereas earlier there had been something in her father's communication that Eva hadn't been able to assimilate, now she saw an example of how experiencing and expressing difficult feelings of her own and others represent real alternatives to trying to carefully manage those feelings.

Further, Eva saw that overreliance on the latter approach had contributed both to her decision-making paralysis and to barriers to intimate relationships. As mentioned earlier, as a result of Eva's travels and her efforts to avoid saying hurtful things, there were three young men in three different countries who all had the expectation that Eva was going to marry them after her graduation. As the therapy continued through the spring of Eva's senior year, fears of facing these young men, as well as her sense that particular choices might disappoint parents, teachers, and others who cared about her, made the prospect of graduating a threatening one for Eva.

In the months that followed, Eva impressed both the therapist and herself with her way of dealing with this threatening prospect. Part of her work entailed challenging but successful, according to Eva, conversations with all three young men involved. These conversations enabled her to graduate and to move forward into the rest of her life, without having destroyed these valued relationships (as she feared), but also with the sense that they no longer had "strings attached"—a feeling that Eva experienced as "liberating." She also used the therapy relationship to express her own feelings about different career paths, and to separate these feelings from the expectations of others. Ultimately, she chose to begin a PhD program in her country of origin, and as of last report, during her second year in the program, felt very good about this decision.

Eva's Therapy: Implications for Understanding Psychotherapy as a Developmental Process

At the most general level, this case analysis illustrates the central claim of this book (which we propose any case would illustrate)—that it is possible to track developmental changes in psychotherapy. Furthermore, one way of understanding what all successful cases of psychotherapy have in common is that they can be seen to foster development, and in any given case, it is "what develops" that is at the core of the therapeutic value. As indicated above, one function of the DAPP analysis is to provide a set of tools for rigorously analyzing the nature and developmental course of psychotherapy regardless of the therapist's theoretical perspective. The DAPP analysis also clarifies (a) how the therapist's specific actions contributed to developmental movement that occurred within all three dialectics of attention, interpretation, and enactment, which we propose to be the common therapeutic processes across all psychotherapy cases; and (b) that it was the combination of movement within all three dialectics that contributed to the novel syntheses within the critical incident that represented "what developed of therapeutic value" in Eva's case.

Thus, we are offering the DAPP approach as a kind of metatheoretical perspective; within the context of our coactive systems framework for understanding development, DAPP also provides a set of tools for understanding the role that a therapist's theoretical perspective plays over the course of psychotherapy. It is important here to restate that we offer the DAPP framework neither as an alternative theory of therapy nor as a novel therapeutic technique. The DAPP framework *does not* and *cannot* replace practitioners' conceptual and technical tools for conceptualizing and conducting their practices. From our perspective, the therapist's conceptual framework for guiding his or her practice, whether it is an eclectic or largely implicit one and whether it includes one or more formal theoretical or technical "approaches to psychotherapy" to which the therapist subscribes, is essential; we see it as playing a crucial *mediating* role in guiding the therapist's choices of how to respond to a client. Rather than replacing the therapist's theories, the DAPP system provides a set of reflective tools for stepping back and understanding how the therapist's theories function or operate in the course of psychotherapy. From the point of view of "third parties"[6] observing and analyzing the psychotherapy process using the DAPP method, the therapists' understandings (including their "theories of psychotherapy") constitute one factor among many that needs to be understood to make sense of what is occurring in the interaction and why. Clients' meaning making, and the dynamic co-constructive interaction among clients and therapists as coactive systems, constitute other such factors, and the focal questions asked by the DAPP method include the following: (a) What developmental resources is a therapist offering, and what, if any, use of them is a client able to make? (b) Is a therapist able to adjust the level and forms of scaffolding offered, in response to (1) clients' successes and failures in being able to use what the therapist has offered, (2) clients' expressed requests for resources or invitations to join in therapeutic dialectics, and (3) emergent opportunities within the psychotherapy process? (c) How does the therapist's theoretical perspective influence choices of which resources he or she provides? And (d) is the therapeutic process working? If so, what is working? If not, why not?

In the case of Eva, as indicated above, the therapist is one of the book's coauthors. As such, the therapist's theoretical perspective has been articulated at length in the first section of this book. In this concluding section of our efforts to articulate what can be learned from the case of Eva, we examine how one particular aspect of the therapist's theoretical perspective functioned in the course of Eva's therapy.

The first author (Basseches, 1993) initially reported upon this case to illustrate an important aspect of his personal orientation to practice: that it was particularly important for the therapist to be responsive to "emergent disequilibrium" within the therapeutic relationship. This orientation was based not only on the threat such disequilibrium, if unaddressed, could pose to the effectiveness and continuation of therapy, but also, as illustrated in the quotation on page 162 on the developmental potential that such disequilibrium itself contained.

In a therapy relationship, the parties go through a series of transformations in the nature and quality of the relationship. Not only do these transformations *support* the client's emerging developmental needs, but also the challenges of transforming the relationship may themselves represent developmental opportunities. According to the therapist, in successful psychotherapy, the therapist and client must first co-construct a successful initial alliance. In so doing, a way of relating is established in which developmental movement can occur. The therapist offers resources; the client

---

[6] The term *third parties* may include researchers, supervisors, or therapists themselves when they are using the DAPP approach as a means of achieving a more critically reflective stance toward their own work.

either uses or does not use those resources. However, as the relationship evolves, in order for *more* of the client's experience, both outside of and within the therapy, to be addressed within the relationship, the form of the relationship must expand and be transformed to make room. Because this "grow or die" dynamic applies to therapy relationships as well as to organisms, communities, corporations, and so on, emergent tensions can be expected to arise in therapeutic relationships, and may be addressed, ignored, or recognized and put aside. If they are put aside, they can result in unresolved disequilibrium in the therapeutic relationship; if they are addressed directly, they can often operate as a powerful template for personal and interpersonal development.

In the case of Eva, the initial alliance was one in which the client's hope (for the therapist to play the "role" of "my mother") was acknowledged, but "countered" with an offer of more limited attentional support. Eva appeared to make good use of this resource in constructing a "theory of herself," in building self-confidence, and in achieving a temporary resolution to her early questions about what the therapist would offer. However, as the therapy progressed, her expressions of loneliness continued, and she occasionally voiced continuing questions about the nature of the therapeutic relationship. As Eva's self-reliance and self-confidence increased, the therapist began to offer more frequent interpretations (along with handshakes). However, in Session 14 the therapist experienced what he noticed to be a sharp contrast from the early pattern. This reflected his orientation toward recognizing and addressing "emergent disequilibrium." He recognized that he had moved from a stance organized primarily around providing attentional support to one in which the dialectic of interpretation was central to the movement of the session. The client was able to make effective use of the therapist's "spring-loaded knob" metaphor to construct a novel synthesis that helped her to modulate her anxiety about the dance and to approach it in a new way. The client reported a deep sense of satisfaction (shared by the therapist) with the new interpretive and emotional tone that occurred in Session 14. But the therapist's theoretical assumptions suggested a need to not only recognize but also address the change.

The therapist therefore began Session 15 with an orientation toward returning to his earlier emphasis on the dialectic of attentional support, while being "on the lookout" for opportunities to explore the dialectic of enactment as it was evolving within the therapeutic relationship. When the client, in Episode 3, interrupted her ongoing discussion with a self-critical comment that expressed concern about whether the therapist was "getting any message," the therapist sensed the client's discomfort as a manifestation of emergent disequilibrium and chose to ask, "What are you feeling right now?" From the point of view of the therapist's meaning making, this response was shaped by both (a) his internal interpretation of Eva's comment as possibly indicative of her discomfort and (b) his having entered the session with the idea in mind that there was something important to understand regarding what happened in Session 14, and how his relationship with Eva might be changing. From the point of view of the DAPP analysis, the therapist's question represents a choice to "switch gears" in response to an emergent opportunity, and to offer resources to the dialectic of enactment—an invitation to look to present novel experience to generate opportunities for development.

The therapist tells us in his narrative that he viewed Eva's subsequent responses as expressions of a wish to be extricated from an uncomfortable situation, rather than to fully explore and express her feelings. Nonetheless, he experienced himself as both "relentless" and "supportive" in inviting further exploration of the nature of her feelings, which he interpreted as disappointment—an interpretation that she affirmed. From the point of view of the DAPP analysis, when very painful feelings came up in Eva's efforts to speak about her disappointment with the therapist's reaction to what she was attempting to "present," the therapist offered a variety of forms of attentional support. In combination, these forms of support helped Eva to express these feelings. In expressing her feelings rather than managing them while avoiding acknowledging them, she was engaging in novel behavior that was antithetical to her accustomed interpersonal style. Thus, in the therapist's choice to be "relentless" and "supportive," he was essentially scaffolding the expression of novel behavior on Eva's part, rather than colluding with her accustomed process of "managing while avoiding" uncomfortable feelings. In this way, the enactment that occurred between the therapist and client provided a medium for constructing a novel experience. Further reflection upon this experience allowed Eva to synthesize representations of the limitations of her customary style of communication and the possibility of enacting novel forms of communication both in and outside of the therapy sessions.

In sum, our analysis makes evident the roles that the dialectics of attention and interpretation, and the resources that the therapist contributed to these dialectics, played in contributing to the development that we have tracked within the session. However, as is signaled by the standstill that the developmental process reaches at the beginning of Episode 3, the dialectic of enactment also plays an essential role in this developmental process. Beyond providing a system for tracking how the episode-by-episode offering and use of therapeutic resources undergird the developmental changes described, analysis of psychotherapeutic discourse in terms of the dialectics of attention, interpretation, and enactment also provides tools for describing how the therapist's theoretical perspective operates over the course of therapy.

In this case, the therapist's perspective first, in the co-construction of a therapeutic alliance, mediated his observing but resisting the initial pull for a praising and collaborating senior mentor (like Eva's mother) that he felt from Eva. Then it mediated his recognition and embrace of the potential for collaborative meaning making that a therapy relationship offers. Finally it mediated his recognition and exploitation of the opportunity for mutually self-conscious understanding and transformation of the dynamics of the therapy relationship that the changes leading up to the "critical incident" offered. To restate, we see the therapist's theoretical perspective as playing a *mediating* role in what he brought to his interaction with Eva. If Eva had not been able to use the resources he offered, he would have had to recognize this and adjust in order for the therapy to succeed. As Basseches (1997b) has discussed at length elsewhere, in some cases the therapist's theoretical perspective may facilitate such adjustment, whereas in other cases it may obstruct such adjustment. For this reason, reflective frameworks such as DAPP, along with reflective contexts such as consultation and supervision, may play important roles in increasing success rates for psychotherapy.

CHAPTER **8**

The Lady Cloaked in Fog
Developing a Construction of the
Therapist as a "Harbor Light"

In this chapter, we extend the developmental analysis of psychotherapy process (DAPP) to the analysis of a case of McCullough's (1999) short-term "anxiety-regulating" dynamic therapy. McCullough bases her approach on an integration of principles from psychoanalytic, cognitive-behavioral, and experiential therapies. Central to the model is the idea of an affect phobia. McCullough (1999) has suggested that many individuals who seek psychotherapy fear experiencing their own feelings. Since McCullough's work, a related literature on "experiential avoidance" has burgeoned (e.g., Chawla & Ostafin, 2007; Kashdan, Barrios, Forsyth, & Steger, 2006; Tull & Roemer, 2007). In McCullough's view, different clients exhibit fears of different emotions. For example, individuals may experience fear of feeling anger, grief, closeness, or positive feelings about the self. An individual's avoidance of different classes of strong emotions impairs the capacity for adaptive activity in the world. McCullough's therapeutic approach entails combining increased exposure to the avoided feelings with a careful use of the therapeutic relationship for anxiety regulation to facilitate tolerance of the exposure. In what follows, we examine the case of the "Lady Cloaked in Fog" (McCullough,

1999),[1] a 42-year-old depressed woman who exhibited difficulty experiencing feelings of closeness.

We will provide a detailed DAPP analysis of the client's development over the course of a single pivotal session of short-term dynamic therapy, tracking microdevelopmental changes in the client's capacity to experience feelings of closeness with the therapist, as well as the therapeutic processes that spurred these transformations. We also use the DAPP framework to elucidate the work done in prior sessions that provided a foundation for the pivotal session.

Case Background

Identifying the client as "The Lady Cloaked in Fog," McCullough (1999, p. 40) used the following case material as an illustration of her own therapeutic approach, which she described as "an 'anxiety-regulating' model of short-term dynamic psychotherapy." McCullough provided the description that follows below of the client and her presenting problem, the course of treatment, and the role of the "pivotal session" which we will analyze in depth to illustrate the DAPP method. She also mentions the difficulties of the previous sessions when the therapist "did not have a clear idea about how to proceed" and the "client became more despairing and suicidal." After the analysis of the development occurring in the "pivotal session," we will use the DAPP method to consider the nature of the difficulty in the previous sessions.

McCullough (1999) described the client as follows:

> The Lady Cloaked in Fog was a 42-year-old unmarried female who had been in some form of therapy for the last 24 years. She had been seriously and intractably depressed all of her adult life. During treatment we realized that she was a therapy "junkie" who never really wanted to get better or take on more responsibility in a relationship than she had with her therapist. She felt she did not matter to

---

[1] The authors would like to acknowledge our tremendous gratitude to Dr. McCullough for making available to us to analyze the videotapes of her work with this client. In this book, we are presenting a framework and method that we claim permits analysis of the common processes that characterize all psychotherapy. But it will only be possible to adequately demonstrate the validity of the claim, as well as the usefulness of the methods, if courageous therapists like Dr. McCullough are willing to share the raw data of their work with others for purposes of examination. We hope that Dr. McCullough will serve as a role model for others, in both her generosity and her courage.
[From McCullough, L. (1999). Short-term psychodynamic therapy as a form of desensitization: Treating affect phobias. *In Session: Psychotherapy in Practice, 4*(4), 35–53. Reprinted with permission of John Wiley & Sons, Inc.]

anyone—and this resulted in chronic suicidal feelings. She repeatedly said, I do not "want to be here," and felt cheated when medical tests would show her to be healthy because she so desperately wanted her "ticket out." She referred to herself as a "toxic waste dump." When her younger and more favored sister died, she felt that she should have died instead to take the burden off her depressed mother. She was socially isolated and had chronic job conflicts, resulting in having to leave many jobs.

She had been non-responsive to medication. A pharmacology case conference was devoted to her case with the resolution that no medication was workable with her. Her pharmacologist told her she did not need any more individual therapy, and that she should "quit her bellyaching, and get on with her life." This indictment felt devastating to her—especially because her therapist had just moved away. Because I had seen her for some consultation sessions many years earlier and had consulted with her therapist, she came to me for treatment.

Her presenting problems included: (i) depression—unresponsive to medication; (ii) a wish to die, and (iii) chronic conflicts with bosses. All problems received a rating of "severe." She met criteria for Depressive Disorder NOS, and met criteria for 43 Axis II items (that is, a moderate to high number of personality disorder criteria, which indicates high levels of defensiveness). She met criteria for personality diagnoses of Obsessive, Depressive, Borderline, and Schizotypal with traits in most other categories. Her admission Global Assessment Form Rating was 42, reflecting "serious impairment in functioning." (pp. 40–41)

The initial course of treatment lasted 64 sessions, a more extended period of time than is typical of "short-term" treatment. The therapist made the judgment that there was a need for extensive work to rebuild the client's sense of self in relation to others before addressing experiences of grief and anger that were the result of past relationships. According to the therapist,

Improvement in the first fifteen sessions was less than optimal because I did not have a clear idea about how to proceed. The client became more despairing and suicidal. However, after a pivotal session, I call the Harbor Light session (no. 16), she began to feel that she mattered to people, and she began to slowly improve. In sessions 20 to 30 she focused on mattering and building some new relationships in her life. During sessions 30 to 50 she made many life changes; became less isolated—building friendships and moving to a better place. She stopped group therapy, joined a book club, took up sculpture as a hobby, and began taking art classes. However, she was unable to face the grief of her childhood or her feelings of anger—though I repeatedly addressed these issues. Then between sessions 50 and 53, strong feelings of grief emerged. Following this, in sessions 54 to 60, she was able to access angry feelings for the first time and began to stand up for herself.

At one year after termination the client's functioning continued to improve—with many indications of deep changes in character structure. She had made friends, and had become quite close to them. She had totally changed the nature of her work relationships, and now was on excellent terms with the boss she had once hated. She had occasional bouts of depression, but after a couple off [sic] booster sessions could quickly return to stable functioning. (p. 42)

Developmental Analysis of the Pivotal "Harbor Lights" Session

In presenting our analysis, we will begin with a broad overview of the major microdevelopmental changes that occurred over the course of the pivotal "harbor light" session (Session 16) of therapy. Second, we will provide a detailed analysis that tracks, episode by episode, the microdevelopmental movements through which the overall novel syntheses in this session were co-constructed. Following the therapist's naming of the session, we give the name *harbor light insight* to the meaning-making structure that organizes this set of developmental syntheses. In a final section of our session analysis using DAPP, we will discuss the developmental relationship between the initial conflict introduced and the harbor light insight through which the initial conflict was resolved.

Overview: The Development of the Harbor Light Insight

Figure 8.1 provides a representation of nine episodes of interaction that occurred over the course of the harbor light session. At the end of this pivotal session, imagining herself as the captain of a ship in stormy and foggy waters, the client was able to represent the therapist as a "harbor light"—a beacon whose "beaming light" reflects the caring feelings of the therapist onshore. By invoking the image of her therapist as a "harbor light," the client is able to feel that she matters to her therapist, even as she navigates her way offshore through the foggy waters of everyday life. Each episode depicted in Figure 8.1 reflects a step in the development of the harbor light insight.

In Episode 1, the client introduced a conflict in her experience that became the focus of the remainder of the session. With deep sadness, the client begins the episode by saying that "my *vote* matters (thesis), but *I* don't matter (antithesis)." Over the course of the episode, the client is able to synthesize multiple examples of each pole of this initial conflict into a higher-order representation of the conflict, "Onstage [at work, doing for

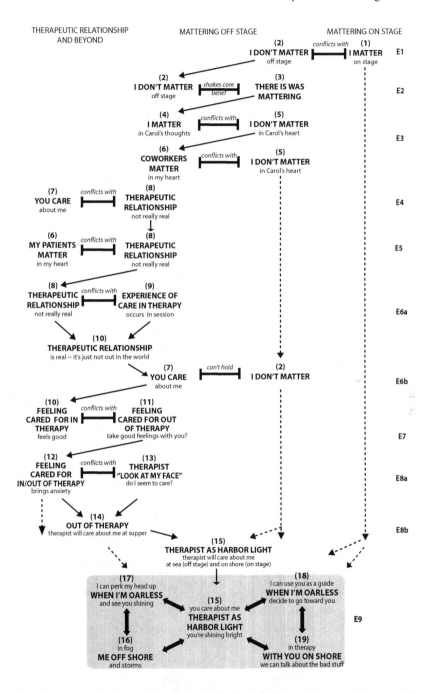

Figure 8.1 Overview of the structural transformations involved in the development of the harbor light insight for the Lady Cloaked in Fog.

others] I matter, but offstage [at home, alone] I don't matter." In Episode 2, building upon this distinction, the client then articulates a counterexample (antithesis) to her statement that "offstage I don't matter." Specifically, she indicates, "It blows my mind to think that there were days ... when I'd go home and like I thought that you and Carol [a previous therapist] were talking on the phone [about me]." When asked to explain the meaning of this counterexample, the client was able to represent the conflict as a clash between "feeling as though I don't matter" and "there I was mattering."

In Episode 3, the therapist and client work together to deal with the disequilibrium that accompanied this conflict. In Episode 3a, probing the client's sense that "there I was mattering [offstage]," the therapist asked the client if, when she was home alone, she felt that she mattered to her previous therapist—that she was in the therapist's "thoughts and in her heart?" The client responded by making a further differentiation in her experience: "Even just that question ... thoughts yes, but heart? Oh well, I don't know about heart." In making this expression, the client creates a distinction within her feelings of "mattering offstage"—her therapist may think about her, but doesn't necessarily care about her in her heart. In Episode 3b, the therapist invites the client to consider that it is possible for people who have primarily professional relationships to care about each other when they are "offstage." In responding, the client is able to acknowledge that when she herself is not at work or on duty, she both thinks about and cares emotionally for patients who may be "hurting" or "in pain." This realization stands in conflict with her previous doubts that her previous therapist—someone with whom the client has a professional but not personal relationship—can nonetheless care deeply about the client.

Episode 4 represents a continued exploration of this theme. Acknowledging that a therapist (an "onstage" relationship) may be able to care about a client (when the therapist or client is "offstage"), the client questions whether the therapist–client relationship can be considered a "real" relationship. Thus, the notion that the therapist–client relationship is not a "real" relationship stands in conflict with the therapist's expression that both the therapist and the client's past therapist experienced feelings of genuine care for the client. In the dialogue that follows (in Episodes 4, 5, and 6), the therapist plays the role of directing the client's attention to (a) the feelings involved in and challenged by the therapist's expressions of care, (b) the client's attempts to avoid these feelings, and (c) the feelings that arise as the therapist challenges the client's marginalization of the therapy relationship as unreal. In so doing, the therapist again invokes the client's own feelings of being able to care about patients in her heart when she is "offstage." This statement then stands in conflict with the client's sense that the therapy relationship is unreal. By the end of Episode 5, the client is able to make use of the therapist's resources to come to the realization that to experience herself as being loved makes her feel uncomfortable; she says, "I could go to beating up on myself and making it wrong (to entertain feelings that I matter)."

A pivotal realization is constructed in Episode 6a as the initial formulation of "mattering versus not mattering" is juxtaposed with all the discomfort, vulnerability, and risks of disappointment involved in allowing oneself to feel cared for. As the exploration of these latter feelings are very new to the client, the current therapeutic relationship provides an avenue of exploration of new experiences. Thus, "enactment" as a form of therapeutic contribution to development assumes a more central role in the therapeutic process. The relationship with the therapist allows for a fuller development of the client's repertoire for experiencing and expressing care, and the vulnerabilities and self-doubts that go with it. As a result, a major synthesis occurs in the client as she again asserts the unreality of the therapist–client relationship:

C: You're telling me that this is real, and I'm saying, "Well, it is real and I can really feel it." Oh, but then it's also not really real and, in that it's bounded.… You're not going to invite me for dinner, and I'm not going to invite you for dinner. You know.

T: That's right. Our experience will be here.

C: Yeah, right and that is very real, and I don't mean … but it is also not out in the world. So my real thing will … my next challenge will be to find whatever thing is here out in the world.

In this remarkable yet subtle exchange, the client's characterization of the therapy relationship as unreal is challenged by the therapist's statement that "yes, our experience will be here." The client's response reflects her first genuine acceptance of the therapist's expression of care. This is made possible by the client's construction of a novel synthesis, namely, that *the therapy relationship* is *real; it's simply not "out in the world."* This synthesis leads to the client's deeper realization of this contradiction: "I mean, I can't … I can't hold feeling good about being cared about and thought about and feeling like I don't matter. They're just … I can't hold those two things at the same time." In so doing, Episode 6b proceeds as a revisiting and restating of—indeed, a dwelling in—the conflict, this time with a full acknowledgment of the risks and the discomfort, both in the therapy relationship and in the rest of life, of allowing herself to matter in relationships (and allowing relationships to matter to her).

Episode 7 begins as the client and therapist explore the positive feelings that are engendered in the client by her ability to accept feelings of care from the therapist. The therapist then asks the client if she would be able to "take these feelings with you" outside of therapy sessions. This creates a conflict between the "safety" of the therapeutic session and the anxiety, fear, and doubt engendered by invoking the therapist's care outside of therapy sessions. This conflict provides the foundation for a novel synthesis that arises over the course of Episode 8.

Episode 8 involves the articulation of the synthesis that was sought throughout the previous episodes. All three conflicts—(a) the conflict between mattering onstage/at work and not mattering offstage/at home, (b) the conflict between allowing oneself to experience mattering in relationship and relying on the old onstage/offstage construction, and (c) the conflict between being supported in developing new capacities in therapy and the demands of facing emotional challenges in the rest of life—are organized in the novel synthesis that is created in Episode 8. Interestingly, the therapist and client appear to be working in a more integrative, collaborative, and interdependent fashion, in the very process of co-constructing and articulating this synthesis.

Episode 8 begins as the client articulates the anxiety, fear, and doubt that she experiences as she contemplates bringing the therapist's feelings of care outside of the therapy session. To counter these feelings, the therapist works to make the client *feel* the depth of the therapist's care. She prompts the client to look at her (beaming) face, and says, "If you really look at my face, [do] I seem like I enjoy seeing you feel joy [about my feelings of care]?" In this context, in being able to accept these feelings of care by the therapist, the client constructs a novel synthesis in which she is able to imagine that the therapist continues to care about her when the therapist is home at supper (offstage):

C: So, I would imagine that you're sitting down at dinner and you would feel good about the session and that you would hope and wonder how I was doing. And you would want [speaking very haltingly here] for me, that I go to group and do my work there knowing that I matter at least to you [nervous laugh].

Episode 8b builds further on this novel synthesis. The episode begins with a statement consisting of both some words of the therapist and some words of the client. Neither party's words are very intelligible without those of the other. But together they create a powerful metaphor describing the role that the client's experience of, and with, the therapist is now playing in the client's psychic life.

T: That I would be ...
C: And it's all mine. One harbor light!

The harbor light metaphor begins to bring together a variety of strands in the microdevelopmental process. Throughout the remainder of the episode, therapist and client continue to collaborate in (a) fleshing out the meaning of the metaphor of the therapist's care as a harbor light for the client, and (b) bringing the metaphor to bear on the various other aspects of her life that the client has been discussing. The final structure of the harbor light insight is depicted in Figure 8.1 (Episode 9). The client represents herself as rowing through foggy and stormy seas and the therapist as a harbor light. As a harbor light, the therapist provides a source of stable beams of light (care) that are available whether or not the client is onstage or offstage (onshore or offshore). When the client feels oarless (helpless) in foggy seas (experiencing depression and feelings of not mattering), she can invoke the therapist's care, as represented by the light beaming onshore. The client can then decide whether to move toward the light onshore, or to use the light to support her independent attempts to navigate through the stormy seas herself.

The Microdevelopment of the Harbor Light Insight

Using the overview of the session provided in the previous section as a roadmap, we now move to a more detailed look at each episode of this pivotal session. We will illustrate the DAPP method's major coding categories for identifying how therapists do or don't contribute to the ultimate creation of novel developmental syntheses, such as the harbor light representation, that address clients' adaptive challenges. Although we focus on DAPP's major categories, for the sake of easier reading we omit the rigorous detailed coding process for tracking (a) action or meaning elements and microdevelopment in the relationships among them, as well as (b) individual discursive acts and the changes in level of scaffolding in the relationship that they reflect. In this chapter, our emphasis is on how DAPP analysis can shed light on particular cases and the common dialectical-developmental processes that exist across cases. In contrast, we provided the detailed coding for Chapter 7 to offer readers a model that they could subject to critical scrutiny for the rigorous use of DAPP methods.

Episode 1: Mattering "Onstage" Versus "Offstage"   The client begins the episode by expressing a differentiation between the ways in which the client feels she matters, and the sense in which she feels she doesn't matter.

C1: Essentially me, my vote matters, but *I don't matter* … the things I can do, and um, changes I can make and uh stuff I do to make the world a better place.

T1: Your actions matter.

C2: My actions matter and stuff but …

T2: I know, uh-huh. But there is a part of you that doesn't [feel you matter]. It's important … because your actions are you, too. But something you were saying, the core of you, the feeling of like of you, your feelings don't matter. I'm just trying to narrow it down.

C3: Yeah. I guess that's it. It's like I, it's like when I'm at work, I matter, and when I go home, am by myself, I don't matter. It's sort of on or off. Um, onstage or offstage.

A detailed DAPP analysis of the ways in which the client made use of the resources offered by the therapist was provided earlier when this initial episode was used as an exemplar of our coding process in Chapter 6 (see Figure 6.1). At this juncture, we note the ways in which constructive activity on the part of the client was supported by the therapist's provision of attentional support and interpretation. The client offered the initial conflict between "my vote matters," and "I don't matter." The therapist, in acts of restatement and interpretation ("Your actions matter ... but your feelings don't"), offers an alternative way of framing the client's stated conflict. In C3, the client abstracts across the various concrete examples of "mattering" (i.e., "my vote," "the changes I make," "what I do to make the world a better place," "my actions," and "at work") and "not mattering" (i.e., "I" and "at home alone") to construct a more generalized representation of her conflict in terms of the metaphors of mattering "onstage" versus "offstage."

Episode 2: An Instance of Mattering "Offstage"   In Episode 2, the client generates a counterexample—an antithesis—to her previous sense that "offstage, [I don't matter]":

C4: It blows my mind to think that there were a lot of days like that when I'd go home and, my God, you and Carol [client's previous therapist] were talking on the phone. It blows me away.

T4: Yeah, that you might have been at home while Carol and I were talking about you ...

T6: ... Those were heartfelt conversations. Now, how did that feel, thinking about that?

C7: Well, it's new and different and ... and, um, shakes something very deep. Some real deep core belief.

T7: Uh-huh. Put some words on it?

C8: That I don't matter—and there I was mattering and I didn't even know it.

T8: For years.

By restating the client's antithesis, and by probing the client's statement further, the therapist provides attentional support in inviting the client to articulate the emotional significance of this realization. In so doing, she fosters an important microdevelopmental movement. The client is able to move from her identification of her concrete counterexample to an articulated and generalized representation of the conflict between her deep core belief that she doesn't matter when she is home alone and the realization that she mattered to her previous therapist. Although attentional support is the major resource that the therapist is contributing to this developmental movement, in her statement that "those were heartfelt conversations," the therapist is also beginning to offer the resource we term *enactment* to the therapeutic process. Here, the therapist expresses her own feelings about the client mattering to her. She thereby steps into the role of relational partner to the client, presumably in an effort to foster in the moment the feeling of "mattering."

Episode 3: Marginalizing the Counterexample I: Mattering in the Head but Not the Heart It appears that the client responds to the therapist's effort to move into the role of relational partner (and thereby to employ enactment as a mode of offering a resource to the client's developmental process) by first distinguishing her relationship with her past therapist from that with her present therapist. The therapist follows the shift of focus to the past therapist, while still probing the extent to which the client *felt* she mattered. At this point it is worth noting that this therapist's particular theoretical orientation (McCullough, 1999) is influencing the process of attentional support. This particular therapist understands much therapeutic work as treating "affect phobia," and therefore directs her own attention and invites the client's attention to the extent to which the client experiences strong feeling. The therapist's enactments are also directed at evoking novel experiences of strong feeling, and as we will see, her interpretations are oriented toward ways in which the client may avoid or defend against strong feeling. A therapist with a different orientation might well selectively direct and support the client's attention to different aspects of the client's experience, as well as offer different kinds of interpretations and enactments. In our view, what matters for effective therapy is not necessarily the theory that guides the therapist, but whether the client is able to make developmental use of the resources the therapist offers, and whether the therapist can adapt his or her offerings to what the client can use. The DAPP method focuses on and reveals these latter processes. The therapist following the client's shift at this point is an example of such adaptation.

C9: I mean I did know it. But ...

T9: You didn't feel it?

C10: Well, that's not even true either. I mean, I didn't know you were so involved until later ... that ... you know.

T10: I see, yeah.

C11: But I knew I mattered to Carol.

T11: When you were home alone, did you feel like you mattered to Carol? That you'd be in her thoughts and in her heart?

C12: Even just that question. Thoughts, yeah. Heart, oh well, I don't know about heart [laughs nervously].

In the previous exchange, the therapist has adapted to the client choice to focus on "Carol," rather than to engage in an exploration of potentially novel experience within the enactment with the current therapist. At the same time, the client has made use of the therapist's attentional support to construct an important differentiation (antithesis) between her reactions to questions about thoughts and to questions about "mattering" in a more heart–feeling sense. Once the client has made this differentiation between thoughts and heart, the therapist combines offering the resources of attentional support, interpretation, and higher-level (guiding) enactments in the remainder of Episode 3 to advance the microdevelopmental process.

T16: Well, let's just think about it this way. Is there somebody whom you work with in your job, that you know is hurting or in pain, someone … and then that you've gotten involved with and really want to see feel better or feel sad about their pain? And when you think about them off hours you feel it in your heart?

C17: Yeah.

T17: It's not some act—or just intellectual thought.

C18: Oh yeah.

T18: So you know that and so it's important.

C19: Yeah and I do feel and I do know that … that I did know at the time … it was hard to … I, I wouldn't do it and eventually when times were tough I would actually call her and she would call me back.

T19: Um-huh.

C20: But even that was a struggle at first.

In T16, the therapist directs the client's attention by inviting her to discover her own emotions in relation to people with whom she works. She asks the client to reflect on her own emotional reaction to patients in her own work setting who are "hurting" or "in pain." In so doing, the therapist moves beyond mere interpretation and enters into the realm of a higher-order enactment (i.e., *directing* the client's actions, Scaffolding Level 6). The therapist essentially directed the client to imagine a situation in which she could anticipate caring for others in ways that she could not imagine her therapists caring for her. The client's capacity to experience caring for the patients at work (part of her onstage existence), even when the client is "offstage," creates a context for the genuine consideration that the client's "onstage" therapists could actually care for her "offstage." The client and therapist begin to confront this issue more deeply in Episode 4.

At this point, the client has been guided by the therapist's attentional support to a discovery of a conflict that she is now holding in consciousness: At times she experienced it as hard, and as a struggle, to call her previous therapist, but "eventually when times were tough I would actually call her and she would call me back." In the excerpt that follows, the therapist first provides attentional support in response to the client's articulation of this conflict:

T20: Um-huh.
C21: It didn't seem fair and …?
T21: What didn't seem fair?
C22: Well she was off duty and she didn't have to answer the phone for me.
T22: Somehow you would … you'd … that's a way of not taking in that she did call. She was and you would matter, so you do know the feelings.
C23: So I sort of conquered that slowly.

The client uses the therapist's attentional support to begin to explain why calling Carol was a struggle. Then, the therapist offers an interpretation from the therapist's own vantage point and theoretical perspective. Consistent with the therapist's view that the client exhibits a fear of accepting feelings of care from others (a type of "affect phobia"), the therapist offers the psychodynamic interpretation that she views the client's explanation as serving a defensive function. The therapist's interpretation essentially functions as an antithesis to the client's explanation.

Episode 4: Marginalizing the Counterexample II: Is the Therapy Relationship "Artificial"?   In Episode 4, the therapist engages the client in a form of enactment. She prepares the client by telling her that she's asking her "to go on a deeper level now." Then, in this enactment, the therapist induces novel experience by first articulating how she views the situation (interpretation), then asking the client to respond to her framing, then offering the client attentional support to further explore the newly induced experience. At this point, the client has (a) first discovered the antithesis to her feeling she doesn't matter offstage, in saying that it "blows my mind" to think about Carol's care; then (b) followed the therapist's guidance in using her own experience to discover that the therapist's care may go beyond thoughts to "heartfelt" emotions; and (c) finally transcended the attempt to dismiss the antithesis by conceptualizing the therapy relationship as unreal. Having brought the client to a point where she is able to appreciate that it is possible for "onstage" people to care about others when they are "offstage," the therapist asks,

T23: Yeah, but, I'm asking you to go on a deeper level now. It's been with you for 5 years now and it's … this presence has been in your life.… Carol's presence and in the background mine has been in your life and how does it feel to think about her having the same feeling for you that you have toward people you're involved with and care about?

C24: Well, I like it.

T24: Hmm. How do you experience it? What's it like when you let yourself have it?

C25: Sometimes it just feels real good and I can sort of cuddle up in the feeling and sometimes it gets confusing because it's not … it's such a … it's such a … it's not artificial, it's such a … structured relationship or something.

T25: You mean therapy.

C26: Yeah, so it felt good and I … it.

T26: Let's just stay with that, 'cause your mind is … starts immediately to devalue [these feelings].

C27: Right, and so most of the time or some of the times it felt really good and some of the times I would kick myself for feeling … letting it feel good because it was such an artificial kind of relationship.

Episode 5: Using the Therapy Relationship to Induce Novel Experiences of Care Episode 5 takes the transition to the dialectic of enactment between the client and the therapist several steps further. Throughout Episode 5, the therapist attempts to induce in the client the novel experience of confronting the therapist's expression of feelings of care for the client. We divide Episode 5 into three segments. In Episode 5a, the therapist works to induce the client to accept "feeling cared about" by the therapist and to take note of feelings of embarrassment that arise from that acceptance. In Episode 5b, the client and therapist explore experiences of embarrassment and shame that arises as the client works to accept such feelings of care. In Episode 5c, the dyad explores the anxiety engendered in the client as she works to accept feelings of care from the therapist.

Episode 5a: Confronting the Experience of Being Cared For In much of Episode 4, the client seemed not to use the therapist's interpretations (while not explicitly rejecting them).

T22: Somehow you would … you'd … that's a way of not taking in that she did call. She was and you would matter, so you do know the feelings.

C23: So I sort of conquered that slowly.

Instead, she continued to use the therapist's attentional support to elaborate her own explanation of the conflict. Perhaps in recognition that the interpretation, by itself, is not being used by the client, the therapist reemphasizes the resource of enactment by first introducing her own feelings, presumably to provide the client with an opportunity for a novel, fuller experience of someone expressing care toward her than she typically has had in the past. To help the client deal with emerging conflicts about the nature of professional relationships, the therapist offers her interpretation that such relationships entail "human feelings" as well. Thereafter, in continuing the enactment, the therapist proceeds by asking the client about her experience in the moment, that is, of what is going on in the current therapeutic relationship. Drawing upon her theory of therapy as a process of "desensitizing" the client who exhibits a type of "affect phobia," the therapist's questions function to induce the client to attend to feelings of being cared for. Eventually, by C30, bolstered by the experience of the enactment, the client seems finally ready to use at least some of the interpretations offered by the therapist to help the client articulate the antithetical relationship between her inclination to devalue the experience of care, and the possibility of having the experience of being cared for, which she describes as "hard."

T27: Hmmm. Does this ... do I seem artificial to you?
C28: No, but the relationship and the ... it's not like we're friends, I was paying her.
T28: Yes, this is a professional relationship. But does that mean there aren't human feelings?
C29: No.
T29: People are paying you, I mean you're working for a salary, but you, just you know the feelings you have, there's human involvement there and ... and somehow when it comes toward you, you want to push it away ... I'm saying open wide (laugh), don't spit it out. Don't throw it off the plate.... It's hard isn't it?
C30: It is ... it is hard, it's yeah ... It feels ... I—I—I could go to beating up on myself and making it wrong.

In what follows, now that the conflict has been acknowledged by both parties, in varying forms, the therapist continues to offer interpretations similar to those of Episode 4, but adds in her interpretation the therapist's way of understanding the conflict in relation to the client's past. At the same time, the therapist continues to offer attentional support, and the opportunity to attend to novel experiences of feeling cared for in the therapeutic relationship itself (enactment), as resources to the client's developmental process.

T30: Making it wrong for you to let yourself have the good feelings that are just pouring out toward you. Here, from me—from Carol. What was going on you know without your realizing it ... here that was all around you. It's going to be so important to let yourself savor some of it. How much are you letting yourself savor it right now?

C31: It's ... it's ... um ... I have to be embarrassed. I feel embarrassed. It feels ... I feel embarrassed.

T31: Okay, well, let's look at that because this is something you've never been able to let yourself do. It makes sense that you'd be embarrassed, self-conscious.

C32: Yeah.

T32: You know, when you've been in the shadows so long and you were with your mother. You were "out there." Then I say, "Let's shine the light on you"—and it's glaring, isn't it?

This section of the episode is pivotal. Consistent with her attempt to desensitize the client with respect to her presumed fear of feeling cared for, the therapist engages in the dialectic of enactment by treating the client as a direct relational partner. In so doing, she also offers both interpretation (T30) and attentional support to express her feelings of care for the client. In T30, the attention-directing question "How much are you letting yourself savor it right now?" while functioning as a form of attentional support, is a central part of the enactment that occurs between the client and the therapist. The therapist uses this question to direct the client's attention to her ongoing feelings about being cared for in the moment. The client responds with verbal and nonverbal indicators of *embarrassment*. The embarrassment suggests the client's felt acceptance of the therapist's feelings of care in the moment. This acceptance appears to set the stage for the subsequent development of the harbor light insight. Indeed, in T32, the therapist introduces the metaphor of care-as-beaming-light when she says, "You know, when you've been in the shadows so long and you were with your mother. You were 'out there.' Then I say, 'Let's shine the light on you'—and it's glaring, isn't it?"

Episode 5b: Exploration of Embarrassment and Shame At this point, the enactment between the client and the therapist shifts to a focus on the source of the embarrassment that the client experiences as a result of accepting feelings of being cared for as expressed verbally and nonverbally by the therapist:

T36: So. Let's go to what's the embarrassment here with me when you just let yourself feel like you matter you know. One human being to another, one woman to another. What—what's the uneasy part of enjoying that?

C37: Well, I feel like a virgin. (Laugh)

T37: Uh-huh, yeah, a virgin. Yeah, that's a good word for it, isn't it?

C38: (Laughing) Yeah, and I'm fragile and it's—

T38: Yeah.

C39: —unknown territory and I don't have the right words. (teary) Hum, and its so quick, that I go into the beating up of myself.

T39: Yeah, let's hear it. How?

C40: I'm 44-years-old, I should have the words.... It's stupid. (Crying)

T40: Yeah, you know, you don't have to have the words. It's OK.

C41: I mean ... (Moving around in the chair)

T41: Yeah, yeah, the shame is so strong, the beating up is strong, let's just push it away. That's good. You don't want to go down that road, just stay here with me. It's embarrassing to feel (laugh) the good feelings. And none of us have the words when we've had to close off to protect ourselves. Yeah, maybe it is a little foolish for you ... you feel silly?

C42: Yeah, I think, I feel a little ...

T42: Your feelings here [you feel silly here before me].

C43: No.

T43: So it's not that.

C44: No that feels OK.

Now that the client accepts—at least provisionally—feeling cared about by the therapist, within the context of the enactment, the therapist offers attentional support in directing the client's attention to her experience of embarrassment. The client's statement "I feel like a virgin" is accompanied by signs of embarrassment (e.g., laughter inconsistent with negative statements). In this context, the sense of being a "virgin" may reflect an unwanted identity in the client; it elicits an experience of shame. In the context of further attentional support by the therapist, the client's sense of shame is borne out through her statements that "I'm fragile" (C38); "I could go on beating myself up over it" (C39); and "I'm 44 years old; I should have the right words ... It's stupid" (C40). By C29, the client's sense of shame is felt deeply and is accompanied by feelings of sadness (e.g., tears, crying, and thin and trembling voice) and anxiety (e.g., increased activity, fidgeting, and moving around in chair). Within the context of the enactment, in T41, the therapist responds to the client's feelings by offering interpretation (e.g., "The shame is so strong...."). She then explicitly guides the client to experience the emergent novelty (higher-level enactment) in their relationship—positive feelings existing between the client and therapist in the here and now (e.g., "Let's just push it away. That's good. You don't want to go down that road ... just stay here with me").

Episode 5c. Exploring Anxiety Over Mattering   In Episode 5c, the client's emotional state shifts from shame over issues related to her history of feeling uncared for to anxiety about actually feeling cared for within the therapeutic relationship:

T44: Hm. Now what part's hard for you?

C45: I'm aware, there's this little sensor in my head that's saying, "This is really weird. This is really outside the bounds of therapy. What the hell is she doing?" (Laugh) That's all right.

T45: So, it's anxiety too. It's unfamiliar.

C46: Exactly.

T46: Yeah, what is this strange thing that I am doing? Talking about the real relationship.

C47: Here I—

T47: It's something therapy has truly ignored, or doesn't talk about, don't talk about the possible feeling but, but look in your case. Isn't it—

C48: Right.

T48: —absolutely tragic what has happened to you because it's so hard to take these things. But at—

C49: Yeah.

T49: —any rate let me hear about the fears. Isn't this what therapy is supposed to do? What is the anxiety there? Let's look at some of the fears that naturally come up with close fears.

C50: Um, it gets all tangled, so I just start.

T50: Uh-huh.

C51: I'm afraid (pause) um, maybe it's boundaries?

T51: Uh-huh, yeah.

C52: I'm afraid of being set up for getting hurt again.

T52: Uh-huh.

C53: So but that's sort of gone or going and that ... meanwhile I have got you now.

T53: Another problem here.

In Episodes 5a and 5b, the client worked to accept the therapist's care and to deal with the feelings of embarrassment and shame that arise from accepting such care. Having provisionally accepted the therapist's care, the client then becomes anxious. In the context of the client–therapist enactment, the therapist offers attentional support to probe the origins of the client's anxiety and fear (T44, T49) and offers a series of interpretations regarding the origins of those fears (T46–T48). In the early part of Episode 5a, the therapist couched her interpretations in terms of the novelty of the client's sense of feeling cared about. The client, however, now offers an alternative interpretation—an antithesis—suggesting that she may be afraid of "getting hurt again," an interpretation that the therapist acknowledges and appears to accept, framing it as a new conflict (i.e., "Another problem here").

Overall, the enactment that occurs in Episode 5 is an important one. In the enactment, the client confronts the experience of being cared for by her therapist and experiences and reflects upon the meaning of her embarrassment, feelings of shame, and anxiety. Although the client was able to use the therapist's provision of attentional support and interpretation, it was through the dialectic of enactment that the client initially became convinced that she mattered to her therapist.

Episode 6: Accepting Care in Therapy as "Real"   Having now become convinced that she matters in the "mind and heart" of her therapist, the client now confronts a new conflict: Even if her therapists have cared about her, such care is "artificial" and "unreal." As long as such care is unreal, the client continues to experience herself as not mattering. This conflict is rather abruptly resolved in the first few conversational turns of Episode 6:

C54: And you're telling me that this is real, and I'm saying, "Well, it is real and I can really feel it." Oh, but then it's also not really real and, in that it's bounded. (Well) You're not going to invite me for dinner, and I'm not going to invite you for dinner. You know.

T54: That's right. Our experience will be here.

C55: Yeah, right and that is very real, and I don't mean … but it is also not out in the world. So my real thing will … my next challenge will be to find whatever thing is here out in the world.

The episode starts with the client articulating a conflict between her sense that the therapist's care is "real" (i.e., "Well, it is real and I can really feel it") and her sense that it is also bounded (i.e., "You're not going to invite me for dinner") and thus not "really real." The client is able to use the therapist's interpretive response (i.e., "That's right. Our experience will be here") to begin to resolve this conflict: The relationship is real and the feelings are real, "but it is also not out in the world." This leads to her next differentiation. Although she can bear the conflictual feelings of care, vulnerability, and shame that come up in the therapy relationship, and the "glaring" contrast to her past, her "next challenge will be to find whatever thing is here out in the world."

In the excerpt that follows, as the client looks at the issue of relationships in the outside world, the enduring feelings about herself with which she started the session return. She then articulates and holds in attention the conflict (C61) between that enduring experience of herself, and the novel experiences that the enactment just completed in therapy brought about. The client experiences a resurfacing of feelings of shame about herself and anxiety about being able to sustain relationships of care outside of therapy:

T55: Exactly, but, but first here there is some fears that came up and see the talking came up around the fears ... the fears of boundaries.

C56: Yeah, I don't want to ever quit working with you. And I don't want to ever have to say goodbye to this. I'm afraid that that's going to happen. I don't ever want more responsibility than is in the rules of this relationship.

T56: Uh-huh, in regards to what, more responsibility?

C57: Well, carrying some shame from the question about do I ever call Audra, I do not want the responsibility of that.

T57: Yeah, of a friendship? Yeah, Because of the give-and-take?

C58: Yeah, so that's a big fear.

T58: So there is a feeling of never wanting to leave?

C59: For the safety-ness of this.

T59: And never wanting the responsibility of the give-and-take.

C60: Because I'm a shit.

T60: Because you're a shit?

C61: (Laughing) Does not make sense. Oh but is right there ... yeah because in the real world then.... I do not want to say that, it's just not right ... it's not a real world, this is very real ... and I don't want to keep talking about Carol.... I mean, I can't ... I can't hold feeling good about being cared about and thought about and feeling like I don't matter. They're just ... I can't hold those two things at the same time.

Throughout this segment of the episode, the therapist provides attentional support in the form of questions, probes, and restatements of the client's utterances. The client uses the therapist's attentional support to articulate a series of antitheses and conflicts, which ultimately move toward a resolution of these conflicts in C61. In C56, the client articulates (a) her fear of losing the therapist and (b) her fear of having more responsibility in a relationship than she has in the therapy relationship. These are antitheses, respectively, (a) to the experience of accepting her therapist's care, and (b) to her wish to find care out in the world. In elaborating on the thought that "I don't ever want more responsibility than is in the rules of this relationship," the client articulates a fear that she would be unable to sustain a relationship involving enduring mutual care because "I'm a shit" (C60). Then, in C61, in response to the therapist's probing acknowledgment, the client immediately brings back into attention the experience of being cared for by the therapist (i.e., "Does not make sense. Oh but is right there ... yeah because in the real world then.... I do not want to say that, it's just not right ... it's not a real world, this is very real"). This halting articulation of the client's awareness that the therapist's care is real provides an antithesis to the client's characterization of herself as "a shit." Now that her efforts to minimize the contradiction or conflict that she identified in Episode 2 have failed, and she has experienced the conflict more fully and poignantly, she is able to restate the conflict in more general terms: "I can't hold feeling good about being cared about and thought about and feeling like I don't matter ... I can't hold those two things at the same time." It is upon this restatement of the fundamental conflict and its being held in attention that the development that occurs in the remainder of the session is built.

Episode 7: Imagining Care Beyond the Therapy Relationship Episode 7 is divided into two parts. In Episode 7a, the therapist introduces the suggestion that the client can "take me with you" in the client's quest to develop caring relationships outside of therapy. The client immediately experiences anxiety when confronted with this suggestion. In Episode 7b, the therapist appears to assuage the client's anxiety by reinducing feelings of being cared for in the client.

Episode 7a: Anxiety About Moving Beyond the Therapy Relationship In Episode 6, the client holds in her attention the experience of the conflict that is the product of all the microdevelopmental processes in the session up until this point. The therapist mainly offers attentional support to the process of holding this conflict, though in T64 she significantly deepens the experience of conflict through offering an interpretation that ties the present experience to the client's past, and to the loss that would be entailed by developmental change in the future.

T63: They're mutually exclusive, aren't they?

C64: Right.

T64: Yeah, you'd have to give up something that's been you your whole life.

C65: Right.

T65: Yeah.

C66: It doesn't make me want to stay right here forever, but I am not in a real rush to go home, to be alone, and play Tetris, and watch ...

In C66, the client uses both the therapist's attentional support and interpretation to explicitly connect the experience of the conflict regarding who she has been, is, and will be, to the process of therapy. In doing so, she holds two kinds of discomfort in tension simultaneously, thus articulating a new conflict, and thereby transforming the experience of conflict to a more complex level of development. On the one hand, being with the therapist entails the experience of conflict between her existing self-concept and the experience of the therapist's care. On the other hand, going home would be a return to the experience of not being cared about. Neither of these feels entirely good to the client. Now that the client has made explicit the tension between the novel experience that she has just enacted in the session and her experience of her life outside of therapy, the therapist offers an interpretation, envisioning the possibility of a synthesis:

T66: Um-huh, but I wonder if you can take me with you, and take these feelings with you?

It is worth noting that this interpretation is stated very gently, and in an open-ended way that invites the client's collaboration in the construction of a synthesis. It begins with the words "I wonder if." Through the lens of the DAPP mode of analysis, this way of offering an interpretation is seen as very likely to be helpful, and as representing an important skill on the therapist's part. At the same time, the DAPP perspective also suggests that a more clumsy and heavy-handed interpretation (such as might be offered by a less experienced therapist) might or might not be equally facilitative of the client's development. From our perspective, an interpretation does not contribute to a client's development until the client actively uses the interpretation in the process of constructing his or her own experience. If, at a point such as this, a therapist presented a fully articulated synthesis describing her view of exactly how a client might take the novel experience in therapy back to her life, different clients might respond in different ways. Some clients might be able to use such an interpretation to begin a process of reorganizing their experience, thereby making the interpretation their own; others might reject the interpretation completely; and still others might use the interpretation as a jumping-off point for constructing their own syntheses. The advantage of the way the interpretation in T66 is offered is that it invites the client *at the outset into the active collaboration* that is ultimately needed for a client to make developmental use of an interpretation.

The client's next statement is equally tentative. In terming it "the next adventure," she endorses the idea that creating the kind of synthesis the therapist suggested might be possible and valuable. So she is definitely not rejecting the interpretation, and her words can be construed as an invitation to the therapist to take the lead in exploring how taking "me with you" might be possible. However, the client does not herself advance the process of envisioning *how* she might take the therapist with her.

C67: That would be the next adventure.

T67: From both Carol and me and then we will think about Audra and Kate as well. But just say if you took these feelings with you, and if it is good why would you ever want to leave these feelings. And I do you no service if I, you know, set it up that this is the only place that you can have them, and you know that you would be coming forever and that is not the goal here.

C68: Right.
T68: Yeah, we need to set you free but not without these feelings, not with-
out ... not with loss or misery.
C69: All of this comes right up there working its (pause) fear.

In T67, the therapist provides an interpretation of why it is important for
the client to move beyond the therapy relationship. In so doing, as she had
indicated earlier in her phrase "Can you take me with you?" the therapist is
careful to note that her suggestion about finding caring relationships outside of therapy would not be a solitary one. The client would be "set ... free
but not without these [positive] feelings" that result from the therapist's
care. Despite this caveat, the idea of seeking caring relationships beyond
the therapy relationship evokes feelings of anxiety in the client.

Episode 7b: Reexperiencing Care and Bolstering Feelings in the Self In
response to the client's increasing anxiety, continuing to work within the
dialectic of enactment, the therapist works to create a bridge between the
good feelings the client experiences within therapy and the attempt to
imagine life outside of therapy. In so doing, using attentional support, the
therapist again draws the client's attention to the therapist's care toward
the client and the resulting positive feelings in the client.

T69: Yeah, I mean are you ever able to let yourself feel like this when you're
at home, like right now, just feeling safe and good and close to
me? Is that, is that ... am I saying it right?
C70: Oh, yeah.
T70: Yeah. It feels good to hear me say that?
C71: Yeah.
T71: Yeah, where do you feel it?
C72: It's ... it's not belly and it's not up here. It's somewhere center.
T72: Hm. Yeah. Right in the center. What is in—
C73: Yeah.
T73: —the center? Here, I'm intentionally having you put words to make
it conscious. What's there.
C74: Um what's there?
T74: What good feelings are there?
C75: Well, a sort of a power, sort of a ... I know it's—
T75: (Hm)
C76: —a chakra for power, isn't it? But ...
T76: (Um, huh) Maybe so, but you know exactly.
C77: It ... it's sort of a, um, it's sort of a strong, sort of a self, kind of place.
Today it's not feeling all, necessarily warm and heart.... It's feel-
ing more—okay sort of.
T77: A strong self, kind of place.

C78: It is kinda nice. I ought to hang out there more often.
T78: Now what is your sense of it … I mean is …Where's the embarrassment and the anxiety? What's happened?
C79: It is not much a fact now.

The conversation that occurs throughout this segment of the episode serves several simultaneous functions: It reduces the client's level of anxiety; it addresses the source of the client's anxiety in her fear of losing positive feelings of care from the therapist; and it replaces the client's fear and anxiety with more positive feelings (e.g., feelings of confidence and being cared for). Most importantly, using attentional support, the therapist helps the client to use language to construct an explicit representation of her inner emotional state. As a result, the client is able to represent her inner state as a "strong, sort of a self, kind of place" and a "chakra for power." One might suggest that this representation of a sense of inner power—having its origins in the enactment between the client and therapist—can serve as a type of inner resource for "mattering" and seeking caring relationships outside of therapy.

Episode 8: The Therapist as a "Harbor Light"   Episode 8 contains two segments. In Episode 8a, the client is able to imagine the therapist's genuine feelings of care for her when the client and therapist are outside of therapy sessions. This imagining provides the foundation for the client's capacity, in Episode 8b, to construct an initial sense of the therapist as a harbor light—a source of care whether the client is in therapy or outside of therapy.

Episode 8a: Imagining the Therapist's Care Offstage   In Episode 8a, the client and therapist explore ways in which the client can "take me [the therapist] with you" in the client's life outside of therapy. Building upon her newfound sense that (a) the therapist cares about the client, (b) such care is real, and (c) it endures after therapy sessions have ended (offstage), the client is able to construct a novel synthesis. Specifically, the client is able to imagine specific ways in which the client resides in the "mind and heart" of the therapist outside of therapy sessions. In this episode, the therapist engages in an enactment in which she affirms an alliance with the client regarding elaborating the envisioned synthesis as an important aspect of their joint work in the therapy. The therapist and client do work together on construing the nature of the relationship between therapy— and the novel experiences that it has entailed—and the client's life outside of therapy. The process of this work is marked by the kind of collaboration that ensures that the client is creating a synthesis that she can use outside of the therapy session. The episode begins as follows:

T80: Bring this with you. This may not be as deep as it can go, but certainly it is a nice—

C81: Right.

T81: Pleasant ... (Lost words) ... Yeah it's wonderful, that's lovely.

C82: Yeah.

T82: Yeah, and how, how can yeah what.

C83: (Deep sigh)

At this point, the client's sigh is a cue for the therapist to attend to the client's experience in the moment, and to move toward further opportunities that may be offered for development through enactment:

T83: What's coming up right now?

C84: I, um, get nervous and embarrassed again.

T84: Umm, just out of the joy ... of the joy of it?

C85: I know but, now I feel like, oh my God, she's seeing me enjoy it.

T85: How do you think I feel seeing you enjoy it?

C86: (Sigh) Huh, how do you feel? It probably—

T86: Um-huh.

C87: —feels good.

T87: Huh, the problem is does it seem like it does?

C88: No, not when I am being all in myself ... no.... But if I step out a little bit of course it feels good.

T88: Yeah and look at me, yeah of course.

C89: I would be there to see you actually.

T89: Yeah right, if you really look at my face, I seem like I enjoy seeing you feel joy?

C90: Right, right.

T90: Intellectually you know that....

C91: Well, and it feels good to have love received (embarrassed).

T91: Yes, it does.

C92: The gifts received.

T92: And it's been so long absent ... you're just so to afraid look for it—or ask for it. Now this is between us. These are the warm feelings between us for you. And you for me—

C93: Right.

This segment of the episode recapitulates the type of enactment that occurred in Episode 7. With the onset of anxiety and embarrassment that arises from confronting feelings of care from the therapist, the therapist draws the client's attention to the therapist's caring words and gaze. Having renewed the client's sense of feeling cared for, the therapist uses attentional support to prompt the client to connect the close feelings that occur in the here and now of therapy to the client's and therapist's experience outside of therapy:

T93: And there they are back and forth, and why will they go away. Tonight while I'm having—

C94: Right.

T94: —supper, will, you know, when you come to mind, what do you think I'll feel?

C95: (Hesitating, and struggling to answer) You'll probably feel good and probably think this was a nice piece of work. You'll probably feel good about it. And you'll wonder how I'm doing—probably.

T95: Yes, absolutely, I will wonder. And what will I want?

C96: You'll want me … Oh … (she looks very embarrassed and laughs).

T96: It's harder, isn't it, to let yourself—

C97: Yeah!

T97: —to think what would be in my heart.

C98: I would want you to want me. Um, I'll start—

T98: Um-huh.

C99: —with what would (wincing and looking away from therapist).

T99: (Lost words) What would I be wanting for you? You would want me? What would you want me to want for you?

C108: …So, I would imagine that you're sitting down at dinner and you would feel good about the session and that you would hope or wonder how I was doing. And you would want—(speaking very haltingly here) for me, that I go to group and do my work there knowing that I matter at least to you (nervous laugh).

So at this point the client and therapist have used the enactment process to create a "starting point" regarding what it would mean for the client to take the therapist with her. This is the synthesis that would organize the differentiation the client made earlier between how she has felt with the therapist today and how she typically feels about herself. That starting point is the construction articulated by the *client* in C108 within the context of the therapist's attentional support and willingness to act as a willing relational partner. In so doing, the therapist is able to support the client as she works through strong emotion in order to construct a novel synthesis, namely, the idea that the therapist would want the client to "go to group and do my work there knowing that I matter at least to you."

Episode 8b. Therapist as "Harbor Light" Episode 8a ended with the client stating what she imagines the therapist would want for her, after the session. The therapist then appears to begin a simple acknowledgment of what she has understood the client to be saying:

T108: Um-hum, but that would be a good starting point wouldn't it?
C109: That would be a good place to start.
T109: That I would be ...
C110: And it's all mine. One harbor light.

But the client finishes the therapist's sentence by taking an enormous developmental step, expanding a great deal on the recently constructed synthesis. In articulating that in her imagination, the therapist is having dinner, feeling good about the session, thinking about her, and wishing her well, the client represents the meaning that this has for her using the metaphor of the harbor light. The therapist would be "one harbor light" that is all hers. The harbor light metaphor brings together a variety of developmental strands. The therapist's *care* is represented in terms of the "light beaming" from ashore. Characterizing the therapist as a harbor light suggests that the therapist's care can be experienced whether or not the client is near (e.g., "onshore," or in therapy) or far ("offshore," or outside of therapy). This metaphor is extended and elaborated in the remainder of the session. In the interaction that follows, the therapist suggests that there may be multiple "harbor lights" in the client's life.

T110: One harbor light, but I think even in that you know that there is others too.
C111: Yeah, yeah, not quite so explicit. And not quite so ...
T111: Yes, I'm shining bright, but I'm explicit.
C112: You're shining ... you're shining bright. Sometimes it gets a little foggy.
T112: Yeah.
C113: You're shining very bright. My ability to see you is sometimes ...
T113: It's foggy. I see, yeah, but ...
C114: And you say I know about it other places, and I do, but it is not as explicit.
T114: Yeah.

Although the client, to some extent, is willing to follow the therapist's invitation to look at other relationships, she also uses the therapist's attentional support to articulate the meaning of the harbor light metaphor as a novel synthesis integrating the conflicts she has been addressing in this session.

Episode 9: Elaboration of the Harbor Light Insight In Episode 9, in the context of modest degrees of attentional support provided by the therapist, the client is able to elaborate the metaphor of the therapist as a harbor light into what we have called the *harbor light insight.* The harbor light insight provides a grand synthesis that coordinates a variety of conflicts and developmental strands articulated over the course of the entire session:

T124: How does it hear ... feel ... hearing me say that?

C125: Um, it's nice, it's very nice because you feel good shining.

T125: Yeah.

C126: I could use it (laugh).

T126: Yeah.

C127: Sounds like a good deal.

T127: Yeah.

C128: And I also have to say that as a metaphor it's like a breath of fresh air.

T128: Yeah.

C129: I've never … I hear this light at the end of the tunnel thing, and I … it's painful to me because it is not an image that is helpful.

T129: Yeah.

C130: But harbor light is really helpful.

T130: Yeah, so there is a storm?

C131: Storms and fog.… It's the fog that is bothering me the most right now.

T131: Yeah.

C132: The fog.

T132: Yeah the fog, it's less stormy than it used to be, but there is the, you know, sometimes a dense fog.

C133: Yeah and it, right now I'm not feeling like that skulpy thing of being oarless in the boat. But sometimes I do, and how nice to think that if I just perk my little head up, that there's going to—

T133: Yeah.

C134: be a harbor light somewhere. And that we can … we can talk about the bad stuff. But …

T134: Um-hum.

C135: But, at the same time I don't have to go in that particular direction. A harbor light is—

T135: Yeah, yeah.

C136: —useful because you know where it is and you can decide where you want to go relative to it

T136: Um-hum.

C137: So I don't have to aim right for you. You can just be there.

The harbor light insight is reflected in the conversation that occurs between C133 and C137. Through this dialogue, the client articulates how the harbor light image provides a synthesis to the conflict between at times (including within the therapy relationship in the recent enactment) feeling that she matters, and at other times when she has difficulty experiencing both that she matters and that she has agency (e.g., "oarless in the boat"). In C134–C137, with the therapist's attentional support, she articulates the harbor light metaphor as a synthesis for the conflict between focusing on her relationship with the therapist and attending to the ways in which the client can use her image of the therapist's enduring care to feel a sense of mattering as the client navigates her way through other relationships outside of the therapeutic context. We will further discuss the structure and importance of the harbor light insight below.

Now that the client has more fully articulated how the harbor light metaphor serves as a novel synthesis that enables her to meet adaptive challenges, the therapist tries to expand the metaphor of "lights" to describe both the client's relationship with her and the client's other relationships. As can be seen below, the client expresses conflict over whether she can accept the therapist's interpretation and expansion of the metaphor. Addressing this conflict remains as work to be done in future sessions.

T137: There is all kinds of lights twinkling onshore. Right, yeah.

C138: Oh yeah, that's right.

T138: You know now I … you know you could.… Uhh …(laughing that covered up the words) So you know that I'm a beacon now? Saying, OK, you're working with me, you're using me to guide you, I'll be a north star or a harbor light. You going in the direction of where people are shining.

C139: Right.

T139: Where faces are shining at you. Where there is … there's a lot of us here.

C140: Yeah, I have to say that I am with you until you say, "There is a lot of us here," and then I say—

T140: Yeah.

C141: I have to take that one on faith. I mean I'm so quick, but I will take it on faith.

T141: Yeah you will because you know Carol, you know Kate, you know Audra, but there may be others. But those are three you talked about. Is there any real doubt? We know can get flipped and dismiss it, but …

C142: That's pretty rich huh?

T142: It's pretty rich.

Relationship Between the Initial Conflict and the "Harbor Light" Insight

As indicated above, at the time of therapy, the client had been chronically depressed and had had multiple hospitalizations. She was currently not so impaired that she could not function effectively at work. The felt sense of mattering and yet not mattering, which she expresses at the outset of Episode 1, is an expression of at least one aspect of the experience of depression with which the client is struggling to cope. Figure 8.2 illustrates

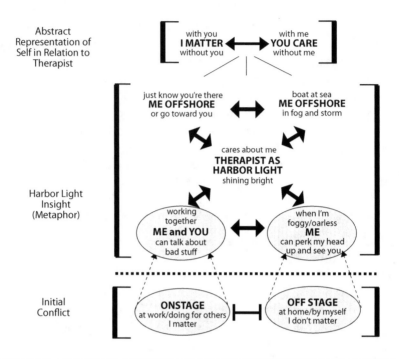

Figure 8.2 Structural transformation from the initial conflict to the harbor light insight for the Lady Cloaked in Fog. At the beginning of the session, the client represented her circumstances in terms of a conflict between mattering onstage but not mattering offstage. By the end of the session, this conflict was resolved through its transformative incorporation into a larger synthesis. Within the final "harbor light insight," the client's sense of mattering on stage was represented in terms of the client and therapist working together (on shore) to talk about the bad stuff; the client's sense of not mattering off stage was represented in terms of being temporarily "foggy" and "oarless" in a boat at sea. However, through its incorporation into the larger "harbor light insight," the client's feelings of not mattering could be mitigated through her capacity to "perk my head up and see you [shining on shore]."

the way in which this initial expression is reconstructed and transformed into the harbor light insight.

The harbor light insight provides a framework for resolving the primary conflict introduced by the client at the beginning of the session, namely, the conflict between "mattering onstage" but "not mattering offstage." The overarching organization of the initial conflict is the distinction between being at home by myself, feeling that I don't matter, versus doing for others—at work, by voting, or in other ways of being "onstage"—and feeling that I matter. The overarching organization of the harbor light insight is the acknowledgment that the therapeutic relationship is one in which my therapist cares and I matter, whether I am with her or not. This organization integrates the differentiated experiences of being away from the therapist, with all of the feelings that that entails, and being with the therapist, working together. As part of the new organization, which the client articulates during Episode 9, she describes the experience of "storms and fog.... It's the fog that is bothering me the most right now." Having co-constructed the belief that the client always matters to the therapist, the initial experience of being at home by myself and feeling I don't matter is thus now recast as being in fog, and not being able to see clearly the way in which I matter. How the novel synthesis represents a solution to the adaptive challenge posed by the experience of feeling I don't matter is clearest when the client describes how she anticipates coping with the negative feelings of being home by herself: "right now, I'm not feeling that skulpy thing of being oarless in the boat. But sometimes I do, and how nice to think that if I just perk my little head up, that there's going to be a harbor light somewhere." This step, of being aware of the therapist's care when feeling I am alone and feeling bad, is then integrated in a new way with what can happen when I am "onstage" with the therapist when the client continues, "And that we can … we can talk about the bad stuff."

Thus, a bridge is created between the new feelings experienced in therapy, and the old onstage–offstage construction of her life. At the same time, the constancy of the awareness of the therapist's care allows for other options for the client's life besides being alone or being with the therapist. This is where the antithesis between the client's experience in therapy and her experience outside of therapy (the focus of Episode 8) is resolved. The client goes on to say, "A harbor light is useful because you know where it is and you can decide where you want to go relative to it. So I don't have to aim right for you. You can just be there."

The client's sense that "Offstage, I Don't Matter" (Initial antithesis in Figure 8.2) is transformed into an experience of being "foggy" and "oarless," but nonetheless able to "Perk Up and See You." At the same time, the old experience that "Onstage, I Matter" is transformed within the new organization by the inclusion of the new fuller experience of being in a relationship with the therapist and is now described as including being able to "talk about the bad stuff." The awareness of the therapist's care, supported by the enactment that just took place within the therapy—the client allowing herself to more fully experience that care—now becomes a constant, represented by the harbor light shining. The stability this constancy provides to the entire representational structure that now coordinates the client's experience is represented in the diagram by the location of the shining harbor light in the center.

The final structure constructed in Episode 9 represents a dramatic developmental advance in relation to the structure expressed in Episode 1, in that it portrays a meaning-making framework that is more complex, more differentiated, and more integrated. It addresses the adaptive challenge that the client brought into the session by both recognizing the chronic painful experience, previously represented as "not mattering," yet transforming it by placing it into a context in which something can be done to ameliorate the pain. Though this challenge may represent just one aspect of the client's depression, according to the therapist's case narrative (McCullough, 1999), this session marked a turning point in a very successful treatment.

Intratheoretical and Pan-Theoretical Analysis of the Psychotherapeutic Process

In Chapter 7, we located the role of the therapist's theoretical perspectives and ways of making meaning within the context of the relational, developmental movements that DAPP analyzes. Although Eva's therapist was one of the authors, in the case of the "Lady Cloaked in Fog," DAPP is used as an alternate pan-theoretical perspective to analyze the work of a therapist (McCullough, 1999) who originally presented the case to illustrate her own theoretical perspective in action. As we begin to examine the context for the development of the harbor light insight, it may be helpful to reaffirm the complementary nature of intratheoretical and pan-theoretical analyses by conceptualizing the foci of each in the context of the other.

The DAPP method of analysis has two primary foci. The first focus is the process of development: Are novel syntheses being created that reflect increased differentiation and integration, and facilitate the client's assimilation and accommodation to adaptive challenges? These adaptive challenges may be the ones that brought the client to therapy to begin with, or others that may have emerged in the course of therapy. The second focus is the interaction between therapist and client. What resources is the therapist offering? Is the client able to make developmental use of those resources? How does the therapist respond to the client's success or failure in using the resources offered, and to the client's implicit or explicit feedback regarding what resources he or she needs?

These foci differ significantly from the foci of many approaches to, or theories of, psychotherapy. Psychotherapy approaches typically focus, *to highly varying degrees*, on (a) the formulation of the client's difficulties and (b) an implicit or explicit taxonomy of therapeutic techniques, and their appropriateness to the nature of varying client difficulties. At one extreme, therapy theories may prescribe using the same techniques or approach for all clients. At another extreme, appropriate techniques may be seen as highly client specific or diagnosis specific. From the DAPP perspective, regardless of what theory a therapist holds, the entire cognitive and personality structure of the therapist (the therapist's patterned forms of meaning making) is what mediates the therapist's response to the behavioral feedback provided by the client. The therapist's explicit psychotherapy theories represent one very important component, though surely not the only one, of the therapist's overall meaning-making structure. The therapist's theories may play a positive mediating role in the therapist–client interaction by helping the therapist to assimilate the client's responses in ways that lead to effective accommodations. Alternatively, the therapist's theories may play a negative mediating role when they lead to understandings of the client's behavior that justify persisting with ineffective therapist responses rather than accommodating to negative feedback.

Because of the crucial role that they play in mediating therapists' responses, therapists' theoretical perspectives and skill repertoires are very important. Nothing in the DAPP approach is intended to devalue the importance of training and experience in psychotherapy theory and technique. At the same time, it is equally important to be able to step outside the linguistic and conceptual frameworks of the approaches in which therapists are typically trained. This is necessary, from a research point of view, in order to address pan-theoretical questions of how, in general, psychotherapy works. It is also important, from the perspective of psychotherapy practice, to be able to address questions regarding how to improve the effectiveness or developmental value of a particular psychotherapy process in which a particular therapist and client are engaged. By entailing a shift in focus, both to the interaction of therapist and client and to the developmental impact of that interaction, the DAPP method provides for this kind of stepping outside of the therapist's theory. DAPP relativizes the therapist's theory, by viewing it as one dynamic, changeable element (equal in importance to the client's meaning-making structures) within the overall dialectic of the therapist–client relationship and their efforts at adaptive co-construction of meaning.

The complementary nature of intratheoretical and pan-theoretical approaches can be illustrated by returning to our case example of the "Lady Cloaked in Fog." In the context of the paper designed to illustrate her own theoretical approach (McCullough, 1999), the therapist discussed her "case formulation" as follows:

> At first, the formulation of her core issues was quite unclear to me. This incredibly sad woman had been in therapy for many years and reported that she had discussed her feelings of anger at length. Therefore, I thought she might be phobic about positive feelings in general—that is, that she could not bear to be excited or joyful because she had never been. I spent the first ten sessions on this focus with no results. She remained as depressed as ever, and I was concerned about her suicide potential. I realized that my formulation had been overly simplistic. The focus I switched to resulted from her repeatedly saying that she didn't matter to anyone. In terms of an affect phobia, this would mean that she was phobic or unable to

face the feeling that someone else cared about her. The second main conflict that was dealt with late in treatment involved the grief—but particularly the anger—at her parents that she was totally unable to acknowledge early in treatment. (p. 41)

We may note that from the therapist's perspective, the change that made possible the progress in the harbor light session was a change in the therapist's formulation. The therapist shifted from viewing the client as phobic regarding positive feelings in general, to viewing her as phobic regarding the feeling that someone else cared about her. It is indeed clear that the client *began* the harbor light session by denying the feeling of being cared about, or mattering when "offstage." It is also clear that the novel synthesis created during the session incorporated the client feeling cared about by the therapist. Therefore, the therapist's responses did illustrate, as intended, the effective use of techniques of exposure and desensitization to feeling cared about. But the DAPP analysis complements the therapist's theoretical analysis by also revealing how much work needed to be done to resolve the conflict between these novel experiences and the client's prior view of herself. Furthermore, in contrast to the focus on formulation, the DAPP analysis of the interaction between therapist and client *in prior sessions* highlighted the grueling work done by both therapist and client to achieve the level of attunement that made possible the effective developmental collaboration that occurred in the harbor light session.

Negotiating Conflicts and Impasses: How Foundations for the Pivotal Session Were Built

The first session we will discuss is one we called the "Eleanor Roosevelt" session, and it occurred approximately 5 weeks before the harbor light session. Viewing the session from a DAPP perspective, we see that the client begins by discussing her passive suicidal feelings, and then introduces the *antithetical idea* (italicized below) that these feelings provide her with some kind of anchor or sense of comfort or familiarity:

T1: OK, you were just saying that you know who you are when you feel like killing yourself—when you want to die.

C1: Yeah, yeah.

T2: It's familiar.

C2: Yeah and I need … I need to keep clarifying that … I don't … I don't know that it's killing myself.

T3: Uh-huh.

C3: I mean I think about it. There are the ideas. But it's not anywhere close to a plan or—

T4: Uh-huh.

C4: I walk over the railway bridge I think, "Ah, I could die if I jumped."

T5: Yeah.

C5: I don't ... I don't get like that.

T6: Yeah.

C6: I don't get anywhere close to that kind of thing.

T7: Right, no. OK.

C7: It's mostly a real passive wishing I was dead.

T8: Mhm.

C8: Um, hoping a drunk driver finds me first.

T9: Sure.

C9: That kind of real passive stuff.

T10: It's real passive, but it's intense.

C10: It's very intense.

T11: Yeah.

C11: And it's constant.

T12: Yeah.

C12: And that's what's familiar.

T13: Yeah.

C13: And so when I'm thinking about that I can't think who would be fun to talk to—

T14: Yeah.

C14: And I can't think about, um, calling you and getting an answering machine.

T15: Yeah.

C15: So then, talk about it tomorrow and then oh well, I had a bad night.

T16: Yeah.

C16: *So there must be something ... I don't want to say useful ... But there must be something that anchors me when I'm doing that... And you know what this also reminds me of ... is ... there was a time ... I can't even remember the details were. But at one point you said, "I really question your motivation for this work given that...."*

DAPP analysis suggests that during the remainder of the session after articulation of this antithesis, the client was able to make *limited* use of the resources of attentional support, interpretation, and enactment that the therapist offered. In the excerpt that follows, the therapist's initial offerings of attentional support did facilitate microdevelopment leading to the client naming the "anchor" as a "familiarity" and connecting it to issues related to her mom.

T27: So let's look at what the ... ah ... what's in it for you. And not that it's going to be on the tip of your tongue ...

C27: It ... it is familiar ... there is a kind of safety.

T28: Yeah.

C28: And I ... I know who I am.

T29: Yeah ... those are very strong things.

C29: But I don't like who I am.

T30: Uh-huh.

C30: And I'm not moving forward in any way.

T31: Hm, this is very familiar ... feeling like this ... yeah ... what thoughts come up?

C31: Mom stuff.

But at this point, we see through the lens of the DAPP perspective that the therapist's primary response is to move away from offering attentional support and instead to offer the resource of interpretation, specifically in the form of the idea that the client's depression represents a way of staying connected to her mother. However, efforts such as this on the part of the therapist appear to lead the client to feel worse and to experience the conflict more intensely, rather than help her to construct an adaptive novel synthesis. This process occurs for approximately 10 minutes and includes the client discussing her retreat from work challenges and feeling like a failure, and the therapist exploring the ways this represents following her mother's example. Soon after, the following interchange occurs:

T74: Right, but for your life now we're saying, "What's the glue here, what's the magnet?" Y'know, and what I'm seeing is that there is some unconscious choosing of doing what your mother did. And that ... that ... and that ... let's not look at that as something critical, but rather that that might be the most fundamental piece of all of us. That's close to your mother.

C74: Mhm.

T75: Somehow that's an identification. Something's bringing up pain, what is it?

C75: I ... ah ... cause it's true and she was such a horrible person. I don't want to be like her.

T76: But don't we all long for our mother?

C76: Not that one.

Though the therapist notices the client's pain at recognizing similarities and wishing to reject her mother, the therapist then continues with more comments that reinforce her interpretation regarding the longing for closeness to mother. Peters (2003), who analyzed this session as part of his master's thesis, suggested that perhaps at this point (in contrast to later in the therapy, e.g., the harbor light session), "The therapist was more ardent in attempting to implement her therapeutic technique (cf. McCullough, 1999) instead of paying more attention to the dyadic process of the session in order to attend to the client's communicated needs" (p. 44).

The client ultimately responds by changing the subject to a book she was reading about Eleanor Roosevelt, hence the name we gave the session. The client explains that reading the book left her experiencing more intensely her own antithetical feelings of comfort with her depressed life. She feels worse about herself because she feels she has chosen to accept her situation. She states about Ms. Roosevelt that "her life was really fucked up in the beginning, really a mess. And her choice was a life-affirming choice out of it instead of my choice." To us as observers, the client appears to be trying to express to her therapist the degree of her self-critical attitude, in saying that a hard childhood does not feel to her like an acceptable excuse for living a life of depression. We may hypothesize that at this point the client has experienced the therapist's "mother interpretations" as not acknowledging the full depth of the client's negative feelings toward herself (and her mother).

Subsequently, in the annotated excerpt below, we see a cycle in which the therapeutic relationship has been repeatedly stuck. In the first part, the therapist's attentional support allows for more expression of the depth of these feelings. But in the second part, the therapist switches back to interpretation, leading to a series of rejections of the interpretations by the client. Through this process, tension and conflict in the therapeutic relationship are reinforced. However, this time, the client blurts out her experience of what is happening in her relationship with the therapist, thereby essentially switching the therapeutic dialogue into the dialectic of enactment. From our perspective of DAPP analysis, as important as any change in theoretical formulation is the therapist's responsiveness to this shift on the part of the client, and her willingness to engage in this process of enactment and to offer resources to it. This appears to us to be what allows some progress to be made in the remainder of this session. In our observer's-eye interpretation, this movement also begins to establish the foundations in (a) the therapist's capacity to respond to the client and (b) the dyad's capacity to use the enactment process effectively, on which the development of the "harbor light" session is subsequently built.

T92: Mhm (offer of attentional support).
C92: And I don't get it....
T93: Mhm.
C93: I don't get how that happens. Even my crazy sister, A—, is ambitious as hell.
T94: Yeah, mhm.
C94: Her depression tends toward the anxiety side of things. But she's gonna do it and she wants to get rid of her depression—
T95: Mhm.
C95: —and I don't ...

T96: Yeah, yeah.

C96: And I don't get it.

T97: Uh-huh.

C97: It's so ... it's so painful.

T98: Mhm.

C98: Because I just don't see any way out.

T99: Yeah.

C99: I really was so hopeful with you and me working together—

T100: Uh-huh.

C100: —and starting to turn it around.

T101: Mhm.

C101: And here I am again. It just feels ...

T102: Yeah.

C102: ... I don't ... I ... I can't keep doing it. It just doesn't seem worth doing.

T103: Turning it around, you mean.

C103: No! Living!

T104: Living.

C104: Living this life anymore if—

T105: Yeah, yeah.

C105: —I can make progress and then—

T106: Mhm (15th consecutive offering of attentional support by therapist).

C106: —it wash out.

The therapist then switches to offering an interpretation of the client's psychological makeup:

T109: Y'know, there is this Eleanor Roosevelt part of you. There is that ambitious part of you that gets things moving. And there's the part of you that shares her pain. Now, there's a reason that Eleanor Roosevelt was able to, y'know, pick up and go. I mean her dynamics weren't identical I'm sure ...

C109: No. (Client rejects interpretation.)

T110: Yeah.

C110: The stories are ... not similar at all. (Client rejects interpretation.)

T111: Right, yeah. But she had something that made it easier for her to dissociate to hard work, ah, and—

C111: Passion ... and relationship.

T112: Yeah ... well ... but let me digress for just a moment (anticipating further discussion of the therapist's interpretation of Eleanor Roosevelt)...

C112: OK. [Puts hand to mouth as if to say, "I'll stop talking now"] (Client communicates nonverbally her ambivalence about listening to the discussion.)

T113: That's all right ... Eleanor Roosevelt ... (Therapist "excuses" ambivalence and starts to plunge forward with her interpretive analysis.)

C113: Don't you see how rotten I am? (Client, unable to contain ambivalence, blurts out what she's experiencing in the moment, thus creating opportunity for development through enactment.)

T114: No. (Therapist joins in the relational experience of the moment.)

C114: I'm sorry. (Client apologizes for interrupting the therapist's interpreting, offering opportunity to move away from the enactment dialectic back to the interpretive one.)

T115: But ... yeah, let's just stay with that a minute. Don't I see how—does it seem like I think you're rotten? (But the therapist, apparently appreciating the developmental opportunity that the enactment process offers, opts to stay in it, rather then return to her interpretations.)

C115: No, I haven't convinced you of how rotten I am.

T116: Uh-huh.

C116: I really want to try to do that.

T117: Yeah, and how about ... you're really convinced that you're rotten?

C117: Yeah—

T118: Mhm.

C118: I'm doing my toxic waste dump thing again. (Makes connection between what is going on in the here and now and previously identified patterns.)

T119: Yeah, that you're rotten in what way? Tell me about it. (Therapist offers further attentional support to explore connections client has made.)

C119: I'm impaired, I'm damaged goods, I am bad news for anybody to get into a relationship—work or anything.

T120: You're impaired ... you're damaged goods ... you're not good for anybody to get into a relationship with.

C120: I'm bad news.

T121: That you're bad news ... and how do you think I see you? (Therapist brings the attention back to what is happening in their relationship now—a possible antithesis to the relational pattern the client has identified as her "toxic waste dump thing.")

C121: I think you probably see me as someone who is struggling.

T122: Mhm.

C122: And you probably can hold the good stuff with the pain that I'm feeling much better than I can.

T123: Yeah ... but I'll hold that for you and remind you of it in ... and tell you that you can hold it too. (Therapist becomes explicit in articulating the possibilities for novel experience in the therapeutic relationship.)

Presaging another of the challenges transcended in the harbor light session, the client goes on to reframe what is novel by distinguishing the therapeutic relationship from relationships in the "outside world." She says the former is easy but she can't do it in the outside world, and then she experiences hopelessness again. This leads to another cycle in which the therapist counters the client's hopeless view with her more positive view of the client, and they become stuck with the same gap between them again. This piece of dialogue ends as follows:

T139: And that's when it's important for me to also remind you that this is where you've been, this new way of being, so it can spread and right now it seems impossible. And you're again so down right now that you're forgetting how good you are with people and how good you do with relationships and skills management and the … the leadership abilities—these are tremendous relationship skills you have—you are disagreeing with me inside?
C139: Yeah.
T140: Uh-huh … but—
C140: I feel I'm good at snapshots.
T141: Uh-huh.
C141: A true leader doesn't quit.
T142 Mhm.
C142: Just quit all the time.

Some progress was made through the enactment dialectic, but it seems to have reached its limit. With the enactment stalled and the therapist's interpretations rejected, the therapist faced a challenge here. One approach would be to acknowledge how negatively the client views herself and how bad she is feeling. This would involve joining the client on her side of the conflict between them. However, instead, the therapist moved to interpreting the impasse by interpreting the client's reactions in the enactment process. Again, we may note that the interpretation offered—that the client has trouble taking in positive feelings—is one that is consistent with the therapist's theory regarding treating affect phobia and its relevance to this client. It is also a line of interpretation that the client will be able to make even greater use of in the process of constructing a novel synthesis during the later harbor light session.

At this point, the client still cannot use the therapist's more positive view of the client in constructing a synthesis. However, the interpretation does foster the continuation of the enactment process (acknowledgment of conflict between client's and therapist's perspectives). In the course of this continuation, the client makes an important differentiation (antithesis) regarding what is new in her relationship with the current therapist, in contrast to her previous therapist. Even amidst being in conflict, the client says that her relationship with the current therapist feels more "adult," whereas her relationship with the previous therapist entailed more "mommy stuff."

Further exploration of this differentiation then led the client to articulate the syntheses within the enactment dialectic that her relationship with her therapist was *novel* in two ways. First, it was different from the relationship with her previous therapist in the client's experience of being more peer-like amidst conflict—"I had ground to stand on, and I knew that you would acknowledge that ground." Second, it differed from her relationship with her sister in that the therapist could hold positive experiences that the client shared, without the client feeling that sharing the experiences led to higher expectations of her that she would fear failing to meet. This latter distinction was represented in the images of the therapist as a "safe-deposit box" or a "low-interest bank account" in which expectations would not grow too fast.

Thus although the fundamental conflict between the client's experience and understanding of herself and the therapist's view of her was never transcended through the creation of novel syntheses in the "Eleanor Roosevelt" session, important work was nevertheless accomplished. In enacting and examining this conflict between them, novel recognitions of important qualities of this therapeutic relationship were established. Both the substance of these recognitions and the processes that led to them were foundations that were built on in the later pivotal session.

Furthermore, when the time for this session to end arrived, the client was again submersed in passive suicidal ideation:

C: And I have to give myself credit ... for valiantly bucking to this point, but I can't do it anymore.... And it's just really hard to up—get up and go to work and face this shit when I don't want to be here.

In response, the therapist chose to extend the session for an additional 15 minutes.[2] She didn't end it until she elicited from the client a positive thought about her mother. In the final interchange of the session, this thought, along with a mutual acknowledgment of the growing strength of the therapeutic relationship, and a "homework assignment" from the therapist and spontaneous response from the client, further established

---

[2] See Peters (2003) for valuable commentary regarding this decision, based on both the DAPP perspective and subsequent discussions with the therapist.

the groundwork for the next session one week later (which we named the "reconstructing mother" session):

T342: I just … just conjecturing. But yeah … it'd be important to get a clear view of this mother. There's something in you that loves her and wants to be close to her. And those first few years probably were quite good … 'cause you love children for a reason.

C342: And I do know that I was wanted.

T343: Mhm.

C343: She really wanted another kid.

T344: Yeah … so I think we did a nice hunk of work today.

C344: I'm exhausted.

T345: Yeah, oh, I know what it is … dream on it.

C345: I remember doing stuff like this and I couldn't do eyes with you, remember that? I couldn't do eye contact.

T346: Yeah.

C346: Anyway.

T347: That's not the case anymore, is it?

C347: No.

T348: So …

C348: You were saying something.

T349: I forgot … oh, dream on it.

C349: OK.

T350: Y'know, see what you can evoke from your mother. You may have repressed all kinds of things … little things.…

C350: Holy shit!

T351: What?

C351: Write down that I had a dream about a baby and putting it up for adoption.

T352: Uh–huh.

C352: That's good one. I didn't remember that until …

T353: Uh-huh, yeah.

To review, in the "Eleanor Roosevelt" session, the client (a) demonstrated to the therapist the limited usefulness to the client of the therapist's interpretations regarding her relationship with her mother, (b) insisted on drawing attention to the conflict between the therapist's view of the client and the client's own very negative self-perception, and (c) appealed for the use of the therapeutic resource of enactment when she blurted out to the therapist, "Don't you see how rotten I am?" The therapist responded to this appeal and, after taking their work using enactment as far as was possible, facilitated the client's articulation of what was novel and hopeful in the therapeutic relationship. The client expressed her experience of the therapist's acknowledgment of their differences in articulating that their relationship was more "peer-like" with less "mommy stuff" than her previous therapy relationship—that "I had ground to stand on, and I knew that you would acknowledge that ground." At the same time, in describing their relationship as a "low-interest bank account" or "safe-deposit box," the client expressed trust that the therapist could hold what the client shared without adding on the expectations she had experienced in other relationships. This helped establish the foundations for the harbor light session, by establishing a way of dealing with differences in interpretation that may have previously inhibited the client's full engagement in therapy. By the therapist acknowledging the differences in interpretation, and then offering the resource of enactment in exploring the implications of such differences for the client's relationship with her, both the value of the use of enactment, and the novel experience of this relationship that differentiated it from previous therapy relationships, were established as foundations for future work.

Between the "Eleanor Roosevelt" session and the "reconstructing mother" session, the client did important developmental work outside of session that prepared her to revisit her relationship with her mother. Perhaps this was in response to the therapist's suggestion and homework assignment, "Dream on it." Early in the "reconstructing mother" session, the client reported on the thoughts she had about her relationship with her mother. This report culminated with expressing to the therapist the realization, "I don't get to bury her. I don't get to just close the door and forget about that I have that of her in me and I have to think about it and not that I have to carry it with me all the time, but … it's not a finished piece that you … just seal over." The dialogue that ensued reflected the therapist's effort to again work through the dialectic of interpretation. She reintroduces and "normalizes" her interpretations from the previous session.

T23: Uh-huh, and what we talked about was that you might be unconsciously close to her.
C24: Well, that I don't like to think about.
T24: No, that was an uncomfortable feeling.
C25: Yeah.
T25: That … does it seem possible, though? That you … maybe …
C26: That being depressed is a way of being close to her?
T26: Mm, wanting to die, being hopeless.
C27: If I say yes it's saying horrible things about me that I don't want to think.
T27: Oh really? Why would it be saying horrible things about you?
C28: Because … she was … she was awful. I mean I'm saying all these things about how she shouldn't have given up on me and she shouldn't have done all these things.

T28: Mhmm.

C29: And I'm saying I'm trying to be like her.

...

T33: So, it's not that you selected this out of some conscious choice. I am trying to raise your consciousness about this because people inadvertently do these things.

C34: Yeah.

T34: I mean are you aware of that—that people wear their watch like their father ...

C35: Yes.

T35: Or dress like their mother dressed ...

C36: Yes.

T36: Y'know, or on a deeper level—live like their mother lived—you— saying that this would mean awful things about you. What does it really mean when the child imitates the parent?

C37: If it's not me? (Laughs.) It may be a wonderful thing.

The therapist's interpretations were developmentally helpful, supporting the client's recognition, at this point, that the attitude she holds toward others is antithetical to the one she holds toward herself. Interestingly, this recognition is followed by a reenacting of the conflict that dominated the "Eleanor Roosevelt" session, in which the client's view of herself as "horrible" for being like her mother seems unappreciated in the therapist's more sympathetic understanding of the situation as "sad." However, this week the therapist's attentional support as the reenactment occurred facilitated the client's articulation of the bind in which the therapist's invitation to build on her interpretation places the client: "that if I join you in this work, then I have to let go of this self-criticizing shit." In response, the therapist expressed her commitment to the use of interpretation being a collaborative process: "If it doesn't ring true to you—let's wait until we find what it is that does fit."

From the DAPP perspective, all of the work cited above established a context for the remainder of the "reconstructing mother" session—a truly collaborative experience of revisiting the client's mother's life, and her impact on the client's childhood. Over the course of 30–40 minutes, this revisiting yielded dramatic new discoveries that transformed both parties' image of the client's mother. A "spunky, ambitious" mother was recalled, prior to the client's younger sister sustaining a traumatic head injury at the age of 6. The injury was followed by 2 ½ years of conflict between her mother, who continued to seek diagnosis and treatment for the sister's head injury, and her father, who "minimized" the injury and traveled a lot. The client remembered that her mother's depression began during this period and worsened when the younger sister died at 8 ½ years of age. Subsequent to the sister's death, the client became closer to her father and two surviving sisters, whereas the mother's depression and emotional withdrawal continued until she herself died of cancer when the client was 17. In our view, this collaborative, transformative work of co-construction was built upon the struggles therapist and client went through in the "Eleanor Roosevelt" session, the between-session work that the client did, and both parties' ability to reestablish collaboration and attunement in the early part of the "reconstructing mother" session. Further, we see the experience of successful collaboration and attunement in the latter session as in turn establishing the foundation that made the developments of the "pivotal" 16th (harbor light) session possible.

So, in sum, the therapist's formulation and her theory may have been useful in guiding her responses; and a shift may have indeed occurred in the therapist's formulation, simultaneously with the therapy process becoming unstuck in the pivotal session. But the DAPP method complements the therapist's theoretical analysis by rejecting the idea that the therapist's shift in formulation was *the fundamental cause* of therapeutic progress. Instead, the DAPP method provides a basis for examining the *interpersonal* processes of negotiating what resources the therapist could offer and what resources the client could use. It locates in these processes the source of all three developmental results: (a) the increased attunement and capacity to collaborate in the therapeutic relationship, (b) the client's articulation of the harbor light insight and the relief that it offered from her depressive and suicidal symptoms, and (c) the therapist's construction of a more sophisticated understanding of the client that allowed for more effective use of her preferred therapeutic techniques.

The discussion above illustrates the potential role for DAPP in psychotherapy training. We will return to this topic in Part 3 of the book. For now, it suffices to say that we believe this case illustrates that training in psychotherapy theory and technique, as well as diagnosis and formulation of client difficulties, is of clear importance. However, it is equally important for therapists to be trained in methods of monitoring ongoing psychotherapy processes that entail therapists stepping out of their preferred frameworks for understanding both clients' dynamics and specific therapeutic methods. DAPP provides one clear example of such a monitoring method, one that has the capacity to reveal and address therapeutic progress, and the absence thereof, in any given treatment.

CHAPTER **9**

Tracking the Role of Emotion
in Psychotherapy

Case Illustrations

Emotion plays a central role in psychotherapy processes. The adaptational conflicts that bring people into psychotherapy are frequently organized around core meanings that evoke strong feeling. Across cases, the feelings expressed in psychotherapy reflect the full range of emotional experience. Further, the organization of these feelings is often the product of long personal and social histories. Regardless of the approach, psychotherapy typically involves identifying strong emotions and in some way reorganizing either the emotional experience itself or the role it plays within a client's life. The DAPP approach attends to all of the interrelated aspects of human activity and experience that undergo differentiation and integration in the course of successful psychotherapy. Emotion is part and parcel of all human experience. The transformation of emotion is part of the process of the transformation of activity and experience. Emotional transformations necessarily contribute to the transformation of action, meaning, and experience; conversely, the transformations in action and meaning entail changes in emotional experience as well. Because the challenges of psychotherapy typically center around conflicts that entail great emotional intensity, and the most important transformations in psychotherapy profoundly influence clients' emotional lives, we devote this chapter to articulating how strong emotions are understood and tracked within the context of DAPP analysis.

In an effort to locate our approach within the context of recent work on the relationships among neuroscience, emotion, and psychotherapy, we begin with a consideration of six principles articulated by Cozolino (2002). These principles were articulated to provide a cohesive framework for understanding the role of emotion in psychotherapy. These principles can be classified into three groups. The first group articulates general principles describing the ways in which emotion organizes interaction between clients and therapists. The second group addresses how psychotherapy prompts transformation in core emotional meanings and experiences of the client over the course of psychotherapy. The third addresses the role of language in integrating affect, meaning, and action.

Affective Co-Regulation Between Therapist and Client

Cozolino (2002) introduced three basic principles that describe how emotion operates within therapeutic relationships over the course of psychotherapy. The first is the principle that optimal development, defined in terms of increasing differentiation and integration of psychological structures, *occurs best within relationships that balance support and optimal stress.* This idea is consistent with how a wide range of traditions within developmental psychology have drawn implications of developmental theory for designing environments and curricula that support development. Balancing challenge and support is consistent with the concepts of equilibration (Piaget, 1985), moderate discrepancy (Hopkins, Zelazo, Jacobsen, & Kagan, 1976; McCall and McGee, 1977), distancing (Sigel, 2002), zone of proximal development (Vygotsky, 1978), goodness of fit (Chess & Thomas, 1991), and scaffolding (Mascolo, 2005; Rogoff, 1990), among others. Each of these ideas or concepts implies that development occurs best in contexts that both *challenge* and *support* an individual's ongoing activity. Events and social interactions whose meanings and demands are too far beyond an individual's level of development or coping skill engender overwhelming emotions; in contrast, events that provide little challenge fail to stimulate the level of cortical arousal required for attention and development (Lewis & Todd, 2007; Mateo, 2008).

Cozolino's (2002) second principle holds that empathic attunement by a therapist provides the foundation for the development of a trusting, therapeutic alliance between the therapist and client. From the DAPP perspective, some therapists explicitly make empathic attunement the highest priority in establishing a therapeutic relationship, whereas other therapists may conceptualize hierarchies of what is helpful in other ways. What turns out to be helpful, in terms of achieving that optimal balance of challenge and support, may vary a great deal from client to client. For example, for a client who experiences a great deal of emotional support in the context of other relationships, confrontative interpretations and enactments in psychotherapy may be of most value in achieving that optimal balance of challenge and support. In contrast, other clients may be very aware of and unable to manage the emotional stress that they are experiencing in other relationships, and may feel quite desperate to find emotional support. For them, empathic support within the therapy relationship may turn out to be the *sine qua non* that Cozolino claimed it to be. Regardless of what resources therapists offer to clients, DAPP analysis closely attends to the client's emotional response to the therapist's way of treating the client. This is important for answering a fundamental DAPP question: To what extent is the client able to use the resources that the therapist is offering? We also advocate that therapists attend to clients' emotional responses to answer this question.

Cozolino's (2002) third principle states that the capacity to tolerate, cope with, and regulate affect is essential not only in the formation of social relationships, but also to create conditions that support the brain's capacity to function effectively and forge new synaptic connections. In normative samples, social demands stimulate the hypothalamic-pituitary-adrenal (HPA) axis to secrete stress hormones such as cortisol. An increase in cortisol stimulates sympathetic nervous system functioning that provides bodily support for mobilizing against stressful events (Cozolino, 2006). Recent research demonstrates that continued and prolonged exposure to high levels of stress or trauma can prompt brain damage. Research (Kocijan-Hercigonja, Sabioncello, Rijavec, & Folnegovic-Šmalc, 1996; Yehuda, 2004) suggests that cortisol functioning is attenuated among individuals who have had prolonged exposure to sustained levels of trauma or stress (e.g., maltreatment, witnessing acts of homicide, or military battle). Further, prolonged trauma has also been associated with a decrement in hippocampal volume, suggesting that trauma can modify brain structure as well as brain functioning (Joseph, 1998; Winter & Irle, 2004). In some cases, one of the important outcomes of psychotherapy is the development of novel organizations of meaning that provide adaptive effectiveness in regulating affect. Sometimes, this is done directively, as in the context of behavior therapy when enactments are created that foster the development of alternatives to phobic reactions. In other circumstances, the development of affective regulation proceeds as a more indirect process. Emotional regulation arises dyadically—between the therapist and the client—through co-regulated exchanges that occur spontaneously throughout the course of psychotherapy (Fogel, 1993). In some approaches to therapy (e.g., CBT and DBT), the client may be explicitly taught particular strategies for regulating affect. In less didactic forms of therapy, affective regulation may arise less directly. Although the therapist may respond in a variety of ways to a client's emotional displays, in some cases, through mutual adaptation, a coordinated pattern of interaction (emotional attunement) and the co-construction of shared ways of attending to core emotional meanings and experiences occurs. In these cases, client and therapist may be seen as jointly creating organizations of activity for regulating the client's affective experience. Over time, the client may become progressively able to become the primary agent of increasingly integrated forms of affect regulation that have their origins in the client–therapist relationship. Unless directly taught, the client does not acquire these strategies from the therapist; she appropriates modes of affect regulation from her participation in emotional exchanges that occur between the therapist and client. The development of increasingly self-regulated forms of affect regulation—either in children or in adults engaged in psychotherapy—allows for more adaptive functioning of the HPA axis. In this way, the activation of stress responses can function in the service of learning and development, rather than against it. Because emotional regulation plays a central role in providing a foundation for doing all aspects of the developmental work of psychotherapy, DAPP pays close attention to the co-construction of novel syntheses that result in improved affect regulation.

Developmental Transformation of Emotion in Psychotherapy

Cozolino (2002) articulated two additional principles related to the processes by which emotional experiences undergo change within psychotherapy. First, interaction between affect and cognition is necessary to achieve integration of subcortical and neocortical neural networks. Second, the *simultaneous activation* of subcortical and neocortical neural networks is necessary to achieve such interaction (see also Ecker & Toomey, 2008). A large body of research (LeDoux, 2008; McGaugh, 2003; Phelps, 2006) suggests that memories for emotional events can be created both *explicitly* and *implicitly*.[1] *Explicit* knowledge of emotion involves conscious awareness and is mediated by the pathways that lead from the sensory thalamus to higher cortical areas. The *implicit* construction of

---

[1] Memory researchers have differentiated between two broad classes of systems involved in remembering: These include *implicit* and *explicit* memory (Berry & Dienes, 1991; Smith & Grossman, 2008). *Explicit* rememberings are those that are able to be articulated by the experiencing individual. The content of explicit remembering often involves verbal declarative knowledge (i.e., "knowledge that"). Explicit knowledge consists of knowledge for constructing and reconstructing consciously available perceptual, semantic, episodic, and autobiographical experiences (e.g., "that a dog bit me yesterday"). In contrast, *implicit* remembering involves the nonconscious construction and use of nondeclarative (and primarily nonverbal) knowledge, including sensorimotor and procedural knowledge (i.e., knowing *how* rather than knowing *that*). Implicit memory systems also mediate the construction and maintenance of primitive sensory, emotional, and bodily associations to experience, including those that have been acquired as a result of early relationships with caregivers (Cozolino, 2006; Gallagher, 2005; Kihlstrom, Mulvaney, Tobias, & Tobis, 2000; LeDoux, 2008).

primitive emotional associations occurs without conscious participation and is mediated by limbic system structures (see MacLain, 1990), including the amygdala, thalamus, and prefrontal cortex (Radwanska, Nikolaev, Knapska, & Kaczmarek, 2002; Repa et al., 2001; Rogan, Stäubli, & LeDoux, 1997). Recent research suggests that the amygdala is involved in the latter form of nonconscious production and retention of emotional associations, whereas the hippocampus is involved in the formation of explicit representations (Phelps, 2006; Phelps & LeDoux, 2005).

Informed by a growing literature addressing emotional change in psychotherapy (Cozolino 2002; Ecker & Toomey, 2008; Greenberg & Pascual-Leone, 2006), the DAPP analysis tracks development in psychotherapy that entails transformation of emotion through five basic steps.[2] These steps are described in Table 9.1. They include (a) co-constructing representations of feeling that have their origins in core emotional processing that typically occurs at preconscious levels and may have never been represented linguistically and conceptually (offering support for attention to emotional experience and contributing interpretations to the process of representing them), (b) maintaining representations of core emotional meanings in conscious awareness so that they can be transformed in psychotherapy (attentional support), (c) creating experiences that disconfirm and conflict with the client's core emotional experiences (creating *antitheses* through enactment), (d) maintaining *conflict* within the attentional field, and (e) resolving the conflict through *novel syntheses* entailing the transformation of core emotional meanings.

The first step in the process consists of articulating representations of feeling states that arise from nonconscious (and presumably precortical) processes. At the neurobiological level, such processes are mediated by fast-acting, subcortical pathways involving the amygdala, cingulated cortex, hypothalamus, and related limbic structures (LaBar & LeDoux, 2003; LeDoux, 2000; Repa et al., 2001). Such structures mediate rapid processing of the emotional significance of events, the retention of such emotional significance in memory, and the production of the felt aspects of such emotional experience (LaBar & LeDoux; McGaugh, 2003). As indicated in Chapter 3, emotional experiences serve important functions for conscious activity; they amplify and select appraisals of significant events for further conscious analysis (Freeman, 2000; Lewis, 1996). Emotional experiences direct and organize a person's conscious awareness in rapid and broadly adaptive ways. *However, because the appraisals that mediate emotional*

---

[2] It is important to underscore the idea that the "steps" outlined in Table 9.1 can only be taken to reflect an idealized sequence that rarely if ever unfolds as a linear process. In actual development, the steps form a loose and cascading sequence of forward and backward movement, depending upon the constraints of the context and the particular elements of experience under development (see Lewis, 1997; Schwarz, 2003).

Table 9.1 DAPP Representation of Steps Involved in the Therapeutic Transformation of Emotion

Step	Description	Therapeutic Resources
1	Co-constructing representations of feeling. Client and therapist co-construct representations of core emotional processing that typically occurs at preconscious levels and that may not have been represented linguistically and conceptually.	Attentional support and interpretation. Therapist offers support to help client attend to emotional experience; therapist contributes interpretations to the process of representing feeling.
2	Maintaining representations of feeling. Maintaining representations of core emotional meanings in conscious awareness over time so that they can be transformed in psychotherapy.	Attentional support. Therapist provides attentional support to ensure that articulated representations are not lost from consciousness.
3	Creating emotionally disconfirming experiences. Creating experiences that disconfirm and conflict with the client's core emotional experiences.	Enactment. Creating emotional *antitheses* through enactment.
4	Maintaining emotional conflict. Maintaining a representation of the *conflicting emotional experiences* within the attentional field.	Attentional support within enactment. Therapist provides attentional support to ensure that *conflicting emotional representations* are maintained in consciousness during enactment.
5	Resolving emotional conflict. Resolving the conflict through the construction of *novel syntheses* entailing the transformation of core emotional meanings.	Enactment.

reactions are nonconscious and often unelaborated, such appraisals are not necessarily apparent to the experiencing individual. Through the use of attentional support and interpretation, a therapist can assist the client in articulating the meanings of the often inchoate feelings that inform conscious awareness. To use language to represent and articulate the meaning of felt experience is to begin the process of forging connections between subcortical neural networks that mediate the implicit construction and representation of knowledge and higher-order cortical networks that are involved in the construction of explicit, conscious, and verbal representations of experience.

For example, in the case analysis of the Lady Cloaked in Fog, after the client has described an example of when she "mattered" to her therapists when she was "offstage" and home alone, the therapist asks, "How does it feel to think about her [your prior therapist] having the same feeling for you that you have toward people you're involved with and care about?" This question prompts the client to put presumably subcortically mediated elements of her emotional experience of the therapist's care into words and to relate it to an experience she has previously represented—her care for her own clients. After the client responds by providing a relatively unelaborated global evaluation (i.e., "Well, I like it"), the therapist presses for more elaboration: "How do you experience it? What's it like when you let yourself have it?" At this point, the client elaborates a more explicit representation of her experience:

> Sometimes it just feels real good and I can sort of cuddle up in the feeling and sometimes it gets confusing because it's not … it's such a … it's such a … it's not artificial, it's such a … structured relationship.

These acts of construction and interpretation, guided by the therapist's provision of attentional support, reflect the process of identifying core implicit emotional meanings.

The next step in the process of emotional transformation is *maintaining or consolidating newly constructed representations of core emotions in consciousness over time.* Once core emotional meanings have been constructed and represented in consciousness, unless they are attended to, they will often be forgotten or otherwise lost or overshadowed in consciousness. This occurs for many reasons. Emotions that arise during therapy are often painful and dysregulating. One way to restore the quality and intensity of one's emotional experiences to a prior level is simply to remove the difficult thoughts from consciousness, either through distraction, changing the subject, or related means. Further, core emotional meanings are often the products of long histories. As a result, people have often developed powerful ways to manage such feelings. Still further, it has been well established that people function at a higher developmental level when assisted by more accomplished others than when working alone (Fischer, Bullock, Rotenberg, & Raya, 1993; Mascolo, 2005; Vygotsky, 1978). When a client constructs a novel representation of experience with the support of a therapist, it will often be difficult to maintain the representation in consciousness without the further support of the therapist. To facilitate the construction of stable explicit representations of core emotional meanings, the therapist can work to repeatedly direct the client's attention to the newly constructed emotional meaning. To direct attention to the newly constructed meaning is not simply to think or talk *about* the core meaning; it is also important for clients to subjectively experience the core emotional feelings.

The process of consolidating newly constructed explicit knowledge is mediated by a variety of brain structures, including the hippocampus, the prefrontal and frontal cortex, and the language-processing areas, which are often located on the left temporal lobe (Cozolino, 2006; LaBar & LeDoux, 2003; McGaugh, 2003). At the neurological level, the consolidation of newly constructed knowledge functions according to a basic rule first formulated by Hebb (1949): Synaptic connections strengthen if conjoined neurons repeatedly fire together; neural connections weaken when coupled neurons do not fire together. When a therapist provides attentional support to prompt a client to represent implicitly constructed emotional memories in a conscious and verbal mode, the therapist facilitates the process of forging new connections between subcortical emotional processing and conscious, explicit cortical processing. The process of constructing stable, enduring patterns of neural firing (potentiation) among neurons that mediate learning and memory is called *long-term potentiation* (LTP). Among corticolimbic structures, studies suggest that LTP occurs not only in the hippocampus (which plays a role in the representation of explicit memory; Cozolino, 2006; Phelps, 2006), but also in the amygdala (which plays a role in implicit processing of the emotional significance of events; LaBar & LeDoux; McGaugh; McGaugh & Cahill, 2003; Phelps & LeDoux, 2005). According to Ecker and Toomey (2008), the key process in creating LTP is the act of directing *attention* to elements of novel experiences, and to emotionally salient experiences (Phelps, Ling, & Carrasco, 2006). In any given experience, the activation of existing neural networks that mediate long-term retention renders those networks more labile and changeable. Once such networks are reactivated, the process of repeatedly allocating attention to a given experience functions to reorganize patterns of neural firing into more stable and enduring long-term structures (LTP). At the level of conscious experience, the conscious construction of stable and enduring representations of core emotional experience requires multiple acts of consciously attending to, reattending to, and integrating those constructed representations and their relations to other aspects to a person's subjective experience. At the neurological level, such acts orchestrate the creation of new patterns of LTP between cortical and subcortical neural networks (Lewis & Todd, 2004).

As an example of the process of consolidating explicit representations of implicit emotional meanings, we return again to the case analysis of the Lady Cloaked in Fog. In the excerpt described above, the client was able to consciously represent the emotionally charged idea that she "mattered offstage" to her former and present therapists. The client experienced considerable difficulty in maintaining this awareness throughout the first half of the therapy session. Confronting the idea that she had indeed mattered to other people in her life, the client experienced both anxiety and doubt. She raised a series of objections to the idea that she could have genuinely mattered to her prior therapist (e.g., being cared about by a therapist is "artificial"). In response to this doubt, the therapist asked directly, "Do I seem artificial to you?" again inviting the client to attend to and represent what she was feeling in that moment. Each revisiting of the issue addressed somewhat different aspects of the client's experience. Nonetheless, without continually reintroducing this newly discovered emotional insight to the client, the insight eluded her grasp. Repeated attention to this novel emotional insight throughout a series of different iterations was necessary to achieve explicit consolidation of the representation in conscious awareness, and to articulate the relations of this novel meaning to the client's sense of "not mattering" to other people.

The integration and consolidation step prompts the construction of an enduring conscious representation of a core emotional meaning that has its basis in previous patterns of implicit emotional learning. The fact that the client is able to construct conscious representations of emotional meanings does not render those meanings less salient, painful, or difficult. It does, however, provide the conscious tools needed to begin the third and fourth steps of enacting novel experiences and maintaining awareness of the conflict between novel experiences and established core emotional patterns. When the therapist looked in the client's eyes and directly asked the question, "Do I seem artificial to you?" we can assume that this represented a novel and antithetical emotional experience. First, it was a direct expression of care from another. But more importantly, if it were simply stated as an expression of care, it might be easier to dismiss as something people just say but don't mean. But by the therapist asking the question "Do I ..." the client was invited to answer the question herself by attending to her own emotional experience of the relationship. In accepting this invitation, the client had the opportunity to experience side by side in her awareness her established emotional pattern of feeling she didn't matter to others, and her novel experience of *feeling* that she represented as mattering to the therapist—a real person. Steps 3 and 4 created the conditions for the fifth step in the process of *transforming emotional meanings*, which happened later in the "harbor light" session.

At the phenomenological and social-relational levels of analysis, the task of transforming emotional meanings requires the prior introduction of experiences that *conflict* with and *disconfirm* constructed conscious representations of the client's core emotional meanings (Step 3), and maintaining the conflict in attention (Step 4) so that the client can be supported in finding ways to coordinate or otherwise resolve the contradiction between conflicting experiences (Step 5). As documented in previous chapters, in psychotherapy, this can be done in many ways. Through the use of attentional support, a client herself can construct novel representations that conflict with explicit representations of core emotional meaning. Similarly, the offering of novel interpretations by the therapist can introduce meanings and experiences that conflict with entrenched modes of feeling and knowing. Through successive acts of differentiation and coordination of novel elements of meaning and experience, higher-order structures are constructed that resolve intra- and interpersonal conflicts. Attentional support and interpretation both play an important role in introducing novel experiences and meanings that challenge entrenched emotional meanings. However, a neuropsychological level of analysis suggests that the dialectic of *enactment* is essential for transforming entrenched core emotional meanings. The dialectics of attentional support and interpretation are directed toward reflecting *upon* or talking *about* emotional meanings and experience. The *actual transformation of core emotional meanings occurs through the process of experiencing the juxtaposition of current emotional meanings and novel experiences that juxtapose new neural connections with established and frequently reinforced neural pathways.*

According to Ecker and Toomey (2008), the neurological process that leads to the transformation of long-held implicit core emotional meanings is *long-term depression* or *depotentiation* (LTD) of existing patterns of neural connections, and the reconsolidation of new such patterns (LTP). As indicated above, LTP refers to the consolidation of patterns of neural firings among any given network of neurons involved in the representation of implicit or explicit memory. The activation of any system of neural networks renders the patterns of potentiation among constituent neurons more labile, changeable, and plastic. According to Alberini (2005), "the stronger the reactivation of the learned experience, the more labile the memory becomes" (p. 54). It is during such reactivation of established long-term memory structures that such patterns of neural firings can be modified by novel experiences, particularly by experiences that are *incompatible* with previously acquired patterns of neural firing. The LTD of neural networks is the inverse of the process of LTP. LTP occurs with the weakening of synapses between and among neurons.

In elaborating this proposition, Ecker and Toomey (2008) drew upon neuroscientific studies using Pavlovian conditioning procedures. They noted that traditional extinction procedures—in which "conditioned stimulus" (CS; e.g., a tone) is presented in the absence of an "unconditioned stimulus" (US; e.g., electric shock)—do not result in permanent removal of emotional memories. This is evidenced by the well-known phenomenon of spontaneous recovery. After a period of delay subsequent to having extinguished a "conditioned response" (CR; e.g., fear) through the repeated decoupling of a US and a CS, the presentation of the CS alone results in a reemergence of the conditioned response. Ecker and Toomey drew upon research that suggests that the retention of long-term emotional memories can be greatly attenuated or even reversed under conditions in which, instead of mere extinction, a CS is paired with an experience that is *incompatible* with the initial conditional response. Although this line of thinking has long been employed in forms of psychotherapy such as systematic desensitization (Zimbarg & Griffith, 2008), flooding (Saigh, 1998), prolonged exposure therapy (Nemeroff et al., 2006), and short-term dynamic theory (McCullough et al., 2003; McCullough & Magill, 2009), Ecker and Toomey reviewed neuroscientific evidence that suggests such effects are mediated, in part, by changes in corticolimbic ("implicit") memory systems.

To illustrate the ways in which the therapist may introduce conflicting and incompatible emotional experiences, we return again to the Lady Cloaked in Fog. Over the course of the pivotal harbor light session, the client was able (a) to articulate and make explicit a set of previously unarticulated emotional meanings (e.g., "I mattered to my previous therapist," and "being cared about in therapy is artificial"), and (b) to consolidate and organize these representations into stable structures. The client was able to construct these insights largely but not exclusively within the dialectics of attentional support and interpretation. Through attentional support and interpretation, the client was even able to reflect upon and represent a challenge to her own sense of "not mattering" offstage. At one point, the therapist asks the client, "Now, how did that feel, thinking about [your previous therapist thinking about you when you were home alone]?" The client responded by saying that "it's new and different and ... and, um, shakes something very deep. Some real deep core belief ..." [T: "Uh-huh. Put some words on it."] *"That I don't matter—and there I was mattering and I didn't even know it."* However, although groundbreaking for the client, this mere conceptualization was insufficient to prompt a core change in the client's experience of not mattering. The core change—including a noticeable change in expressed affect—developed over the course of the session within a series of emotionally rich *enactments* that occurred between the client and the therapist. Within face-to-face emotionally embodied exchanges, the therapist enacted her feelings of care for the client. The therapist's actions evoked feelings of both joy and embarrassment in the client, which the client directly linked to feeling cared for by the therapist. Through these enactments, the therapy brought into awareness the *felt contradiction* between, on the one hand, the client's feelings of joy and embarrassment over being cared for, and, on the other hand, her feelings of sadness over "not mattering" to others. Over the course of the enactments that occurred in this session, the client came to no longer feel the negative feelings in the moment. However, their residue remained, represented by the metaphor of "fog," and she expected to experience the old feelings of sadness in an entirely different way—in the context of contradictory experiences of joy and feeling cared about. The client's use of the harbor light metaphor to organize and relativize her feelings of sadness was most evident when she said,

> Storms and fog … It's the fog that is bothering me the most right now…. Yeah the fog, it's less stormy than it used to be, but there is the, you know, sometimes a dense fog. Yeah and it, right now I'm not feeling like that skulpy thing of being oarless in the boat. But sometimes I do, and how nice to think that if I just perk my little head up, that there's going to … be a harbor light somewhere. And that we can … we can talk about the bad stuff.

Integrating Affect, Cognition, and Action

Cozolino's (2002) final principle for integrating neuroscience, affect, and psychotherapy involves the role of language and narrative in the therapeutic process. Mediated by higher-order cortical systems, the capacity for language is founded upon prelinguistic patterns of intersubjectivity that have their origins in subcortical processes as they are deployed and co-regulated within infant–caregiver interaction (Bråten, 2007). The interactions that occur in psychotherapy often include a great deal of nonverbal communication and communication through actions, all of which may have considerable emotional impact. However, typically, therapeutic change takes place within the medium of language. Because of its capacity to generate and represent shared meanings, language functions as the quintessential vehicle of social interaction and higher-order development. Words are not simply conduits for transmitting already existing thoughts and feelings to others; through words, we jointly create new systems of meaning on which further patterns of thinking, feeling, and acting are predicated. Words operate as a nexus for integrating experience, meaning, and action as they emerge and change both within and between people. Words are vehicles of reflection and praxis. It is through the use of words that we are able to create novel, socially shared meanings of our experiences and relations with others, and to then carry those novel meanings into relationships outside of the therapy session (McNamee, 2003). The DAPP analysis focuses on the role of linguistic exchanges in the process of evoking emotions within relationships, representing the emotions that have been created, and reorganizing and giving novel meaning to emotional experience.

The Role of Emotion in Psychotherapy: Case Illustrations

Building upon the approach to analysis elaborated above, we examine the role of emotion in psychotherapy with the clients discussed in Chapters 7 (Eva), and 8 (the Lady Cloaked in Fog). Our examination is guided by two basic questions: (a) How, if at all, do the clients' and the therapists' emotions change over the course of therapy? (b) What dominant emotions are exhibited over time? And (c) how are core emotional themes identified, consolidated, and transformed over the course of therapy? To address these questions, we examine developmental changes in the production of emotional experience over the course of therapy sessions for each of the three clients discussed in this book. First, we trace changes in positive, negative, and neutral affect exhibited by both the client and the therapist over the course of conversational turns within a given therapy session. Second, we identify specific episodes involving the production of strong emotion on the part of the client, or that otherwise appear to be emotionally significant for understanding the developmental process that occurs within the target session. Third, we will consider the role of the therapist in processes of emotional change over the course of each psychotherapy session, including the resources offered to the five steps in the emotion transformation process that we have described above.

Identifying Emotional States in Clients and Therapists

For each episode within a given psychotherapy session, we identified the emotions exhibited by the client. We adopted a discursive-interpretive methodology (Mascolo, 2008b) to identify and track emotional changes over the course of psychotherapy encounters. The discursive-interpretive approach builds upon the presupposition that—for laypersons and psychological scientists alike—the process of understanding the inner life of others is founded upon the human capacity for establishing *intersubjectivity* with others. From this view, any attempt to understand the experience of others is mediated by everyday emotion concepts and founded upon an individual's unique and shared history of intersubjective interactions with others. Drawing upon such experience, in any given social encounter, our initial sense of the emotional life of the other is often intuitive and implicit. Even when we categorize another's emotion using everyday (or more technical) emotion language, we are not always aware of the conceptual basis of our categorizations. The discursive-interpretive method proceeds by making *explicit* what is often only *implicit* in our intersubjective experience of the other. This includes identifying the specific (and often highly subtle) *aspects of the other person's expressed emotion* on which our implicit sense of the other's emotion is based. It also involves articulating the (often implicit) *conceptual criteria* that we use to classify the emotional states of others into any given emotional category. In so doing, the discursive-interpretive method operates as a collaborative process in which researchers use *their own intersubjective experience* as the primary research instrument (Hammersley & Atkinson, 1995).

Through careful observation of the expressed emotion of another person, researchers (a) gain an initial intuitive sense of the emotional state of the other; (b) draw upon everyday emotion terms to form an articulated sense of the other's emotional experience; and, (c) having done so, test and retest their articulated emotional categorizations against the data of the other person's expressed emotion. In so doing, the researcher's activities are guided by a series of questions designed to facilitate the process of articulating the conceptual and empirical bases of their use of everyday emotional terms to classify the experience of the other. The researchers ask, "Upon what specific expressive acts do I rely to support my statement that this person is experiencing X?" This question forces the researcher to focus closely upon particular elements of expressed action (including verbal action) to support his or her emotional ascription. This question naturally prompts a related question, "What conceptual criteria do I draw upon in order to make the assertion that this person is experiencing X?" This question prompts the researcher to articulate the often implicit conceptual criteria that define one emotion category in contradistinction to another (e.g., "Is this an expression of embarrassment or shame? What criteria differentiated these two emotions? What aspects of the person's expressed emotion fit these criteria?"). These questions inevitably lead to *conflicts* between a researcher's provisional emotional categorizations and the "data" of the target person's expressed emotion. The attempt (d) to *resolve* such conflicts drives the process of *reflecting* upon, *revising*, and *refining* the researcher's increasingly articulated emotion concepts against the data of the other person's expressed emotion. In so doing, however, researchers must not only seek to resolve conflicts between their own emotion attributions and the data of the other's expressed experience, but also seek to resolve conflicts that arise among the co-researchers themselves. The discursive-interpretive interactions continue until all conflicts are resolved, or until some threshold degree of intersubjective agreement among researchers is established. (For further theoretical justification and illustration of the discursive-interpretive method, see Mascolo, 2009.) The identified emotions reported in Figures 9.1 and 9.2 represent the final intersubjective agreement among the co-researchers.

Case Illustration 1: Emotional Transformations in the Lady Cloaked in Fog

During the harbor light session, the client exhibited four main classes of emotion: depression/sadness, anxiety/fear, embarrassment/shame, and positive affect.[3] Using the interpretive-discursive method, Table 9.2 depicts

---

[3] Given the availability of videotaped emotional interactions of the target therapy session, we begin with an analysis of the Lady Cloaked in Fog.

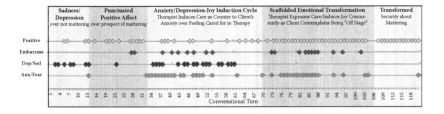

Figure 9.1 Emotional transformations en route to the harbor light insight. Changes in the configuration of expressed anxiety/fear, depression/sadness; embarrassment, and positive affect over the course of the harbor light session for the Lady Cloaked in Fog.

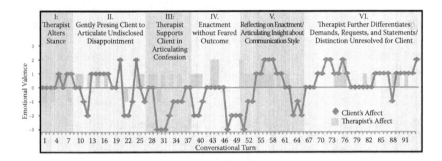

Figure 9.2 Emotional changes over the course of the "critical incident" session for Eva. Although the therapist's emotional demeanor was guarded at the beginning of the session (see text for explanation), his affect ranged from neutral to slightly positive over the course of the session. After the client's "confession," her affect shifted from positive to deeply negative during which time the therapist, within the dialectic of enactment, supported the client's attempt to express her fear of rejection by the therapist. A cognitive-emotional transformation occurred after the client found her fears of rejection disconfirmed over the course of an enactment with the therapist.

the expressive acts that co-researchers identified as manifestations of these four emotion families. The distribution of these emotions as expressed by the client over the course of the pivotal harbor lights therapy session is depicted in Figure 9.1. (The therapist's affect, not exhibited in Figure 9.1, fluctuated between positive and neutral throughout the course of the session.) Over the course of the session, the client's emotional state evolved in a series of five basic phases. The first phase was marked mainly by expressions of *sadness/depression* over not mattering.[4] It was during this first phase that the client and therapist constructed a representation of the client's core emotional theme—"not mattering offstage." The main moment of affective intensity occurred when the client said, with deep sadness,

---

[4] In the analyses that follow, in order to highlight the emotional elements of the analysis, all descriptions of acts that are considered to be expressions of emotion are identified in italics.

Table 9.2 Emotion Families Exhibited by the Lady Cloaked in Fog

Emotion	Expressive Elements
Positive affect	Smile; laughter; increasing pitch; statements expressing positive emotion (e.g., "It feels good")
Sadness/depression	Crying; tears; thin, constricted voice, as if about to cry; soft thin voice; tremor in voice; low or guttural voice; downturned lips; sitting back heavily in the chair as if difficult to lift arms or body; long pauses between speech; staring into space during long pauses; sigh or heavy breaths
Anxiety	Closed, tight posture, arms closing around body with muscles tight; increase in bodily movement; increase in pace of speech and/or decrease in clarity of speech; gaze aversion during speech; verbal expressions of anxiety or fear (e.g., "all this bringing up its fear again")
Embarrassment	Laughter or smiling inconsistent with utterances; smiling with gaze aversion; verbal expressions of embarrassment (e.g., "I would have to be embarrassed")

"Essentially me, my vote matters, but *I don't....*" In making this statement, the client's voice was clear and forthcoming until she said, "*I don't.*" At this point, her voice *choked*; the "*I don't*" was stated so *softly* that it was barely audible, almost as if it were almost unspeakable by the client. The client's utterance reflects a clear statement of the client's core emotional meaning. As the phase moved onward, the client generated her own counterexample to feeling as if she did not matter offstage (i.e., that her present and past therapists would talk about her when the client was at home). As discussed above, it was at this point that when asked by the therapist to "put words on" her feelings, that the client indicated the counterexample "shakes a core belief ... *that I don't matter—and there I was mattering and I didn't even know it.*"

In articulating the latter antithethical side of the conflict that she had generated, the client exhibited brief signs of positive affect that contrasted with her sadness over not mattering. However, when the therapist asked, "When you were home alone, did you feel like you mattered to Carol? That you'd be in her thoughts and in her heart?" the client responded as follows:

"Even just that question—thoughts, yeah. Heart?" Lifting her hands in front of her upper torso and lower face, with her palms up, the client emitted a "pushing away" gesture; concurrently, starting in a high pitched voice and descending slowing to a low pitch, she said, "Oooooooh..." Then, speaking very quickly, she said, "well, I don't know about heart." The client then looked away from the therapist, closed her eyes and emitted a brief laugh ("hih hih"). Then, the client tilted her head and moved it back and forth, alternatively looking toward and away from the therapist. Again, she held her hands in front of her body, palms toward the therapist, and made a gesture as if she were pushing away something coming toward her. As she did this, in an increasingly guttural and choking voice (as if about to cry), [she] said, "You, I just, I can do just so much, it's just a delicate answer." The client then looked away from the therapist, smiled briefly, and modified her body into a closed posture (shoulders raised and tight; fidgeting body movements; hands and arms together and placed between her legs; muscles tight). She let out a deep breath, and, as if trying to calm herself, and said "Jeez."

In this brief moment, the client exhibited two broad categories of emotion. Her choking voice reflected deep *sadness* over her sense of not mattering. Her closed posture, increased tightness, and bodily movement indicated *anxiety* as she "pushed away" the "delicate question" of whether her prior therapist actually cared in her heart. The client's laughter and gaze aversion also indicated a degree of *anxious embarrassment*. Thus, in this initial phase, the client, with the support of the therapist, (a) constructed a clear representation of the client's core emotional theme (Step 1), (b) maintained that representation in mind over the course of the phase (Step 2), and (c) constructed an emotional antithesis to her painful disclosure about not mattering offstage (Step 3). However, the client's self-generated emotional antithesis was short-lived; it was instantly challenged by the therapist's question about mattering in her previous therapist's heart. The emotions of sadness and anxiety over not mattering set the stage for the remainder of the session.

The second phase consisted of *tentative feelings of joy over feeling cared for*. As a counterpoint to the previous phase, the therapist asked the client to verify whether or not she (the client) had ever cared deeply for coworkers who were in pain when the client was at home. In response, *gazing at the therapist*, the client *smiled* and emitted a *soft* and *breathy* "Oh yeah." In response to the therapist's query about how it felt to have her therapists care about the client in the same way, the client *smiled, pursed her lips*, and *nodding her head slowly* said, "*Well, I like it.*" During this phase, the client exhibited an increase in positive affect. Again, however, her positive feelings were short-lived and unstable. Immediately after indicating her positive feelings about being cared for, the client expressed some feelings of *sadness/depression* when contemplating how she would "*kick herself*" for not letting herself feel good about her therapist's feelings of care for her. Nonetheless, during this second phase of emotional engagement, the therapist was successful in introducing an incompatible emotional state (*joy over mattering*) as a counterpoint to the client's verbally and nonverbally expressed feelings of *sadness and anxiety* over not mattering (Step 3).

The third phase consisted of what might be called an *anxiety/joy induction cycle*. During this phase, although the client was intellectually able to accept the idea that her therapist indeed cared about her, the client repeated exhibited feelings of *sadness/depression* and *anxiety* related to her sense that being cared for in therapy was "artificial" or "not real." In response to the client's expressed sadness and anxiety, the therapist adopted the strategy of all but forcing the client to attend to and experience the therapist's overt enactment and emotional expression of care for the client. In this way, in the context of a series of emotional enactments, the therapist directly induced feelings of *joy* and *embarrassment* as *counterexperiences* to the client's palpably expressed feelings of *sadness* and *anxiety*. For example, in response to the client's statement that she experienced therapy as an artificial relationship, the therapist countered by asking, "Do I seem artificial to you?" and by reminding the client of the feelings of care that are "pouring out toward you, here, from me—from Carol [previous therapist]." In response to the question, "It's going to be so important to let yourself savor some of it. How much are you letting yourself savor it right now?" the client responded, "It's … it's … um … *I have to be embarrassed. I feel embarrassed. It feels … I feel embarrassed.*" The client's embarrassment signals a degree of acceptance of the therapist's expression of care. As part of the process of emotional transformation, the therapist introduced yet another novel experience (*joy and embarrassment over feeling cared for*) as a counter to the client's feelings of *sadness and anxiety* (Step 3). In addition, the therapist continues to maintain an explicit representation of the client's emotional conflict in mind as they reflect upon the client's feelings. For example, in response to the client's feelings of embarrassment, the therapist said,

> Okay, well, let's look at that because this is something you've never been able to let yourself do. It makes sense that you'd be embarrassed, self-conscious. [C: Yeah] You know, when you've been in the shadows so long as you were with your mother. You were 'out there'. Then I say "Let's shine the light on you"—and it's glaring isn't it?

Throughout this phase, there are several reiterations of Steps 3 and 4 involving the expression of sadness/anxiety over not mattering followed by the direct induction of positive affect resulting from the expressed care of the therapist. By the end of the third phase, as the client appeared able to accept the feelings of care from the therapist, the client's feelings of *sadness/depression* all but disappeared. Although the client was able to accept and feel good about feeling cared for within the therapeutic relationship, the client experienced high levels of anxiety about her capacity to experience such feelings of care outside of the therapeutic relationship.

During phase 4, *emotional transformation,* a significant transformation in the client's emotional meaning system occurred. During phase 4, the dominant emotions expressed by the client were *anxiety, embarrassment,* and *positive affect.* The client's anxiety was exacerbated by the therapist's suggestion that the client "take these [good] feelings with you" when she left the therapy session. Although the client was able to feel good about being cared for within the therapy relationship, the client was unable to imagine that the therapist would continue to have positive feelings for the client after she left the session. The idea of imagining what the therapist might feel for the client after the session had ended produced observable levels of *anxiety* for the client. With sensitivity and in the context of overtly expressed feelings of care, the therapist guided the client through the process of imagining what the therapist would think and feel about the client that evening at dinner. Over and over again, as the client attempted to imagine how the therapist might feel out of session, the client experienced heightened levels of *anxiety*; in response, the therapist redirected the client's attention to the therapist's expressed feelings of care. This produced feelings of *joy and embarrassment* in the client. At a pivotal point in this phase, *in the context of sustained levels of anxiety in the client,* the therapist was able to help the client to imagine that, at dinner that evening, the therapist would want the client to feel that she mattered to the therapist. This is illustrated in the following exchange:

T: And there they are back and forth, and why will they go away. Tonight while I'm having [C: Right] supper will you know when you come to mind, what do you think I'll feel?

C: (*Hesitating, and struggling to answer*). You'll probably feel good and probably think this was a nice piece of work. You'll probably feel good about it. And you'll wonder how I'm doing—probably.

T: Yes, absolutely, I will wonder. And what will I want?

C: You'll want me...Oh... (*she looks very embarrassed* and *laughs*).

T: It's harder, isn't it, to let yourself.

C: Yeah!

T: To think what would be in my heart.

C: I would want you to want me Um, I'll start—

T: Um huh.

C: With what would ... (*wincing and looking away from therapist*)

T: What would I be wanting for you? You would want me? What would you want me to want for you?

C: So, I would imagine that you're sitting down at dinner and you would feel good about the session and that you would hope or wonder how I was doing. And you would want—(*speaking very haltingly* here) for me, that I go to group and do my work there knowing that I matter at least to you (*nervous laugh*).

Throughout this period of the episode, the client simultaneously exhibited signs of anxiety over the prospect of imagining the therapist's care, embarrassment over the feelings of care expressed by the therapist, and positive affect (joy) in her articulated anticipation of the therapist's feelings of care. Through this enactment, the client experienced the simultaneous juxtaposition of anxiety/fear over not mattering to the therapist and the incompatible experience of joy over feeling cared for. This enactment illustrates Steps 4 (maintaining the conflict over time) and 5 (resolving the emotional contradiction) in the process of emotional transformation.

The fifth and final phase involved the experience of *transformed affect*. Within the session, the client no longer exhibited sustained signs of anxiety or sadness/depression. Instead, with *positive emotion*, the client was able to articulate the harbor light insight without any significant assistance from the therapist. However, more important than the mere shift in affect from negative to positive within the session, this episode marked the transformation of a core emotional meaning that, from the perspective of the therapist (McCullough, 1999), provided the emotional foundation for the client to begin to develop a sustained sense that she could matter to other people outside of the therapy relationship.

The DAPP analysis of emotional development makes it extremely clear that the harbor light insight, discussed at length in Chapter 8—the idea that the therapist cares about the client both "onstage" and "offstage"—is something far more than a "cognitive achievement." Instead, the harbor light insight comprises a novel synthesis that builds upon and resolves the *emotional* conflict between, on the one hand, *sadness/anxiety* over not mattering and, on the other, *joy/acceptance* over mattering to the therapist. It was achieved through the enactment of novel emotional experience with the therapist.

The transcendent power of the harbor light insight is clearly evident in the "reviewing-and-wrapping-up" part of the session, which comes after the utterances representing the emotional transformation itself that are coded in Figure 9.1. In her statements, the client makes clear that she is now prepared for dealing, within the context of the overall emotional structure of the novel synthesis, with the *sadder, more depressed* emotions that she anticipates. As quoted above, she states,

But there is the, you know, *sometimes a dense fog* (stated with *somber tone* and the same emotional signs of *sadness and depression* as accompanied her expressions of not mattering). Yeah and it, *right now I'm not feeling* (*positive affect*) like that skulpy thing of being oarless in the boat. But sometimes I do, and *how nice to think* that if I just *perk my little head up*, that there's going to … *be a harbor light somewhere* (*positive affect*). And that we can … we can talk about the *bad stuff* (the *negative emotions* are now both acknowledged and *represented* in a way that the client and therapist can proactively work with them, rather than the client be taken over by them).

Case Illustration 2: Transcending Eva's Fear of Rejection in Communicative Exchanges

Over the course of the "critical incident" session analyzed in detail in Chapter 7, there was a transformation in Eva's emotional repertoire. The dominant emotional theme that arose in the discussion between Eva and her psychotherapist was the fear of offending others within communicative exchanges and being rejected as a result. As indicated in Chapter 7, this fear was played out in an enactment with the therapist. The client, disappointed with the flow of the psychotherapy session, was reluctant to reveal her feelings to the therapist out of fear of appearing aggressive. When she was able to disclose her disappointment to the therapist, she found not only that her fear of rejection was unfounded, but also that she was accepted and affirmed by the therapist, and her honest expression of emotions was appreciated. Similar to the case of the Lady Cloaked in Fog, Eva's emotional transformation occurred when her fear of rejection was first fully attended to and represented, and then juxtaposed with an incompatible emotional state (evoked by the therapist's acceptance of Eva's expression of disappointment in the session).

Figure 9.2 tracks the emotional valence (positive versus negative) of the vocalizations expressed by the client and therapist over the course of the session. Table 9.3 describes criteria for identifying the valence and level of intensity of any given vocal expression. The emotional changes can be organized into six phases. To understand how the emotions that were transformed during the critical incident (Session 15) were first evoked, it is necessary to review events that transpired during the previous therapy session. In the 14th therapy session, the therapist experienced himself as both offering much more interpretation than in previous sessions and finding the accompanying interaction to be emotionally gratifying. During the 14th session, the discussion focused on a dance that the client was set to attend with a young man (Steve). The client expressed a felt need to figure out in advance whether she should expect the date to be "platonic" or romantic. The therapist suggested an alternative to the client's expressed need to decide upon the nature of the relationship with Steve in advance. He indicated that one alternative would be to attend to her own feelings over the course of the evening, and to allow the decision-making process to emerge in response to the feelings. The client was excited to receive this

Table 9.3 Classifying Affective Valence for Eva and Her Therapist

		Expressive Elements	
Emotional Valence		**Eva**	**Therapist**
(3)	Very positive	NA	NA
(2)	Positive	Laughter; high pitch; relative increase in volume; fast pace; high level of fluctuation in loudness and inflection (animated voice)	Laughter; high pitch and increase in volume; fast pace with higher level of fluctuation in loudness and inflection (animated voice)
(1)	Slightly positive	Increase in pitch and pace; slight increase in volume; chuckle or brief laugh.	Somewhat higher volume, pace of speech, and pitch of speech (in comparison to neutral). High, brief, and empathic vocal tone, especially when saying "Mm-hm."
(0)	Neutral	Even pace and moderate tone; no significant fluctuations of voice; voice of moderate volume; vocal quality is clear.	Even paced and moderate tone; no significant fluctuations of voice; voice of moderate volume; vocal quality is clear.
(−1)	Slightly negative	Softer tone; slightly slower rate of speech; tone sometimes slightly more "round" and sometimes slightly more "thin." Narrow range of fluctuation, but within higher or lower register of volume and pitch; sigh; trailing off of words.	Low guttural tone; slightly "heavy" voice, as if fatigued; slow speaking pace; somewhat long pauses between utterances.
(−2)	Negative	Laughter inconsistent with content of speech; thin voice, as if near tears; high pitch; constricted throat; tremor; childlike, plaintive tone.	NA
(−3)	Very negative	Crying; sobbing; very slow or very fast pace; rushed voice; very loud or very soft voice.	NA

"advice"; she gratefully accepted the therapist's suggestion as a novel and helpful solution to her problem.

In reflecting upon the session, the therapist experienced a series of concerns about the way he engaged in the dialogue with Eva. First, he was aware of the client's previously expressed wish to view the therapist as a kind of "competent problem solver" auxiliary ego. Feeling that such a conception of the therapist was reminiscent of the client's relationship with her mother, the therapist, early in the therapy, had formulated the goal of assisting the client in finding ways to attend to and manage her own feelings and decisions in the course of everyday problem solving—a goal that had been endorsed by the client. The therapist was further wary of the possibility that he himself might come to enjoy the role of acting as a "competent problem solver" for the client and the explicit adulation expressed by the client when the therapist played such an interpretive role. The therapist's second concern was informed by his having reflected on the content of the session using a "transference" lens. The therapist wondered about the extent to which the drama between the client and Steve was also being played out in the client's mind with reference to the therapeutic relationship itself. If this were the case, the therapist's advice about the relationship between the client and Steve (to allow the question of a platonic versus romantic relationship to be settled over time) would not be appropriate when applied to the therapeutic relationship. The therapist felt the need to communicate, however indirectly, the bounded nature of the therapeutic relationship. Informed by a discussion of these concerns during peer supervision, the therapist decided to approach the next therapy session in a more observant and less active fashion.

It was with this intention that the therapist entered the critical 15th session. In the first phase of the session (*Therapist Alters Stance Pulls Back*), the therapist altered the behavior of active interpretation accompanied by excitement about the process that evolved during the previous therapy session. He relied on attentional support that was accompanied by a more emotionally reserved demeanor. In our analysis of the therapist's verbal behavior for emotional expression, we identified a slightly *negative* tone that was characterized by a *soft and low pitch*, a *graveled quality*, a *slow pace*, and *relatively long pauses* before speaking. In contrast, the client spoke in a predominantly direct tone, fluctuating from neutral to slightly positive, within a moderate range of rising and falling intonation. This pattern continued until the beginning of the second emotional phase (*Client's Unstated Disappointment*). In an apparent response to the therapist's relatively muted affect, the client raised the question (accompanied by somewhat *self-deprecatory content*) of whether or not the therapist was "getting any message" from the client. As indicated in Figure 9.2, the client's statement, which marked the beginning of the second phase of affective engagement, was accompanied by a shift in affective tone from positive to *slightly negative.*

C: (Pause) I don't know if you're getting like any message.... I mean I sort of feel like this whole ... like all of what I've been saying has been very like not organized or anything (client *shifts* from an animated voice with rising and falling intonation to a *soft voice* with *descending volume* until almost *inaudible*) and sort of like jumping from one thing to another, but ...

Sensing a change in the client's *affect* (as well as a discrepancy between the client's previous articulateness and her calling herself "not organized"), the therapist asked, "What are you feeling right now?" At this point, the client's affect began to become more *negative*, exhibiting signs of *sadness*:

C: Well, I guess I'm feeling that I wanted to like present to you, like, specific topics for today, or something or, or, or a case or whatever, and then we would talk about that. But I find myself ... like now this is sort of like the third thing I'm talking about, and we haven't really like talked about one thing (again, the client *shifts* from an animated voice with rising and falling intonation to a *soft voice* with *descending volume* until almost *inaudible*) which is probably fine too I guess.

T: But there, there was this hope that you could come in with a topic and you could [C: Yeah *(drawn out)*] something would happen [C: Yeah *(drawn out)*] between us around that topic, that would ...

C: Yeeah (voice moving from very high pitched to low pitched in less than a second, plaintive, almost childlike)

Sensing this change, throughout the course of the second phase, the therapist gently pressed the client to articulate her concerns about the course of the therapy session. Over the next several turns, the therapist continued to gently request through questions and probes (Sc4) that the client articulate her felt concerns, despite his recognition that the client was starting to express *anxiety.*[5] With each attempt, the client resisted with a chuckle, as if to gently resist the therapist's persistence. At this point in the session—somewhat ironically—without either the client's or therapist's knowledge, the client was engaged in an enactment of the adaptive and emotional conflict that she had begun the session by articulating. In her first few turns of the session (Phase 1), she had used the therapist's attentional support

---

[5] Although the therapist felt that he was communicating empathy with Eva's anxiety with his eyes, this was a case where he judged that confrontation with and identification of the unpleasant emotion were important enough to eschew joining in Eva's efforts to minimize her discomfort.

to construct a clear representation of the conflict—namely, a sense of not asserting herself in social interactions out of fear of appearing aggressive and offending social partners (see Chapter 7) and then feeling devalued relative to those partners. Neither the client nor the therapist knew yet that this very conflict would continue to be played out in the subsequent series of enactments between the client and the therapist. Thus, although the client was able to construct a conceptual representation of her adaptive conflict, the dyad had not yet co-constructed a representation of the emotional dynamics upon which this conflict was founded (Step 1 of the process of emotional transformation).

Phase 3 (*The Confession*) began as the client appeared to yield to the therapist's gentle and persistent questions about the nature of the client's disappointment with the session. In response, the client offered her "confession," namely, that it had crossed her mind twice that "this topic just bored you … and I didn't want to talk about something that you'd be bored about." Once the client had "confessed," the therapist shifted his stance and responded empathically with attentional support and explicit approval and encouragement. The client in turn expressed her *emotional difficulty* in making this disclosure to the therapist. In what might be an emotional turning point of the session, the therapist said emphatically, "I *feel* this is so important for you to … to be able to say that." At this point, the client began to *sob*, saying, "It, it's so hard for me, that *I have to cry!* (Through *sobbing*) It's like very hard for me to say this to you, you know? (short pause) … I don't know why."

After the client regained her composure, the therapist probed the client further about her *feelings*. At this point, after the client reiterated her sense that the therapist may have been bored, the client began *sobbing* again, this time *in silence*. She also expressed *embarrassment*. Phase IV began as the therapist gently invited the client to articulate what she was *embarrassed* about. After a series of conversational turns in which the client was able to successively reformulate her sense of what she was embarrassed about, the dyad was able to co-construct a clear representation of her feelings in terms of the client's *fear of being aggressive toward the therapist and as a result being rejected by him*:

C: (*In a slightly high-pitched, as if about to cry, yet graveled tone*) I mean what really was hard for me … is to say … *that you felt I was being aggressive toward you*, right? Like by telling you oh, you're bored, you're bored about what I'm saying.

T: That that would be aggressive?

C: Yeah, because that would mean that I wasn't perceiving the attention you were giving me, or that I was demanding like, some kind of (*becoming graveled despite high pitch*) like expression

of your attention that you didn't give me. (*Becomes more animated again*) You know like, "oh," you know like, I don't know
[T: Mm-hm], and that would be sort of like aggressive towards
you because I was telling you that you hadn't shown to me what
I was expecting.

T: You were feeling disappointed in my reaction.

C: Yeah, (said quickly) so that would be hurtful to you.

T: Why … (interrupts self) … Mm-hm, mm-hm.

C: So, (*in a high-pitched, slightly singsong voice, as if nearing tears*) but of
course now after we've talked more, I feel comfortable that you
don't think I'm being aggressive, so it doesn't bother me that
much anymore. [T: Mm-hm mm-hm] But I couldn't even bring
myself to say it.

T: It was so scary at that moment that I might feel it as aggressive.

C: (In a higher pitch with a tremor in her voice, as if about to cry, and in
a singsong voice involving rising and falling intonation, where
the rising is indicated in italics:) Yeah, and *obviously*, and I think
obviously the *fear* is that if you felt that I was being ag*gres*sive
(voice is thin, cracking, as if about to cry) then what you would
do maybe is just like shut yourself off and like never [T: Protect
myself] never be like interested in any of like, whatever I talked
about a*gain*. (Voice falling in volume, becoming progressively
softer over time.) You can say, "Oh well, you know, if she's going
to be like this, you know, I don't want to have to deal with her,"
kind of thing.

Through Phases III and IV, the dyad embarked upon several important
elements of the emotional transformation process. First, the dyad was able
to co-construct a clear representation of the source of the client's embarrassment, namely, the client's fear of appearing aggressive to the therapist
and thus being rejected by him (Step 1). In so doing, the dyad maintained
the focus of their joint attention on the client's representation of her feeling state (Step 2). Throughout the process, the client exhibited strong signs
of negative emotion, primarily fear and embarrassment over the possibility of offending the therapist. In the context of the client's strong emotion, and in contrast to the client's expectations, the therapist responded
with compassionate acceptance and support. As a result, throughout the
phase, the therapist's responses within the enactment functioned to introduce experiences that were incompatible with the client's core emotional
themes (Step 3). The client was able to articulate a clear representation of
how the therapist's responses within the enactment process disconfirmed
her emotional expectations:

I mean, like, (voice is still a little *choked* and *high pitched*, in some-what *rapid singsong* voice) just the way, um, like things are turning out right now. It's so much better to talk about it, because you're not being offended at all. But I thought that you might be offended, right? And so *I feel a lot better* that we could talk about something.

During Phase V (*Reflecting Upon the Enactment*), the therapist and client were able to hold a representation of the client's emotional conflict in mind (Step 4) as they reflected upon the client's fears of offending others in communicative exchanges. Reflecting upon the just completed enactment, the client was able to form a clear representation of how her fear of offending others placed limitations on her relationships. Building upon the therapist's suggestion that the client could simply "state her feelings" in communicative exchanges that occurred both in and out of therapy, the client was also able to identify prior occasions in which she was able to assert her agenda without offending her communication partners (see Chapter 7). Throughout this phase, the client exhibited primarily *positive affect*. The positive affect that accompanied the client's reflection on her enactment with the therapist signaled the experience of emotional transformation (Step 5).

This transformation in emotional experience soon led to awareness that the transformation was in conflict with Eva's self-representation. She had for as long as she could remember thought of herself as "demanding," in fact "demanding" in a "neurotic" way. Thus, work had emerged that needed to be done integrating Eva's novel emotional experience with her established construction of self. This work in part proceeded through attentional support to the etiology of her self-representation (e.g., the therapist's question "Someone has told you you're demanding?"—leading to a long discussion of her childhood experience with her father and his wife). It also proceeded through the therapist offering interpretations (e.g., of how he saw the difference between making a demand, making a request, and sharing an emotional response). From this interpretation, conflicts not only with Eva's self-representation but also with her representations of her cultural background emerged. Eva stated her understanding that demands, requests, and simple statements of feeling are all equivalent from the standpoint of her culture of origin, implying that to state a feeling is equivalent to making a demand.

According to the therapist's account (see Chapter 7), much of the therapeutic work arising from the conflicts among her emotional transformation, her self-identity, and her cultural identity was accomplished in the few months following the critical incident. Her self-representations were reconstructed in a more complex way that included greater appreciation of the triangle among her father, his wife, and herself, and she was able to develop a relativistic understanding of communication styles in relation to cultural context that gave her much more of a sense of choice regarding communication of feelings in various contexts. The case of Eva illustrates that although novel experience is essential in bringing about emotional transformation, and emotional transformation can provide a foundation from which further therapeutic work often proceeds more easily, conflict requiring further psychotherapeutic work may evolve from emotional transformation when novel emotional experience conflicts with well-established representations of oneself and one's cultural identity.

How Emotions Organize and Are Organized by Psychotherapy

The primary medium of much psychotherapy is talk. In psychotherapy, talk serves many functions. The case analyses provided in Chapters 7 and 8 demonstrate ways in which development can be tracked through the detailed analysis of discourse. Although we often hear a distinction made between speech and action, we think it more important to remember that speaking is both a *form* and a *tool* of action. Our higher-order thoughts, feelings, and activities in the world are *mediated* through the use of speech. In this way, speech is not an encased or disembodied module that operates separately from other psychological processes. As a tool of action, thought, and feeling, speech functions *in medias res*—in the middle of everything. Speech carries with it the capacity to *develop* and *transform* meaning-dependent organismic processes. This chapter is intended to underscore the point that emotion is central among the organismic processes that are brought forward and transformed in psychotherapy.

As they do in everyday life, emotions serve central functions in psychotherapy. Emotions consist of different *felt* relations between a person's circumstances and her goals, motives, and concerns. The production of emotion is generally rapid and nonconscious. Emotional processes immediately direct one's attention to important motive-relevant circumstances. Without conscious effort or awareness, emotions precipitate changes in consciousness and adaptive action.[6] The *experience* of emotion is immediate; however, because of the neurological levels at which the experience occurs, the *meanings* of emotional experience are often not constructed prior to or simultaneous with the experience. To construct a sense of the meaning of emotional experience, it is generally necessary to engage in acts of reflection and identification.

In psychotherapy, such acts of reflection are facilitated by the offering of attentional support and interpretation. However, the offering of such

---

[6] It is for this reason that emotions are generally experienced as *happenings* rather than as active *doings* (Averill, 1982; Sarbin, 1989; Solomon, 1976).

resources by therapists is an act whose impact is not limited to the level of making abstract meaning. Such acts by therapists (as well as by clients) produce emotional reactions. Not only does the production of emotional reactions in clients organize clients' conscious experience and action, but also the expressive aspects of clients' emotions play a direct role in organizing therapists' sense of clients' emotional states (and vice versa). This is accomplished in part by modifying therapists' own emotional experience, which thereupon plays a role in structuring their actions toward clients. Like clients, therapists may not be immediately aware of the meaning of their own emotional reactions. Articulation of the nature and meaning of the emotional experiences of clients and/or therapists thus becomes an important element of the dialectics of attentional support and interpretation.

In this way, the direct experience of emotion plays a central role in both organizing psychotherapeutic exchanges and in providing an object of focus for therapeutic inquiry. Similar processes are operative for what we have called *core emotional themes*. Core emotional themes reflect more enduring and often nonconscious assemblies of emotional meaning. The conflicts and issues that bring people into therapy are generally organized in relation to strong, painful, and often tender feelings with reference to some area or domain of functioning. The process of consciously identifying and articulating the nature of these more enduring and often implicit emotional themes often occurs within the dialectic of attentional support and interpretation. Through the offering of attentional support and interpretation, the therapist was able to assist the Lady Cloaked in Fog in identifying the core emotional meaning of "not mattering offstage." Eva's therapist was able to support their joint identification of Eva's fear of being rejected by others if she appeared too aggressive.

Although the offering of attentional support and interpretation often facilitates the process of identification and consolidation of emotional experiences and core emotional themes, the process of enactment is important in fostering novel experiences that lead to emotional transformation. In their analysis of the process of emotional transformation, Ecker and Toomey (2008) suggested that core emotional meanings can be transformed and not simply counteracted during psychotherapy. By offering resources that help clients bring core negative emotional themes into contact with novel and incompatible emotional experiences, a therapist assists in the emergence of emotional conflict. In the face of novel and incompatible emotional experience, a client experiences the limitations of existing emotional meanings. Emotional transformation occurs in successful psychotherapy as a product of the conflict between existing emotional meanings and novel incompatible experiences. The production of such novel experiences often occurs within the therapeutic dialectic of enactment. For example, in the case of the Lady, the client's capacity to experience and accept feelings of care from her therapist proved incompatible with her core emotional stance of "not mattering offstage." The emotional transformation that evolved from this conflict created the experiential conditions for the client's construction of the harbor light insight at the end of the psychotherapy session. Similarly, in the enactment process with her therapist, Eva's experience of her therapist's acceptance and understanding directly conflicted with her ongoing fear of offending the therapist and being rejected by him. The enacted disconfirmation of Eva's fear of rejection produced an emotional transformation that created the conditions for the developmental construction of Eva's insight about her communicative style. In each of these cases, representational development was founded upon the results of enactment processes that resulted in foundational emotional transformations in the client.

PART V
Implications

CHAPTER 10

Psychotherapy as a Developmental Process

Implications and Future Directions for Psychotherapy Research, Practice, and Training

In seeing this book as a journey that is nearing its close, we must first acknowledge that we have spent time in many lands, including discussions of purposes, conceptual frameworks, research methods, and case illustrations. We recognize that for varying readers' tastes, we quite likely have spent too much time in some of these lands and not enough time in others. Now we reach this concluding chapter on implications and future directions for research, practice, and training. Our goal is to offer some differentiation of potential directions for communities of practice, research, and study, while reaffirming that this book is fundamentally an offer of an alternative paradigm for all those who think about psychotherapy process and outcome. Within this paradigm, the implications for the relationship of researchers and practitioners, and for the activities of communities of both beginning students of psychotherapy and experienced professionals who want to learn from each other, remain intertwined. All the parties to these relationships have an impact on one another.

We stated in the introduction that this book is an effort to provide a *descriptive* framework that can be used to appreciate the highly varied ways in which particular therapists tailor their work to unique clients' developmental needs, while at the same time offering a *prescription* of a more rigorous method for recognizing and correcting the problem when a particular therapist's way of working is not serving a client well. Studying, describing, and appreciating both similarities and differences across therapy approaches, particular therapists, and particular clients are clearly appropriate tasks for psychotherapy researchers, practitioners, and students alike.

We will suggest below a range of types of research studies that can lead to a kind of mapping of the highly variegated field of psychotherapy practice. Studies of some of these types are already under way. Researchers will also be interested in the integration of the methods and results of such studies with other research in psychotherapy (e.g., large N studies comparing therapy approaches in terms of prespecified outcome measures) and developmental psychology (e.g., how development is facilitated or obstructed by other forms of human relationships).

DAPP provides practitioners a method for describing their own work. In doing so, they may simultaneously be able to contribute to the research enterprise of creating the map of similarities and differences, while using the results of previous research to locate their own work on the map. Finally, for students newly developing their own skills and approaches as psychotherapists, the map can function as a kind of menu of possibilities to explore, comparable within a common language, whereas DAPP provides a method to chart their own progress and challenges encountered as they study themselves putting into practice the approaches and techniques described by the map.

The "prescription" offered by the book is that psychotherapy cases in which effectiveness of therapy is blocked be recognized, reflected upon, and scrutinized for the nature of the blockages and "unblocking alternatives," all using the DAPP method. This also is an appropriate task for researchers, practitioners, and students alike. However, whereas researchers might be seen in a "lead role" in the descriptive task, the roles may be reversed for the prescribed task.

Students typically have the fewest number of ongoing psychotherapy cases, combined with the greatest amount of time to reflect on these particular cases. Also, unlike experienced practitioners, who are typically functioning in communities of practice that employ a shared language for discussing their work that may differ dramatically from the language used in other communities of practice, students' training typically occurs within academic communities in which they are exposed to a wide range of ways of understanding and discussing psychotherapy, and not asked to narrow their conceptual framework to that of a particular approach until, perhaps, late in their training. Teachers who are familiar with using the DAPP framework may be of tremendous help in students' processes of critical self-reflection and professional growth.

Although experienced practitioners may have larger caseloads and less time for reflection than students, the importance of continued scrutiny of their success in working with clients, and continued openness to lifelong learning from colleagues who may be approaching their psychotherapy practices in different ways, is equally if not more important for the well-being of psychotherapy clients. DAPP not only provides practitioners with a method of scrutinizing and reflecting on their work, but also provides a common language for discussing their work with colleagues who organize their practical work as psychotherapists using very different conceptual models and technical languages.

Because of the time constraints under which they operate, practitioners could benefit greatly through collaboration with researchers both who are familiar with the DAPP approach, and for whom scrutinizing new cases to help develop their maps of varieties of psychotherapy practice is a professional activity that is compensated as part of their jobs. However, as we stated in Chapter 1, collaboration between researchers and practitioners is typically discouraged by currently dominant paradigms. Relationships between researchers and practitioners are typically tension-filled, if not downright adversarial. This is because researchers are typically experienced as prescribing that practitioners change their practices—that they do something new that is sometimes quite discrepant from the approaches on which the practitioners have come to rely. These prescriptions are based on results of empirical research conducted in settings and using methods that are often so discrepant from what is familiar to the practitioners that the research is often dismissed by the practitioners as irrelevant to them, or lacking ecological validity (Neisser, 1976). The practitioners are then often regarded disdainfully by the researchers as "closed-minded," "unscientific," or "antiscientific."

Because the DAPP approach takes as its starting point close and careful observation of the interaction between a particular therapist and a particular client, rather than a manual that has been employed in randomized control trials by large numbers of other therapists working with even larger numbers of other clients, DAPP analyses and their implications clearly have relevance and ecological validity for the particular therapist involved. As long as practitioners are among the many who are motivated to reflect critically upon and improve their service to clients, they are likely to find the DAPP analyses relevant and useful. And yet the language of the analyses is neutral with regard to extant theories of psychotherapy. If obstructions to development are identified, this allows the therapist either to generate ways of addressing or removing the obstructions from his or her own conceptual models, or to consider suggestions drawn from a map of a wide variety of psychotherapy approaches. If, upon reflection, the therapist can see any relationships between the specific obstructions identified and his or her choice to operate on rigidly held theoretical models, this provides a meaningful research basis for gaining more critical distance on those models.

Before further differentiating the implications for researchers, practitioners, and students, it is important to review the values and philosophical and psychological assumptions that underlie the new paradigm we are offering, in which psychotherapy is viewed and studied as a developmental process. For members of any of these constituents of our audience, the implications are meaningful only if the underlying assumptions are seen to have merit. Thus, this will be the focus of the next section of this chapter.

Using DAPP as a Paradigm for Research and Reflection on Practice

Kohlberg and Mayer (1972), investigating the value assumptions and philosophical models underlying approaches to education, claimed that all such assumptions and models—whether implicit or explicit—could be organized into the categories of developmental models, socialization models, or romantic models. They argued that the philosophical grounding for the former category was sounder than for the other two. We hold that the same is the case for approaches to psychotherapy as is the case for approaches to education.

We have spoken of a dominant paradigm for psychotherapy research and practice, to which the developmental approach that we propose represents a novel alternative. We see this dominant paradigm, in which what we have termed a *medical model* plays a central role, as resting on a philosophical foundation of a socialization model, with some elements of a romantic model sometimes added in. The following paragraphs flesh out our understanding of the dominant paradigm.

The medical model assumes that therapy is designed to treat symptoms (or identified syndromes) composed of symptoms as well as, in some cases, underlying disease processes, if they are adequately understood. It is the exception in psychiatry rather than the rule that assumed underlying disease processes can be understood and measured apart from symptoms. In these cases, the medical model may suggest that the goal is to cure the underlying disease process. However, for most psychotherapy, the medical model assumes that short-term and long-term reduction of symptoms represents the desired outcomes. Research then takes changes in symptoms (usually specific to the diagnosed syndrome or reflective of the assumed underlying disease process) as dependent variables, and studies the independent or mediating variables that best predict symptom reduction. Because the interacting variables studied include psychotherapy length, psychotherapy approaches and techniques, and diagnosis and initial severity of presenting symptoms, both large numbers of cases and standardization of therapeutic approaches are necessary to determine statistically significant predictors of changes in symptoms.

In Chapter 1, we noted that this dominant paradigm receives very substantial support from third-party payers for psychotherapy, who not only are familiar with operating within the medical model but also have their own vested interest in paying as little as possible for treatment that will most effectively and efficiently relieve symptoms. Such third parties support research aimed at empirically validating the effectiveness and efficiency of broad general forms and techniques of treatment. They also, through their reimbursement policies and procedures, selectively support those practitioners who present their work within a medical model of diagnosis, treatment plans, and measuring symptom reduction, and who claim to employ empirically supported treatments that have been standardized and then found to be effective and efficient for large numbers of clients with particular diagnoses.

But what are the value assumptions and commitments that underlie this paradigm and the activities supported by it? We would argue that first and foremost, it is a socialization model. Socialization models, in education as well as psychotherapy, are characterized by socially designated experts defining what is "normal" and "healthy" in terms of behavioral functioning and psychological experience, and then tailoring interventions to promote such normal outcomes and to prevent or remediate deviations. For educational interventions, the designated experts may be those who design curricula and standardized tests. For psychotherapy interventions, the experts are those psychiatrists and psychologists who codify normality and disorder through projects like creating the *Diagnostic and Statistical Manual of Mental Disorders*, or DSM (American Psychiatric Association, 1952, 1968, 1980, 1994, 2000), and those researchers and mental health practitioners who develop and use measures of disorders and normality, supplemented by their own "expert judgment," to assess mental health. Because in socialization models, the norms that represent goals of education or psychotherapy are derived from the societies in which individuals are expected to participate, it is expected that definitions of disorder versus desired outcome will change as societies evolve, and may vary from one culture to another. These variations need no philosophical justification, other than changes in social norms, and changes in the personal values of socially designated experts. The nature of the revisions of the DSM over time are consistent with the philosophical arbitrariness of an underlying socialization model. For example, in 1973, homosexuality was converted from a "disorder" to a "healthy life-style orientation" (Drescher & Merlino, 2007). Critics have suggested ways in which the DSM reflects cultural and gender biases (Cosgrove & Riddle, 2004; Dana, 2002).

What Kohlberg and Mayer (1972) called the "romantic model" and traced to Rousseau (1762/1979) essentially assumes that it is "natural" for each human being to achieve the knowledge, modes of behaviors, and forms of psychological experience that are healthiest for that individual. Disorders, and departures from what is "natural," are seen as caused by negative experiences with the environment, especially the social environment, which may be traumatic. In the romantic view, just as it is assumed to be natural for trees to grow up straight and that external assaults result in deviation, it is assumed natural for humans to grow up "healthy," and deviations are seen as caused by social assaults. That "healthiness" is different for each person is reflected in modern psychological theories such as Maslow's (1943), for example in its treatment of "self-actualization," and that social factors function to impede self-realization is reflected in ideas such as Rogers' (1959) views of the roles of "conditions of worth" in the etiology of psychological problems, and the importance of removing them in psychological treatment. Rogers (1959) assumed that an "organismic valuing system," unique and internal to each individual, is responsible for the choices an individual makes, once the effects of socially derived "conditions of worth" are mitigated. Thus, a significant contrast exists. In socialization models, the needs and norms of society provide the basis for definition of health and disorder, social conditioning is assumed to be a central means by which health is achieved, and socially designated experts are expected to diagnose and treat disorder, which represents deviation from normality. In romantic models, health and disorder are defined and judged by the experience of the individual, and social conditioning is seen as a major obstacle to health and source of disorder.

Although we see the dominant paradigm as founded on values derived from the socialization model, it also occasionally appeals to romantic models for support. In these cases, symptoms are defined (as problems) *because* they are experienced by the individual as discomfort, not because they are deviant from the behavioral patterns and psychological experiences of others. Removal of those symptoms associated with the individual's experience of suffering and lack of well-being is thus seen as the central goal of therapy. It is assumed that once such symptoms are removed, something like the individual's "organismic valuing system" (Rogers 1951, 1959) will take over and provide the basis for his or her subsequent life choices. Thus, when symptoms, disorder, and health are understood in this different way from socialization models, the goal of symptom reduction may still be seen as the primary desired outcome of psychotherapy, and the paradigm of research on techniques and approaches to therapy that may be found to decrease suffering for various subsets of clients may be embraced.

We reject the socialization model as an adequate fundamental basis for our thinking about psychotherapy practice for several reasons. Most important is that the socialization model rests on a foundation of psychotherapy practice, which clearly involves therapists making many value judgments, on what happen to be current shared cultural norms. This makes the foundation of the entire discipline relative to time and place, and also to the particular communities of valuing with which particular therapists identify. We find the romantic model to be even more relativistic. Only the individual client is in a position to judge what is healthy, and what is healthy depends on what feels good. This places the therapist in the role of technician, who simply places the techniques in which he or she has expertise in the service of the client's goals. It leads to the view that the therapist ought to make no value judgments at all, a standard that we see as ultimately unjustifiable and, even if it were justifiable, impossible to achieve. This model, in taking discomfort as the appropriate basis for mental health diagnosis, also assumes that all discomfort and suffering are bad things. In the alternative developmental model that we are about to present, discomfort regularly, and even suffering at times, may be seen to play a positive role in the process of development.

As was suggested in Chapter 2, at the core of the developmental model we propose is a fundamental philosophical commitment to valuing (a) the *processes* of mutual adaptation in the relationships of individuals with their changing social and physical environments, *and* (b) the more complex, differentiated, and integrated *organizations* of human psychological and physical activity that are both the product of the processes of adaptation, and the means by which such adaptation is achieved.

All of the implications for research, practice, and training that we propose in this chapter are based on viewing psychotherapy as a developmental process, which entails valuing the processes of adaptation through which human development occurs, and valuing the more complex organizations of human activity and meaning that allow all individuals to individually and collectively survive and thrive in their changing environments. This leads to our foundational claim that the development of such organizations, seen as the creation of adaptive novel syntheses, is the common outcome of all successful psychotherapy. This is fundamentally a tautological claim, because we are suggesting replacing the goal of "symptom reduction" with the goal of "development."

However, we are not suggesting any need for "conversion" on the part of therapists or therapy researchers who pursue the value of symptom reduction and try to track the process.

We assume, with no evidence to the contrary, that all reductions of symptoms are associated with adaptive (at least in the short run) novel syntheses that integrate new activities or ways of thinking into clients' repertoires, or integrate existing activities and ways of thinking in new ways. In each case that we have examined, or that has been described to us in detail, symptom improvement was associated with or itself constituted an observable microdevelopmental movement. We have heard references to "inexplicable" symptom change, but haven't examined any such cases in detail.

Sometimes, of course, as when one symptom decreases while another emerges or increases, the microdevelopmental movement may be unstable and quickly lead to the emergence of new antitheses and new conflicts. We hope some readers will be willing to continue to entertain our view that development is a common outcome of all successful psychotherapy because we have demonstrated that it is a plausible complement to other ways of evaluating psychotherapy process and outcome, and indeed it is one that allows tracking all forms of therapy using the same set of concepts, in contrast to definitions of success that are couched in the terminology of the particular therapeutic approach employed. We hope that others will share our view that either (a) allowing privileged representatives of a given society to establish the criteria by which the mental health of others will be judged or (b) allowing individuals to be the sole judges of their own mental health, without regard for considerations such as the impact that they have on others (their social environment) or on our shared natural environment, is less adequate than judging the success of psychotherapy based on criteria of mutual adaptation that considers both the evaluation of the client of his or her own success in adaptation and the impact one is having on one's environment.

We hope that both groups will recognize that criteria of mutual adaptation are functional, in that the methods presented in the book demonstrate how both the microdevelopmental movements and the constructions of novel syntheses that are all part of processes of adaptation can be rigorously tracked and described. Also, these criteria are functional even in those cases in which an adaptation that is achieved and recognized by DAPP analysis turns out to be not so adaptive (leaving or leading to new internal and external conflicts for the client). Such adaptations and syntheses are characterized by instability and will be manifest quickly in the appearance of new adaptive challenges, either recognized by the client or made evident by subsequent unforeseen or undesired events in the client's life, which will then need to be overcome for the therapy to have more lasting positive results.

Restating a point made in Chapter 2, developmental frameworks do incorporate evaluative perspectives and assumptions. We hold that it is precisely because these frameworks have this *prescriptive* aspect that developmental approaches are (and we hope and expect that they will be so experienced by psychotherapists) appropriate frameworks for *describing* psychotherapeutic practice. Psychotherapeutic practice, like all educational practice, is not a value-neutral enterprise. It will inevitably be guided either by values that can be articulated and subjected to consensual affirmation, or by values that remain unarticulated and are more likely to be idiosyncratic, ethnocentric, or shared only by self-defined communities of "experts." Viewing psychotherapy as a developmental process represents an alternative, or complement, to the implicit prescriptivity of the "medical model," which has a significant impact on how psychotherapy is currently and has historically been conducted.

One implication of adopting the values we propose above is that when one attempts to document what is successful within cases or processes of psychotherapy, one focuses on the developmental movement that can be identified, and then considers the roles of clients and therapists in fostering that movement. Another implication involves ways for practitioners, researchers, and students to express a commitment that we strongly advocate—to improving success rates of psychotherapy, on behalf of all future therapy clients. The way we have proposed is to reflect critically on therapy cases and processes, identifying and analyzing periods in which developmental movement appears to be absent, or blocked. We have suggested that failure of therapists' and clients' utterances to remain for any period of time within the same therapeutic dialectic (attentional support, interpretation, or enactment) is one likely indicator of the absence of developmental movement. Rambling across thesis and antithesis statements, with an absence of statements of conflicts or efforts to resolve them, is a second indicator. Negative feedback from client to therapist that appears to be ignored, rather than adapted to, is yet another indicator. Once indicators have been observed, informed by the DAPP framework, studying how therapists and clients seem to be reacting to these indicators within sessions may be helpful in pursuing the goal of improving psychotherapy success rates.

In sum, the use of a developmental model for understanding psychotherapy process and outcome is both a descriptive enterprise that helps us see the similarities and differences across all therapy cases, and an affirmation of values that have prescriptive implications for practitioners, researchers, and students. It rests on the assumption that the observation of microdevelopmental movement, in which the step-by-step co-construction of more adaptive, complex, differentiated, and integrated organizations of activity and meaning occurs, is indicative of successful therapy. This is true regardless of the form of therapy observed, and the therapist's and the client's goals, although developmental movement is expected in every case to coexist with, and in fact explain, therapeutic gains and accomplishments defined in other terms (including those of the "medical model"). Furthermore, the absence of such movement, which a developmental approach defines as indicative of unsuccessful therapy and expects to coexist with and to explain other negative outcomes, represents a problem to be ameliorated.

The alternate developmental paradigm for conceptualizing the outcomes and processes of psychotherapy proposed by this book also has significant implications for how the roles of therapists' theoretical frameworks, assumptions, and technical skills are understood. This general issue merits some discussion here. Implicit or explicit within much psychotherapy research and practice conducted within the dominant paradigm is the following assumed starting point of the therapeutic process (see Figure 10.1): An (ideally)[1] well-assessed patient presents for psychotherapy, accompanied by a diagnosis, history, and set of presenting problems. These may be determined by an intake and/or, if appropriate, by additional testing using paper-and-pencil instruments and/or formal test batteries. This patient is then met by a therapist, ideally well trained in psychotherapy theory and technique, who has used or will use such training to develop a treatment plan that is understood as an "intervention" designed to improve the patient's disordered symptoms. The success or failure of the treatment that ensues is thus a measure of some combination of the worth of the theory and technique that the therapist employed, the competency of the therapist in implementing the theory or technique, and the appropriateness of

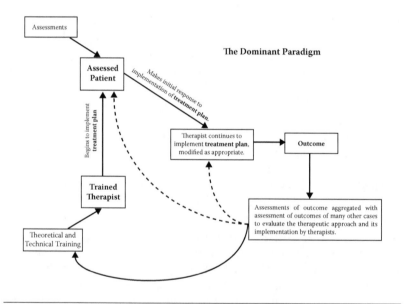

Figure 10.1 The dominant paradigm. Within the dominant paradigm, the theories and techniques in which the therapist is trained (validated in previous outcome research with many other clients), and the therapist's capacities to translate these theories and techniques into an appropriate treatment plan, are seen as at the core of what accounts for positive outcomes.

[1] Although this separation between assessment and psychotherapy may be the ideal implicit in many training programs, clinic operating procedures, and research designs, the reality of how therapy occurs in the world is that the ongoing processes of assessment and psychotherapy are often intertwined within a single relationship.

the theoretical or technical approach to the particular patient and his or her diagnosis. The paradigm presented in this book for viewing psychotherapy as a developmental process entails a sharply contrasting view of the therapist's theoretical assumptions and technical training. In the dominant paradigm, represented in Figure 10.1, the focus is on the impact of the treatment provided (input) on the patient's symptoms (outcome). The therapist's theoretical approach and technical training are usually seen as central processes influencing the input. In contrast, the paradigm we propose focuses on tracking the moment-to-moment interaction of therapist and client and the microdevelopmental movement that may occur during such interaction (see Figure 10.2). In the developmental study of interaction using a coactive systems model, each party's actions, understood as communicative acts, are assumed to be the major inputs influencing the other parties' responses. The client and therapist interaction forms a coactive system. However, each party is also recognized as himself or herself organized as a system. Thus, how each input from another is interpreted is influenced by the entire organization of the interpreting party's forms of meaning making, including forms of understanding shared with communities in which the interpreting party has participated, and more individualized meaning structures. Currently stimulated emotional states and expectations also influence the interpretation of input. How each party responds to the interpreted input of others is then influenced by the entire organization of

CLIENT-THERAPIST SYSTEM

CLIENT (SYSTEM)		THERAPIST (SYSTEM)
Responses to therapist's communicative acts are mediated by client's previously developed and currently developing forms of meaning making and organized repertoires of activity. Simultaneously, novel input from the therapist may lead to current development.	Communicative Act 1 / Communicative Act 2 / Communicative Act 3 / Communicative Act 4 / Communicative Act 5 / Communicative Act 6 — MICRODEVELOPMENTAL MOVEMENT?	*Responses to client's communicative acts are mediated by therapist's previously developed and currently developing forms of meaning making and organized repertoires of activity. Simultaneously, novel input from the client may lead to current development.*

Figure 10.2 The developmental coactive systems paradigm. Within the proposed alternative paradigm theories and techniques are viewed as important components (among others) of the system by which the therapist organizes himself or herself. Such theories and techniques play important roles in maintaining coherence within the therapist's activity as he or she interacts with the client. However it is the interaction of the client and therapist as coactive systems that is responsible for developmental movement that occurs in the course of therapy, both within the relationship and in each party's organization of his or her activity and experience.

that party's repertoire of activity, including practices shared with communities and more idiosyncratic activity schemes and structures. Here again, currently stimulated emotional states and expectations in the actor also influence the next communicative act.

As represented in Figure 10.2, clients and therapists are not in any way fundamentally different in regard to the role of systemic structure in mediating communication with the other. However, both the therapist's theoretical understandings of his or her own therapeutic practice and his or her technical training represent *parts* of the meaning-making organization and the repertoire of activity that mediate the therapist's responses (represented in Figure 10.2 as THERAPIST (SYSTEM)). Of course, other aspects of the therapist's conceptions of human nature, personality, history, values, current emotional states, expectations, and so on are equally important parts of the whole system that will mediate every response on the part of the therapist. Furthermore, as indicated by Figure 10.2, it is expected that therapists' meaning-making schemes and activity repertoires will develop in response to novel experiences of communication with the particular client, just as it is expected that the client's meaning-making schemes and activity repertoires will develop in response to novel experiences of communication with the particular therapist.

The focus of the paradigm we have proposed entails viewing the role of psychotherapy theory quite differently from the dominant paradigm. But this does not imply seeing such theory as unimportant. First of all, having a coherent theory of psychotherapy and having some confidence in one's repertoire as a therapist enable a therapist usually to remain reasonably well organized in his or her responses to clients. This is very important, as clients often come to therapy experiencing a great deal of disequilibrium, disorganization, or threats to sense of self-coherence in the organization of their meaning making and activity. The therapist is often able to exert a calming influence, making the feelings of disorganization and threat more manageable, because he or she brings to bear ways of making sense of the encounter with the client's experience.

However, from our perspective it is equally important to recognize that what is usually a resource that a well-trained therapist brings to work with clients can become an obstacle as well (Basseches, 1997b). This can happen when the therapist's theories begin to interfere with the client's sense of being understood in his or her experience, or when techniques that the therapist relies upon are experienced as unhelpful by the client. If therapists are so dependent for their professional identity on the sense of organization that their theories and techniques provide that they are only able to defend against, rather than adapt to, the novel information that clients are providing, from the DAPP perspective the therapy is more likely to be destructive than helpful.

Furthermore, with respect to the role that theoretical understanding and technical skills play in enabling a therapist usually to remain well organized in interactions with clients, from the DAPP perspective it does not matter which theoretical understanding or technical skills the therapist relies on, as long as he or she has some sufficient foundation. Regardless of approach, successful psychotherapy depends on the therapist being able to offer a combination of resources of attentional support, interpretation, and enactment to the client, and to adapt these resources to the client's needs such that the client can make use of them. DAPP looks at each case and asks the fundamental research question of whether there is evidence that successful adaptation is occurring, or whether the therapist is unable to offer resources that the client is able to use. This is very different from the dominant paradigm, which assumes that some theories or techniques are "better" than others, and takes as a fundamental research question for various relatively large populations of clients, "Which theories and techniques work best?"

A second way in which the therapist's theoretical orientation and training are also of great importance from the DAPP perspective is that therapists with different backgrounds are likely to make different choices with regard to how to respond to particular situations. In each case we have analyzed in this book, we have looked carefully at the question of how the therapist's orientation influenced the implicit or explicit choices that the therapist made in crucial moments in the therapy. Such questions are not only important for appreciating both the power and the limitations of various theoretical perspectives and techniques, but also important for understanding the process of mutual adaptation between therapist and client that we argue takes place in every successful psychotherapeutic process.

We have argued that DAPP, pan-theoretical analysis, and analyses in the languages of particular theories play important complementary roles in approaching any particular case. The theoretical analysis provides the therapist with a basis for organizing his or her approach to a particular client, generating ideas for forms of resources to offer that are expected to be appropriate to the client's particular situation, conflicts, and needs. The DAPP pan-theoretical analysis provides a basis for therapists and researchers across orientations to look at the raw data of therapeutic interaction and assess whether the resources offered by the therapist are in fact used by the client in ways that realize the potential of the therapeutic resource to foster development.

Implications and Future Directions for Research

In this section, we will consider the many kinds of research studies we see as made possible by DAPP methods, and their potential value. Where possible, we will note examples of current studies that have been done, are being planned, or are under way. The set of research possibilities is so large and variegated that it is somewhat challenging to organize such a discussion. We have decided to organize them according to the goals of the research and the types of research questions asked. However, it is also important to keep in mind that different types of studies may be used to address these goals and questions: for example, case studies; comparative case studies; incorporating DAPP methods within process and outcome studies with large samples, either examining single approaches or comparing approaches; reliability studies; and studies of group therapies. One implication is that we will consider the role of studies with these formats under more than one side heading. Another is that the same research study can be used to address different types of questions.

Understanding Similarities and Differences Across Instances of Psychotherapy

The majority of studies using DAPP thus far have been case studies. This book has included two as illustrations of the method presented in Chapters 7 and 8. Each case study makes a contribution to the fundamental argument of this book, which is essentially one about similarities across psychotherapies. This is the argument that all successful psychotherapy can be understood as based on the foundation of three fundamental dialectics, in which three different types of relational resources (attentional support, interpretation, and enactment) are offered to clients, and the clients make use of these resources in the service of their own development. For each case, it is possible to track two essential processes: (a) the microdevelopmental movements entailed in work within all dialectics, as conflicts emerge within the clients' and therapists' attentional fields and novel syntheses are co-constructed that transcend these conflicts; and (b) the adaptations entailed in the offering and use of resources as clients try to use the resources that therapists offer, therapists try to offer resources that clients can use, and blockages to the movement tracked in (a) are identified.

Every future case study of a successful therapy adds to the establishment of both the fundamental similarities of all forms of therapy, and the power of DAPP analysis to interpret both the precise nature of the therapeutic success and the central processes that led up to it. Currently, three case studies are under way, being conducted in collaboration with the first author of this book. One, by Ilana Licht (a Ph.D. student) and Joan Wheelis, M.D., is a study of "The Developmental Analysis of Psychotherapy Process (DAPP) in Dialectical Behavioral Therapy (DBT)"; a second, by Shana D'Angelo (a Ph.D. student) and Leslie Greenberg, Ph.D., is a study of "Developmental Processes in Emotion-Focused Therapy"; a third, by Anthony Annunziata (a Ph.D. student) and Allison Berger, Ph.D., is a study of "Assessing the

Developmental Processes of Adjunctive Mindfulness Therapy: A Single-Case Design" (Annunziata, 2009). Any other researcher (or practitioner qua researcher) who has case material in verbatim form—videotape, audio-tape, or transcription—can make important contributions to this corpus of work. Furthermore, the more the cases accumulate, the more each new case contributes to the claim of relevance across approaches, modalities, therapists, and clients of DAPP analysis.

There have been no case studies of group therapy, couple therapy, and family therapy completed to date, although we have been in touch with several researchers interested in adapting DAPP methods to studies of therapies including more than one client. Such studies will be of great value for demonstrating the similarities in therapeutic processes across modalities. From a theoretical perspective, the same processes of attentional support, interpretation, and enactment would be expected to foster each client's development in these multiclient settings. Such modalities offer the potential of more enactment partners and more emergence of conflicting interpretations, while challenging therapists' skills of allocating their own attention and guiding clients' attention in such a way as to optimize the development of all clients. This requires skills in allowing and facilitating the resources that group members offer to each other to realize their developmental potential, while remaining sufficiently attuned to all clients' individual needs and developmental processes to adapt the resources offered by the therapist to the needs of all. For researchers, it should not be hard to adapt the tracking process of numbering of thesis, antitheses, conflicts, and syntheses, though these elements of microdevelopmental movement will come from more sources. However, it may be more of a challenge to adapt the coding methods to track the resources offered and used, as the same comment by one participant may simultaneously trigger a novel experience (enactment) for one participant, constitute an antithetical interpretation for another client, and offer attentional support to a third.

Of course, case studies not only contribute to the claim for similarities or "common factors" (Carere-Comes, 1999, 2001) across all psychotherapy, but also help us to understand the differences across approaches to therapy. For example, the Licht, Basseches, and Wheelis study mentioned above entails (a) identifying "uniquely DBT" interventions in the course of the therapy, tracking their impact, and speculating on what might have been the impact of alternative responses; and (b) identifying the most developmentally significant therapeutic interactions within the case, and interviewing the therapist regarding these interactions in order to understand the role her training in DBT theory and technique played in influencing the implicit choices she made in these critical interactions. In the Annunziata, Basseches, and Berger study (Annunziata, 2009), key moments have been identified in which the therapist made a very different response—one consistent with the emphasis on enactment (novel experiences) in the mindfulness training approach—from what one would expect from therapists whose approaches put more emphasis on discussing the client's understanding, history, cognitions, or past emotional experience. The microdevelopmental processes that followed these responses have helped clarify the more unique aspects of what the mindfulness approach has to offer.

As DAPP analyses of case material accumulate, they will provide a basis for illustrating the dimensions along which psychotherapy process differs in different cases, as well as some of the strengths and weaknesses of various approaches. They will also provide a basis for generating hypotheses, for testing in larger samples, and regarding how systematic differences among therapeutic approaches, therapeutic modalities, groups of individual therapists, and groups of individual clients may be observed within the close analysis of therapeutic process, and described using the language of DAPP.

To summarize the recommended method for case studies, described in detail in Chapter 6, the case study begins with the review of all material related to a given case. As a result of that review, important sessions or parts of sessions are identified for closer analysis, based either on their perceived importance within the overall development of the clients, on their containing evidence suggesting that the processes of developmental movement are being blocked, or in their perceived importance in the process of mutual adaptation in which therapists alter or integrate the resources offered in response to perceptions of the extent and the limits of the usefulness to the clients of resources thus far offered. A current study by Carla Gabris, Adriana DeAmicis, Michael Basseches, and Matthew Jerram, to be discussed further below in the context of other reliability studies, is investigating the extent to which trained coders agree in their judgment of the parts of sessions most important for detailed analysis.

Once important segments are identified, the segments identified may be divided into episodes, and movement through the episodes tracked in detail. The methods explained in Chapter 6 and illustrated with the cases in this book, such as tracking the relationship of utterances to each other in terms of theses, antitheses, conflicts, and syntheses; tracking discursive acts among clients and therapists; diagramming movement within episodes; and recognizing changes over time in the complexity of utterances and the levels of scaffolding provided, may all be used for this detailed analysis.

A second approach to understanding similarities and differences among psychotherapy cases is to design studies that explicitly compare cases to one another. The dimensions along which kinds of cases might be distinguished from each other and compared, while other variables are kept common across the cases, are almost endless. What would distinguish such comparative research using DAPP from other comparative psycho-therapy research is that the cases would be compared using the pan-theoretical process models of DAPP. Such research would contrast on the one hand with research that compares psychotherapy process and outcomes using constructs drawn from one theoretical approach to understanding and implementing psychotherapy, and on the other hand from research that compares psychotherapies using very general outcome measures (like general symptom reduction, global assessment of functioning (GAF), quality of life, or satisfaction with therapy) that are not at all specific to the particular issues that brought clients to therapy or that they addressed in the course of their therapies. For example, one could hypothesize ways in which the developmental processes involved in psychodynamically ori-ented therapy for depressed clients systematically differ from the develop-mental processes involved in cognitive-behavioral therapy for depressed clients, even if all rely on some combination of attentional support, inter-pretation, and enactment. One could test these hypotheses by examining a few cases in each category. Although the capacity to generalize from small numbers of cases is strictly limited, whether the predicted differences could be observed in the small sample of cases, or whether instead the pro-cesses that led to development in key moments of the therapies were not sufficiently different to distinguish between the therapeutic approaches, would represent useful interesting results for the overall goal of mapping the terrain of psychotherapeutic practices.

Peters' (2008) doctoral dissertation included the first efforts to compare therapies conducted from different theoretical approaches using DAPP methods. His was a pilot study, rather than a hypothesis-testing effort, and he used videotapes of single therapy sessions placed into the public domain as useful-for-teaching-purposes illustrations of solution-focused therapy, cognitive-behavioral therapy, reality therapy, and motivational interview-ing. Nonetheless, Peters found that he was able—using an earlier version of the DAPP coding system that coded each utterance in terms of whether, and in what form, therapists offered attentional support, interpretation, or enactment, and whether clients made use of the resources offered—to meaningfully describe the similarities of the approaches in terms of the integration of all codes, and the differences in terms of the frequency with which utterance fell into different coding categories.

An earlier study (Richard, 2005) was a comparative case study of two cases conducted by the same therapist, subjected to DAPP analysis. Both cases were intended to illustrate the implications of the therapist's "spiritual orientation" by examining how it was translated into practice. DAPP analyses revealed *similarities* with other therapies in the offering of resources of attentional support, interpretation, and enactment in the service of the clients' development, whereas *differences* represented in the therapist's spiritual orientation were mostly evident in the content of his interpretations, and the interactions that ensued. However, the study also illustrated important differences between the two cases that seemed attributable to *differences between the two clients*. Differences between the two clients' organizations of experience, meaning, and activity, and more specifically the roles that religion played in these organizations, led the same spiritually oriented therapist into very different responses, interpretations, and relational enactments with these two clients, all of which were evident in the DAPP analyses.

Understanding Success and Failure in Psychotherapy

One goal of this book is to provide a method for describing in a common language and appreciating the widely varied ways in which different psychotherapies accomplish successful results. We expect that as the range of case studies and comparative case studies accumulate, they will show that there are many alternative feasible pathways for making use of psychotherapy relationships to foster development. What we expect successful cases to have in common is the use of some combination of resources of attentional support, interpretation, and enactment, offered by therapists, and a process whereby therapists adapt the resources offered, and the forms in which they are offered, to feedback regarding what clients are and are not able to use.

A second goal is to provide a method for understanding, and if possible remedying the process, when psychotherapy fails. A great deal of research thus far (e.g., Seligman, 1995; Joyce et al., 2006; Carr, 2009) has demonstrated that psychotherapy in general, and specific forms of therapy, have significantly positive results in comparison to no treatment. Such results provide encouragement to therapists in offering therapy, and clients in seeking it. However, even success rates in the 70–80% range are seen by the authors of this book as posing an extremely important challenge to researchers, as well as students and practitioners of psychotherapy. Such results indicate that 20–30% of clients are either being adversely affected by psychotherapy, or spending a great deal of time, and often money, without receiving satisfactory results. Just as the effort to conduct studies using large numbers of cases and symptom reduction outcome measures to isolate predictors of therapeutic success is of value, so is the use of such studies to isolate predictors of psychotherapeutic failure.

But we believe that such studies, by themselves, not only are insufficient for understanding why a wide range of therapists, using very different approaches and techniques, all succeed some of the time, but also are insufficient for understanding why psychotherapy fails as often as it does. DAPP provides a complementary method for understanding psychotherapeutic failure. If offers of attentional support, interpretation, and enactment opportunities typically lead to conflicts—which then, if given sufficient attention, generate novel adaptive syntheses—why does this not occur in so many cases? It is our expectation that by applying DAPP methods to the analysis of unsuccessful psychotherapy cases, we will be able to track microdevelopmental movements to the point where they cease to occur, and examine what the patterns are in the responses of clients and therapists that block further movement.

However, there have been no DAPP analyses of unsuccessful cases performed thus far. This would require therapists and clients being willing to make available for analysis verbatim data (videotapes, audiotapes, and transcripts) of cases in which psychotherapy has failed to bring about positive outcomes. We would especially welcome such data. Based entirely on anecdotal evidence, we would suggest that unsuccessful psychotherapy is part of the experience of even the most experienced and well-regarded therapists. We have never heard any therapist claim that his or her personal success rates are significantly better than the success rates found in systematic studies of large numbers of cases. This suggests that having unsuccessful cases is not a sign of being an inadequate therapist. If this is commonly understood, and it encourages the presentation of detailed data regarding cases of failure for individual case-by-case DAPP analysis, this would be a tremendous boon for the field of psychotherapy research and practice. Both individual case studies and comparative case studies using DAPP methods to analyze cases of psychotherapeutic failure represent a very important direction for future research.

Another form of research that can be helpful in understanding psychotherapeutic success and failure entails incorporating DAPP methods within process and outcome studies with large samples, either examining single approaches or comparing approaches. Such studies are usually intended to assess the overall effectiveness of psychotherapeutic approaches and techniques, or the relevance of particular process measures (e.g., the successful formation of a therapeutic alliance), using general measures of outcome. However, collecting verbatim data on smaller subsamples of cases makes it possible to go back and compare more successful with less successful cases, both within and across the subsets into which samples were divided for the planned statistical analyses. Such comparisons are likely to shed light on why a similar approach is successful in some cases and unsuccessful in others, by tracking the developmental processes by which the successful therapies achieved their results and ways in which the unsuccessful therapies became stuck.

Using DAPP to Elucidate Other Aspects of Therapeutic Process

The framework we have proposed for seeing psychotherapy as a developmental process, and the methods we have proposed for tracking that process, may be generative of a wide range of questions for psychotherapy research. For example, "Does emphasizing attentional support at the outset of a relationship make the development of a stronger therapeutic alliance more likely?" "When therapists move away from attentional support to offer other resources, to what extent is this a response to cues from clients, to case formulations, and/or to styles and approaches that the therapist has developed independently of clients?" and "What factors, over time, influence changes in what we have called (see Chapter 6) the level of scaffolding that therapists provide?" Peters' (2008) dissertation suggests some of these types of questions. Such questions entail joining DAPP with other systems for coding aspects of the psychotherapy process to specifically answer questions about the key concepts in the framework and methods we have proposed.

DAPP analysis may also be used as a resource in addressing a variety of different research questions, not specifically about DAPP concepts. For example, previous research (e.g., Harned et al., 2008; Miller, Rathus, & Linehan, 2007) has shown that DBT is effective in changing suicidal clients' experience of and actions in response to suicidal urges. Consider the question "How does this change occur?" One way of answering this question is to ask what new developmental skills and structures account for this change in clients who experience it, and to use DAPP analysis of relevant DBT cases to describe such skills, and to show the role of the DBT therapist in their development.

As another example, Angela Brandao has begun research aimed at understanding the role that "emotional attunement" between therapists and clients plays in therapeutic success. One part of this research involves conceptualizing and tracking movements in and out of attunement. A second aspect entails using DAPP to track (a) the microdevelopmental movements, or lack thereof, that occur; as well as (b) stability or changes in resources offered and used, during (1) periods of attunement, (2) periods of lack of attunement, (3) periods of moving out of a state of attunement, and (4) periods of reestablishing attunement.

Vasco's (2005) theory of paradigmatic complementarity is another theory regarding common factors across all therapies. He has suggested that one thing that all forms of therapy have in common is movement through a series of universal phases, though such movement typically takes a more cyclical than linear form. This is confirmed by factor analyses of designated "markers" within therapeutic processes of work being done on phase-specific issues. This theory suggests that the appearance of markers of a new phase may result from the partial or complete resolution of previous phase-specific issues, and return to work on earlier issues may be based on novel events that disrupt previous resolutions. If this is the case, DAPP analysis of the dialogue should be able to detect the resolutions and disruptions created by therapist and client that accompany changes in the markers from session to session, and such research is currently in the planning stage.

Finally, in the previous section, we have stated that our perspective on psychotherapy as a developmental process leads us to view theoretical orientation and training as mediating variables that intervene between clients' actions and therapists' responses. We have affirmed the important roles that these mediating structures play in successful psychotherapy, while also claiming that at times these structures may interfere with effective adaptation on the part of the therapist, and lead to cases of psychotherapeutic failure. Questions about the roles of theory and training have been concerns of psychotherapy research for a long time. Combining in-depth DAPP analyses of case material with developing more systematic tools for gathering data from therapists in which they both retrospectively and prospectively express the role of personal experience, theoretical rationales, and so on in their action choices and plans would represent a form of research that could shed light on such questions.

Researching the Continuum of Developmental Interventions

In the context of viewing psychotherapy of all types as developmental processes, Chapter 2 acknowledged a continuum of developmental interventions. At a more "constrained" end, interventions are directed toward bringing about preformulated outcomes using more or less prescribed pathways and developmental mechanisms. At a more "open-ended end," developmental changes occur in a relatively open-ended fashion in the absence of prescribed or preformulated goals and pathways. In cases toward the latter end of the continuum, it is more likely that one must wait until after the developmental process has been completed to identify the nature and the adaptive significance of the development that has occurred. For example, in a psychotherapy intervention toward the more "constrained" end of the continuum, a therapist may set out to help a client remediate a social skills deficit in order to be able to function effectively in a classroom. In contrast, toward the more open-ended end, a therapist may join with a client in an investigation into why all his intimate relationships seem to "end in disappointment."

Although across this entire continuum, when psychotherapy is successful, the more developed outcome will be characterized by increased differentiation, integration, and hierarchical integration, with respect to the initial state, there may be interesting differences among therapy cases, depending upon the degree to which the intended outcome is specified in advance. These differences can be researched both through the accumulation of individual case studies and through comparative case studies that examine cases all along the continuum, examining both the nature of therapists' treatment plans and the evolution of the therapy that ensues.

Comparing Psychotherapy With Other
Relationships That Foster Development

We have advocated understanding the nature of therapeutic processes in the context of the coactive systems model of human development presented in Chapter 3 because of the new light this lens sheds on the psychotherapy process, which, for the most part, has been the focus of our examination in this book. However, the same understanding also brings psychotherapy research into the context of a broader field of research in developmental psychology aimed at understanding the nature of development in the context of human relationships (Fogel, Garvey, Hsu, & West-Stromming, 2006; Sroufe, 2005; Stern, 1985; Wozniak & Fischer, 1993; Zlatev, Racine, Sinha, & Itkonen, 2008). Although contributing to this body of research, the kinds of studies we have discussed above also raise two equally important types of research questions for future study.

First is the question of whether the DAPP method is equally useful for studying other kinds of helping relationships, such as clinical supervision, coaching, mentoring, leadership development, and the like. As long as verbatim data are collected, data from any kind of relationship may be used to test the usefulness of adapting DAPP methods.

Second, if DAPP methods are equally relevant to understanding how development occurs in the context of various types of "helping relationships," this raises the question of what, in fact, differentiates such relationships from one another. Some may see the answer as largely a matter of the training of the helper. Because psychotherapists are trained in knowledge of psychopathology and theories of psychotherapies, this makes psychotherapy different from, say, "executive coaching" conducted by practitioners who are trained in knowledge of organizations and theories of leadership development. This could be a focus of research with DAPP, extending beyond the comparison of the differing training backgrounds of different therapists, and the role such differences play, to include differences in training between psychotherapists and other helping professionals. On the other hand, if one accepts our suggestion that the conceptual frameworks and techniques learned in explicit psychotherapy training are just one aspect of the organizations of meaning and activity that mediate therapists' response to clients, *focusing* research on training differences may lead to missing other similarities and differences that exist across helping relationships. Research comparing DAPP analyses of psychotherapy relationships and other relationships can investigate the commonalities and the differences in professionals drawing on their past knowledge in mediating their responses, while also investigating the roles within the developmental processes of the unique social expectations, social meanings, and relationship boundaries that characterize psychotherapy, as well as the constraints on the psychotherapy relationships imposed by the involvement of outside parties, such as third-party payers. The comparison between psychotherapy and developmentally oriented clinical supervision is a particularly interesting one from a DAPP perspective, as in this case the issue is clearly more one of role definitions and boundaries rather than a difference in theoretical orientation and training.

Toward Intersubjectivity in Understanding Psychotherapy

Part of what DAPP offers psychotherapy research is the promise of a common language for understanding the details of psychotherapeutic interaction across theoretical and technical approaches and therapeutic modalities. This provides an alternative to the choices between studying therapy at the macroscopic level, using non-theory-specific outcome measures (e.g., symptoms and client satisfaction) to compare approaches, or studying the more microscopic details of the therapy process, which is usually done using constructs drawn from the theory of psychotherapy being employed. However, the promise of this new alternative is entirely dependent on researchers finding the language of DAPP to be comprehensible and useful. For this reason, intersubjectivity has been an important ongoing concern in psychotherapy research. Several training studies have been conducted in which coding manuals and training procedures have been developed; trainees have coded case material using DAPP methods, first separately and then together; and the consensual understanding achieved through this process has been evaluated.

In examining these studies, it is important to distinguish between intersubjective understanding as (a) the ability to understand and communicate using the technical language of DAPP (this is comparable to the tradition of the psychoanalytic community's ability to communicate meaningfully about clients using psychoanalytic terminology), and (b) the ability to achieve statistically significant levels of interrater reliability among coders independently coding the same material using DAPP coding methods (this is comparable to the research tradition of establishing interrater reliability for coding systems that are designed to be used by multiple coders for making categorical summary comparisons across multiple instances within a data set). The former is important for the kind of accumulation of case study research to create a map of similarities and differences across therapies. In order for case studies to be used in that endeavor, readers must be capable of understanding and critically responding to case analyses presented to them. The latter is important when summary data provided by different coders for different verbatim material are to be compared to each other (as in the research proposed above, for comparative case studies of work with depressed clients by therapists with psychodynamic and behavioral orientations). If it is hypothesized that there will be proportionately more interpretation offered in the psychodynamic cases, and more explicit attention to enactment opportunities in the CBT cases, and different coders are counting the instances of interpretation and explicit attention to enactment opportunities for different cases, interrater reliability in the traditional sense is important for the numbers counted to be compared.

Some studies of reliability among trained coders of DAPP coding methods have already been conducted, indicating scores for Cohen's (1960) kappa in the "fair to good" range (Fleiss, 1981). These studies are summarized by Peters (2008). Other studies now being conducted by (doctoral students) Carla Gabris and Adriana DeAmicis, in collaboration with Matthew Jerram, Ph.D., are intended to use "signal detection" theory to improve the methods of calculating reliability and make them more appropriate to the way DAPP is currently being used (and intended to be used) in the contexts of research and practice.

DAPP as Formative Evaluation

This final category of future research directions largely overlaps with the future directions and implications for practice and training that will be discussed in the rest of this chapter. The authors' ultimate hope is that the DAPP framework will be useful for critically evaluating therapy in progress. Where microdevelopment is occurring, identifying the conflicts and syntheses emerging may allow therapists to build more effectively on them in subsequent sessions. Identifying what therapeutic resources clients are able to use under what conditions and what else they might be expressing the need for can also enhance therapeutic effectiveness. Similarly, identifying blocks to microdevelopment or limitations encountered in offering resources in particular forms, combined with using the DAPP framework to consider a broad set of possible options, may help therapies to become unstuck.

The ideal format for a "DAPP as formative evaluation" research study might entail the following steps: A therapist videotapes his or her sessions. Immediately after each session, a first viewing of the videotape by therapist and DAPP coders takes place in which the coders and the therapist note what parts they found most significant. The coders then continue to study the tape, and they present an analysis to the therapist prior to the next session with the client. In the analysis they note their observations of what conflicts have emerged, what syntheses have been constructed, and what resources offered by the therapist have been used by the client. They also have the opportunity to suggest possible ways of building on the work of the previous session, or addressing problems that developed in the previous session, during the next session. The therapist also has an opportunity to share his or her reactions to the analysis, and thoughts about the next session, before it takes place. Over the course of the therapy, each of these steps in the process would be documented, so conclusions may be drawn regarding how the analyses of previous sessions influenced subsequent sessions.

Although a team of volunteers ready to carry out such a project has not yet been assembled, and funding has not yet been sought, initial explorations of aspects of such a project, asking how feedback from coders may be useful and used by therapists, are under way.

Implications and Future Directions for Practice

At the risk of being repetitious, we feel it is important in introducing the section to restate clearly a point made in Chapter 1: Unlike many other writings and research on psychotherapy, this book is *not* suggesting that psychotherapy practitioners substitute any particular other way of engaging with their clients from what they already do. We see value in every theory and technique of psychotherapy that any therapist may be using to organize what he or she offers to clients, and how he or she understands what particular clients need. Although Chapter 5 merely touched the surface of our efforts to view all approaches to psychotherapy through the lenses of DAPP, it suggests how in *every* approach to psychotherapy we see the therapist offering to clients some combination of (a) support in attending more fully and more simultaneously to varying aspects of the clients' activity and experiences, (b) alternate ways of understanding the clients' activity and experience, and (c) opportunities to engage in and reflect upon novel activities and experiences. These are the resources that therapists offer to the three fundamental dialectical processes through which development in psychotherapy occurs.

The major implications of this book for practitioners include (a) encouraging psychotherapists to refrain from defining their approaches in opposition to or as exclusive from other approaches, thereby paying *more attention* to the commonalities and continuities across what all psychotherapists fundamentally do; and (b) encouraging psychotherapists to *reflect critically* on what they are doing with each client, while offering to therapists *a novel framework for such critical reflection* that allows such reflection to occur *within broader communities of discourse* than the psychotherapy "camps" in which critical reflection typically occurs. We view all critical reflection, in whatever communities and relationships in which it occurs, as not only valuable but also essential to the ideal of being a scientist-practitioner. However, we see reflection that occurs within communities that speak in the specific languages of particular approaches as limited, in that the languages themselves often contain implicit or explicit assumptions that narrow the scope of the discourse, without adequate validation to justify doing so. We are offering a way to move beyond the narrowness. This is most important both for identifying when work with a client is not fostering developmental progress, and for considering the full range of possible alternative tacks that might more effectively address the clients' developmental needs and potentials.

We recognize that this offer comes at a cost. Readers who have read this book so far have already started to pay that cost. It is the cost of learning a whole new language for conceptualizing psychotherapy process. This cost may seem quite expensive for a practitioner who by and large feels that the language in which he or she already speaks and thinks about psychotherapy in general and his or her work with clients is perfectly adequate. Furthermore, at the same time we are claiming that other languages contain implicit and explicit assumptions, we are also acknowledging the assumptions underlying the developmental framework we have proposed. We have tried, both in the beginning of this chapter and in the earlier chapters of the book, to be as clear and explicit as possible as to what these assumptions are, the nature of the prescriptivity the assumptions entail, and our view of their justification. It is our hope that enough practitioners will be willing to learn this language to create a much more inclusive community of discourse about psychotherapy, which will in turn lead to increased richness in research and practice.

For those who make the effort, and sufficiently learn a language that allows them to conceptualize psychotherapy as a developmental process, the immediate payoff will be of two types. First, they will be able to present case analyses that rigorously demonstrate the value and process of their work to this inclusive community of discourse. They will thereby transcend the dichotomy between psychotherapy that follows the manual representing a particular empirically supported treatment, and psychotherapy that merely represents the practitioner's personal preferences and lacks scientific validation. Second, they will be able to use DAPP as a tool in the formative evaluation of their work with clients, which is likely to be of greatest value when work is not going so well. This process would be similar to what was proposed in the "DAPP as Formative Evaluation" section of the implications for research discussed above, but much less expensive. The therapist himself or herself could review tapes (made with clients' permission) or even process notes of his or her work with clients, assess which developmental resources were being offered and the extent and limits to which they are being used, and, using the model of three central therapeutic processes, consider alternative resources that could be offered to transcend identified limits. He or she also could observe, within all three processes, conflicts that have been expressed but not yet resolved with novel syntheses. By maintaining focus on such conflicts, opportunities for novel syntheses will be supported. Finally, opportunities to consult with diverse members of the inclusive community of discourse could further augment the process of generating alternatives.

In suggesting the value of the developmental language we offer, we are suggesting that therapists become "bilingual," rather than proposing that this language can substitute for the more content-rich languages through which the knowledge and skills developed by generations of therapists have been passed down from each generation to the next. Furthermore, even though the underlying individual-case-focused developmental paradigm has been presented as an alternative to the medical model, the realities of psychotherapy practice in the United States and many other countries will continue to require that therapists who conceptualize their work developmentally *also* be able to translate back and forth to the language of the medical model. As long as psychotherapy is practiced in medical settings and paid for by health insurance companies, rather than practiced in educational settings and supported in the manner of public education, the language of diagnosed problems, treatments, and symptom-related outcomes will be essential for psychotherapists to speak. Even if one understands the underlying psychotherapy process in developmental terms, the way in which the development that occurs translates into improvement of symptoms will need to be expressed to outside parties who, thinking in medical model terms, are assessing effectiveness.

Implications and Future Directions for Training

The implications for training follow from all we have said above about theory, technique, practice, and reflection. We view it as no less important for students to learn modalities, theories, and techniques of psychotherapy, as is currently recognized by most psychotherapy training programs. In fact, we expect that such learning requires developing fluency in speaking multiple languages for articulating case formulations, treatment plans, and bases for altering formulations and treatment plans. However, we see as an implication of this book that it is equally important to create learning environments in which students can engage with what they learn within a dialectical-constructivist epistemological context. Doing so entails being able to "read," speak, and think in another language, which we hope to articulate in what follows.

First, central to viewing psychotherapy in a constructivist-epistemological context is the recognition that the modalities, theories, and techniques of psychotherapy learned are all forms of organization constructed by therapists, individually and in communities, to serve the purpose of mediating therapists' responses to clients in the context of therapeutic relationships. Although some constructivist epistemologies are relativistic (see Neimeyer

& Mahoney, 1995), with the implication that there are no transcontextual criteria for evaluating the different forms of knowledge created by different human communities, this is not the case with the dialectical-constructivist epistemological framework that we propose.

Assumptions regarding two dialectical contexts for evaluation are central to what we view as an adequate epistemological context for psychotherapy training. First is the context of the individual psychotherapy relationship, which we believe is the fundamental context in which the forms of organization that therapists bring both are expected to function effectively and, in the process of coming to function effectively, are expected to evolve. In other words, it is appropriate to judge the frameworks and repertoires that mediate therapists' responses to clients in therapy, according to whether they foster the realization of the potential of psychotherapy relationships to serve as a context for clients' development. We have discussed at length how clients can make use of the resources of attentional support, interpretation, and enactment opportunities to bring conflicts into focus and to create novel syntheses. Training in psychotherapy must include learning the capacity to *monitor* the extent to which these processes are occurring, and to *adapt* what one is doing to better facilitate these processes.

Essential to these capacities are, first of all, being able to read the *cues of equilibrium and disequilibrium*, and of *conflict and synthesis*, both *within the therapeutic relationship itself* and in the *organizations* of activity clients are trying to maintain or achieve and the *emergent conflicts* to which they are trying to adapt. Therapists in training must learn to ask and answer the question, "When are my client and I working together, and when are we not?" Trainees must learn to recognize and attend to tensions that emerge in the therapy relationship, and to collaborate with clients in processes of seeking syntheses when they do. In both the cases of Eva and the Lady Cloaked in Fog presented in Chapters 7 and 8, we have illustrated through detailed DAPP analysis how the recognition by the therapist of emergent disequilibrium within the therapy relationship led to shifts in attention or response on the part of the therapist. Addressing the disequilibria together with the client then opened up major developmental opportunities that helped realize the developmental potential of the therapy, and in the process transformed the therapy.

Along with learning to read the cues of equilibrium, disequilibrium, and transformation, it is crucial that therapists in training be supported to gain a reflective distance from the conceptual and technical structures that they use to mediate their responses, so that they can question these structures and allow them to evolve in collaboration with clients' input, in response to conflicts within the therapy relationship that emerge. This is what makes space for the process of mutual adaptation of therapist and client that we have tried to demonstrate above is central to therapeutic success. If therapists in training are taught theories as if they are "truths" about psychotherapy, or techniques as "proven to work if properly applied," this will not allow them that crucial reflective distance when they put what they have learned into practice. On the other hand, if they understand the therapeutic relationship as where the development that constitutes successful therapy occurs, and theories and techniques as transient forms of organization that operate within such relationships until they reach their limits, and then they adapt and grow, this will provide an epistemological context for them to become the most effective therapists they can be, without the sources of their professional identifies and indeed world coherence being threatened by the process of adaptation. Such an epistemological context will also enable them to notice the parallel and intertwined processes of clients' struggles to conserve a sense of meaning while adapting to the situations they face, with therapists' struggles to conserve their sense of meaning while adapting to all that they have to learn from each particular client.[2]

There is a second dialectical context in which approaches to psychotherapy operate that is equally important to their evaluation and evolution. A relativistic approach to psychotherapy typically asserts, "I (we) work the way I work; it is helpful to some clients but not all; if my approach doesn't work for particular clients, they should go see someone else." The costs of such relativistic approaches to psychotherapy, in terms of limiting psychotherapy success rates, the sometimes traumatic losses of what clients have invested in therapy relationships, and the losses of developmental opportunities for both therapists and clients, are discussed in greater detail in earlier work (Basseches, 1997b). Here, our goal is to simply contrast such relativistic approaches with a dialectical-constructivist one that assumes that if there are different therapists or therapeutic communities with different approaches, each with their own strengths and limits, this represents a conflict with developmental potential within the field of psychotherapy, as a science and as a practice. It is not epistemologically acceptable to merely accept this state of affairs, with the recommendation that there be mutual respect across approaches. Rather, the challenge, within a dialectical-constructivist epistemology, that follows from this conflict is to create a metaframework within which the strengths and limits of each approach by itself can be understood, and an integrative approach that embraces the strengths of each while guiding adaptive responses when limits are encountered can be constructed. We have suggested that our view of psychotherapy as a developmental process offers such a metaframework and language for constructively organizing the similarities and differences

---

[2] See Basseches (1997b) for a fuller discussion of the challenges of developing a dialectical-epistemological perspective for therapists, and the potential costs of not doing so.

among different therapists' approaches. But as mentioned in the previous section, the creation of inclusive communities of psychotherapists in which such a framework can be used is important to realizing the potential of this developmental framework.

Psychotherapy training programs are ideal places in which to create such communities. Mentors from the worlds of psychotherapy research and practice, with expertise in different approaches, can be brought together to offer their expertise to students. The challenge is to do this with a spirit in which the expectations of students are that they will integrate what they are exposed to, both to advance the field of psychotherapy and to become the most effective therapists that they can be for all the clients that they see, rather than one in which students are expected to decide to which "camp" to declare their allegiance. If this challenge can be met, training programs represent opportunities to create spaces in which the time for detailed reflection on cases is available, and an inclusive community of psychotherapists can participate in the discourse. To those involved in psychotherapy training in particular, faculty, and students, we offer this book as providing a framework that we believe can play a central role in such crucially important processes of communal reflection.

References

Ackerman, B. P., Abe, J. A., & Izard, C. E. (1998). Differential emotions theory and emotional development. In M. F. Mascolo & S. Griffin (Eds.), *What develops in emotional development?* New York: Plenum.

Ainsworth, M. D. S., Blehar, M. C., Waters, E., & Wall, S. (1978). *Patterns of attachment.* Hillsdale, NJ: Erlbaum.

Alberini, C. (2005). Mechanisms of memory stabilization: Are consolidation and reconsolidation similar or distinct processes? *Trends in Neurosciences, 28,* 51–56.

American Psychiatric Association. (1952). *Diagnostic and statistical manual of mental disorders.* Washington, DC: American Psychiatric Association.

American Psychiatric Association. (1968). *Diagnostic and statistical manual of mental disorders* (2nd ed.). Washington, DC: American Psychiatric Association.

American Psychiatric Association. (1980). *Diagnostic and statistical manual of mental disorders* (3rd ed.). Washington, DC: American Psychiatric Association.

American Psychiatric Association. (1994). *Diagnostic and statistical manual of mental disorders* (4th ed.). Washington, DC: American Psychiatric Association.

American Psychiatric Association. (2000). *Diagnostic and statistical manual of mental disorders—TR* (4th ed.). Washington, DC: American Psychiatric Association.

Annett, J. (1995). Motor imagery: Perception or action? *Neuropsychologia, 33,* 1–23.

Annunziata, A. J. (2009). *Assessing the developmental processes of adjunctive mindfulness therapy: A single-case design.* Unpublished report on early research project, Suffolk University.

Arbib, M. A (2006). *Action to language via the mirror neuron system.* Cambridge University Press.

Averill, J. R. (1982). *Anger and aggression: An essay on emotion.* New York: Springer.

Bandura, A. (1977). *Social learning theory.* New York: General Learning Press.

Bandura, A., Blanchard, E., & Ritter, B. (1969). The relative efficacy of desensitization and modeling approaches for inducing behavioral, affective, and attitudinal changes. *Journal of Personality and Social Psychology, 13,* 173–199.

Bandura, A., Ross, D., & Ross, S. (1963). Vicarious reinforcements and imitative learning. *Journal of Abnormal and Social Psychology, 67,* 601–607.

Basseches, M. (1984). *Dialectical thinking and adult development.* Norwood, NJ: Ablex.

Basseches, M. (1989). Toward a constructive-developmental understanding of the dialectics of individuality and irrationality. In D. A. Kramer & M. J. Bopp (Eds.), *Transformation in clinical and developmental psychology* (pp. 188–209). New York: Springer-Verlag.

Basseches, M. (1993). Disequilibrium and transformation. In A. Lipson (Ed.), *Critical incidents in psychotherapy* (unpublished collection).

Basseches, M. (1997a). A developmental perspective on psychotherapy process, psychotherapists' expertise, and "meaning-making conflict" within therapeutic relationships: A two-part series. *Journal of Adult Development, 4,* 17–33.

Basseches, M. (1997b). A developmental perspective on psychotherapy process, psychotherapists' expertise, and "meaning-making conflict" within therapeutic relationships: Part II. *Journal of Adult Development, 4,* 85–106.

Basseches, M. (2003). Adult development and the practice of psychotherapy. In J. Demick & C. Andreoletti (Eds.), *The handbook of adult development.* New York: Plenum.

Basseches, M., Mascolo, M., Dooley, C., Peters, T., Rideout, M., Sharma, R., et al. (2002). Therapeutic processes coding manual. Unpublished manuscript.

Bearison, D. J., & Dorval, B. (2001). *Collaborative cognition: Children negotiating ways of knowing.* Westport, CT: Ablex.

Becker, J. (2004). Reconsidering the role of overcoming perturbations in cognitive development: Constructivism and consciousness. *Human Development, 47,* 77–93.

Beebe, B., Knoblauch, S., Rustin, J., Sorter, D., Jacobs, T., & Pally, R. (2005). *Forms of intersubjectivity in infant research and adult treatment.* New York: Other Press.

Beebe, B., & Lachman, F. M. (2002). *Infant research and adult treatment: Co-constructing interactions.* New York: Analytic Press.

Berger, D., & Wilde, J. (1987). A task analysis of algebra word problems. *Applications of cognitive psychology: Problem solving, education, and computing* (pp. 123–137). Hillsdale: Erlbaum.

Bergman, L. R., Cairns, R. B., Nilsson, L-G., & Nystedt, L. (Eds.). (2000). *Developmental science and the holistic approach.* Mahwah, NJ: Erlbaum.

Berry, D., & Dienes, Z. (1991). The relationship between implicit memory and implicit learning. *British Journal of Psychology, 82,* 359–373.

Bertenthal, B. I. (1996). Origins and early development of perception, action and representations. *Annual Review of Psychology, 47,* 431–459.

Bickhard, M. H. (2005). Consciousness and reflective consciousness. *Philosophical Psychology, 18*(2), 205–218.

Bidell, T. R., & Fischer, K. W. (1996). Between nature and nurture: The role of human agency in the epigenesis of intelligence. In R. Sternberg & E. Grigorenko (Eds.), *Intelligence: Heredity and environment* (pp. 193–242). Cambridge: Cambridge University Press.

Blasi, A., & Glodis, K. (1995). The development of identity: A critical analysis from the perspective of the self as subject. *Developmental Review, 15,* 404–433.

Bowen, M. V.-B. (1996a). Foreword. In B. A. Farber, D. C. Brink, & P. M. Raskin (Eds.), *The psychotherapy of Carl Rogers: Cases and commentary* (i–ix). New York: Guilford.

Bowen, M. V.-B. (1996b). The myth of nondirectiveness: The case of Jill. In B. A. Farber, D. C. Brink, & P. M. Raskin (Eds.), *The psychotherapy of Carl Rogers: Cases and commentary* (pp. 84–94). New York: Guilford.

Bowlby, J. (1980). *Attachment and loss* (Vols. 1–3). New York: Basic Books.

Bowlby, J. (1998). *A secure base.* New York: Basic Books.

Bråten, S. (Ed.). (2007). *On being moved: From mirror neurons to empathy.* Philadelphia: John Benjamins.

Brentano, F. (1973). *Psychology from an empirical standpoint* (T. Rancurello, D. Terrell, & L. McAllister, Trans.). Atlantic Highlands, NJ: Humanities Press. (Originally published in 1874)

Brink, D. C. (1987). The issues of equality and control in the client- or person-centered approach. *Journal of Humanistic Psychology, 27,* 27–41.

Broca, P. (1878). Anatomie comparée des circonvolutions cérébrales: le grande lobe limbique. *Revue anthropologique, 1,* 385–498.

Brody, L. R. (1981). Visual short term cued recall memory in infancy. *Child Development, 52,* 242–250.

Bromberg, P. M. (1998). *Standing in the spaces: Essays on clinical process, trauma, and dissociation.* Hillsdale, NY: Analytic Press.

Bronfenbrenner, U., & Morris, P. A. (2006). The bioecological model of human development. In W. Damon & R. M. Lerner (Series Eds.) & R. M. Lerner (Vol. Ed.), *Handbook of child psychology: Vol. 1. Theoretical models of human development* (6th ed., pp. 793–828). Hoboken, NJ: Wiley.

Bruner, J. (1986). *Actual minds, possible worlds.* Cambridge, MA: Harvard University Press.

Bruner, J., & Kalmar, D. (1998). Narrative and metanarrative in the construction of self. In M. Ferrari & R. J. Sternberg (Eds.), *Self-awareness: Its nature and development* (pp. 308–331). New York: Guilford.

Bucci, W. (1995). The power of the narrative: A multiple code account. In J. W. Pennebaker (Ed.), *Emotion, disclosure and health* (pp. 71–92). Washington, DC: APA Press.

Buck, R. (1980). Nonverbal communication of emotion. In S. Weinberg (Ed.), *Messages: A reader in human communication* (3rd ed.). New York: Random House.

Burgdorf, J., & Panksepp, J. (2006). The neurobiology of positive emotions, *Neuroscience and Biobehavioral Reviews, 30,* 173–187.

Cacioppo, J. T., Visser, P. S., & Picket, C. L. (Eds.). (2006). *Social neuroscience: People thinking about thinking people.* Cambridge, MA: MIT Press.

Campos, J. J., Anderson, D. I., Marianne, A., Barbu-Roth, M. A., Hubbard, E. M., Hertenstein, M. J., et al. (2000). Travel broadens the mind. *Infancy, 1,* 149–219.

Campos, J. J., Barrett, K. C., Lamb, M. E., Goldsmith, H. H., & Steinberg, C. (1983). Socioemotional development. In M. M. Haith & J. J. Campos (Eds.), *Handbook of child psychology: Vol. 2. Infancy and developmental psychobiology* (pp. 783–915). New York: Wiley.

Carere-Comes, T. (1999). Beyond psychotherapy: Dialectical therapy. *Journal of Psychotherapy Integration, 9,* 365–396.

Carere-Comes, T. (2001). The logic of the therapeutic relationship. *Journal European Psychoanalysis, 12/13,* 91–104.

Carr, A. (2009). *What works with children, adolescents and adults?: A review of research on the effectiveness of psychotherapy.* New York, NY US: Routledge/ Taylor & Francis Group.

Carver, C. S., & Scheier, M. F. (2002). Control processes and self-organization as complementary principles underlying behavior. *Personality and Social Psychology Review, 6,* 304–315.

Case, R. (1992a). *The mind's staircase: Exploring the conceptual underpinnings of children's thought and knowledge.* Hillsdale, NJ: Erlbaum.

Case, R. (1992b). Neo-Piagetian theories of child development. In R. J. Sternberg & C. A. Berg (Eds.), *Intellectual development* (pp. 161–196). Cambridge: Cambridge University Press.

Case, R., & Okamoto, Y. (1996). *The role of central conceptual structures in the development of children's thought* (Monographs of the Society of Research in Child Development, Vol. 61). Chicago: Society for Research in Child Development.

Chawla, N., & Ostafin, B. (2007). Experiential avoidance as a functional dimensional approach to psychopathology: An empirical review. *Journal of Clinical Psychology, 63,* 871–890.

Chess, S., & Thomas, A. (1991). Temperament and the concept of goodness of fit. In J. Strelau & A. Angleitner (Eds.), *Explorations in temperament: International perspectives on theory and measurement* (pp. 15–28). New York: Plenum.

Clark, A. (1997). *Being there.* Cambridge, MA: MIT Press.

Clark, K., & Holquist, M. (1984). *Mikhail Bakhtin.* Cambridge, MA: Harvard University Press.

Cocking, R. R., & Renninger, K. A. (Eds.) (1993). *The development and meaning of psychological distance.* Hillsdale, NJ: Erlbaum.

Cohen, J. (1960). A coefficient of agreement for nominal scales, *Educational and Psychological Measurement, 20,* 37–46.

Cole, M. (1996). *Cultural psychology.* Cambridge, MA: Harvard University Press.

Commons, M. L., Trudeau, E. J., Stein, S. A., Richards, F. A., & Krause, S. R. (1998). The existence of developmental stages as shown by the hierarchical complexity of tasks. *Developmental Review, 8,* 237–278.

Cosgrove, L., & Riddle, B. (2004). Gender bias and sex distribution of mental disorders in the DSM-IV-TR. In P. J. Caplan & L. Cosgrove (Eds.), *Bias in psychiatric diagnosis* (pp. 127–140). Lanham, MD: Jason Aronson.

Cowley, S. J., Moodley, S., & Fiori-Cowley, A. (2004). Grounding signs of culture: Primary intersubjectivity in social semiosis. *Mind, Culture and Activity, 11,* 109–132.

Cozolino, L. (2002). *The neuroscience of psychotherapy.* New York: Norton.

Cozolino, L. (2006). *The neuroscience of human relationships: Attachment and the developing social brain.* New York: Norton.

Csíkszentmihályi, M. (1991). *Flow: The psychology of optimal experience.* New York: Harper & Row.

Cuijpers, P., van Straten, A., & Warmerdam, L. (2008). Are individual and group treatments equally effective in the treatment of depression in adults? A meta-analysis. *European Journal of Psychiatry, 22*, 38–51.

Dana, R. (2002). Examining the usefulness of DSM-IV. In K. Kurasaki, S. Okazaki, & S. Sue (Eds.), *Asian American mental health: Assessment theories and methods* (pp. 29–46). New York: Kluwer Academic/Plenum.

Davanloo, H. (1994). *Basic principles and techniques in short-term dynamic psychotherapy*. Northvale, NJ: Aronson.

Davidson, R. J. (2000). Cognitive neuroscience needs affective neuroscience (and vice versa). *Brain & Cognition, 42*, 89–92.

Dawes, R. M. (1994). *House of cards: Psychology and psychotherapy built on myth*. New York: Free Press.

Dawson, T. L., Fischer, K. W., & Stein, Z. (2006). Reconsidering qualitative and quantitative research approaches: A cognitive developmental perspective. *New Ideas in Psychology, 24*, 229–239.

Dawson-Tunik, T. L., Fischer, K., & Stein, Z. (2004). Do stages belong at the center of developmental theory? A commentary on *Piaget's stages. New Ideas in Psychology, 22*, 255–263.

Demetriou, A., Shayer, M., & Efklides, A. (1992). *Neo-Piagetian theories of cognitive development: Implications and applications for education*. London: Routledge.

Dewey, J. (1916). *Democracy and education: An introduction to the philosophy of education*. New York: Macmillan Publishing.

Dewey, J. (1922). *Human nature and conduct*. New York: Henry Holt and Company.

Dewey, J. (1999). *Liberalism and social action*. New York: Prometheus. (Originally published in 1935)

Diaz, R. M., & Berk, L. E. (1992). *Private speech: From social interaction to self-regulation*. Hillsdale, NJ: Erlbaum.

Dimaggio, G., Salvatore, G., Azzara, C., & Catania, D. (2003). Rewriting self narratives: The therapeutic process. *Journal of Constructivist Psychology, 16*, 155–181.

Dodge, K. (2006). Translational science in action: Hostile attributional style and the development of aggressive behavior problems. *Development and Psychopathology, 18*, 791–814.

Drescher, J., & Merlino, J. P. (2007). *American psychiatry and homosexuality: An oral history*. Binghamton, NY: Harrington Park.

Druyan, S. (2001). A comparison of four types of cognitive conflict and their effect on cognitive development. *International Journal of Behavioral Development, 25*, 226–236.

Ecker, B., & Hulley, L. (1996). *Depth-oriented brief therapy: How to be brief when you were trained to be deep—and vice versa*. San Francisco: Jossey-Bass.

Ecker, B., & Hulley, L. (2008). Coherence therapy: Swift change at the roots of symptom production. In J. D. Raskin & S. K. Bridges (Eds.), *Studies in meaning 3: Constructivist psychotherapy in the real world* (pp. 57–84). New York: Pace University Press.

Ecker, B., & Toomey, B. (2008). Depotentiation of symptom-producing implicit memory in coherence therapy. *Journal of Constructivist Psychology, 21*, 87–150.

Edwards, D., & Potter, J. (2005). Discursive psychology, mental states and descriptions. In H. te Molder & J. Potter (Eds.), *Conversation and cognition* (pp. 241–59). Cambridge: Cambridge University Press.

Ekman, P. (1993). Facial expression and emotion. *American Psychologist, 48,* 384–392.

Ellsworth, P. C., & Scherer, K. R. (2003). Appraisal processes in emotion. In R. J. Davidson, H. Goldsmith, & K. R. Scherer (Eds.), *Handbook of affective sciences.* New York: Oxford University Press.

Emde, R. N. (1983). The prerepresentational self and its affective core. *Psychoanalytic Study of the Child, 38,* 165–192.

Farber, B. A. (1996). Introduction. In B. A. Farber, D. C. Brink, & P. M. Raskin (Eds.), *The psychotherapy of Carl Rogers: Cases and commentary* (pp. 1–14). New York: Guilford.

Field, T., Lasko, D., Mundy, P., Henteleff, T., Kabat, S., Talpins, S., et al. (1997). Brief report: Autistic children's attentiveness and responsivity improve after touch therapy. *Journal of Autism and Developmental Disorders, 27,* 333–338.

Fischer, K. W. (1980). A theory of cognitive development: The control and construction of hierarchies of skills. *Psychological Review, 87,* 477–531.

Fischer, K. W., & Bidell, T. R. (2006). Dynamic development of action, thought, and emotion. In W. Damon & R. M. Lerner (Eds.), *Theoretical models of human development: Handbook of child psychology* (6th ed., Vol. 1, pp. 313–399). New York: Wiley.

Fischer, K. W., Bullock, D. H., Rotenberg, E. J., & Raya, P. (1993). The dynamics of competence: How context contributes directly to skill. In R. Wozniak & K. W. Fischer (Eds.), *Development in context: Acting and thinking in specific environments* (pp. 93–117). Hillsdale, NJ: Erlbaum.

Fischer, K. W., & Hogan, A. (1989). The big picture for infant development: Levels and variations. In J. Lockman & N. Hazen (Eds.), *Action in social context: Perspectives on early development* (pp. 275–305). New York: Plenum.

Flavell, J. H. (1982). On cognitive development. *Child Development, 53,* 1–10.

Fleiss, J. L. (1981). *Statistical methods for rates and proportions* (2nd ed.). New York: John Wiley.

Fodor, J. (1980). On the impossibility of acquiring "more powerful" structures. In M. Piatelli Palmarini (Ed.), *Language and learning: The debate between Jean Piaget and Noam Chomsky* (pp. 142–162). Cambridge, MA: Harvard University Press.

Fogel, A. (1993). *Developing through relationships.* Chicago: University of Chicago Press.

Fogel, A. (2006). Dynamic systems research on interindividual communication: The transformation of meaning-making. *The Journal of Developmental Processes, 1,* 7–30.

Fogel, A., & DeKoeyer-Laros, I. (2007). The developmental transition to the secondary subjectivity in the second half year: A microdevelopmental study. *The Journal of Developmental Processes, 2,* 63–90.

Fogel, A., Garvey, A., Hsu, H-C., & West-Stromming, D. (2006). *Change Processes in relationships: A relational-historical approach.* New York: Cambridge University Press.

Fogel, A., Lyra, M. C. D. P., & Valsiner, J. (Eds.). (1997). *Dynamics and indeterminism in developmental and social processes.* Mahwah, NJ: Erlbaum.

Freeman, W. (2000). Emotion is essential to all intentional behaviours. In M. D. Lewis & I. Granic (Eds.), *Emotion, development, and self-organization* (pp. 209–235). New York: Cambridge University Press.

Freud, S. (1965). *New introductory lectures on psychoanalysis.* New York: Norton. (Originally published in 1917)

Freud, S. (1990). *Beyond the pleasure principle.* New York: Norton. (Originally published in 1920)

Frijda, N. H. (1986). *The emotions.* Cambridge: Cambridge University Press.

Frijda, N. H. (1987). Emotion, emotion structure, and action tendency. *Cognition and Emotion, 1,* 115–143.

Gagne, R. M. (1974). Task analysis: Its relation to content analysis, *Educational Psychologist, 11,* 11–18.

Gallagher, S. (2005). *How the body shapes the mind.* Oxford: Oxford University Press.

Gallagher, S., & Hutto, D. D. (2008). Understanding others through primary interaction and narrative practice. In J. Zlatev, T. Racine, C. Sinha, & E. Itkonen (Eds.), *The shared mind: Perspectives on intersubjectivity.* Amsterdam: John Benjamins.

Gallese, V. (2005). "Being like me": Self-other identity, mirror neurons and empathy. In S. Hurley & N. Chater (Eds.), *Perspectives on imitation: From cognitive neuroscience to social science* (Vol. 1, pp. 101–118). Cambridge, MA: MIT Press.

Gallese, V., Eagle, M. N., & Migone, P. (2007). Intentional attunement: Mirror neurons and the neural underpinnings of interpersonal relations. *Journal of the American Psychoanalytic Association, 55,* 131–176.

Garon, N., & Moore, C. (2007). Awareness and symbol use improves future-oriented decision making in preschoolers. *Developmental Neuropsychology, 31,* 39–59.

Gelman, R., & Baillargeon, R. (1983). A review of some Piagetian concepts. In J. H. Flavell & E. Markman (Eds.), *Handbook of child psychology: Vol. 3. Cognitive development.* New York: Wiley.

Gergen, K. J. (1989). Social psychology and the wrong revolution. *European Journal of Social Psychology, 19,* 463–484.

Gergen, K. J. (1991). *The saturated self.* New York: Basic Books.

Gergen, K. (2001). *Social construction in context.* London: Sage.

Gergen, K. J. (2006). *Therapeutic realities, collaboration, oppression and relational flow.* Chagrin Falls, OH: Taos Institute.

Gergen, K., & Gergen, M. (2003). *Social construction: A reader.* London: Sage.

Ginsberg, H. P., & Opper, S. (1988). *Piaget's theory of intellectual development* (3rd ed.). Englewood Cliffs, NJ: Prentice Hall.

Glenberg, A. (1999). Why mental models must be embodied. In G. Rickheit & C. Habel (Eds.), *Mental models in discourse processing and reasoning.* New York: Elsevier.

Gonçalves, O., & Ivey, A. (1993). Developmental therapy: Clinical applications. *Cognitive therapies in action: Evolving innovative practice* (pp. 326–352). San Francisco, CA US: Jossey-Bass.

Gottlieb, G., & Lickliter, R. (2007). Probabilistic epigenesis. *Developmental Science, 10,* 1–11.

Gottlieb, G., Wahlsten, D., & Lickliter, R. (2006). The significance of biology for human development: A developmental psychobiological systems perspective. In W. Damon & R. M. Lerner (Series Eds.) & R. M. Lerner (Vol. Ed.), *Handbook of child psychology: Vol. 1. Theoretical models of human development* (6th ed., pp. 210–257). Hoboken, NJ: Wiley.

Gouin-Decarie, T., & Ricard, M. (1996). Revisiting Piaget revisited or the vulnerability of Piaget's infancy theory in the 1990s. In G. G. Noam & K. W. Fischer (Eds.), *Development and vulnerability in close relationships* (pp. 113–132). Mahwah, NJ: Erlbaum.

Granott, N. (1993). Patterns of interaction in the co-construction of knowledge: Separate minds, joint effort, and weird creatures. In R. Wozniak & K. W. Fischer (Eds.), *Development in context: Acting and thinking in specific environments* (pp. 183–207). Hillsdale, NJ: Erlbaum.

Granott, N. (1998). Unit of analysis in transit: From the individual's knowledge to the ensemble process. *Mind, Culture, and Activity: An International Journal, 5*(1), 42–66.

Granott, N. (2002). How microdevelopment creates macrodevelopment: Reiterated sequences, backward transitions, and the zone of current development zone. In N. Granott & J. Parziale (Eds.), *Microdevelopment: Transition processes in development and learning* (pp. 213–242). New York: Cambridge University Press.

Granott, N., Fischer, K. W., & Parziale, J. (2002). Bridging to the unknown: A fundamental mechanism in learning and problem-solving. In N. Granott & J. Parziale (Eds.), *Microdevelopment: Transition processes in development and learning.* Cambridge: Cambridge University Press.

Granott, N., & Parziale, J. (2002). *Microdevelopment: Transition processes in development and learning.* New York: Cambridge University Press.

Greenberg, L., & Elliott, R. (2002). Emotion-focused therapy. In F. W. Kaslow & J. W. Lebow (Eds.), *Comprehensive handbook of psychotherapy, Vol 4. Integrative/eclectic* (pp. 213–240). Hoboken, NJ: John Wiley.

Greenberg, L. S., & Goldman, R. (2008). *Emotion-focused couples therapy: The dynamics of emotion, love and power.* Washington, DC: APA Press.

Greenberg, L., & Pascual-Leone, J. (1995). A dialectical constructivist approach to experiential change. In R. Neimeyer & M. Mahoney (Eds.), *Constructivism in psychotherapy* (pp. 169–191). Washington, DC: APA Press.

Greenberg, L., & Pascual-Leone, A. (2006). Emotion in psychotherapy: A practice-friendly research review. *Journal of Clinical Psychology, 62,* 611–630.

Greenberg, L. S., Rice, L. N., & Elliot, R. (1993). *Facilitating emotional change: The moment by moment process.* New York: Guilford Press.

Guerin, P., & Chabot, D. (1997). Development of family systems theory. *Theories of psychotherapy: Origins and evolution* (pp. 181–225). Washington, DC: APA Press.

Habermas, J. (1971). Knowledge and human interests. Boston: Beacon Press.

Habermas, J. (1995). *Moral consciousness and communicative action* (C. Lenhardt & S. W. Nicholsen, Trans.). Cambridge, MA: MIT Press.

Hammersley, M., & Atkinson, P. (1995). *Ethnography: Principles in practice* (2nd ed.). New York: Routledge.

Harned, M., Chapman, A., Dexter-Mazza, E., Murray, A., Comtois, K., & Linehan, M. (2008). Treating co-occurring Axis I disorders in recurrently suicidal women with borderline personality disorder: A 2-year randomized trial of dialectical behavior therapy versus community treatment by experts. *Journal of Consulting and Clinical Psychology*, 1068–1075.

Harré, H. R., & Tissaw, M. (2005). *Wittgenstein and psychology*. Basingstoke, UK: Ashgate.

Harré, R. (1983). *Personal being: A theory for individual psychology*. Oxford: Blackwell.

Harré, R., & Gillett, G. (1994). *The discursive mind*. London: Sage.

Hassin, R., Uleman, J., & Bargh, J. (Eds.). (2005). *The new unconscious*. New York: Oxford University Press.

Hastings, P. D., Zahn-Waxler, C., & McShane, K. (2006). We are, by nature, moral creatures: Biological bases of concern for others. In M. Killen & J. G. Smetana (Eds.), *Handbook of moral development* (pp. 483–516). Mahwah, NJ: Erlbaum.

Hatano, G., & Amaiwa, S. (1987). Formation of a mental abacus for computation and its use as a memory device for digits: A developmental study. *Developmental Psychology*, *23*, 832–838.

Hebb, D. O. (1949). *The organization of behavior*. New York: Wiley.

Hegel, G. W. F. (1977). *Phenomenology of spirit* (A. V. Miller, Trans). New York: Oxford University Press. (Originally published in 1807)

Heidegger, M. (1962). *Being and time*. New York: Harper & Row.

Hensler, J. (2006). Serotonergic modulation of the limbic system. *Neuroscience & Biobehavioral Reviews*, *30*, 203–214.

Herman, J. L. (1992). *Trauma and recovery*. New York: Basic Books.

Hobson, P. (2007). On being moved in thought and feeling: An approach to autism. In J. M. Perez, M. L. Comi, & C. M. Nieto (Eds.), *New developments in autism: The future is today* (pp. 139–154). London: Jessica Kingsley.

Hobson, P., & Hobson, J. (2008). In the beginning is relation … and then what? In U. Müller, J. I. M. Carpendale, N. Budwig, & B. Sokol (Eds.), *Social life and social knowledge: Toward a process account of development* (pp. 103–122). New York: Erlbaum.

Hopkins, J. R., Zelazo, P. R., Jacobsen, S. W., & Kagan, J. (1976). Infant responsivity to stimulus schema discrepancy. *Genetic Psychology Monographs*, *93*, 27–62.

Horney, K. (1950). *Neurosis and human growth*. New York: Norton.

Hume, D. (1998). *Enquiry concerning the principles of morals* (Tom L. Beauchamp, Ed.). Oxford: Oxford University Press. (Originally published in 1751)

Hume, D. (2000). *A treatise on human nature*. Oxford: Oxford University Press.

Husserl, E. (1966). *The phenomenology of internal time consciousness* (J. Churchill. Trans.). Bloomington: Indiana University Press. (Originally published in 1928)

Inhelder, B., Sinclair, H., & Bovet, M. (1974). *Learning and the development of cognition*. Cambridge, MA: Harvard University Press.

Izard, C. E. (1977). *Human emotions*. New York: Plenum.

James, W. (1884). What is an emotion? *Mind*, *9*, 188–205.

James, W. (1890). *The principles of psychology*. New York: Holt.

James, W. (1922). *Pragmatism*. New York: Longmans, Green.

Joseph, R. (1998). Traumatic amnesia, repression, and hippocampus injury due to emotional stress, corticosteroids and enkephalins. *Child Psychiatry & Human Development, 29,* 169–185.

Joyce, A., Wolfaardt, U., Sribney, C., & Aylwin, A. (2006). Psychotherapy research at the start of the 21st century: The persistence of the art versus science controversy. *The Canadian Journal of Psychiatry, 51,* 797–809.

Kagan, J. (1974). Discrepancy, temperament, and infant distress. In M. Lewis & L. Rosenblum (Eds.), *The origins of fear.* New York: Wiley.

Kagan, J. (2002). *Surprise, uncertainty, and mental structures.* Cambridge, MA: Harvard University Press.

Kagan, J. (2008). *What is emotion?* New Haven, CT: Yale University Press.

Kashdan, T., Barrios, V., Forsyth, J., & Steger, M. (2006). Experiential avoidance as a generalized psychological vulnerability: Comparisons with coping and emotion regulation strategies. *Behaviour Research and Therapy, 44,* 1301–1320.

Kauffman, S. (1995). *At home in the universe: The search for laws of self-organization and complexity.* New York: Oxford University Press.

Kegan, R. (1982). *The evolving self.* Cambridge, MA: Harvard University Press.

Kegan, R. (1994). *In over our heads: The mental demands of modern life.* Cambridge, MA: Harvard University Press.

Kihlstrom, J., Mulvaney, S., Tobias, B., & Tobis, I. (2000). The emotional unconscious. In E. Eich, J. F. Kihlstrom, G. H. Bower, J. P. Forgas, & P. M. Niedenthal (Eds.), *Cognition and emotion* (pp. 30–86). New York: Oxford University Press.

Kisley, M. A., Noecker, T. L., & Guinther, P. M. (2004). Comparison of sensory gating to mismatch negativity and self-reported perceptual phenomena in healthy adults. *Psychophysiology, 41,* 604–612.

Kochanska, G. (2001). Emotional development in children with different attachment histories: The first three years. *Child Development, 72,* 474–490.

Kocijan-Hercigonja, D., Sabioncello, A., Rijavec, M., & Folnegovic-Šmalc, V. (1996). Psychological condition hormone levels in war trauma. *Journal of Psychiatric Research, 30,* 391–399.

Koestler, A., & Smithies, J. R. (Eds.). (1969). *Beyond reductionism: New perspectives in the life sciences.* Boston: Beacon.

Kohlberg, L. (1969). Stage and sequence: The cognitive developmental approach to socialization. In D. Goslin (Ed.), *Handbook of socialization theory and research* (pp. 347–480). New York: Rand McNally.

Kohlberg, L., & Mayer, R. (1972). Development as the aim of education. *Harvard Education Review, 42,* 449–496.

Kozulin, A., Gindis, B., Ageyev, V. S., & Miller, S. (Eds.). (2003). *Vygotsky's educational theory in cultural context.* Cambridge: Cambridge University Press.

Kuo, Z-Y. (1967). *The dynamics of behavioral development.* New York: Random House.

LaBar, K. S., & LeDoux, J. E. (2003). Emotional learning circuits in animals and humans. In R. J. Davidson, K. Scherer, & H. H. Goldsmith (Eds.), *Handbook of affective sciences* (pp. 52–65). New York: Oxford University Press.

Lave, J., & Wenger, E. (1991). *Situated learning: Legitimate peripheral participation,* Cambridge: Cambridge University Press.

Lazarus, R. S. (1984). On the primacy of cognition. *American Psychologist, 39,* 124–129.

Lazarus, R. S. (1991). *Emotion and adaptation.* New York: Oxford University Press.

LeDoux, J. E. (2000). Emotion circuits in the brain. *Annual Review of Neuroscience, 23,* 155–184.

LeDoux, J. (2008). Remembrance of emotions past. In Jossey-Bass Publishers (Eds.), *The Jossey-Bass reader on the brain and learning* (pp. 151–179). San Francisco: Jossey-Bass.

Legerstee, M. (2005). *Infants' sense of people: Precursors to a theory of mind.* Cambridge: Cambridge University Press.

Lerner, R. (1991). Changing organism-context relations as the basic process of development: A developmental contextual perspective. *Developmental Psychology, 27,* 27–32.

Lerner, R. M. (2006). Developmental science, developmental systems, and contemporary theories of human development. In W. Damon & R. M. Lerner (Series Eds.) & R. M. Lerner (Vol. Ed.), *Handbook of child psychology: Vol. 1. Theoretical models of human development* (6th ed., pp. 1–17). Hoboken, NJ: Wiley.

Lewis, M. (1990). Intention, consciousness, desires and development. *Psychological Inquiry, 1*(3), 278–283.

Lewis, M. D. (1995). Cognition–emotion feedback and the self-organization of developmental paths. *Human Development, 38,* 71–102.

Lewis, M. D. (1996). Self-organising cognitive appraisals. *Cognition and Emotion, 10,* 1–25.

Lewis, M. D. (1997). Personality self-organization: Cascading constraints on cognition-emotion interaction. In A. Fogel, M. C. D. P. Lyra, & J. Valsiner (Eds.), *Dynamics and indeterminism in developmental and social processes* (pp. 193–216). Hillsdale, NJ: Erlbaum.

Lewis, M. D., & Granic, I. (Eds.). (2000). *Emotion, development, and self-organization.* New York: Cambridge University Press.

Lewis, M. D., & Todd, R. M. (2004). Getting emotional: A neural perspective on emotion, intention, and consciousness. *Journal of Consciousness Studies, 12,* 210–235.

Lewontin, R. C. (2000). *The triple helix: Gene, organism and environment.* Cambridge, MA: Harvard University Press.

Linehan, M. M. (1993a). *Cognitive behavioral treatment of borderline personality disorder.* New York: Guilford.

Linehan, M. M. (1993b). *The skills training manual for treating borderline personality disorder.* New York: Guilford.

Lipson, A. (Ed.). (1993). *Critical incidents in psychotherapy* (unpublished collection).

Loar, B. (1997). Phenomenal states. In N. Block, O. Flanagan, & G. Guzeldere (Eds.), *The nature of consciousness.* Cambridge, MA: MIT Press.

Lompscher, J. (2002). The category of activity as a principal constituent of cultural-historical psychology. In D. Robbins & A. Stetsenko (Eds.), *Voices within Vygotsky's non-classical psychology: Past, present, future* (pp. 79–99). Hauppauge, NY: Nova Science.

Luborsky, L., Rosenthal, R., Diguer, L., Andrusyna, T., Levitt, J., Seligman, D., et al. (2003). Are some psychotherapies much more effective than others? *Journal of Applied Psychoanalytic Studies, 5*(4), 455–460.

Lucas-Thompson, R., & Clarke-Stewart, K. A. (2007). Forecasting friendship: How marital quality, maternal mood, and attachment security are linked to children's peer relationships. *Journal of Applied Developmental Psychology, 28*, 499–514.

MacLean, Paul D. (1990). *The triune brain in evolution: role in paleocerebral functions.* New York: Plenum Press.

Macfie, J., Toth, S., Rogosch, F., Robinson, J., Emde, R., & Cicchetti, D. (1999). Effect of maltreatment on preschoolers' narrative representations of responses to relieve distress and of role reversal. *Developmental Psychology, 35*, 460–465.

Magnusson, D., & Stattin, H. (2006). The person in the environment: Towards a general model for scientific inquiry. In W. Damon & R. M. Lerner (Series Eds.) & R. M. Lerner (Vol. Ed.), *Handbook of child psychology: Vol. 1. Theoretical models of human development* (6th ed., pp. 400–464). Hoboken, NJ: Wiley.

Mahler, M., Pine, F., & Bergman, A. (1975). *The psychological birth of the human infant.* New York: Basic Books.

Mahoney, M. (2003). *Constructive psychotherapy: A practical guide.* New York: Guilford.

Malan, D. (1994). The case of the secretary with the violent father. In H. Davanloo (Ed.), *Basic principles and techniques in short-term dynamic psychotherapy.* Lanham, MD: Jason Aronson.

Malan, D. (2001). *Individual psychotherapy and the science of psychodynamics* (2nd ed.). London: Arnold.

Mancia, M. (Ed.). (2006). *Psychoanalysis and neuroscience.* New York: Springer.

Mascolo, M. F. (2004). The coactive construction of selves in cultures. In M. F. Mascolo & J. Li (Eds.), *Culture and self: Beyond dichotomization* (New Directions in Child and Adolescent Development Series, pp. 79–90). San Francisco: Jossey-Bass.

Mascolo, M. F. (2005). Change processes in development: The concept of coactive scaffolding. *New Ideas in Psychology, 23*, 185–196.

Mascolo, M. F. (2009). Wittgenstein and the discursive analysis of emotion. *New Ideas in Psychology, 27*, 258–274.

Mascolo, M. F. (2008). The concept of domain in developmental models of hierarchical complexity. *World Futures: The Journal of General Evolution, 64*(5), 330–347.

Mascolo, M. F., Craig-Bray, L., & Neimeyer, R. (1997). The construction of meaning and action in development and psychotherapy: An epigenetic systems approach. In G. Neimeyer & R. Neimeyer (Eds.), *Advances in personal construct psychology* (Vol. 4, pp. 3–38). Greenwich, CT: JAI.

Mascolo, M. F., & Fischer, K. W. (1998). The development of self through the coordination of component systems. In Ferrari, M., & Sternberg, R., Self-awareness: Its nature and development, (pp. 332–384). New York: Guilford.

Mascolo, M. F., & Fischer, K. W. (2004). Constructivist theories. In B. Hopkins, R. G. Barre, G. F. Michel, & P. Rochat (Eds.), *Cambridge encyclopedia of child development.* Cambridge: Cambridge University Press.

Mascolo, M. F., & Fischer, K. W. (2007). The co-development of self-awareness and self-evaluative emotions across the toddler years. In C. A. Brownell & C. B. Kopp (Eds.), *Transitions in early socioemotional development: The toddler years.* New York: Guilford.

Mascolo, M. J., Fischer, K. W., & Li, J. (2003). Dynamic development of component systems of emotions: Pride, shame, and guilt in China and the United States. In R. J. Davidson, K. Scherer, & H. H. Goldsmith (Eds.), *Handbook of affective science*. Oxford: Oxford University Press.

Mascolo, M. F., Fischer, K. W., & Neimeyer, R. (1999). The dynamic co-development of intentionality, self and social relations. In J. Brandstadter & R. M. Lerner (Eds.), *Action and development: Origins and functions of intentional self-development* (pp. 133–166). Thousand Oaks, CA: Sage.

Mascolo, M. F., & Griffin, S. (1998a). Alternative trajectories in the development of anger. In M. F. Mascolo & S. Griffin (Eds.), *What develops in emotional development?* (pp. 219–249). New York: Plenum.

Mascolo, M. F., & Griffin, S. (Eds.). (1998b). *What develops in emotional development?* New York: Plenum.

Mascolo, M. F., Harkins, D., & Harakal, T. (2000). The dynamic construction of emotion: Varieties in anger. In M. Lewis & I. Granic (Eds.), *Emotion, self-organization and development* (pp. 124–152). New York: Cambridge University Press.

Mascolo, M. F., & Mancuso, J. C., & Dukewich, T. (2005). Trajectories in the development of anger in development: Appraisal, action and regulation. In J. Cummins (Ed.), *Working with anger: A practical perspective*. New York: John Wiley.

Mascolo, M. F., & Margolis, D. (2004). Social meanings as mediators of the development of adolescent experience and action: A coactive systems approach. *European Journal of Developmental Psychology, 1*, 289–302.

Mascolo, M. F., Pollack, R., & Fischer, K. W. (1997). Keeping the constructor in constructivism: An epigenetic systems approach. *Journal of Constructivist Psychology, 10*, 25–29.

Maslow, A. H. (1943). A theory of human motivation. *Psychological Review, 50*, 370–396.

Maslow, A. H. (1970). *Motivation and personality* (2nd ed.). New York: Harper & Row.

Mateo, J. (2008). Inverted-U shape relationship between cortisol and learning in ground squirrels. *Neurobiology of Learning and Memory, 89*, 582–590.

Matusov, E. (1996). Intersubjectivity without agreement. *Mind, Culture and Activity, 3*, 25–45.

McCall, R. B., Kennedy, C. B., & Appelbaum, M. I. (1977). Magnitude of discrepancy and the distribution of attention in infants. *Child Development, 48*, 772–785.

McCall, R., & McGhee, P. (1977). The discrepancy hypothesis of attention and affect. In F. Weizmann & I. Uzgiris (Eds.), *The structuring of experience*. New York: Plenum.

McCall, R. B., & Nelson, W. H. (1970). Complexity contour and area as determinants of attention infants. *Developmental Psychology, 3*, 343–349.

McCullough, L. (1999). Short-term psychodynamic therapy as a form of desensitization: Treating affect phobias. *In Session: Psychotherapy in Practice, 4*(4), 35–53.

McCullough, L., Kuhn, N., Andrews, S., Kaplan, A., Wolf, J., & Hurley, C. (2003). *Treating affect phobia: A manual for short-term dynamic psychotherapy*. New York: Guilford Press.

McCullough, L., & Magill, M. (2009). Affect-focused short-term dynamic therapy. *Handbook of evidence-based psychodynamic psychotherapy: Bridging the gap between science and practice* (pp. 249–277). Totowa, NJ: Humana Press.

McGaugh, J. (2002). Memory consolidation and the amygdala: A systems perspective. *Trends in Neurosciences, 25*, 456–461.

McGaugh, J. (2003). *Memory and emotion: The making of lasting memories.* New York: Columbia University Press.

McGaugh, J. L., & Cahill, L. (2003). Emotion and memory: Central and peripheral contributions. In R. Davidson, K. Scherer, & H. Goldsmith (Eds.), *Handbook of affective sciences.* New York: Oxford University Press.

McNamee, S. (2003). Therapy as social construction: Back to basics and forward toward challenging issues. In T. Strong & D. Pare (Eds.), *Furthering talks: Advances in the discursive therapies* (pp. 253–269). New York: Kluwer Academic/Plenum.

McNamee, S., & Gergen, K. J. (Eds.). (1992). *Therapy as social construction.* London: Sage.

McNeill, D. (1996). *Mind and hand.* Chicago: University of Chicago Press.

Mead, G. H. (1934). *Mind, self and society from the standpoint of a social behaviorist.* Chicago: University of Chicago Press.

Meltzoff, A. N. (2002). Elements of a developmental theory of imitation. In A. N. Meltzoff & W. Prinz (Eds.), *The imitative mind: Development, evolution, and brain bases* (pp. 19–41). Cambridge: Cambridge University Press.

Meltzoff, A. N., & Brooks, R. (2007). Intersubjectivity before language: Three windows on preverbal sharing. In S. Bråten (Ed.), *On being moved: From mirror neurons to empathy* (pp. 149–174). Philadelphia: John Benjamins.

Meltzoff, A. N., & Moore, M. K. (1977). Imitation of facial and manual gestures by human neonates, *Science, 198*, 75–78.

Meltzoff, A. N., & Moore, M. K. (1983). Newborn infants imitate adult facial gestures. *Child Development, 54*, 702–809.

Meltzoff, A. N., & Moore, M. K. (1999). Persons and representation: Why infant imitation is important for theories of human development. In J. B. G. Nadel (Ed.), *Imitation in infancy: Cambridge studies in cognitive perceptual development* (pp. 9–35). New York: Cambridge University Press.

Menninger, K. (1958). *Theory of psychoanalytic technique.* New York: Basic Books.

Merleau-Ponty, M. (1945). *The phenomenology of perception* (C. Smith, Trans.). London: Routledge and Kegan Paul.

Merleau-Ponty, M. (1962). *The phenomenology of perception* (C. Smith, trans.) London: Routledge and Kegan Paul.

Miller, A. L., Rathus, J. H., & Linehan, M. M. (2007). *Dialectical behavior therapy with suicidal adolescents.* New York: Guilford.

Miller, G. A., Galanter, E., & Pribram, K. H. (1960). *Plans and the structure of behavior.* New York: Henry Holt.

Monin, B., Pizarro, D. A., & Beer, J. S. (2007). Deciding versus reacting: Conceptions of moral judgment and the reason-affect debate. *Review of General Psychology, 11*, 99–111.

Morra, S., Gobbo, C., Marini, Z., & Sheese, R. (2007). *Cognitive development: A neo-Piagetian perspective.* Mahwah, NJ: Erlbaum.

Müller, U., & Runions, K. (2003). The origins of understanding self and other: James Mark Baldwin's theory. *Developmental Review, 23*, 29–54.

Neimeyer, R. A. (1995). Constructivist psychotherapies: Features, foundations, and future directions. In R. A. Neimeyer & M. J. Mahoney (Eds.), *Constructivism in psychotherapy.* (pp. 11–38). Washington, DC: APA Press.

Neimeyer, R., & Baldwin, S. (2003). Personal construct psychotherapy and the constructivist horizon. In F. Fransella (Ed.), *International handbook of personal construct psychology* (pp. 247–255). New York: Wiley.

Neimeyer, R., Herrero, O., & Botella, L. (2006). Chaos to coherence: Psychotherapeutic integration of traumatic loss. *Journal of Constructivist Psychology, 19,* 127–145.

Neimeyer, R. A., & Mahoney, M. J. (Eds.). (1995). *Constructivism in psychotherapy.* Washington, DC: APA Press.

Neisser, U. (1976). *Cognition and reality.* San Francisco: Freeman.

Nelson, D. L., & Brooks, D. H. (1973). Functional independence of pictures and their verbal memory codes. *Journal of Experimental Psychology, 98,* 44–48.

Nelson, K. (2005). Emerging levels of consciousness in early human development. In H. Terrace & J. Metcalfe (Eds.), *The missing link in cognition: Origins of self-reflective consciousness* (pp. 116–141). Oxford: Oxford University Press.

Nemeroff, C., Bremner, J., Foa, E., Mayberg, H., North, C., & Stein, M. (2006). Posttraumatic stress disorder: A state-of-the-science review. *Journal of Psychiatric Research, 40,* 1–21.

Noam, G., & Fischer, K. (1996). *Development and vulnerability in close relationships.* Hillsdale, NJ: Erlbaum.

Ogawa, J. R., Sroufe, L. A., Weinfeld, N. S., Carlson, E. A., & Egeland, B. (1997). Development and the fragmented self: Longitudinal study of dissociative symptomatology in a nonclinical sample. *Development and Psychopathology, 9,* 855–879.

Overton, W. F., Mueller, U., & Newman, J. (Eds.). (2007). *Developmental perspectives on embodiment and consciousness.* Mahwah, NJ: Erlbaum.

Oyama, S. (2000). *Evolution's eye: A systems view of the biology-culture divide.* Durham, NC: Duke University Press.

Panksepp, J. (1998). *Affective neuroscience.* New York: Oxford University Press.

Parker, I. (Ed.). (1999). *Deconstructing psychotherapy.* London: Sage.

Pedreira, M. E., Perez-Cuest, L. M., & Maldonado, H. (2004). Mismatch between what is expected and what actually occurs triggers memory reconsolidation or extinction. *Learning & Memory, 11,* 579–585.

Pepper, S. C. (1942/1961). *World hypotheses.* Berkeley: University of California Press.

Pepper, S. (1961). World hypotheses: A study in evidence. Los Angeles: University of California Press.

Perinbanayagam, R. S. (1991). *Discursive acts.* Hawthorne, NY: Aldine de Gruyter.

Peters, T. Q. (2003). *A fundamental component analysis of microdevelopment: A case of successful therapy.* Unpublished master's thesis, Suffolk University, Boston.

Peters, T. Q. (2008). *Developmental analysis of psychotherapy process (DAPP): A methodology for psychotherapy integration with specific application to therapy disruption.* Unpublished doctoral dissertation, Suffolk University.

Phelps, E. (2006). Human emotion and memory: Interactions of the amygdala and hippocampal complex. *Current Opinion in Neurobiology, 14,* 198–202.

Phelps, E. A., & LeDoux, J. E. (2005). Contributions of the amygdala to emotion processing: From animal models to human behavior. *Neuron, 48,* 175–187.

Phelps, E., Ling, S., & Carrasco, M. (2006). Emotion facilitates perception and potentiates the perceptual benefits of attention. *Psychological Science, 17,* 292–299.

Piaget, J. (1932). *The moral judgment of the child.* London: Kegan Paul, Trench, Trubner.

Piaget, J. (1952). *The origins of intelligence in children.* New York: IUP Press.

Piaget, J. (1954). *The construction of reality in the child.* Oxford: Basic Books.

Piaget, J. (1960). *The child's conception of the world.* Oxford: Littlefield Adams.

Piaget, J. (1966). *Play, dreams and imitation in childhood.* New York: Norton.

Piaget, J. (1970a). *Structuralism.* New York: Harper & Row.

Piaget, J. (1970b). *Genetic epistemology.* New York: W.W. Norton & Company.

Piaget, J. (1973). *The child and reality.* New York: Viking.

Piaget, J. (1981). *Intelligence and affectivity: Their relationship during child development.* Palo Alto, CA: Annual Reviews.

Piaget, J. (1985). *Equilibration of cognitive structures.* Chicago: University of Chicago Press.

Piaget, J. (1995). *Sociological studies.* New York: Routledge.

Piaget, J., & Inhelder, B. (1971). *Mental imagery in the child* (P. A. Chilton, Trans.). New York: Basic Books. (Originally published in 1966)

Plutchik, R. (2000). *Emotions in the practice of psychotherapy: Clinical implications of affect theories.* Washington, DC: APA Press.

Radwanska, K., Nikolaev, E., Knapska, E., & Kaczmarek, L. (2002). Differential response of two subdivisions of lateral amygdala to aversive conditioning as revealed by c-Fos and P-ERK mapping. *Neuroreport: For Rapid Communication of Neuroscience Research, 13,* 2241–2246.

Repa, J., Muller, J., Apergis, J., Desrochers, T., Zhou, Y., & LeDoux, J. (2001). Two different lateral amygdala cell populations contribute to the initiation and storage of memory. *Nature Neuroscience, 4,* 724–731.

Richard, D. (1995). *The translation of spiritual orientation into psychotherapeutic practice: How developmental process analysis can help clarify therapists' contributions and clients' responses.* Unpublished doctoral dissertation. Suffolk University.

Rigazio-DiGilio, S., & Ivey, A. (1993). Developmental counseling and therapy: A framework for individual and family treatment. *The Family Journal, 1,* 209–219.

Rizzolatti, G. (2005). The mirror neuron system and imitation. In S. Hurley & N. Chater (Eds.), *Perspectives on imitation: From neuroscience to social science* (Vol. 1, pp. 55–76). Cambridge, MA: MIT Press.

Rizzolatti, G., & Sinigaglia, C. (2008). *Mirrors in the brain: How our minds share actions, emotions, and experience.* Oxford: Oxford University Press.

Rochat, P. (2008). Mutual recognition as foundation of sociality and social comfort. In T. Striano & V. Reid (Eds.), *Social cognition: Development, neuroscience and autism.* Oxford: Blackwell.

Rochat, P., & Striano, T. (2000). Perceived self in infancy. *Infant Behavior and Development, 23,* 513–530.

Rogan, M., Stäubli, U., & LeDoux, J. (1997). AMPA receptor facilitation accelerates fear learning without altering the level of conditioned fear acquired. *Journal of Neuroscience, 17,* 5928–5935.

Rogers, C. (1977). *Carl Rogers on personal power*. Oxford, England: Delacourt.

Rogers, C. R. (1942). *Counseling and psychotherapy*. Boston: Houghton Mifflin.

Rogers, C. R. (1951). *Client-centered therapy*. Boston: Houghton Mifflin.

Rogers, C. R. (1954). The case of Mrs. Oak: A research analysis. In C. R. Rogers & R. F. Dymond (Eds.), *Psychotherapy and personality change* (pp. 259–348). Chicago: University of Chicago Press.

Rogers, C. R. (1957). The necessary and sufficient conditions of therapeutic personality change. *Journal of Consulting Psychology, 21*, 95–103.

Rogers, C. R. (1959). A theory of therapy, personality and interpersonal relationships, as developed in the client-centered framework. In S. Koch (Ed.), *Psychology: A study of science* (pp. 184–256). New York: McGraw-Hill.

Rogers, C. R. (1986). Reflection of feelings. *Person-Centered Review, 1*, 375–377.

Rogers, C. R. (1961/1995). *On becoming a person: A therapist's view of psychotherapy*. Boston: Houghton Mifflin. (Originally published in 1961)

Rogers, C. R. (1996a). The case of Jill [1983]. In B. A. Farber, D. C. Brink, & P. M. Raskin (Eds.), *The psychotherapy of Carl Rogers: Cases and commentary* (pp. 74–83). New York: Guilford.

Rogers, C. R. (1996b). The cases of Mary and Louise [1986]. In B. A. Farber, D. C. Brink, & P. M. Raskin (Eds.), *The psychotherapy of Carl Rogers: Cases and commentary* (pp. 95–119). New York: Guilford.

Rogers, C. R. (1997). *Carl Rogers on personal power*. New York: Delacorte.

Rogers, C. R. (2001). The case of Mrs. Oak. In D. Wedding & R. J. Corsini (Eds.), *Case studies in psychotherapy* (3rd ed., pp. 57–78). Belmont, CA: Wadsworth/Thomson. (Originally published in 1961)

Rogoff, B. (1990). *Apprenticeship in thinking: Cognitive development in social context*. New York: Oxford University Press.

Rogoff, B. (1993). Children's guided participation and participatory appropriation in sociocultural activity. In R. H. Wozniak & K. W. Fischer (Eds.), *Development in context* (pp. 121–153). Hillsdale, NJ: Erlbaum.

Rogoff, B. (2003). *The cultural nature of development*. New York: Oxford University Press.

Rommetveit, R. (1979). On the architecture of intersubjectivity. In R. Rommetveit & R. M. Blaker (Eds.), *Studies of language, thought and verbal communication*. New York: Academic Press.

Rommetveit, R. (1985). Language acquisition as increasing linguistic restructuring of experience and symbolic behavior control. In J. V. Wertsch (Ed.), *Culture, communication and cognition* (pp. 57–68). Cambridge: Cambridge University Press.

Rousseau, J. J. (1979). *Emile: or, on education*. New York: Basic Books. (Originally published in 1762)

Saigh, P. (1998). Effects of flooding on memories of patients with posttraumatic stress disorder. In J. D. Bremner & C. R. Marmar (Eds.), *Trauma, memory, and dissociation* (pp. 285–320). Washington, DC: APA Press.

Salomon, G. (Ed.). (1993). *Distributed cognitions: Psychological and educational considerations*. Cambridge: Cambridge University Press.

Sarbin, T. R. (1952). A preface to a psychological analysis of the self. *Psychological Review, 59*, 11–22.

Sarbin, T. R. (1972). Imagination as muted role taking. In P. W. Sheehan (Ed.), *The function and nature of imagery* (pp. 333–354). New York: Academic.

Sarbin, T. (1989). Emotion as situated action. In L. Cirillo, B. Kaplan, & S. Wapner (Eds.), *The role of emotion in ideal human development* (pp. 77–99). Hillsdale, NJ: Erlbaum.

Sarbin, T. R., & Allen, V. L. (1968). Role theory. In G. Lindzey & E. Aronson (Eds.), *The handbook of social psychology* (2nd ed., pp. 488–567). Reading, MA: Addison-Wesley.

Saxe, G. B. (1982). Developing forms of arithmetic operations among the Oksapmin of Papua New Guinea. *Developmental Psychology, 18,* 583–594.

Scheff, T. (2003). Shame in self and society. *Symbolic Interaction, 26,* 239–262.

Schwarz, W. (2003). Stochastic cascade processes as a model of multi-stage concurrent information processing. *Acta Psychologica, 113,* 231–261.

Searle, J. R. (1969). *Intentionality.* Cambridge: Cambridge University Press.

Searle, J. (1983). *Intentionality: An essay in the philosophy of mind.* New York, Cambridge University Press.

Seligman, M. (1995). The Effectiveness of Psychotherapy. *American Psychologist, 50* (12), pp. 965–974.

Shotter, J. (1997). The social construction of our "inner" selves. *Journal of Constructivist Psychology, 10*(1), 7–24.

Shotter, J. (2000). Wittgenstein and the everyday: From radical hiddenness to "nothing is hidden"; from representation to participation. *Journal of Mundane Behavior, 1,* 116–134.

Shweder, R. A. (1991). *Thinking through cultures: Expeditions in cultural psychology.* Cambridge, MA: Harvard University Press.

Siegler, R. S. (1995). How does change occur: A microgenetic study of number conservation. *Cognitive Psychology, 28,* 225–273.

Siegler, R. S. (2006). Microgenetic analyses of learning. In D. Kuhn & R. S. Siegler (Vol. Eds.), *Handbook of child psychology* (6th ed., pp. 464–510). New York: John Wiley.

Sigel, I., Stinson, E., & Kim, M. (1993). Socialization of cognition: The distancing model. *Development in context: Acting and thinking in specific environments* (pp. 211–224). Hillsdale, NJ: Lawrence Erlbaum Associates.

Sigel, I. (2002). The psychological distancing model: A study of the socialization of cognition. *Culture & Psychology, 8,* 189–214.

Silberg, J. L. (Ed.). (1998). *The dissociative child: Diagnosis, treatment, and management* (2nd ed.). Baltimore: Sidran Press.

Smith, E. E., & Grossman, M. (2008). Multiple systems of category learning. *Neuroscience & Biobehavioral Reviews, 32,* 249–264.

Smith, L. B. (2005). Action alters shape categories. *Cognitive Science, 29,* 665–679.

Solomon, R. (1976). *The passions.* New York: Anchor.

Spiegel, J., Severino, S., & Morrison, N. (2000). The role of attachment functions in psychotherapy. *Journal of Psychotherapy Practice & Research, 9,* 25–32.

Sroufe, L. (2005). Attachment and development: A prospective, longitudinal study from birth to adulthood. *Attachment & Human Development, 7,* 349–367.

Stamenov, N. I., & Gallese, V. (2002). *Mirror neurons and the evolution of brain and language.* Amsterdam: John Benjamins.

Stern, D. N. (1985). *The interpersonal world of the infant.* New York: Basic Books.

Stien, P. T., & Kendall, J. (2004). *Psychological trauma and the developing brain: Neurologically based interventions for troubled children.* Binghamton, NY: Haworth.

Stone, C. A. (1998). The metaphor of scaffolding: Its utility for the field of learning disabilities. *Journal of Learning Disabilities, 31,* 344–36.

Sullivan, H. S. (1940). *Conceptions of modern psychiatry.* New York: Norton.

Tangney, J. P. (2002). Self-conscious emotions: The self as a moral guide. In A. Tesser & D. A. Stapel (Eds.), *Self and motivation: Emerging psychological perspectives* (pp. 97–117). Washington, DC: APA Press.

Ter Hark, M. (1990). *Beyond the inner and the outer: Wittgenstein's philosophy of psychology.* Dordrecht: Kluwer Academic.

Thelen, E. (2000). Grounded in the world: Developmental origins of the embodied mind. *Infancy, 1,* 3–28.

Thelen, E., & Smith, L. B. (2006). Dynamic systems theories. In W. Damon & R. M. Lerner (Series Eds.) & R. M. Lerner (Vol. Ed.), *Handbook of child psychology: Vol. 1. Theoretical models of human development* (6th ed., pp. 258–312). Hoboken, NJ: Wiley.

Thompson, E. (2007). *Mind in life.* Cambridge, MA: Harvard University Press.

Tomasello, M. (2003). *Constructing a language: A usage-based theory of language acquisition.* Cambridge, MA: Harvard University Press.

Tomkins, S. (1962). *Affect, imagery and consciousness* (Vol. 1). New York: Springer.

Toomey, B., & Ecker, B. (2007). Of neurons and knowings: Constructivism, coherence psychology and their neurodynamic substrates. *Journal of Constructivist Psychology, 20,* 201–245.

Trevarthen, C. (1993). The self born in intersubjectivity: The psychology of an infant communicating. In U. Neisser (Ed.), *The perceived self: Ecological and interpersonal sources of self-knowledge* (pp. 121–173). New York: Cambridge University Press.

Trevarthen, C. (1998). The concept and foundations of infant intersubjectivity. In S. Braten (Ed.), *Intersubjective communication and emotion in early ontogeny* (pp. 15–46). Cambridge: Cambridge University Press.

Trevarthen, C., & Aitken, K. J. (2000). Infant intersubjectivity: Research, theory, and clinical applications. *Journal of Child Psychology and Psychiatry and Allied Disciplines, 42,* 3–48.

Trevarthen, C., & Hubley, P. (1978). Secondary intersubjectivity: Confidence, confiding and acts of meaning in the first year. In A. Lock (Ed.), *Action, gesture and symbol: The emergence of language* (pp. 183–229). London: Academic Press.

Tull, M., & Roemer, L. (2007). Emotion regulation difficulties associated with the experience of uncued panic attacks: Evidence of experiential avoidance, emotional nonacceptance, and decreased emotional clarity. *Behavior Therapy, 38,* 378–391.

Van Geert, P. (1991). A dynamic systems model of cognitive and language growth. *Psychological Review, 98,* 3–53.

Van Geert, P. (1994). *Dynamic systems of development: Change between complexity and chaos.* London: Harvester Wheatsheaf.

Van Geert, P. (1998). A dynamic systems model of basic developmental mechanisms: Piaget, Vygotsky and beyond. *Psychological Review, 105,* 634–677.

Vasco, A. (2005). A conceptualização de caso no modelo de complementaridade paradigmática: Variedade e integração. *Psychologica, 40,* 11–36.

Vedeler, D. (1991). Infant intentionality as object directedness: An alternative to representationalism. *Journal for the Theory of Social Behaviour,* 21, 431–448.

Vedeler, D. (1994). Infant intentionality as object directeness: Toward a method of observation. *Scandinavian Journal of Psychology, 35,* 343–366.

von Bertalanffy, L. (1968). *General systems theory.* New York: Braziller.

Vygotsky, L. (1978). *Mind in society.* Cambridge, MA: Harvard University Press.

Vygotsky, L. S. (1981). The genesis of higher mental functions. In J. V. Wersch (Ed. & Trans.), *The concept of activity in Soviet psychology.* Armonk, NY: M. E. Sharpe.

Vygotsky, L. S. (1987). *Thinking and speech.* In R. W. Reiber & A. S. Carton (Eds.), *The collected works of L. S. Vygotsky: Vol. 1. Problems of general psychology* (N. Minick, Trans.). New York: Plenum.

Wallin, D. (2007). *Attachment in psychotherapy.* New York: Guilford.

Wapner, S., & Demick, J. (2000). Person-in-environment psychology: A holistic, developmental, systems-oriented perspective. In W. B. Walsh, K. H. Craik, & R. H. Price (Eds.), *Person-environment psychology: New directions and perspectives* (2nd ed., pp. 25–60). Hillsdale, NJ: Erlbaum.

Watson, M. W., Fischer, K. W., & Andreas, J. B. (2004). Pathways to aggression in children and adolescents. *Harvard Educational Review, 74,* 404–430.

Wedding, D., & Corsini, R. J. (Eds.). (2001). *Case studies in psychotherapy* (3rd ed.). Belmont, CA: Wadsworth/Thomson.

Weiss, M. J., Zelazo, P. R., & Swain, I. U. (1988). Newborn response to auditory stimulus discrepancy. *Child Development, 59,* 1530–1541.

Weiss, P. A. (1977). The system of nature and the nature of systems: Empirical holism and practical reductionism harmonized. In K. E. Schaefer, H. Hensel, & R. Brady (Eds.), *A new image of man in medicine: Vol. 1. Towards a man-centered medical science.* Mount Kisco, NY: Futura.

Wells, G. (1999). *Dialogic inquiry: Towards a sociocultural practice and theory of education.* Cambridge: Cambridge University Press.

Werner, H., & Kaplan, B. (1984). *Symbol formation.* Hillsdale, NJ: Erlbaum. (Originally published in 1962)

Wertsch, J. V. (1985). *Vygotsky and the social formation of mind.* Cambridge, MA: Harvard University Press.

Wertsch, J. V. (1991). *Voices of the mind: A sociocultural approach to mediated action.* Cambridge: Cambridge University Press.

Wertsch, J. V. (1998). *Mind as action.* Cambridge, MA: Harvard University Press

Wertsch, J. V. (2002). *Voices of collective remembering.* New York: Cambridge University Press.

Wilde, L. (1989). *Marx and contradiction.* Aldershot, UK: Avebury.

Winter, H., & Irle, E. (2004). Hippocampal volume in adult burn patients with and without posttraumatic stress disorder. *American Journal of Psychiatry, 161,* 2194–2200.

Wittgenstein, L. (1953). *Philosophical investigations* (G. E. M. Anscombe, Trans.). Oxford: Blackwell.

Wood, D. J., & Middleton, D. J. (1975). A study of assisted problem solving. *British Journal of Psychology, 66,* 181–191.

Wood, L., & Kroger, R. (2000). *Doing discourse analysis: Methods for studying action in talk and text*. Thousand Oaks, CA: Sage Publications.

Wozniak, R., & Fischer, K. (1993). Development in context: Acting and thinking in specific environments. Hillsdale, NJ: Lawrence Erlbaum.

Yalom, I. D. (1980). *Existential psychotherapy*. New York: Basic Books.

Yalom, I. D. (1995). *The theory and practice of group psychotherapy* (4th ed.). New York: Basic Books.

Yalom, I. D. (2002). *The gift of therapy: An open letter to a new generation of therapists and their patients*. New York: Harper Collins.

Yalom, I. D., with Leszcz, M. (2005). *The theory and practice of group psychotherapy* (5th ed.). New York: Basic Books.

Yehuda, R. (2004). Risk and resilience in posttraumatic stress disorder. *Journal of Clinical Psychiatry, 65*, 29–36.

Zahavi, D. (2003). *Husserl's phenomenology*. Palo Alto, CA: Stanford University Press.

Zahavi, D. (2005). *Subjectivity and selfhood*. Cambridge, MA: MIT Press.

Zajonc, R. B. (1984). On the primacy of affect. *American Psychologist, 39*, 117–123.

Zeedyk, M. S. (2006). From intersubjectivity to subjectivity: The transformative roles of imitation and intimacy. *Infant and Child Development, 15*, 321–344.

Zelazo, P. D. (1996). Towards a characterization of minimal consciousness. *New Ideas in Psychology, 14*, 63–80.

Zelazo, P. D., & Lourenco, S. F. (2003). Imitation and the dialectic of representation. *Developmental Review, 23*, 55–78.

Zelazo, P. D., Sommerville, J. A., & Nichols, S. (1999). Age-related changes in children's use of external representations. *Developmental Psychology, 35*, 1059–1071.

Zelazo, P. R., Hopkins, J. R., Jacobson, S., & Kagan, J. (1973). Psychological reactivity to discrepant events: Support for the curvilinear hypothesis. *Cognition, 2*, 385–393.

Zhang, J., & Norman, D. (1994). Representations in distributed cognitive tasks. *Cognitive Science: A Multidisciplinary Journal, 18*, 87–122.

Zimbarg, R. E., & Griffith, J. W. (2008). Behavior therapy. In J. L. Lebow (Ed.), *Twenty-first century psychotherapies: Contemporary approaches to theory and practice* (pp. 8–42). Hoboken, NJ: John Wiley.

Zimring, F. (1996). Rogers and Gloria: The effects of meeting some, but not all, of the "necessary and sufficient" conditions. In B. A. Farber, D. C. Brink, & P. M. Raskin (Eds.), *The psychotherapy of Carl Rogers: Cases and commentary* (pp. 65–73). New York: Guilford.

Zlatev, J. (2007). Intersubjectivity, mimetic schemas and the emergence of language. *Intellectica, 46*, 123–151.

Zlatev, J., Brinck, I., & Andrén, M. (2008). Stages in the development of perceptual intersubjectivity. In F. Morganti, A Carassa, & G. Riva (Eds.), *Enacting intersubjectivity*. Amsterdam: IOS Press.

Zlatev, J., Racine, T., Sinha, C., & Itkonen, E. (Eds.). (2008). *The shared mind: Perspectives on intersubjectivity*. Amsterdam: John Benjamins.

Index